AN INTRODUCTION TO
THE LAW OF TRUSTS

SECOND EDITION

SIMON GARDNER

BCL (Oxford) MA (Oxford)
Fellow of Lincoln College Oxford

OXFORD
UNIVERSITY PRESS

OXFORD

UNIVERSITY PRESS

Great Clarendon Street, Oxford OX2 6DP

Oxford University Press is a department of the University of Oxford.
It furthers the University's objective of excellence in research, scholarship,
and education by publishing worldwide in

Oxford New York

Auckland Bangkok Buenos Aires Cape Town Chennai
Dar es Salaam Delhi Hong Kong Istanbul Karachi Kolkata
Kuala Lumpur Madrid Melbourne Mexico City Mumbai Nairobi
São Paulo Shanghai Taipei Tokyo Toronto

Oxford is a registered trade mark of Oxford University Press
in the UK and in certain other countries

Published in the United States
by Oxford University Press Inc., New York

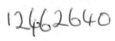

British Library Cataloguing in Publication Data
Data available

Library of Congress Cataloging in Publication Data
Data available
ISBN 0–19–926134–2

1 3 5 7 9 10 8 6 4 2

Typeset in Ehrhardt
by RefineCatch Limited, Bungay, Suffolk
Printed in Great Britain by
Biddles Ltd., Guildford and King's Lynn

Preface

The first edition of this book appeared in 1990. Since then, the law itself has continued to evolve, and so too have the ideas which judges and commentators hold about it. A new edition has in truth been due for some time, but its preparation has been delayed as for some years, until recently, my role in Oxford was a predominantly administrative one. As that period came to its end, however, I was fortunate enough to be granted a year's leave by my college and faculty, which allowed me to give this book the attention it required.

This edition follows its predecessor in attempting to present both an account of the main features of the subject, and some thoughts about how these can be understood and evaluated. The identification of 'the main features' is evidently a contentious operation. My choices are grounded partly in syllabus considerations, and partly in an effort to explain matters revealing what I depict as the subject's most fundamental concerns. I have, I think, given more detail in this edition than in the last: not for its own sake, but so as to provide a more textured and less dogmatic treatment than is otherwise possible. The ideas which I offer about how the law can be understood and evaluated are likewise necessarily selective. They include perspectives of principle, policy, and praxis. In this respect, too, this new edition aims to offer a subtler treatment than its predecessor.

The book is aimed above all at readers studying the subject of trusts at degree level. My hope is that it will help them to understand the subject better than they otherwise might, both by the reflections it makes on the material they are studying and, perhaps more importantly, by encouraging them to develop such reflections for themselves, in giving an example of the kind of thing that is possible. Other readers may also find that it serves their needs: especially those looking for a brief account of this area of the law, explained in terms which may strike chords with other fields of interest. The book should, as its title implies, be one which can helpfully be read before, or (if this is all that is needed) in lieu of, a fuller study. But it will perhaps most rewardingly be read alongside or after such fuller study, for at that stage the reader, being more familiar with the subject, will be much better able to take a personal part in seeking to understand and evaluate it.

In preparing this second edition I enjoyed support in many quarters. I should especially mention the advice unstintingly given by my former colleague, now at McGill University, Lionel Smith; and the scrupulous objectivity of my research assistant, Michael Izzo, who now moves on with his career as clerk to Gleeson CJ of the High Court of Australia; the efficiency of the publishers; and the love of my family.

Simon Gardner
Hallowe'en 2002

Contents

Table of Cases

Table of Statutes

Table of Statutory Instruments

I

The nature of trusts

Our first task is to form a general idea of what trusts are.[1]

1.1 A 'DEFINITION'

The most basic legal concepts are often not easy to define with complete precision, and trusts are no exception. The difficulty arises partly because, in English law, many of the concepts (including trusts) are developed by the judges rather than being established by Act of Parliament, so there is no single, completely authoritative statement of their nature. But it arises also for a more fundamental reason. There can be a variety of different ideas as to the proper policy mission of the law in the area in question—whether it should reflect this consideration, or that—and therefore as to the proper work that the concept should do. These ideas are often in conflict with each other. If one were altogether to vanquish its rivals, none of this would prevent the emergence of a clear-cut definition. But that does not normally happen. For one thing, human affairs are too complicated and compromised to allow for nothing but clean answers. For another, the definition has (as a result of the doctrine of precedent) to be assembled from judicial utterances over many years: some from periods when one policy slant dominated, others from periods when another view had come to the fore.

So no definition of a trust can be given which is beyond contention, either in terms of its technical fit with the substance of the law or in terms of its freedom from political controversy. It would therefore be entirely reasonable not to offer a definition, but to move directly into a discussion of the various points which might feature in any definition, and of the different possible accounts of them. Such a discussion certainly cannot be dispensed with. But it is probably easier to follow, and more rewarding, if

---

[1] The nature of trusts today differs in some respects from that of their ancestors, known originally as 'uses'. On the early period, see A Simpson *A History of the Land Law* (1986) ch VIII.

at the outset we do posit something having the look of a definition, to provide a starting point. The 'definition' thus offered here is as follows.

A trust is a situation in which property is vested in someone (a trustee), who is under legally recognized obligations, at least some of which are of a proprietary kind, to handle it in a certain way, and to the exclusion of any personal interest. These obligations may arise either by conscious creation by the previous owner of the property (the settlor), or because some other legally significant circumstances are present.

The task is now to explain the significance of the various aspects of this 'definition', and to record and explore the ways in which it is contentious.

I.2 AN EXAMPLE

Many of the terms of the 'definition' just offered are abstract or not matters of ordinary usage. So, in order to be able to focus our discussion more solidly, it will be helpful at this stage to give a concrete example of a trust. To do so is itself a contentious undertaking, however.

It will be noted that the 'definition' offers two alternative ways in which a trust can arise: 'either as a result of the conscious creation of these obligations, or because some other legally significant circumstances are present'. The reference to 'some other legally significant circumstances' is unspecific, hinting (accurately) that these circumstances are various in nature. And there is no stipulation as to the content of the obligations which lie at the heart of the 'definition'. Taking all this together, it can be inferred, correctly, that trusts can arise in many situations and be made to do a wide range of work. If we take an example, however, we immediately focus upon the particular kind of situation, and upon the particular kind of work, which the example illustrates. And we thereby tacitly privilege this situation and work over all other situations and work which can in principle equally well be associated with trusts. To explain the danger is, however, hopefully to go some way towards allaying it. At all events, the usefulness of giving an example seems worth the risk.

Imagine that a grandmother, who believes her life to be close to its end, wishes to give her grandson Adam £100,000. But she does not want Adam to have all the money straight away. So she makes a trust for him. She does so by transferring the money to a trustee (a close friend, maybe, or her bank) with instructions how to deal with it: say, to invest it and accumulate the income, to pay Adam the capital and accumulated income on his eighteenth birthday, but meanwhile to pay out anything that might be needed to give him a good education, plus an annual allowance of £1,000 once he reaches his teens. This illustration certainly falls within our 'definition' of a trust. We see that, as a result of the conscious creation of the arrangement by the grandmother, property is vested in a trustee, who comes under obligations not to treat it as his own (this is the essence of the obligations being 'proprietary') but to handle it in a defined way, ie to provide the stated benefits to Adam. But we can also see that there are many respects in which the 'definition' allows for trusts which do not follow the pattern of the example. That is what now needs to be explored.

No other example would have avoided the danger of privileging its content any better than the example just given. But it may nevertheless be asked why the particular kind of situation inherent in that example should have been singled out for attention. This situation features an effort at structuring of the use of wealth between generations of a family. This situation and effort are characteristic of the principal use made of trusts as a matter of history (though the example of Adam and his grandmother is much simpler than most real parallels). The trust concept was thus predominantly developed against the policy considerations relevant to this situation and effort. Beginning from material such as the example should help us, therefore, to understand and appraise many of the concept's features.

1.3 THE WAYS IN WHICH TRUSTS CAN BE ESTABLISHED

The grandmother in the example may have established her trust by paying the money over to the trustee during her own lifetime. If she did, the resulting arrangement (even though designed to endure after her death) is known as an '*inter vivos*' trust. Alternatively, she might have chosen to establish the trust by providing for the payment to the trustee in her will. This would have created a 'testamentary' trust.

In the example, the trust came about as a result of someone wanting to make it. Such a person is called a 'settlor'. The establishment of a trust by a settlor is a very common situation, but it is not essential to the idea of a trust. Trusts are also found in cases where they are not consciously made in this way, but for one reason or another the circumstances demand that the holder of some property should nevertheless be regarded as a trustee and subjected to duties concerning its handling accordingly. Trusts which arise because they are consciously made, like that in the example, are called 'express trusts'. Those arising for other reasons are called 'constructive trusts'.[2] But the underlying point is that these various circumstances in which constructive trusts arise, and the conscious actions of a settlor which are found in express trusts, are all different reasons for coming to the conclusion that someone who holds some property should be under a duty as to its handling.

Sometimes, the idea of 'the circumstances demanding a constructive trust' is read as an invitation to the judges to rely on their own individual notions as to when that is the case. That approach is found more often in the law of the United States and Canada, however, than that of England.[3] Here, with occasional exceptions, 'the circumstances demanding a constructive trust' are regarded as laid down by the law, though of course that does not preclude innovation and development. The bases on which, and the main circumstances in which, constructive trusts arise in English law will be discussed in Chapters 7 and 8. But a few examples of them, drawn from that discussion, may be given now. Where property is transferred to someone on the understanding that she will hold it on an express trust, but this trust is not (as trusts must sometimes be) put into writing, a constructive trust arises to oblige the transferee to hold it on the agreed terms. Where property belongs to one person, but it is understood between him and another person that it should be shared with the latter, and the latter acts to his detriment upon that understanding, a constructive trust arises to give effect to the understanding. Where an agent makes a profit for herself when she should have been acting for her employer, that profit will be subject to a constructive trust. And where a person inherits property after himself murdering the deceased, a constructive trust arises to prevent him enjoying the benefit of it.

It is sometimes said that whilst express trusts (especially within families) were historically the more important species of trust, constructive trusts nowadays occupy that position. How does one measure 'importance', however? Many such statements implicitly look to the relative frequency of litigation. It appears likely that there is nowadays more

---

[2] Left out of account here are 'resulting trusts', which are customarily regarded as a category additional to express and constructive trusts. The basis on which they arise, however, is either (like express trusts) the wish of their settlor, or (like constructive trusts) some other legally significant circumstances. Sections 7.6 and 7.7 discuss which of these is the case.

[3] Constructive trusts imposed because the individual judge thinks it right are called 'remedial' (as opposed to 'institutional'). Remedial constructive trusts are discussed further in section 7.3.

litigation over constructive trusts than over express trusts, and that this reverses the historic position. But although comparison on this ground does possess significance (for example, for priorities in the education of advocates, and for the organization of court business), it is not the only possible approach. If one looks instead to the relative frequency with which clients consult lawyers over the two types of trusts in a non-litigious context, express trusts will probably emerge as the more 'important'. This measure too has its significance (eg for the organization of solicitors' firms). But the real conclusions are that no measure of 'importance' has value outside its own terms, and that neither type of trust can therefore be represented as more 'important' than the other in a global sense. They both matter, but differently.

1.4 THE SETTLOR

An express trust therefore arises as a result of a decision on the part of the settlor to make a trust of it. It follows that an express trust must have a settlor.

In the example given above, the settlor (the grandmother) transferred the property to the trustee in order for the latter to hold it on trust. This step, however, is not essential. It is possible for the settlor and the trustee to be the same person. Instead of transferring his property to a trustee who will then have the duty of dealing with it as specified, a settlor may keep it but undertake the same duty himself. Had the grandmother in the example not perceived her remaining period of life to be short, she might have chosen to do this instead of establishing her trust by transferring the property to a trustee. Proceeding in this way is known as 'declaring a trust': the settlor declares that he holds the property in question as trustee, and stipulates that in that capacity he will deal with it in a certain way for the beneficiary. What is essential, therefore, is not a transfer of property from a settlor to a trustee, but rather for the property to be with the trustee, and for the trustee to be under a duty in regard to its handling.

In a case where a constructive trust arises, indeed, the position will normally be that the owner of some property will come under some duty to deal with the property in a certain way, ie will become trustee of it. There will not be a settlor, ie a person whose intention to place his own property on trust is effectuated by the law.

The grandmother in the example was a human being. Where a trust does have a settlor, that settlor may alternatively be any other entity recognized by the law as having the same capacities, in regard to the enjoyment of property, as a human being. In other words, it might be a 'legal (or juristic) person', notably an incorporated company.

I.5 THE BENEFICIARY

The trust in the example was constructed so as to provide for payments to Adam. A person who has a claim to receive payments from a trust is known as a 'beneficiary'.[4] Many trusts have at least one beneficiary, and of those that do, most have more than one. The beneficiaries' entitlements may be arranged concurrently (eg 'for Adam and Briony in equal shares') or in succession to one another (eg 'to pay the income to Adam for his lifetime, then to pay the capital to Briony'), or be some mixture of the two.

A beneficiary may be either a human being, like Adam, or some other legal person. But many trusts do not have a beneficiary, human or otherwise, at all. A trust might instead provide for payments towards the achievement of some purpose: for example, to investigate whether the plays attributed to Shakespeare were really the work of Bacon, or to establish and maintain a dogs' home, or to provide a public recreation ground, or to further the aims of some organization. Such trusts without beneficiaries are called 'purpose trusts'. Collectively, beneficiaries and such purposes are called 'objects' of trusts. Many purpose trusts have certain characteristics that make them 'charitable', and as such they receive special treatment from the law. We shall examine these in Chapter 6. The law has also accepted non-charitable purpose trusts, but only in the limited way described in section 14.3. It is controversial however whether non-charitable purpose trusts especially should be valid. The thesis against such trusts contends, indeed springs from the view, described in section 14.2, that trusts must by definition feature not merely duties upon the trustees, but rights on the part of beneficiaries amounting to something like an interest in the trust property. The merits of this thesis, and the appeal of the rules antagonistic to it, are discussed in section 14.4. But it is not reflected in our 'definition' as it does not capture the existing state of the law. Instead, the 'definition' stipulates for duties on the part of the trustees, it being possible for these to exist whether or not they mirror, or are mirrored by, rights on the part of any beneficiaries.

---

[4] Or 'cestui que trust', pronounced 'settee key trust'; plural correctly 'cestuis que trust' ('cestuis que trustent' is also found), pronounced (in either case) 'settees key trust'.

A beneficiary of a trust may also be a trustee of it. Such an arrangement makes some sense: since the point of the trust is to provide for the beneficiaries, it is reasonable for them to be involved in running it. So if Adam's grandmother had created a trust for his parents as well as himself, she might have made the parents not only beneficiaries but also trustees. But this effect can occur only in trusts with more than one trustee and/or beneficiary. Otherwise, if a person were both sole trustee and sole beneficiary, the trust would consist in him owing an obligation purely to himself, which dissolves into nothing: he would in effect be absolute owner.

Sometimes, too, a trust's beneficiary may be the same person as its settlor. The settlor of an express trust may stipulate that he will be its beneficiary, ie make a trust for himself. The idea of doing so may at first sound strange. In medieval times, however, it was a common practice, used above all so as to avoid certain forms of taxation. It is also quite common today: for example, when people put money into pension schemes, they can (simplifying somewhat) be seen as essentially placing it with trustees on trust for themselves. Sometimes, too, such a trust will arise without a stipulation by its settlor. Most of the trusts which arise in this way are called 'resulting trusts'. A resulting trust occurs when I give you property to hold on trust, but do not fully specify the objects for whom or for which you are to hold it; or where I give you property, apparently as a gift, but you cannot prove that I meant to make a gift. The law regarding resulting trusts is discussed further in Chapter 7.

1.6 THE TRUSTEE

The trust created by the grandmother in our example had one trustee. A trustee, again, may be either a human being or some other legal person such as an incorporated company. Some companies, known as 'trust corporations', specifically offer their services as trustees of express trusts, but any corporation may find itself trustee of a constructive trust or a resulting trust. If the settlor of an express trust confines herself to human trustees, she is unlikely to have just one: groups of between two and four are commoner.

We have seen that a trust need not have a settlor or a beneficiary, as opposed to a purpose. But in all the variations on the trust theme which we have noticed—express and constructive trusts, trusts for beneficiaries and for purposes, and so on—there has always been a trustee. And amongst all the learning on the subject of trusts, it has never been doubted that a trustee is required. This is not an accident. A trust involves an obligation to handle certain property in a particular way. An obligation is a proposition about what a person ought to do. So there cannot be an obligation to handle property in a particular way unless there is also a person, the trustee, who is subject to that obligation.

It is likely that the trustee in our original example agreed to take on the trust. It is usual for the settlor of an express trust to consult the intended trustee, and obtain his agreement to act in that role. If the settlor does not take this step and the intended trustee is not willing to act, the latter may disclaim the trusteeship, in which event the role will fall upon the settlor (or, if the settlor was acting by will, her executors), until someone else can be appointed trustee. Moreover, if a trustee wishes subsequently not to continue to act, it will generally be possible to relinquish the role.[5] So in practical terms, the agreement of the trustee comes close to being a requirement in express trusts. But the trustee's agreement is certainly not required in the case of other kinds of trusts. A constructive trust will arise where the trustee has the relevant property and the circumstances are such that the law imposes such a trust. It is irrelevant whether the trustee agrees to the trust's imposition.[6] On the other hand, such trustees too can normally rid themselves of the role, principally by handing the property over to the beneficiary.

To see the trustee as important only so as to provide a repository of the trust obligations would, however, be to capture only part of the picture. Trustees are important to trusts also for their own qualities, whether as people, in the case of human trustees, or organizations, in the case of trust corporations. The operation of an express trust in particular may, and normally does, require choices to be made. (In the trust in our original example, for instance, the trustee had to choose in what investments to place the trust's assets, and whether and how much to pay out for Adam's education.) The choices made will reflect the individual values and capabilities of the particular trustees. Exceptionable values and low capabilities will lead to trusts being performed unsatisfactorily. The law contains certain measures designed to counteract this possibility.[7] Above the floor created by these measures, however, the operation of trustees' individual values and capabilities is not simply tolerated; it is essential if trusts are to

---

[5] See section 13.1.

[6] The same should be true of resulting trusts. Lord Browne-Wilkinson in *Westdeutsche Landesbank Girozentrale v Islington LBC* [1996] AC 669, 708 asserts that a resulting trust arises only if the trustee so intends, but this is implausible: see section 7.6.

[7] See Ch 13.

function as usefully as we have come to expect. When a settlor selects a trustee, therefore, she will reflect not only on whether the person in question is honest, but also on whether that person will in a more positive sense conduct the trust (make the choices) in a way which the settlor finds congenial. (Adam's grandmother, for example, will have chosen as trustee someone whom she regards as likely to keep Adam's best interests at heart, and whose conception of Adam's best interests is one which, she feels, resonates with her own.) And the law too relies heavily on the contribution that trustees' qualities make to the operation of trusts,[8] above all as implying that trusts can for most of the time be safely allowed to run by themselves, without supervision by the courts. If it were otherwise, the courts would soon be overwhelmed.

1.7 THE TRUSTEE'S DUTIES

Although to mention duties and overlook the importance of the trustee's own characteristics is therefore to miss part of the picture, it remains the case that the trustee, owning the trust property, is under duties to handle it in a certain way. There is much to be said on this topic; Chapters 9–11 are devoted to it.

All trusts require their trustees not to treat the trust property as their own, but to transfer it, if they still have it and are called upon to do so, to the beneficiaries (if they are immediately entitled to it) or to fresh trustees. All trusts, too, require their trustees to safeguard any property known to be trust property: not to use it for themselves, and to try to keep it secure against loss.

Many constructive and resulting trusts will involve no duties beyond these. Most express trusts will demand more, however. The trust in the example was an express trust. Its trustee had further duties of two kinds. He had not merely to refrain from treating the trust property as his own: but also to pay money out to the right person (Adam), in the right amounts, at the right times, under the right conditions; and not to pay it out otherwise, or wrongly withhold it. And he had not merely to safeguard the trust property: but also to manage it, and invest it appropriately so as to produce the income envisaged. Trustees of express trusts generally have duties of both these more demanding kinds, but these will vary in their details from the duties upon Adam's trustee. There will normally be a duty to allow the object of the trust, and no one else, to enjoy the

---

[8] See section 13.8.

trust property in some fashion, and to do so in the right measure, at the right times, under the right conditions. But in another trust the manner of enjoyment might be different (it could aim at providing a house for the beneficiary to occupy, for example); and the designation of the object, amounts, times, and conditions will certainly be different (eg 'to pay half the capital to each of my sons on his marriage, save that if any reaches the age of 40 without having married his share shall be divided equally between his married brothers'). Likewise, there will normally be a duty to manage the trust property so as effectively to allow for the enjoyment of it by the objects; but the exact manner of doing so may differ (eg the trust property may include agricultural land, the trusteeship of which evidently requires different practical steps from the trusteeship of stocks and shares). Chapters 9–11 deal with different aspects of the duties which trustees can incur.

The 'definition' essayed at the outset referred to 'legally recognized duties'. One function of the words 'legally recognized' is to establish a contrast with duties which the holder of some property may owe, but which are morally, not legally, operative. The grandmother's settlement for Adam could take exactly the same form, but be composed of moral, not legal, duties. A person subject to a duty might not wish to make anything of the distinction, and might be equally ready to comply with a moral as with a legal duty. But the distinction matters if the law needs to establish whether there is present something which it regards as a duty: for that purpose, moral duties do not count. In the case of constructive trusts, there will be no confusion over this matter, as all circumstances recognized by the law as giving rise to such trusts will always generate legal duties. The same is true for resulting trusts, in so far as these are not based on the settlor's intention. With express trusts, however, the question could in principle always be asked whether the settlor intended the duties to be legal (so creating a trust) or not. In practice, however, most trust-like arrangements are created in a relatively formal way, which leaves little doubt that legal duties are intended.

1.8 THE OBJECTIVES OF THE TRUST

The device of an express trust lends itself to any purpose which can be translated into the terms of the two principal types of duty discussed above, namely transfer of rights of enjoyment (often, in the form of payment out) and stewardship. So it can be used, as in our original example, to make payments to a person in a pattern more complex than a simple gift; equally, to a number of people, often according to a complicated scheme; or, as noted in the reference to purpose trusts, to provide for spending on an abstract purpose. And the use of trusts in these ways may itself occur for a range of reasons. Trusts for people might be used to distribute wealth amongst a family, for instance. They also provide the legal vehicle for the holding of contributions in a pension scheme, and the payment out of pensions; or for the pooling of investments, and the payment out of the rewards upon them.[9] Trusts for purposes might be used, as already noted, for objects such as investigating whether the plays attributed to Shakespeare were really the work of Bacon, or establishing and maintaining a dogs' home, or providing a public recreation ground, or furthering the aims of some organization.

The element of stewardship is sometimes, as in the case of pooled investments, no less prominent among the reasons for which a trust is employed than that of transfer of enjoyment. Sometimes there will be a desire to procure the talents of the trustee in the active management of the trust's affairs, especially in the matter of investing the money.[10] Sometimes the idea will be more passive, eg to lodge the money with a custodian in such a way that it will remain safe even in the event of the custodian's bankruptcy (such safety being, as explained below, a characteristic of the trust concept).

Sometimes, even when the purposes of the trust are fundamentally ones of transfer of enjoyment and stewardship, the precise arrangement of its provisions is shaped by a collateral aim: the reduction of tax liability. That is, the precise arrangement is chosen, in preference to other possible schemes for producing the same desired package of stewardship and transfer, because it should attract a lower level of tax liability than they.[11] At one time, for example, trust arrangements were used to bring it about that payments, which would otherwise have been classed and taxed as income, appeared instead as a capital gain, which carried a lower tax rate.

There are, however, some objectives for which settlors might wish to use the trust device but which are not permitted by the law. This is the other significance of the stipulation, in the 'definition' essayed at the outset, that the trustee's duties be 'legally recognized'. In brief, it is not

[9] G Moffat *Trusts Law Cases and Materials* 3rd edn (1999) ch 13.
[10] R Cotterrell (1993) 46(2) CLP 75.
[11] J Martin *Hanbury and Martin Modern Equity* 16th edn (2001) ch 9.

permissible to make a trust for a purpose which is itself illegal, such as for the furtherance of a criminal or otherwise illegal activity.[12] Arrangements which, while not otherwise illegal, tend to do social damage are also sometimes declared invalid, but the picture is ill defined. Provisions undermining the institution of the family are sometimes struck down, for example, as are those interfering excessively with the freedom of the beneficiaries (say, by attaching intrusive conditions to their entitlements). There seems also to be evidence of judicial unhappiness at the economic damage which trusts can do. And trusts calculated to avoid tax are not always permitted to operate thus. These matters are considered in more depth in Chapter 2.

It is probably true in the abstract to say that the range of uses to which trusts may (legitimately) be put is infinitely variable. It would therefore be reasonable to suppose that the trust concept itself remains unaltered, no matter what use it is put to. But in practice, particular clusters of use emerge, albeit with detailed differences from one trust to another within each cluster: family settlements, charitable purpose trusts, pension scheme trusts, unit trusts, and so on. To greater or lesser extents, these clusters have attracted rules special to themselves, calculated to deal with concerns special to the area in question. As regards pension scheme trusts, for example, legislation such as the Pensions Act 1995 (introduced in the wake of a scandal, the Maxwell affair) secures that the trust property is better protected, and that scheme members are better informed and more closely involved in the running of the fund, than would be the case under the general law. The existence of such special rules has led some commentators to suggest that instead of thinking about the trust concept, or the law of trusts, as a single entity, we should think about a number of different entities.[13] They undeniably have a point. But it must not be assumed that because some new rule has emerged in a particular context, it cannot apply in other contexts too. If the new rule is compatible with the trust concept (which it must be, to have been accepted even in a limited context), it is worth considering whether it should be extended to some or indeed all other instances of that concept, which is a matter of whether it would advance policy aims favoured in the latter. The move to enhance the rights of pension scheme members, for

---

[12] For a case involving a trust whose object was a fraud on the social security system, see *Tinsley v Milligan* [1994] 1 AC 340; and for one involving a trust whose object was to defraud creditors, see *Tribe v Tribe* [1996] Ch 107.

[13] G Moffat (1993) 56 MLR 471 (pension trusts); J Warburton [1999] Conv 20 (charitable trusts).

example, may perhaps be seen as having catalyzed or accelerated a similar, if less clear-cut, development of the position of trust beneficiaries generally.

1.9 THE PROPERTY

Our original example involved a grandmother placing property on trust for her grandson. And we have continued to discuss trusts in terms of an obligation upon a trustee to handle some property in a particular way. It is implicit in this that there must be some property.[14]

Some legal arrangements create obligations having no reference to property. For example, a singer, hired to perform at a concert, has a duty to do so. His voice is not regarded as property.[15] Such a situation cannot be a trust.

But the fact that an obligation *relates to* property does not on its own qualify it to be a trust obligation. The distinctive characteristic of a trust is that at any rate the trustee's more basic obligations regarding the property (those of not treating it as his own, and of safeguarding it) are *attached to* the property, rather than resting on him personally. Obligations attached to property are known as 'proprietary' (or '*in rem*'); those resting on someone personally are termed 'personal' (or '*in personam*'). If I contract to sell you my car, I have an obligation to you (to perform this contract) which relates to a piece of property (the car), but I do not hold the latter on trust for you. Although it refers to a piece of property, my obligation to sell you the car is as personal as the singer's obligation to let the concert audience have the benefit of his voice.

What does it mean to say that an obligation relating to some property is proprietary rather than personal? The answer is visible in two situations in particular: first, if the owner of the property transfers it to another person; and secondly, if the owner of the property becomes bankrupt, and his property is seized and sold to pay his debts. If I had contracted to sell you my car, the upshot in these circumstances is that the car is validly

---

[14] One sometimes finds the term 'constructive trust' used to describe a situation in which it is asserted not that the 'trustee' holds certain property on trust, but that she owes a purely personal obligation. This usage is nowadays commonly regarded as incorrect, in not conforming with the need for trusts to have certain property as their subject matter; and as meaning that the 'trustee' owes personal obligations to those who are or were objects of a trust and whose interests as such the 'trustee' has infringed. See section 7.1.

[15] The notion of 'property' is not entirely hard and fast, of course: K Gray [1991] CLJ 252; cf J Harris *Property and Justice* (1996).

transferred to the other person, or validly seized in my bankruptcy. Because my obligation to you is only personal, rather than attached to the car, you cannot go after the car itself: you can only have me pay you compensation for the fact that I can no longer perform my duty to let you have the car. On the other hand, if I hold the car on trust for you, the car will commonly[16] not be validly transferred to the other person, and cannot be seized in my bankruptcy. Because my obligation is proprietary, ie attached to the car itself, you can demand that it be vindicated against the very car, and not just against me.

The characterization of trust obligations as proprietary or personal, and their relationship with the beneficiaries' rights, are matters dealt with more fully in Chapter 14.

1.10 THE ABSENCE OF A PERSONAL INTEREST IN THE TRUSTEE

The 'definition' given earlier stipulated that the trustee's obligations must extend 'to the exclusion of any personal interest'. The trust in the original example complied with this: the trustee there had no role other than to provide stewardship of the property and to transfer it as stipulated to Adam.

There are some arrangements which, like trusts, involve the owner of some property being subject to a legal duty, attached to the property, to handle it in a certain way; but where the owner does retain a personal interest in the property. Consider an easement. An easement arises where, for example, the owner of some land undertakes to permit his neighbour to walk across the land (the kind of arrangement known as a 'right of way'). The owner thus incurs an obligation to handle the land he owns in a particular way, for his neighbour's enjoyment, and this obligation is attached to the land. But he himself remains very substantially interested in the land: in all respects other than the inability to prevent the neighbour walking across it, it remains his. In particular, if he sells the land, he takes the proceeds for himself.

In the case of a trust, on the other hand, this will generally not be the case. If a trustee sells trust property, the proceeds will not be hers to keep, but will in turn become subject to the trust. The exception is where the trustee is also one of the beneficiaries, as discussed earlier. In

---

[16] A valid transfer will occur, however, if the transferee is a bona fide purchaser of the car without notice of your claim to it: see sections 8.3, 14.1.

that case, she will obviously have a personal interest, in the latter capacity.[17]

The rule that trustees should have no personal interest is an important one for the trust concept. Because it means there is no legitimate occasion for trustees to promote their own interests, the rule allows trustees' duties to be formulated on the basis that they must act solely for the sake of the trust's objects, and not allow their loyalties to become divided. As will be seen in section 13.10, this is an important element of the law's approach to ensuring a satisfactory performance of trusts. As will be discussed there, however, its functional significance may be overstated, and in practice it is often compromised.

1.11 THE ESSENTIALS OF TRUSTS

We began, albeit with caveats, by offering the following 'definition' of the trust concept:

A trust is a situation in which property is vested in someone (a trustee), who is under legally recognized obligations, at least some of which are of a proprietary kind, to handle it in a certain way, and to the exclusion of any personal interest. These obligations may arise either by conscious creation by the previous owner of the property (the settlor), or because some other legally significant circumstances are present.[18]

The various components of this 'definition' have now been reviewed and explained. Although again with caveats, we took an example, that of the grandmother's trust for Adam: more abstractly, a settlor transferring property to a trustee with instructions to handle it for the benefit of a beneficiary. We then saw how the various features of this may be essential or inessential to trusts. This trust arose because its settlor so intended; but trusts are recognized as arising for other reasons as well. It had a settlor, a trustee, and a beneficiary, who were different people; we have

---

[17] A few cases (*Binions v Evans* [1972] Ch 359; *Swiss Bank Corporation v Lloyds Bank Ltd* [1979] Ch 548; *Lyus v Prowsa Developments Ltd* [1982] 1 WLR 1044; *Ashburn Anstalt v Arnold* [1989] Ch 1) hold a 'trust' to arise where the trustee clearly retains a personal interest, just like the owner of land which is subject to an easement. These cases are discussed in sections 7.1 and 8.8, where it is argued that they do not truly involve trusts, on the ground in the text.

[18] This description of a trust is in most respects similar to that used in Article 2 of the Hague Convention on the Law Applicable to Trusts and on their Recognition. This Convention aims to secure international agreement that countries whose own law does not feature trusts will nevertheless respect trusts emanating from countries whose law does feature them. The principal difference between the description given in the Convention and that given in the text is that the former in effect confines itself to express trusts.

seen that whilst there must be a trustee, there need not be a settlor, and, in place of a beneficiary, the object of the trust might be a purpose. The trust must, however, always (like that in the example) involve some property, which the trustee will own but as regards the handling of which he will be under certain obligations of legal rather than just moral significance, some of which will be attached to the trust property. The example was typical in involving duties to disburse the trust property correctly and meanwhile to manage it, but the details of the duties, and the reasons why people wish to create them, may vary considerably. They must, however, remain within the realm of what is legally permitted, and they must in principle exclude any interest on the part of the trustee.

Taking all this into account, the 'definition' can therefore be seen to cover everything that is meant by the trust concept. Some points now need to be made, however, about two matters which are, deliberately, omitted from the 'definition'. These are matters which have been suggested as being essential to the trust concept, but which are not.

1.12 THE TRUST AS AN EQUITABLE CONCEPT?

First, it might be said that our description should be refined by recording that the trust is an 'equitable' concept, as opposed to a 'legal' one.

'Equitable' concepts are those which, historically, were developed by the Court of Chancery (whose chief, and for a long time sole, judge was the Chancellor), while 'legal'[19] concepts originated in the common law courts: the King's Bench, the Common Pleas, and the Exchequer. Trusts certainly originated in the Chancery,[20] and so count as equitable. Noting this fact would certainly add a true detail to our description of trusts. It is, however, questionable whether it adds information of useful significance.

The fact that the English legal system historically had more than one set of courts may have contributed to the emergence of the trust concept. The multiplicity of courts operating along somewhat independent lines probably allowed for a more enterprising exploration of conceptual possibilities than might otherwise have occurred, and trusts may be seen as one of the products of this process. But it would certainly not be impossible to reproduce the trust concept in a legal system which only ever had one set

---

[19] When that word is used in contradistinction to 'equitable'; in a broader sense, both equitable and legal concepts are legal, as opposed to, say, merely moral.

[20] For an account, see A Simpson *A History of the Land Law* 2nd edn (1986) ch 8. For certain periods of their history, trusts have been operated by the common law courts as well as by the Chancery, but it remains true that they were developed by the Chancery.

of courts;[21] and indeed, in England itself the different courts have been amalgamated for over a century.[22] So one looks rather for evidence that equitable concepts function differently from legal ones in the contemporary law. It is possible to find such evidence, but its power is open to question.

One piece of evidence is this. We have noted that if trust property is passed by the trustee to another person, the recipient will commonly, though not always, incur duties attached to the property.[23] The exact circumstances in which transferees are bound by duties attached to property under equitable concepts are slightly different from those in which they are bound by duties attached under legal concepts. To state that trusts are equitable can serve as a shorthand means of saying that they feature one, rather than the other, set of rules in this respect. But there is nothing in the labels 'equitable' and 'legal' to mean that the two sets of rules, and the differences between them, must be as they are. In fact, the modern tendency is to eliminate the differences, and to subject both legal and equitable concepts to a single regime of rules regarding the circumstances in which duties attached to property under them will affect recipients.[24]

Another piece of evidence is said to be that equitable concepts are less determinate than legal ones. That is, the law's response to a given set of facts is less easily identified when an equitable concept is in play than when a legal one is. This is because, it is in turn said, equity and the common law define their responses in different ways. Whilst the dictates of legal concepts are seen as generally contained in hard-and-fast rules, which the judge has only to identify and apply, the dictates of equitable concepts are seen as generally established by an exercise of creative judgement—discretion—on the part of a judge. It is a commonplace that the law as a whole makes use both of relatively determinate rules and of rules requiring a greater degree of discretion. What requires examination is the thesis that discretion, and so the tendency to indeterminacy, is especially characteristic of equity.[25]

---

[21] For a survey of the occurrence of the trust concept in different countries' legal systems (many of which have never had a separation of courts), see M Lupoi *Trust Laws of the World: A Collection of Original Texts* (1996).

[22] Finally as a result of the Judicature Acts 1873–5, but the assimilation was begun in earlier legislation.

[23] See section 1.9.

[24] Notably, by requiring duties attached to property to be recorded in a national register before they will affect a recipient. This is especially the approach of the Land Registration Acts 1925 and 2002.

[25] For references to literature supporting this thesis, see A Duggan (1997) 113 LQR 601.

One question over the thesis is whether it is factually accurate in the observations it makes about the way in which legal and equitable concepts operate. Presumably the claim is not that discretion is discernible only in equitable doctrines,[26] but that equity uses discretion more than the common law. It is difficult to test this claim. Discretion is not a simple phenomenon;[27] it is straightforward neither to identify nor even to describe, and its use is accordingly hard to quantify. It is clear, in particular, that propositions which do not explicitly call for judicial discretion may nevertheless do so implicitly. For example, a requirement 'to take reasonable care' does not itself tell us exactly what is required in the circumstances of a particular case: that is established rather by a judge, authoritatively interpreting the requirement. At the same time, it is a mistake to regard a doctrine which (explicitly or implicitly) requires judicial discretion in its implementation as therefore indeterminate. Discretions normally are, and it is thought in legal contexts should be, exercised according to fairly clear patterns. This needs to be taken into account when attempting to assess a concept's determinacy.

If, despite these problems, one concludes that equitable concepts are as a matter of fact less determinate than legal ones, a second difficulty arises. Is the relative indeterminacy of equitable concepts a necessary facet of their being equitable, or is the link looser than that? Again, the matter is hard to test, as it is unclear just what it means to say that some characteristic of a doctrine is a 'necessary facet' of its being legal or equitable. But an argument is sometimes made in this vein.

The argument starts from the proposition that, of its nature, equity is a supplement on the law. That is, equity is the vehicle whereby considerations which deserve attention, but which are insufficiently reflected by the law's rules, are given effect. This proposition is undoubtedly an accurate description of the way in which equity first developed, in the late Middle Ages.[28] The ordinary legal regime had become somewhat ossified, and was acknowledged therefore not to do satisfactory justice in all circumstances. Where the Chancellor found that this was likely to be the

---

[26] There are certainly some common law concepts which rely heavily upon judicial discretion, such as the jurisdiction to quash an administrative action upon judicial review. There are also some highly discretionary jurisdictions which cannot sensibly be ascribed either to the common law or to equity (because in their current forms they substantially post-date the amalgamation of the common law and equity courts); eg the sentencing of criminals, and most jurisdictions concerned with family matters.

[27] See generally K Hawkins (ed) *The Uses of Discretion* (1991) especially Part I.

[28] For an account of the history of equity, see J Baker *An Introduction to English Legal History* 4th edn (2002) ch 6.

case, he intervened, essentially under the royal prerogative, making orders calculated to align the outcome better with abstract justice.[29] But to say that equity consists in a set of pronouncements whereby the law is given a more satisfactory shape is not necessarily to say that it is special on account of inherent indeterminacy. The indeterminacy may be only in the short term, while the reform takes hold; thereafter, the new rule may be as determinate as any other.[30] Equity may more easily be seen as special on account of indeterminacy if it is regarded as *constantly* operating to supplement the rules with considerations which those rules do not sufficiently reflect. On that account, it must consist of ideas that are in principle enduringly and necessarily indeterminate, for without that quality they would be unfitted for their work of infinite supplementation.[31] Is there evidence for this version of the account?

It is commonly said that there was a significant degree of indeterminacy about equity as it first developed. This proposition requires careful discussion. The interventions by the medieval Chancellors were aimed at compelling those involved in the matter in question to act in accordance with conscience, in exceptional cases when the common law failed to secure this. This activity can certainly be described as ad hoc. The reference to conscience focused upon what it was right for the individual to do: a person's conscience was conceived as his purest means of perceiving the implications for him of perfect (divine) justice, which, especially where the relevant facts were not publicly known, might even be perceptible by him uniquely. And, almost certainly connected with this concern to require compliance with the dictates of a person's conscience, the Chancellor's instructions were '*in personam*': ie they consisted not in generalized rules but in individual orders issued to individual people, requiring them to perform, or refrain from, certain acts. But although the Chancellor's activity was thus certainly ad hoc, in the sense of

[29] The stock illustration is this. The common law regarded a sealed bond as incontrovertible evidence of the debt to which it testified. So if a debtor failed to get the bond cancelled when repaying the debt, the creditor could, so far as the common law was concerned, require him to pay over again. It was not that this was thought just: only that looking simply to the bond was more certain than looking to the individual facts, and the common law courts had come to attach supreme value to that certainty. For a creditor to act unjustly in this way was, however, against his conscience. The Chancellor, aiming to prevent breaches of conscience, therefore intervened to prevent him.

[30] This account is attractive to many. For one appeal to it, see A Mason (1994) 100 LQR 238: whilst celebrating equity's role in facilitating reform, Mason represents any indeterminacy produced thereby as a short-term price worth paying.

[31] For this version of the argument, see M Halliwell *Equity & Good Conscience in a Contemporary Context* (1997).

individualized, there is nothing which necessarily entails that it was indeterminate. The dictates of conscience, the nature of the exceptional circumstances, and the content of the corrective orders could in principle all have been firmly established. It is in fact hard to believe that, despite the lack of published systematization, there was not in fact a high degree of repetition about the situations eliciting the Chancellor's intervention and about the nature of that intervention.[32] If early equity was indeed indeterminate, the only necessary reason for this was probably the fact that it was naturally somewhat experimental. It is far from clear, then, that we should regard early equity as aimed at constant supplementation, as opposed to de facto substantive reform, albeit by the use of ad hoc techniques.

It seems clear that by soon after the end of the medieval period, equity could at least sometimes have been, and was, accurately described as indeterminate. But the reasons for this indeterminacy seem not to have been intrinsic to a mission of supplementation. One may have been the great increase at this time in the volume of the business brought before the Chancellor, which, in the absence of systematization, will have increased the likelihood of inconsistencies. Another may have been the contemporaneous general movement, epitomized by the Reformation, towards the secularization of the State. As the ideas of justice and conscience thereupon lost the old (divine, and so transcendent) reference point for their content, it was unclear whence they would acquire a new one, other than from the personal opinion of the Chancellor.

During this early modern period, the nature of the cases brought before the Chancellor had become more ordinary; and this ordinariness placed a higher premium on determinacy. It thus came increasingly to be suggested that the indeterminacy of the Chancellor's activities was unsatisfactory. The force of these suggestions, which eventually became associated with the more general movement against rule by personal (most especially, royal) preference in the seventeenth century, elicited a firm systematization of the rules of equity during this period.[33] Thenceforth, equity was, and was applauded for being, generally no less

---

[32] One cannot be positive one way or the other, as there are no records of the Chancellors' early activities. On the other hand, the pleas for such intervention have been preserved. In these, certain kinds of situation are repeatedly referred to in similar terms as meriting the Chancellor's intervention, prompting the conclusion that there was an expectation (both in principle and in practice) that the Chancellor would operate according to a pattern.

[33] D Yale *Nottingham's Chancery Cases* Vol II (1961) Introduction.

determinate than the common law. Subject to the two qualifications about to be discussed, this state of affairs has generally continued to the present day.[34]

The first qualification is that at least some Chancery judges presented equity as inherently indeterminate in the last quarter of the nineteenth century. The context was this. Where a person enters into a contract to buy a piece of land, or to lease it, equity will under certain circumstances regard that person as already the owner or the lessee of the land, even before the legal formalities to that effect are complete.[35] The way in which this doctrine was and is applied assumes that the rights so acquired are reasonably concrete, and this can only be the case if the circumstances in which they are acquired are reasonably determinate. Yet in the last quarter of the nineteenth century, one finds a flurry of judicial statements to the effect that such rights arise only where, if the matter had come before a judge, the judge would have chosen so to order, in the exercise of a discretion. This late outcrop of ostensible affection for indeterminacy was very specific to the area of law in question, however, and it seems to owe nothing to a sense that equity has a peculiar mission of constant supplementation. Rather, it probably sprang from a concern to make the rules of equity difficult to grasp. A recent statutory reform (contained in the Judicature Acts 1873–5) had merged the common law courts with the Chancery, with the aim that the common law and equity should in future be administered by the same personnel. This reform was widely unpopular among Chancery lawyers, and they appear to have played up the indeterminacy and hence impenetrability of this facet of equity as a means of substantiating their claim that equity could never be accessible to common lawyers.[36]

The second qualification is that, since about 1970, a number of judges and commentators (principally in Australia, Canada, and New Zealand, but also in England) have made a point of depicting equity as indeterminate.[37] Much reference has been made to 'conscience', specifically in the form of 'unconscionability'; and although there is nothing about these concepts requiring them to be indeterminate, it is clear that they are so

---

[34] A non-discretionary view of the implications of the trust concept was strongly asserted in *Foskett v McKeown* [2001] 1 AC 102, 108–9, 127.

[35] See section 8.7.

[36] S Gardner (1987) 7 OJLS 60, 92–7.

[37] See the literature collected by A Duggan (1997) 113 LQR 601. The approach is undeniably reflected in some equitable phenomena, including the remedial constructive trust and the doctrine of proprietary estoppel: sections 7.3 and 8.10.

regarded within this movement. It may be possible to ascribe this development too to particular catalysts. One may have been that the equity and common law courts of the dominant Australian jurisdiction, New South Wales, were merged in 1970; like its English counterpart a century earlier, this development was opposed by some Chancery lawyers, who may have found a counter-weapon in the depiction of equity as indeterminate. Another may have been the interest in Australia, Canada, and New Zealand, as they and the United Kingdom increasingly diverged politically, in forming distinctive laws of their own, though at the same time continuing for the most part to claim the legitimacy of historical derivation for these laws. The latter end is served by invoking an established concept such as equity, whilst the former is served by claiming that that concept is indeterminate, and so infinitely capable of producing new effects. A third catalyst may have been the movement, in England from the 1980s on, towards barristers losing their virtual monopoly of audience in the higher courts, instead having to share it with solicitors. Indeterminacy in an area of law favours the specialist in that area (ie the barrister), who is in a position to decipher the unwritten patterns, over the non-specialist (the solicitor).[38] A fourth factor may have been the increased academic interest during this period in deconstructionist and post-modernist styles of thought, a trait of which is to emphasize, and to some degree celebrate, the idea of supplementation. Some adherents to these styles of thought see equity as quintessentially the embodiment of that idea.[39] The sustainability of the latter perspective is, of course, the question currently under consideration.

On the whole, therefore, there is no strong evidence that equity is special—essentially different from the common law—as having a mission of constant supplementation, or on any other account. To put the evidence at its highest, one can satisfactorily say that equity has undoubtedly displayed certain distinctive features. But this does not warrant the crucial conclusion that an approach different from that of the common law is intrinsic to the very idea of equity. So although we can accurately add into our description of trusts the point that the obligations in question must be equitable ones, to do so is not to make a significant contribution to that description.

---

[38] M Galanter (1974) 9 Law and Society Review 95.
[39] eg M Halliwell *Equity & Good Conscience in a Contemporary Context* (1997).

1.13 KNOWLEDGE BY THE TRUSTEE?

The second matter which might be said to be essential to trusts, but which we have omitted from our 'definition', is a requirement that the trustee should know of the facts on account of which the law finds a trust. In the example with which we began, there was no reason to suppose that the trustee was unaware of the trust being created. And that will generally be the case, whether the trust is express, where the trustee will know that the settlor is trying to create a trust; or resulting or constructive, where the trustee will know of, because she will have been involved in, the facts which lead the law to impose the trust.

According to Lord Browne-Wilkinson in *Westdeutsche Landesbank Girozentrale v Islington LBC*,[40] such knowledge is essential to a trust. On this view, an express trust cannot arise unless the alleged trustee knows that he is supposed to hold the property on trust, and a resulting or constructive trust cannot arise unless the alleged trustee knows of the facts by reason of which that trust would arise. So if I make you an apparent gift without your knowledge, it is only from the moment of your enlightenment that you hold the property on a resulting trust.[41] Or if I, already a trustee, give trust property to you, you hold it on trust too only when you know of the trust.[42] Lord Browne-Wilkinson concedes however that in the latter of these two situations, but apparently only there, although you do not hold *on trust* until you know of the trust, meanwhile an innominate situation arises in which you may not treat the property as beneficially your own.[43] This means that so long as you retain the property you can be required to transfer it to the beneficiaries, if they are immediately entitled, or to new trustees; but you have no other responsibilities, so that if you lose the property before attaining the necessary knowledge, you incur no liability to make good the loss. (Though if you give the property to someone else, presumably the same will go for them.)

---

[40] [1996] AC 669, 705–6, 715. Other members of the House of Lords concurred with Lord Browne-Wilkinson: [1996] AC 669, 689, 718, 720. The position taken in the text assumes that the supposed requirement of knowledge by the trustee was not necessary to the court's decision: that the claimant lost because the resulting trust for which it argued could not arise in the circumstances at issue, regardless of the alleged trustee's knowledge (see the discussion in section 7.5). If that is incorrect, and the requirement of knowledge was essential to the decision, there would be no choice but to incorporate it in our 'definition' of the trust concept in at any rate English law.
[41] Section 7.5 describes how resulting trusts arise in cases of apparent gifts.
[42] Section 8.3 describes how a recipient of trust property holds it on trust.
[43] [1996] AC 669, 707.

Lord Browne-Wilkinson's view is generally doubted, however. The commoner opinion is that trusts can arise without the alleged trustee's knowledge,[44] and that is the position taken by our 'definition'. In particular, there seems clear authority that if I make you an apparent gift without your knowledge, you nonetheless hold it on resulting trust.[45]

Lord Browne-Wilkinson based his notion on the idea that trusts, being equitable concepts, can arise only where the alleged trustee's conscience is engaged: which, he continues, is only where the alleged trustee knows of the reasons why it should be engaged.[46] We saw in the last section that attention to conscience was crucial to early equity. But as equitable jurisprudence later underwent the systematization also referred to in the last section, its concepts ceased to be defined by direct reference to the dictates of conscience. At the end of that section we noted however that references to conscience have sometimes continued to be made, in the service of other agendas. The view of Lord Browne-Wilkinson under discussion can be regarded in this way. The reference to conscience provides a vehicle, of a historically resonant and contemporarily fashionable kind, for what seems to be a concern to ensure that trusts operate in a practically acceptable way. It is perhaps aimed at one worry in particular. It would be unsatisfactory if someone having no reason to think herself a trustee was liable for breach of a trustee's duty to keep the property safe. On Lord Browne-Wilkinson's view, she would escape such liability on the ground that she is not a trustee. But the law seems to come to this result anyway. Lord Browne-Wilkinson's opponents assert that whilst someone can be a trustee and so incur the duty whether she knows it or not, she does not *breach* the duty unless she could have known that she held the property in question on trust.[47] This rule is probably the law, though it is little emphasized outside the case of the unwitting recipient of trust property,[48] as most other trustees do realize their status as such, and would-be claimants against those who do not have probably always recognized the unpromising nature of their claim. If this rule is the law, the practical justification for Lord Browne-Wilkinson's view is removed.

---

[44] This view was expressly taken in *Hardoon v Belilios* [1901] AC 118, 123.

[45] *Birch v Blagrave* (1755) 1 Amb 264; *Childers v Childers* (1857) 1 De G & J 482; *Re Vinogradoff* [1935] WN 68.

[46] [1996] AC 669, 705.

[47] R Chambers *Resulting Trusts* (1997) 201–12; C Harpum in P Birks and F Rose (eds) *Restitution and Equity Volume One, Resulting Trusts and Equitable Compensation* (2000) 165–7.

[48] See section 15.9.

2

Policies shaping the express trust concept

In the last chapter we identified what we mean by the trust concept. As we saw, the concept involves certain facts being treated in a particular way by the law, above all by the imposition of a legal duty upon the trustee. We did not, however, address the question *why* the law maintains the trust concept, ie treats these facts in this way.

In addressing this question, we need to distinguish between express and constructive trusts. As noted in the previous chapter, express trusts arise because a settlor decides to create them, while constructive trusts arise for other reasons. In this chapter, we shall consider why such a decision by a settlor elicits the legal response of a trust, and whether it should. The reasons for constructive trusts, and the justifiability of the legal significance of these reasons, will be considered in Chapters 7 and 8.[1]

2.1 EXPRESS TRUSTS AS FACILITATIVE DEVICES

If we accept that an express trust is one which arises because its settlor wishes it to, have we not thereby answered the question why the law recognizes it? No. There are many situations in which I may wish something to occur, but in which the law does not oblige persons concerned to make it occur, as it does when it says that they are trustees. Why, then, does the law impose obligations in aid of my wish to create a trust?

It is sometimes suggested that the obligation in express trusts may be explained in terms of the trustee's being unjustly enriched at the expense of the settlor. The argument is that if the trustee did not observe the settlor's instructions, but kept the property for herself or disposed of it however else she wished, she would have been unjustly enriched at the settlor's expense; and that the trustee's duty arises so as to prevent this

---

[1] The third category of trust, namely the resulting trust, is said by some to arise because its settlor wants it to, analogously to the express trust; by others, because of some other legally significant reason, analogously to the constructive trust. That argument is considered in sections 7.6–7.7.

from occurring. This suggestion, however, makes no sense in the case where the settlor declares himself trustee of some property which she already holds. Here, no one is unjustly enriched at her expense, because she has not parted with the property. Yet she is still under a duty to implement the terms of the trust. Moreover, the trustee's unjust enrichment at the settlor's expense could always be prevented by requiring the trustee to restore the property to the settlor. So this suggestion does not ultimately provide what we are seeking, namely a reason why the trustee should be under a duty actually to carry out the terms of the trust.

Alternatively, it might be suggested that the obligation arises so as to prevent the trustee's unjust enrichment at the expense of the beneficiary, in the form of her intercepting a benefit which would otherwise have gone to the latter. This suggestion too has problems. What if the object of the trust is not a beneficiary but a purpose? Is it possible to be unjustly enriched at the expense of anything but a person? Moreover, except in very simple cases where a straightforward gift would have done as well as a trust, it is hard to see how the benefit could have reached the intended beneficiary unless the trust was effective anyway. So in saying that the trustee is enriched by intercepting that which should have gone to the beneficiary, the argument assumes what we need it to prove—namely, again, a reason why the settlor's intention to create the trust should be legally effective.

One seems to get closer to the point if one suggests instead that the settlor's wish to create a trust gives rise to an expectation on the part of the settlor or beneficiary, against the trustee, that the trustee will perform the trust, and that the trustee comes under a duty to fulfil this expectation. But this answer too will not suffice. One cannot realistically identify any such expectation in at least some cases in which a trust is undoubtedly present. For example, a purpose, as opposed to a beneficiary, cannot have expectations. Where the beneficiary has not yet been born, or his identity has not yet been established (eg 'such person as my daughter may in future marry'), he cannot have an expectation. Even where there is an identified living beneficiary, there is no need for him to know about the trust or its terms, so as to form expectations about it. A settlor making a trust by will cannot have expectations either. And a settlor who makes himself trustee cannot sensibly be said to have expectations against himself. Moreover, this explanation does not suffice even in situations where expectations can meaningfully be said to exist. We wanted to know why the law should translate a wish to create a trust into a legally recognized duty on the trustee to carry out the trust, when it is clear that it does no such thing so far as many wishes are concerned. Speaking in terms of expectations does not answer this question. It merely reformulates it as an inquiry why the law should translate expectations of this particular kind into legally recognized duties.[2] So all the suggestions considered so far fail to answer the question at which they are purportedly aimed, and would still do so even if their other deficiencies were met or overlooked.

It is striking that all the suggestions considered so far envisage the source of the obligation as a natural one, in this sense: they depict the people concerned (especially settlors) as acting in a state of utopian innocence, and then seek to explain, in terms of notions extrinsic to the actions themselves, why their naive actions should have the binding effect that we actually observe. This kind of approach may be appropriate in contexts where the people involved do characteristically act without reference to the question of what their obligations might be: in cases of accidentally or indeed deliberately causing loss, for example—the area of the law of tort. The situations in which constructive trusts arise are often of this kind. There, people who acted with no notion of coming under trust-type obligations may have arrived at a position which seems to demand that such obligations be imposed. But our present concern is with express trusts, which arise in principle only where a settlor wants to make one.

This conscious, voluntary quality of express trusts is the key to understanding the obligation which arises in them. It means that the people concerned (settlors, trustees) are characteristically not acting in innocence, with the trust concept coming in from outside to deal with the consequences of what they have done. Instead, they are acting with their eyes already on the concept, and deliberately interacting with it. They can be seen, therefore, as undertaking roles in an activity with preordained rules.

The idea may become clearer if we draw an analogy with the playing of some recognized sport. There is no natural reason whatever why a certain configuration of people on a field ('an offside situation') should lead to one person kicking a ball in a particular fashion ('taking a free kick'). Explaining the connection between them involves referring to the

---

[2] In the case of contracts, where the law renders the expectation of performance into a legal obligation to that effect, the answer to the question 'Why?' lies in the presence of consideration. The further questions 'What is the essence of consideration?' and 'Why should it have this effect?' are not without difficulty, however. The outstanding literature includes P Atiyah *The Rise and Fall of Freedom of Contract* (1979) and *Promises, Morals and Law* (1981), and C Fried *Contract as Promise* (1981).

internal arrangements of the game, football, to which the participants submit themselves when they elect to play. So the express trust can be thought of as a defined package in which certain actions have certain specified effects, to which people may choose to subscribe. Deciding to create a trust gives rise to a duty of giving effect to the trust's terms because that is the convention that one is opting into. There is thus a crucial difference between the question why an obligation should arise where a settlor wishes to bestow certain benefits upon his objects, to which we are hard put to supply a satisfactory answer; and the question why an obligation should arise where a settlor decides to create a trust, to which the answer is, in effect, 'because that is what making a trust means'.[3]

The idea, then, is that society, through the law, maintains the express trust concept as a packaged arrangement of rules about dispositions of property which those who wish to make such dispositions may use in order to do so, in the foreknowledge of what is entailed. As such, the concept is what is known as a 'facilitative' provision: a facility of which people may take advantage if they wish to achieve the results it comports.

2.2 THE BASIS FOR THE FACILITATIVE PROVISION OF A TRUST DEVICE

But this in turn raises the question why this particular facilitative provision should exist. Why should 'deciding to make a trust' mean something more than 'wishing to bestow certain benefits'? The existence of express trusts enables people to make dispositions of their property of a more complicated kind than simply giving it away; why should the law go to the trouble of providing a facility for doing this? There seems to be an assumption that people have a legitimate interest in being able to do so, for which the law should cater by offering the necessary facilitative device. Why should this be?

The answer lies in liberalism, especially the liberal vision of the institution of property. Liberalism argues that everyone should be permitted the largest possible degree of autonomy. The autonomy of a property owner is protected if we say that she does not lose her property unless she herself intentionally gives it away; but her autonomy is also maximized if

---

[3] There appears to be an analogy between trusts and covenants, ie promises made without consideration but in a deed. It is hard to explain why making a covenant should give rise to a legally recognized obligation to perform it (the deed seems to have no 'natural' importance, in the sense used in the text) except in the terms 'Because that is what making a covenant means'.

we accord her the greatest possible freedom as to how she may intentionally give it away. If she might wish to dispose of it in some elaborately arranged fashion, she should be able to do so. The law provides the vehicle of the express trust in order to permit this.

But it is not enough to locate the basis of express trusts in liberal theory and leave matters there. Trusts—or at any rate some uses of the trust device—can be seen as serving other useful interests besides the liberty of settlors. Pension provisions and charitable initiatives, for example, may be thought 'good things' for reasons over and above the fact that they represent the fulfilment of someone's wishes. At the same time, while trusts serve the liberty of settlors, they—or, again, some uses to which they are put—may harm other wholesome interests. A trust to finance drug trafficking is harmful, for example, although it is just as much an exercise of its settlor's liberty as any other trust.

Recognizing that the express trust concept has its foundation in liberalism does not, therefore, mean that to point to the settlor's wish is always the only justification for a trust. Nor does this recognition provide a sufficient justification for allowing property owners carte blanche to organize the fate of their property in absolutely any way they may fancy. We should look at the other considerations by which the express trust device may be additionally supported or, on the other hand, according to which it may be problematic.

We shall look at these other considerations under four heads (which are doubtless not exhaustive). The first type is paternalist: preventing a settlor from acting against his own interests. The second is communitarian: taking the point that to concentrate exclusively on the wishes of an individual, the settlor, may be to overlook the interests of groups, which may be affected by those wishes. The third type is utilitarian: considerations as to whether trusts' effects are more beneficial than deleterious. And the fourth focuses upon rights, the concern here being whether trusts vindicate or infringe people's rights. We shall see too how the law to some extent reflects these other considerations, rather than assuming a purely facilitative shape.

2.3 PATERNALISTIC CONSIDERATIONS

Paternalism demands an effort to ensure that people act in accordance with their own interests. So on this view, if it seemed that a settlor was acting against his own interests in making a trust of his property, the law ought not to uphold that trust.

There are, however, different kinds of paternalism. The least controversial simply recognizes the natural limitations of liberalism. It is one thing to leave people to decide for themselves how to behave when they possess the usual collection of faculties and fruits of experience which characterize normal adulthood: then, it can be seen as insulting to them not to leave them to their own devices. But it is another thing to take this attitude if they lack these attributes. So freedoms which are accorded to ordinary adults are often withheld from children and sufferers from mental disorders, because it is thought that such people lack the rationality and experience satisfactorily to make judgements about the exercise of such freedoms. There can be debate about where the lines should be drawn, but the general point is commonplace enough.

Thus, in the trusts context, the facilitative project—the law's provision of the liberty to make trusts—does not extend in its full form to children and mental patients. A child can make a trust, but is permitted to disavow it at any time up to, and shortly after, reaching majority (the point being that then, as an adult, he is mature enough to be allowed to commit himself).[4] The position regarding mental patients is not altogether clear, but seems to involve treating such people as to at least some extent of less than full capacity.[5]

The position of a responsible adult who is temporarily disabled from exercising his own judgement is similar. Say a person is instructed to do some act at gunpoint, or misunderstands the nature of what he is doing: although he possesses the normal faculties, he is not in a position to give full rein to them, and so it would be wrong to accord his action dispositive effect. In this vein, there are rules that settlors can disavow trusts made under duress, undue influence, and mistake (either a spontaneous misconception by the settlor, or one induced by some other person's misrepresentation).

Paternalism moves to another level if it requires effect to be denied to a transaction which, although made by a normal adult in full command of the situation, seems improvident according to some external standard. This is a much more controversial idea, for, unlike the situations we have looked at so far, it cannot be put in terms of the natural limitations of liberalism. However, the law of trusts has some features of this cast, albeit presented in the less controversial terms of incapacity or loss of

---

[4] *Edwards v Carter* [1893] AC 360.

[5] Though the Court of Protection, which looks after the interests of such people, may make trusts of their property on their behalf: Mental Health Act 1983 ss 95–6.

command. For example, where the settlor makes the trust on the advice of some person who is in a position to sway his judgement, and the trust appears improvident, the trust is *presumed* to have been made under undue influence, and is therefore invalid unless the presumption can be rebutted. At one time, indeed, there seems to have been a presumption that any trust involving a substantial amount of property was made under a misunderstanding as to its effect, so as to make it invalid unless the presumption could be rebutted;[6] but this is not the modern law.[7]

2.4 COMMUNITARIAN CONSIDERATIONS

'Communitarianism' refers to a collection of ideas having, as their common theme, the perception that well-being is better promoted if the potential role, interests and responsibilities of communities are made part of the reckoning. This perception runs counter to liberalism's thesis that well-being is best served by concentrating on the freedom of individuals, and communitarianism can therefore sometimes indicate prescriptions different from liberalism's.

One natural concern of communitarianism is to protect and foster such institutions as the family. Recognition of this concern would entail allowing or indeed encouraging settlors to make trusts whose provisions are aligned with their family obligations. For centuries, in fact, making family provision has been a very important application of the trust device. Indeed, long ago it would probably have made less sense to justify trusts on the ground that they vindicated settlors' freedoms than on the ground that they provided the vehicle for the fulfilment of settlors' family obligations. And a concern that property should not be alienated from families may have underlain the presumption that property gratuitously transferred is held by the transferee on resulting trust.[8] The idea of the 'family' behind this point is a rather specialized one, however, having a dynastic quality, or at any rate a dimension of wealth serving more than just basic needs. A more down-to-earth idea of the family can also be served by the trust concept, though, and there is some evidence of the law's reacting to this. In one case, an express trust was found on the basis of less than cogent evidence, so that a portion of a man's property did not pass on his death to his estranged wife, but was held on trust for the

---

[6] *Hoghton v Hoghton* (1852) 15 Beav 278; *Price v Price* (1852) 1 De GM & G 308.
[7] *Henry v Armstrong* (1881) 18 Ch D 668; *Dutton v Thompson* (1883) 23 Ch D 278.
[8] See sections 3.7, 7.5.

woman with whom he had been living for nine years.[9] And a type of constructive trust, which in theory requires a common intention that property should be shared, is frequently found on the basis of little real evidence of such an intention, the motive influence apparently being to achieve a just sharing of property among those contributing to a family's well-being.[10]

A concern to protect and foster institutions such as the family would also entail denying settlors the liberty to make trusts where to do so would have a deleterious effect on those institutions. The law takes this line, in a group of rules prohibiting settlors from attaching conditions to beneficiaries' entitlements of a kind which, broadly, would damage the beneficiaries' natural family relationships. So, for example, conditions tending to promote separation or divorce of married couples (eg 'for Adam, as soon as he leaves his wife'),[11] or tending to separate children from their parents ('for Adam, but only so long as he has no contact with his father'),[12] would probably be disallowed. However, we are asked to distinguish such conditions from apparently similar ones which have been allowed. For example, a trust was permitted to stand when it was viewed as containing arrangements for the aftermath of a couple's separation, as opposed to encouraging the separation or discouraging a reconciliation itself.[13] Some of these distinctions seem more plausible than others. In effect, it seems that different judges take different views on the relative weight they give to this communitarian concern on the one hand, and to liberal considerations on the other. A striking example of liberalism being preferred over communitarianism occurred in one case where the House of Lords, having explicitly discussed the issue in these terms, allowed a trust which forfeited the interest of any beneficiary who became a Roman Catholic, thereby interfering with the upbringing of the infant beneficiaries by their parents.[14] The possibility that communitarian thinking may now have been brought into the law by the Human Rights Act 1998 is, however, discussed in section 2.6 below.

Communitarianism also asks that we think carefully whether some desired effect is better delivered by legal rules and remedies, or by some

---

[9] *Paul v Constance* [1977] 1 WLR 527; also *Rowe v Prance* [1999] 2 FLR 787.
[10] See section 8.11.
[11] *Re Caborne* [1943] Ch 224; *Re Johnson's Will Trusts* [1967] Ch 387.
[12] *Re Sandbrook* [1912] 2 Ch 471.
[13] *Re Lovell* [1920] 1 Ch 122.
[14] *Blathwayt v Lord Cawley* [1976] AC 397. Cf *Re Boulter* [1922] 1 Ch 75; *Re Borwick* [1933] Ch 657.

other form of prescription. Specifically, the suggestion is that the law's techniques are (necessarily or otherwise) stiff and commonly adversarial; and that social techniques marked by these qualities may never be unequivocally desirable, and that there are some contexts, especially those which are or ought to be characterized by more humane values, in which they are certainly out of place.[15] This argument is clearly of potential relevance to the treatment of trusts. In particular, the relationships between the settlor, the trustees, and the beneficiaries of a family trust will commonly be of such a kind that legal enforcement could be thought inappropriate.

First appearances are that the law does not reflect this perception. There is substantial authority to the effect that a trust cannot be valid unless it is capable of being enforced in court.[16] Any inference that the courts necessarily keep trustees on a tight rein would be false, however. In a body of decisions largely taken with reference to family trusts, the judges have shown themselves generally reluctant to intervene against trustees.[17] So long as trustees exercising a discretion take the proper factors and only those factors into account, for example, a court will not interfere with the choices they make, even if the judge disagrees with them.[18] Trustees do not generally have to disclose the reasons why they made the choices they did, so that in the absence of other evidence to the contrary their choices are presumed valid.[19] And the court will respect a settlor's stipulation that her trustees' duties shall be almost entirely unenforceable against them.[20]

The law's special provision for charitable trusts can readily be seen in communitarian terms. It may not, however, be correct to conclude that there should therefore be relatively little legal intervention in the case of such trusts. As we shall discover in Chapter 6, the law's treatment of charitable trusts is to a large extent best seen as reflecting a sense that, as

---

[15] This suggestion appears to have been accepted in, especially, the fact that bargains between family members in the family context are often treated as not legally enforceable, as involving no 'intention to create legal relations'.

[16] *Morice v Bishop of Durham* (1804) 9 Ves 399, 404–5, (1805) 10 Ves 522, 539; *Re Astor's Settlement Trusts* [1952] Ch 534, 541–2; *Re Shaw* [1957] 1 WLR 729, 744–5; *Leahy v AG for New South Wales* [1959] AC 457, 479, 484.

[17] See further section 14.6.

[18] *Gisborne v Gisborne* (1877) 2 App Cas 300; *Tempest v Lord Camoys* (1882) 21 Ch D 571.

[19] *Re Beloved Wilkes' Charity* (1851) 3 Mac & G 440; *Re Londonderry's Settlement* [1965] Ch 918. These decisions, regarding a charity and a family trust respectively, were followed—arguably inappropriately—in the pension scheme trust case of *Wilson v Law Debenture Corp plc* [1995] 2 All ER 337.

[20] *Armitage v Nurse* [1998] Ch 241.

well as acts of humanity on the part of their settlors, they represent a valuable part of the nation's social provision. If that is so, it follows that there is a public interest in their satisfactory operation, and it is possible to regard this as not less suitable for legal supervision than the satisfactory operation of those aspects of social provision which derive from the government. The latter have in recent times become the subject of a relatively high degree of legal intervention, in the form of judicial review. And indeed, although the actions of charitable trusts are not tightly controlled by the courts,[21] they have increasingly been supervised by a state institution, the Charity Commission.

Communitarian considerations seem at their least relevant, and from this point of view legal intervention therefore seems least contraindicated, in the case of trusts made in commercial spheres. Unit trusts are of this kind. So may be pension fund trusts,[22] with the demise of the perspective that the provision of a pension is an act of altruism by the employer (which might suggest unenforceability in legal terms) in favour of the perspective that it represents a component of the pay-and-benefits 'package' like any other. The latter description does not fully capture the prevailing perception, however. It misses the points that there is an important social interest in employment conditions (including pension arrangements) satisfactorily reflecting the interests of employees as people; and that the ability of the state to economize on the provision of public pensions depends on their work being done instead by private (including company) pensions, implying that the latter cannot be significantly less fair or secure.[23] Although these considerations have communitarian resonances, this is an instance where communitarianism might be content to recruit the law, so as to see them satisfactorily vindicated.[24] All in all, therefore, one might expect pension fund trusts to attract a relatively high degree of judicial activity. The picture is ambiguous, however. There is a significant body of modern reported litigation regarding the administration of pension fund trusts, as those aggrieved by actions taken

---

[21] *Re Beloved Wilkes' Charity* (1851) 3 Mac & G 440.

[22] G Moffat (1993) 56 MLR 471.

[23] The importance of private-sector pensions to the state is implicit in the material aimed more explicitly at improving their fairness and security of operation, notably Pension Law Review Committee *Pension Law Reform* Cm 2342 (1993); Department of Social Security *Security, Equality, Choice: The Future for Pensions* Cm 2594 (1994); Pensions Act 1995.

[24] The considerations may be promoted by other techniques than judicial intervention, however. The Pensions Act 1995 uses watchdogs in the shape of the Occupational Pensions Regulatory Authority and the Pensions Ombudsman, and provides for some of a pension scheme's trustees to be drawn from among its beneficiaries.

in respect of such trusts have sought judicial relief. But the judicial response has not always been markedly interventionist.[25] This restraint[26] may, however, be best understood less in terms of communitarianism than in those of a free-market ethic, whereby the parties' bargain is to be respected and not interfered in by the law.[27] A communitarian perspective is once again required, though, when it is realized that the bargains looked to here are collective ones, between the employer and the present and prospective pensioners, and that it was therefore not a foregone conclusion that the latter would have a voice at all.[28] The complexity of the overall picture reflects the point that, in the polyvalent nature of our society, it is routine for communitarian concerns and approaches to be inextricably interwoven with those of other types.

2.5 UTILITARIAN CONSIDERATIONS

Utilitarianism demands that we consider the question whether a trust does more good than harm, and proposes that the settlor be permitted to make it if, but only if, the answer is yes.

It is possible to be selective about the kinds of factors to be included in the calculus of good and harm, but at its widest it involves taking account, on the one side, of the general utility of according rights to private property, the more specific social advantages of the trust device in general, and more specifically still the benefits of the particular type of trust in question; and, on the other, of any hurt done to the trust's beneficiaries, to particular other people outside the trust (eg the settlor's creditors), and to society in general.[29]

We cannot attempt anything like a complete assessment of the kinds of social advantage and disadvantage to arise from trusts here: the necessary sociological and economic research has never been done, and it would be a

---

[25] A relatively non-interventionist approach was taken in *Re Courage Group's Pension Schemes* [1987] 1 WLR 495 and *Wilson v Law Debenture Corp plc* [1995] 2 All ER 337; a more interventionist approach in *Cowan v Scargill* [1985] Ch 270, *Mettoy Pension Trustees Ltd v Evans* [1990] 1 WLR 1587, and *Imperial Group Pension Trust Ltd v Imperial Tobacco Ltd* [1991] 1 WLR 589.

[26] Cf the appeal for it in the classic labour law text, K Wedderburn *The Worker and the Law* 3rd edn (1986).

[27] See especially *Re Courage Group's Pension Schemes* [1987] 1 WLR 495. Moreover, the interventionist decision in *Mettoy Pension Trustees Ltd v Evans* [1990] 1 WLR 1587 was overtaken by a collectively bargained compromise pending an appeal.

[28] G Moffat (1993) 56 MLR 471.

[29] For an analysis in economic terms, see A Ogus (1986) 36 U Tor LJ 186.

very major enterprise. But we can look at some particular matters over which there seems to be a live issue.

First, the ways in which trusts may be beneficial. Historically, instances are not difficult to find.[30] In the medieval period, trusts, together with wills, were viewed as a way of ensuring a compliant younger generation: if young people had become absolutely entitled to property, there would have been no check on them, to the detriment of society. Considerations of public order may even have been involved: the withdrawal of the facility of making trusts and wills for a time in the sixteenth century[31] provoked a turbulent reaction, being one of the grievances behind the unpleasantness known as the Pilgrimage of Grace, and the move was quite soon reversed. For a long time, too, trusts were seen as beneficial because they fostered the existence of great dynastic families which ruled the nation, by allowing for their wealth to pass down from one generation of the family to the next, rather than being placed at the entire disposal of individuals. Then again, until matters were reformed in the late nineteenth century, the trust device was the only means by which married women could even come close to owning property. In the modern world, factors such as these have disappeared, but trusts continue to facilitate important social benefits. They provide, for example, the vehicle for many kinds of investments, and for private-sector pensions, and the means whereby people (usually married or unmarried couples) can jointly own property (especially their home). And throughout their history, charitable trusts have, at any rate in broad terms, operated to the general good.

So trusts can certainly be beneficial to society. But they may also have bad effects, which in some cases may outweigh the advantages, warranting withdrawal of the facility to make them. Some of these bad effects are narrow, arising from the trust device being put to a particular injurious application; others are more general, common to most or even all trusts.

One instance of trusts being put to a particular injurious application may be their use in the avoidance of tax. The damage, arguably, lies in obliging the government either to reduce its expenditure on objects which would otherwise have benefited the nation; or to levy higher taxes

---

[30] For discussion of the value of trusts from the mid-seventeenth century, and the law's responses, see M Chesterman in G Rubin and D Sugarman (eds) *Law Economy & Society* (1984) ch 1.

[31] By *Lord Dacre's Case* (1535) YB 27 Hen VIII Pasch f 7 pl 22, and the Statute of Uses 1536. The reversal began with the Statute of Wills 1540. See generally A Simpson *A History of the Land Law* 2nd edn (1986) ch 8.

in those quarters where avoidance is more difficult (eg on people's ordinary salaries, taxed by PAYE); or else to borrow more, with the detriment to the economy, and hence people's lives, that that is said to entail. It is sometimes said that it is not for the law to make value judgements about tax avoidance; that if people can manage their affairs so as to escape taxation, they are entitled so to do.[32] But, at any rate if they use the trust device, to argue thus is to overlook the fact that the law itself, by providing that device, is furnishing them with the means to avoid tax. So the law cannot be neutral on the subject: by maintaining trusts as available for tax avoidance, it abets that avoidance. The law has in fact taken the point, although not wholly consistently. In the early 1980s the judges abandoned their earlier attitude of complaisance,[33] and began to discountenance tax avoidance[34] (though the case law did not arise especially in the trusts context). Later in that decade, albeit with some powerful dissenting voices, they resumed their former attitude.[35] The more recent picture continues to be mixed.[36]

Another harmful use of the trust device might be so as to injure creditors. Say a trader, fearing that his business might run into difficulties, declared a trust of all his assets for his wife. The plan would be that she should continue to let him use them as his own, so that in practice the couple's life would continue much as before. But the assets would now be safe, because the creditors' claims are against the trader, not his wife. Allowing people the freedom to make trusts in this way, then, would be injurious to the economic interests of their creditors. There is thus a strong argument that it is socially disadvantageous, and that the availability of trusts should therefore to that extent be curtailed. And in fact, the law does contain a collection of rules proscribing various forms of such trusts.[37]

The position in this area is not entirely consistent, though. Trusts according people interests only until bankruptcy, so that the money in

---

[32] *IRC v Duke of Westminster* [1936] AC 1, 19.

[33] *IRC v Duke of Westminster* [1936] AC 1; *IRC v Plummer* [1980] AC 896.

[34] *WT Ramsay Ltd v IRC* [1982] AC 300; *IRC v Burmah Oil Co Ltd* [1982] STC 30; *Furniss v Dawson* [1984] AC 474.

[35] *Craven v White* [1989] AC 398.

[36] Cf *Ensign Tankers (Leasing) Ltd v Stokes* [1992] 1 AC 655, *Moodie v IRC* [1993] 1 WLR 266, and *IRC v McGuckian* [1997] 1 WLR 991 (discountenancing tax avoidance) with *Fitzwilliam v IRC* [1993] 1 WLR 1189, *Ingram v IRC* [1999] 1 All ER 297, and *MacNiven v Westmoreland Investments* [2001] 2 WLR 377 (permitting it).

[37] Insolvency Act 1986 ss 339–42, 423–5 (replacing earlier provisions to generally similar effect).

question will not go to their creditors, have long been held valid notwith-standing the injury they may do traders by the false appearance of creditworthiness that they create.[38] And in the contemporary law there is confusion in the context of one creditor injuring his rivals by using a trust to establish a prior claim to the available assets. There have been cases in which suppliers of money[39] or materials[40] on credit have set up their right to payment in a trust, so that in the event of the debtor's bankruptcy the money would be regarded as already theirs, giving them a right to all of it, rather than as part of the debtor's assets which they would have to share with the rest of his creditors.[41] Again, this practice gives a false appear-ance of creditworthiness: the other creditors may have been led to per-ceive the debtor as a viable concern with adequate resources available to meet its liabilities, when in reality these resources are already bespoken under the trust arrangements. The law's reactions have been mixed. Some judicial decisions[42] have begun and ended with facilitative logic, little or no visible attention being paid to the question whether the argu-able injury to other creditors warrants limiting the freedom to make trusts in this respect. Elsewhere,[43] however, judges have refused to give effect to such arrangements.[44] The cases in the former group concern money loans, while those in the latter group concern the supply of materials, but it is not easy to see why there should be a bifurcation on

---

[38] 'Protective trusts' (see further section 11.2). The essential validity of such trusts was reaffirmed in *Re Trusts of the Scientific Investment Pension Plan* [1998] 3 All ER 154. In the United States, while 'spendthrift trusts', operating slightly differently but to the same end, are seen as fundamentally valid, there has been some legislative retrenchment of their effectiveness.

[39] eg *Barclay's Bank Ltd v Quistclose Investments Ltd* [1970] AC 567.

[40] eg *Aluminium Industrie Vaassen BV v Romalpa Aluminium Ltd* [1976] 1 WLR 676, after which such devices became known as '*Romalpa* clauses'.

[41] S Worthington *Proprietary Interests in Commercial Transactions* (1997); cf M Bridge (1997) 17 LS 507.

[42] eg *Barclay's Bank Ltd v Quistclose Investments Ltd* [1970] AC 567; *Re Kayford Ltd* [1975] 1 WLR 279; *Carreras Rothmans Ltd v Freeman Mathews Treasure Ltd* [1985] Ch 207.

[43] eg *Re Bond Worth Ltd* [1980] Ch 228 (which involved a trust), together with eg *Borden UK Ltd v Scottish Timber Products Ltd* [1981] Ch 25; *Re Peachdart Ltd* [1984] Ch 131; *Re Andrabell Ltd* [1984] 3 All ER 407 (which involved other legal devices).

[44] Generally, though, the reasoning has (at least ostensibly) been not that the arrangement came up against the limits of the facilitative project as involving an unacceptable injury to creditors, but instead that the arrangement's terms were not apt to achieve what the parties wanted anyway. Conceding the primacy of the facilitative logic in this way left it possible for equally injurious but better drafted arrangements to succeed in *Clough Mill Ltd v Martin* [1985] 1 WLR 111 and *Hendy Lennox (Industrial Engines) Ltd v Grahame Puttick Ltd* [1984] 1 WLR 485 (again, however, not involving trust arrangements).

this account. There exists some statutory regulation of this type of arrangement, but its impact is hesitant.[45]

These, then, are examples of the arguably injurious effects of particular uses of trusts. But it is also possible to find social disadvantages in the very nature of the trust situation. Perhaps the most prominent perception in this vein is to the effect that trusts may be injurious to the economy, and hence to the well-being of society. This argument depends upon a free-market economic theory, and runs as follows.

The utilitarian goal of making people as happy as possible is seen as promoted by the generation of as much wealth as possible. And this goal is in turn promoted if assets find their way to those who can afford to offer the highest price for them, because this will be a reflection of the fact that the latter will be able to make the largest profits—extract the greatest wealth—from the assets. In order for this to happen, though, the market needs to be as free and efficient as possible: any clogs upon it, or friction within it, will hinder the process. The absolute owner of a piece of property is able to sell it, and a prospective purchaser is able to buy it from him, without any impediment (this is part of what we mean by 'ownership'): so the market can operate freely, and happiness is maximized. But if property is held on trust, there are likely to be problems with its marketability, and thus with the maximization of happiness; so an argument arises against the trust device.

The most extreme impediment to marketability would be for the settlor to stipulate for the trustee to hold on to the particular piece of property indefinitely, rather than treat it as an investment (ie sell it and buy something else, according to what will give the best return). This might occur, for example, if (as was once common) the settlor holds a great estate and makes a trust providing for it to be kept for succeeding generations of his family. No matter how attractive a price might be offered for the land (by someone who wants to erect a factory on it, for example), the fact that it is tied up in trust in this way means that it cannot be sold, and so it is withdrawn from the market altogether. Alternatively, say the terms of the trust do allow the trustee to sell the original trust property so as to reinvest the proceeds, but nevertheless impose restrictions on that ability, such as a requirement that the beneficiaries

---

[45] In the background is the Companies Act 1985 ss 395–6, under which debts secured on a company's assets by means of a 'charge' must be registered; but valid arrangements of the kinds under discussion have been held not to constitute 'charges'. Valid *Romalpa* clauses may not, however, be enforced in the event of the debtor company's insolvency without leave from a court: Insolvency Act 1986 ss 10, 11, 15.

should consent to the sale, or one insisting that the best possible price be obtained. If a sale in breach of these restrictions were defective, a prospective purchaser would have to spend time and money in checking that they had been complied with. This expenditure (known as the 'transaction costs') in effect increases the price that the purchaser has to pay for this piece of property above that of a comparable commodity being sold by an absolute owner, and so reduces the wealth that can be extracted from it, perhaps even preventing it from being a profitable proposition at all. Or again, say sale and reinvestment are allowed, but with restrictions on the sorts of assets in which the reinvestment may be made, perhaps out of a natural desire that the beneficiaries' interests should not be jeopardized by risky ventures.[46] The problem here is that these restrictions might disable the money from being spent on whatever new asset would generate the greatest profit.

And most fundamentally and pervasively, even assuming (as is nowadays normal, but has not always been) that the trust property can be invested by the trustees, it may perform less effectively in the economy than equivalent property invested by an absolute owner. For trustees will often, by reason of their consciousness of their position, be more cautious in their approach than an absolute owner would be. After all, their whole *raison d'être* is to serve the interests of the trust's objects, and they may well as a result feel less ready to take risks.

Wherever there is a trust, then, the assets are to some degree less exposed to the market than assets which are owned absolutely. According to free-market theory, this diminishes the amount of wealth and so happiness which can be derived from it. So a question arises over the acceptability of all trusts: that is, over the facilitative project as a whole. The fact that there are drawbacks to trusts, however, does not automatically mean the abandonment of that project. The drawbacks have always to be balanced against the benefits, or against the argument from liberalism itself. In reality, the case for the availability of trusts evidently is accepted, for better or worse, as ultimately compelling. After all, we do still have a law of express trusts. But the facilitative logic does not carry all before it. The law contains a number of rules, comprehensible in utilitarian terms, declining to give effect to settlors' intentions. The relevant rules fall into two tranches.

The first tranche consists of rules whose effect is to emphasize the

---

[46] Until the Trustee Act 2000 the law itself imposed such restrictions, unless the settlor provided otherwise: see section 9.4.

extent to which property held on trust is nevertheless exposed to the market. In Chapter 9 we shall examine the rules governing the manner in which the trustees are required to manage and invest the trust property. Broadly, they tend to assimilate the treatment of trust property to the way in which an absolute owner would treat it. But, as we have already noted, even though there is thus no legal constraint on the property's exposure to the market, the trustee's own awareness that he is a trustee and not an absolute owner might still have a sobering effect. The law has, however, experimented with a measure calculated to counteract even this latter effect. In a certain kind of land-holding trust known as a strict settlement (now defunct),[47] the law gave the power to sell the land not to the trustees but to the first beneficiary, the 'tenant for life'.[48] Since the tenant for life received the income from the trust's investments for his lifetime, he had a personal interest in maximizing that income, which in turn meant that he would want to sell the land if that was the most profitable thing to do. By placing control over the investment and management of the trust assets not with the trustees, with their natural reticence, but with the tenant for life, with his equally natural self-interest, a closer approach to full marketability should have been achieved.[49] This arrangement had a major drawback: a self-interested tenant for life might have paid attention more to immediate income than to capital growth, to the detriment of the beneficiaries who came after him. But even in market terms, it was not a perfect solution, because a tenant for life might have turned out not to be so self-interested after all. Like the trustees, and even against his own interest, he might have felt a sense of responsibility towards the group of beneficiaries as a whole, or of respect for the settlor's wish that the land should remain in the family. Death duties and similar taxes will commonly have operated to persuade him otherwise in this last respect, however.

[47] The possibility of creating a strict settlement was abolished by the Trusts of Land and Appointment of Trustees Act 1996 s 2.

[48] Settled Land Act 1925, replacing the generally similar Settled Land Act 1882. It is known that economic arguments were amongst those supporting the introduction of this legislation: H Perkin in J Butt and I Clarke (eds) *The Victorians and Social Protest* (1973) 177; F Thompson (1965) *Transactions of the Royal Historical Society* 5th series vol 15, 23. There was a high level of concern at the state of the economy in the last quarter of the nineteenth century: F Crouzet *The Victorian Economy* (1982), especially 47–8, 58–63.

[49] Under the Trusts of Land and Appointment of Trustees Act 1996, the place of the strict settlement is taken by the 'trust of land'. The Act allows for the power of sale to be excluded, or subjected to a consent requirement, by the settlor (s 8), and provides for it to lie with the trustees unless they choose to delegate it to a beneficiary (s 9). The trust of land is thus significantly less aligned to free-market considerations than the strict settlement.

Thus although these rules about investment and management go some way to alleviate the economic disadvantages of trusts, they do not remove them completely. At this point we encounter the second tranche of rules. These are rules limiting the very existence of trusts. So far as presently relevant, they fall into three groups.

The first group is a collection of rules whereby some kinds of dispositions, which might arguably have been intended to create trusts, are instead read as conferring absolute ownership of the property in question. The details of these rules will be examined in Chapter 3. Some of them are expressed in the terms of the facilitative project, referring themselves to the settlor's 'true intention'; but it will be seen that this ascription is dubious. In most of the important decisions on these lines,[50] a man left property to his widow, but apparently on trust so that she should have only the income for her lifetime, with the capital to go thereafter to, say, their son. The courts read the arrangement instead as a bequest of the capital to the widow, she having only a moral obligation to provide in turn for the son.

The second group centres on a rule whereby, under certain (fairly usual) circumstances, beneficiaries can dismantle a trust in their favour and take the capital for themselves as absolute owners.[51] Once again, this rule is sometimes ascribed to the settlor's intentions, but in its developed form it is clear that a settlor's intentions can be simply overridden.

The third group consists in rules collectively known as the rule against perpetuities. This operates to ensure that a settlor cannot legally provide for assets to remain subject to a trust for longer than legal policy will tolerate: there comes a point at which they must return into absolute ownership, and hence full marketability. In its turn, the rule against perpetuities has three main branches: 'the rule against remoteness of vesting'; 'the rule against inalienability'; and 'the rule against accumulation of income'.[52]

---

[50] eg *Lambe v Eames* (1871) LR 6 Ch App 597; *Re Hutchinson and Tenant* (1878) 8 Ch D 540; *Mussoorie Bank Ltd v Raynor* (1882) 7 App Cas 321; *Re Adams and the Kensington Vestry* (1884) 27 Ch D 394; *Re Williams* [1897] 2 Ch 12.

[51] The rule in *Saunders v Vautier* (1841) 4 Beav 115, Cr & Ph 240: section 12.4.

[52] For a full treatment, see R Maudsley *The Modern Law of Perpetuities* (1979). Connected with the rule against perpetuities was the law on entails. An entail was a special kind of settlement designed so that no one might enjoy an absolute interest, at least for many generations, potentially *ad infinitum*. But for most of its history, the law allowed entails to be overridden—'barred'—by those having the interests, permitting them to gain absolute ownership of the property in question. For details, see C Harpum *Megarry and Wade: The Law of Real Property* 6th edn (2000) 72–8. Entails may no longer be created: Trusts of Land and Appointment of Trustees Act 1996 Sch 1 para 5. The rules about perpetuities and entails can also be explained in terms of a rights analysis: see section 2.6.

The rule against remoteness of vesting stipulates that all the interests conferred by the trust must 'vest' within 'the perpetuity period'. This means that within this time, the details regarding the arrangement of interests, such as the identity of the people to whom they will belong, must be finalized. In the case of a trust for 'my first-born grandchild', for example, an actual name must emerge. There are two versions of the perpetuity period: either the life-span of someone connected with the trust, and alive at the time it originally takes effect, plus 21 years; or else, if the settlor prefers, a specific period nominated by her, not exceeding 80 years from the time when the trust originally takes effect.

So say a man dies leaving a widow and a son, the latter being then ten years old. He makes a trust in his will, stipulating for payments first to his widow for her life, then to their son for his life, then to the son's eldest child for its life, then to that child's eldest child for its life. He does not opt for a specific perpetuity period, so it will be the duration of a life in being at the time of his death (when the trust comes into effect)—that is, the life of either the widow or the son—plus 21 years. This trust is certainly valid so far as the provisions in favour of the widow and son are concerned: these entitlements are finalized from the start. The provision for the son's eldest child will be valid too, because if the son has a child at all it will be born, and so this entitlement will also become finalized, within a period of the son's life-span plus 21 years.[53] But the last provision, that for the eldest child's eldest child, is problematic. This child may be born (if at all), and so its entitlement finalized, no longer after the settlor's death than the period of the son's life plus 21 years. Probably it will be: most children are born within their grandparents' lives. If it is, this provision will be valid too. But it might not. Say the settlor's widow dies first, then the son dies immediately after the birth of his own child, and the latter's first child—the one in whom we are interested—is then not born until maybe 30 years later: its entitlement is not finalized until nine years after the permitted perpetuity period of the duration of the son's life plus 21 years. In this event, then, this final provision would be invalid.

The rule against inalienability (or excessive duration) is simpler. It stipulates that purpose trusts may not last for longer than the duration of a life in existence at the time the trust takes effect plus 21 years. This rule is rather tougher than that against remoteness of vesting. Since it deals with trusts for purposes rather than people, there will very often be no

---

[53] Though emerging medical techniques make this less inevitable than hitherto.

relevant life in existence at the time of the trust coming into effect—especially if it is made in the settlor's will, as many are—and so the limit will be the 21 years alone. And the trust will be invalid unless it is certain from the outset that it must terminate within the permitted period. So a trust providing for the care of a testator's (youngish) horse will fail, because it will not be certain that its end, on the death of the horse, will occur within 21 years. There appears to be no option of specifying a period of up to 80 years here, but apparently such a trust can be saved by the settlor's limiting its duration to the permitted 21 years or less. So a trust for the care of his horse for its life or 21 years, whichever is the shorter, would be valid.

The rule against accumulation of income stipulates that a settlor can validly provide for the income upon the trust assets to be accumulated (ie added to the capital, as opposed to being paid out to the objects) only under certain circumstances, and for certain periods. There are two main types of permissible provision to accumulate. One is where the accumulation is limited to the settlor's lifetime, or to a period of 21 years after his death or after the trust coming into effect. The other is where a beneficiary is a child, and the stipulation is for the income to be paid over to him only upon his reaching majority, and in the meantime to be put aside.

The rules against inalienability and accumulation overtly limit the time for which capital and income respectively can be kept out of absolute ownership by being subjected to a trust. In the case of the rule against remoteness of vesting, the point is less obvious. On the face of it, this rule regulates how distantly into the future a settlor's stipulations can come into effect, rather than how long they—and hence the trust, and the keeping of the property out of absolute ownership—can endure. But the ban on stipulations whose effect remains to be finalized beyond the permitted period has to be seen in combination with the fact of human mortality. A settlor who wants his trust to last far into the future will have to stipulate for new beneficiaries to replace those who die. But once they become too remote, these stipulations will be disallowed by the rule, and so such replacement will become impossible. This combination of mortality with a ban on new stipulations beyond a certain point means that the trust will necessarily come to an end, and, once again, the property will come back into absolute ownership.

Seen thus, therefore, the three branches of the rule against perpetuities deal with three different variants of the same phenomenon, the prolonged subjection of property to a trust regime. Their effect is that such subjection will be tolerated so far, but no further, before the property has to be free to come back into absolute ownership, and so marketability. In other words, for the duration of the perpetuity period, the law will accept the degree of damage to social well-being that trusts can entail; but then it draws the line. In terms of the contest of utility, the rule against perpetuities can thus be seen as a compromise (and, when all is said, a fairly arbitrary, rough and ready one), whereby the liberty to make trusts is preserved but its potential for social harm kept within bounds.[54]

2.6 RIGHTS CONSIDERATIONS

To state that some interest of a person constitutes a 'right' is to assert that that interest should be respected. An interest's identity as a right does not spring from a perception that respecting it conduces to the greatest overall happiness; that may or may not be the case. Rather, it springs from the interest's being of such a kind that respect for it is the due of each individual person. An interest might be viewed as of such a kind on more than one basis, but in our culture the salient basis is a perception that the interest captures a facet of what it is to be human. For instance, a person's interest in life (especially, in not being killed) is regarded as a right because life is held to be of the essence of the human condition. There can of course be controversy over whether any given interest meets this description and so qualifies as a right. It is also possible to argue that, although rights do not depend on any identification with the greatest happiness and so are not traversed simply by a demonstration that they are inconsistent with the greatest happiness, rights may under certain circumstances be overridden.

It may be possible to regard the liberty to make trusts as springing from a right on the part of the settlor: the right to dispose of his property as he wishes. It is, however, uncertain whether the analysis just offered supports the existence of a right to property.[55] But in principle it is clear

---

[54] A number of jurisdictions have in fact abolished or substantially curtailed the rule against perpetuities. For England and Wales, retention (with certain, essentially technical, reforms) is recommended by the Law Commission Report No 251 *The Rules Against Perpetuities and Excessive Accumulations* (1998) (that report's recommendations being broadly adopted by the ensuing Government White Paper, Lord Chancellor's Department *The Rule Against Excessive Accumulations* (2002)). The Commission were unsure about the balance of economic advantage surrounding the rule, and were instead influenced by an argument that the rule achieves maximum happiness by compromising between the desires of different generations for complete freedom with the property in question. For the argument, see L Simes *Public Policy and the Dead Hand* (1955); for criticism, see T Gallanis [2000] CLJ 284.

[55] For discussion, see J Waldron *The Right to Private Property* (1988); J Harris *Property and Justice* (1996).

that the exercise of the settlor's liberty, the making of a trust, may infringe another person's rights. In this event, we should expect the law to limit the settlor's liberty and refuse to recognize the trust in question. Say a settlor tried to create a trust for the purpose of killing certain people. The proposition that the law should uphold that trust, under facilitative logic, would be assailed by the argument that to do so would involve infringing the right to life. It may be presumed that the law would not uphold such a trust.

In practice, of course, trusts are not found pitted against the right to life. But take trusts which injure creditors, discussed above. Some such trusts operate by contracting the pool of assets from which debtors are obliged to pay their debts. By upholding such trusts, the law could be said to infringe the creditors' right to the secure enjoyment of their property. Other such trusts accord more favourable treatment to some creditors than to others. So the law, if it upholds these trusts, may be said to contravene a right to equal treatment.

Indeed, trusts may injure the rights of their own beneficiaries. This can occur in two ways. First, if the settlor gives a beneficiary his interest only on specific terms, the terms may violate some right of the beneficiary. For example, a condition that the beneficiary shall forfeit his interest unless he espouses a particular religious faith (eg 'for Adam on condition that he remains a member of the Church of England') may infringe the beneficiary's right to freedom of conscience; and a condition making the beneficiary's interest depend on his family status (eg 'for Adam, once he is divorced from his wife') may infringe his right to a private and family life. Secondly, beneficiaries' rights may be violated by the very fact that the settlor makes his disposition to them under a trust at all, rather than as an absolute gift. Under a gift, they would have had access to the capital, but under the trust they are confined to the income, and may have to wait for that. This limitation may be seen as violating their right to the full enjoyment of their property.[56]

It might be said that these suggestions cannot be valid, for the following reason. To become a beneficiary under a trust is to be given the certainty or possibility of receiving greater wealth than one already has. If someone does not like the arrangement in question (the restriction on her religious freedom, for example, or the restriction to income, rather than

---

[56] In the United States, such limitation is termed 'the dead hand', and in some minds particularly disfavoured as aristocratic and unrepublican. See G Alexander (1985) 37 Stanford LR 1189.

capital), she can decline her interest. In that event, she will merely remain in her existing position, both financially and in terms of her various freedoms. There is nothing about being proposed as the beneficiary of a trust to erode that position, however constricting the trust's terms may be.

But this answer may be too crude. Even if one concedes that a beneficiary who declines the proffered interest loses nothing to which she is actually entitled, one may argue that rights to religious freedom, family life, and the like can be infringed by a bribe (the offer of a beneficial interest on the relevant terms) as much as by aggression. Moreover, one might not wish to make that concession. It is possible to argue that control of property should naturally be vested in those who have a present attachment to it (the beneficiaries), rather than remaining with someone who has parted with it and may indeed be dead (the settlor).[57] On this view, a beneficiary would be essentially entitled to full ownership of the property in question. To grant her the property in question under a trust, rather than by way of absolute gift, would be to infringe her right fully to enjoy that entitlement. The implications of especially the latter perception are profound. The basis of express trusts is the facilitative thesis, the idea that people's rights in respect of their property should be vindicated to a maximal degree, by allowing them to make not only simple but also complex dispositions of it. This, we now see, can readily conflict with the project of vindicating the rights of the recipient of the property likewise to a maximal degree. There are, it is evident, the makings of a struggle here.

In fact, it seems that the law of trusts has so far toyed with but not fully accepted the view that conditions of this kind constitute an infringement of the beneficiary's rights, and as such should be disallowed. There have been many reported cases in which religious conditions have been involved but have attracted no animadversion from the judges; their permissibility has occasionally been questioned, but the answer has tended to be that facilitative logic should prevail.[58] Conditions damaging to family

[57] Note also that, under appropriate (eg dynastic) circumstances, the settlor may be thought to owe a duty to settle the property in question upon the beneficiaries (cf *Re Brocklehurst's Estate* [1978] Ch 14, 32). But that duty might be to confer only an entitlement which was itself subject to a similar duty, rather than absolute ownership.

[58] See eg *Blathwayt v Lord Cawley* [1976] AC 397. However, at any rate conditions removing a beneficiary's entitlement (as opposed to conferring it) have always been subjected to very strict requirements as to the clarity with which they must be expressed before they will be accepted as valid. This rule may have been used as a surrogate means of screening them on policy grounds (see eg *Clayton v Ramsden* [1943] AC 320, where a condition whereby the entitlement was forfeited if the beneficiary married someone not of Jewish parentage and faith was struck down in this way). However, if so, the tide has turned back in favour of the facilitative logic again: modern decisions have been more easygoing

life have been treated more sternly, though still not consistently so.[59] The Human Rights Act 1998 may, however, now require or precipitate a more sceptical view of conditions of these kinds.[60] Conditions as to race and sex (eg 'for Adam's future wife, so long as she is white', or 'for my first-born female grandchild') have also been accepted without demur, and generally speaking the relevant modern anti-discrimination legislation, the Race Relations Act 1976 and the Sex Discrimination Act 1975, does not touch such stipulations in trusts.[61]

The law seems, however, to have been much more impressed by the idea that a person's rights may be infringed by the very fact of her being placed in the position of a beneficiary, rather than enjoying full dominion over the property in question. This can be seen in the collection of rules, discussed in the previous section of this chapter, whereby the very existence of trusts is curtailed. The first is the rules whereby some kinds of dispositions, which might arguably have been intended to create trusts, are instead read as conferring absolute ownership of the property in question. As a result, for example, an apparent stipulation that a widow should enjoy only the income from her deceased husband's estate for her lifetime, holding the capital for their children, is read as an absolute bequest to the widow, with a moral obligation to provide in turn for the children. The second is the rules whereby, under certain (fairly usual) circumstances, beneficiaries can dismantle a trust in their favour and take

over the degree of clarity required, so that such conditions have been able to survive (see eg *Blathwayt v Lord Cawley*; *Re Tuck's Settlement Trusts* [1978] Ch 49; *Re Tepper's Will Trusts* [1987] Ch 358).

[59] *Re Caborne* [1943] Ch 224; *Re Johnson's Will Trusts* [1967] Ch 387; *Re Sandbrook* [1912] 2 Ch 471; but cf *Re Lovell* [1920] 1 Ch 122.

[60] The European Convention on Human Rights protects the rights to respect for private and family life (Art 8); to freedom of thought, conscience, and religion (Art 9); and to marry and found a family (Art 12). The 1998 Act may not make these rights enforceable between private individuals, such as parties to litigation over the validity of a term in a trust. But it does require public authorities, including courts, to act consistently with Convention rights (s 6); and the argument of this chapter is that the facilitative project, under which property owners are enabled to create trusts and so impose such conditions, has to be seen as a set of acts on the part of the courts.

[61] Both Acts do have some, fairly modest, application to charitable trusts (ss 34 and 78 respectively). The point is presumably that, as we shall see in Ch 6, there is a more direct public interest in such trusts than in private ones, as a result of which the facilitative approach has always been more strongly qualified in respect of them. (For a manifestation of the same point before the advent of legislation in the race relations field, see *Re Dominion Students' Hall Trust* [1947] Ch 183.) The Human Rights Act 1998 is not strongly effective against such conditions: Article 14 of the ECHR prohibits discrimination, but only as regards the extent to which the law secures the enjoyment of another Convention right.

the capital for themselves as absolute owners.[62] The third is the rule against perpetuities, which ensures that property cannot be subjected to a trust indefinitely, but must at a point prescribed by the law return into absolute ownership.[63] These can all be seen as calculated to vindicate the rights of those in whose favour they operate.

It is perhaps curious that the law should reflect the argument that beneficiaries have a right to dominion over the property in this way, but not concern itself so much over matters of religious, racial, and sexual discrimination. Perhaps the explanation is that the project of vindicating beneficiaries' dominion over trust property frequently shares goals (above all, finding absolute transfers rather than trusts) with another powerful consideration, the utilitarian economic argument.

---

[62] *Saunders v Vautier* (1841) 4 Beav 115, Cr & Ph 240; see section 12.4. The case for viewing this provision in terms of rights is especially strong. It *permits* the property to come into absolute ownership, at the option of the beneficiaries, rather than *requiring* it to, as the economic argument would wish; derived from it is a rule enabling beneficiaries merely to modify their trust, if they prefer, rather than dismantle it altogether, in which event there may be no economic gain; and judges have put the matter in rights terms: *Gosling v Gosling* (1859) John 265, 272; *Wharton v Masterman* [1895] AC 186, 192–3.

[63] A rights analysis does not, however, offer the best account of the rule against perpetuities. The rule gives complete primacy to the settlor's liberty over the liberty of those beneficiaries whose interests vest within the perpetuity period, then the reverse in respect of beneficiaries whose interests vest thereafter. There is something here, however, of two wrongs (not) making a right.

3

Finding settlors' intentions

As we have seen, the law recognizes an express trust because a settlor intends to create it. Evidently, that raises a need to say when a settlor has the required intention. This chapter considers how the law goes about that.

3.1 THE NORMAL STANDARD OF PROOF

How certain is it necessary to be as to the relevant intentions, whether regarding the creation of a trust at all or regarding its terms? In civil cases, such as those about trusts, the law normally requires proof on the balance of probabilities. This means accepting whichever view of the facts is more probable than the other (though the onus is on a person asserting a proposition to prove that it is more probable than not, so if the probabilities are even, inertia prevails). This has been accepted[1] as the standard of proof applicable to the discovery of a settlor's intentions. Following the balance of probabilities in this way can readily be seen as consonant with facilitative thinking. This aims to find an express trust where one is intended and not otherwise, so is neutral as between the two outcomes.

There will often be no difficulty. When a person wants to make a trust, it is in her own interest to make this and the trust's terms clear, so as to avoid the possibilities both of wasteful arguments about what she intended, and of her intentions being frustrated by a false conclusion (and equally, where a trust, or some detail, might be expected but is not intended, to make this clear). To this end, she will probably employ solicitors, who will use a formal document, stating unmistakably what is meant, using words such as 'trust', 'trustee', 'beneficiary', and so on.

Where evidence of that clarity is lacking, a court may find it helpful to address the abstract question of whether a trust was intended in terms of more concrete issues. Two of these have been identified by experience as

[1] *Re Snowden* [1979] Ch 528.

regularly likely to be useful points to concentrate on.[2] One is whether the alleged settlor intended her wishes to be enforceable by legal sanction. A trust is a legal obligation, and a breach of it will, at any rate in principle, entail legal liability for the trustee. So, for example, if I bequeath all my property to my sister, instructing her to give a quarter of it to charity, we can focus on the question whether the obligation so imposed on her was meant to be a legal one, enforceable in court, or merely a moral one. Finding it to be merely moral tells us that I did not intend to create a trust. Another such indicator is how specific the instructions are. If they are vague, or contradictory, it is generally less likely that they are intended to comprise a trust as opposed to an expression of wishes of at most moral force. Of course, it is not impossible that they were intended to amount to a trust: sometimes one comes across dispositions which are quite clearly meant to be trusts, but whose terms are poorly expressed. But where the intention to create a trust is questionable, such difficulty does point against it.

3.2 OTHER APPROACHES

Whilst proof on the balance of probabilities is thus the principal tool for discovering settlors' intentions, different approaches are frequently visible. In particular, the judges operate 'rules of construction', requiring that in a certain type of situation, a person shall normally be held to have intended to create a trust; or not, as the case may be. They also follow other, less well crystallized, practices inconsistent with the normal standard of proof.

  These rules and practices do not ultimately part company with facilitative logic, as they have effect only in cases where it is not completely clear whether someone intended to create a trust, or what he intended its terms to be: where the intention has been made unmistakable, it will be respected, except if it contravenes a rule which avowedly overrides intention, such as that against perpetuities. If our rules and practices rested on an empirical observation that in the kind of situation concerned, people normally do have a certain kind of intention, they could even be ascribed to facilitative logic. But, as we shall see, that is not the case. They instead load the perception of the relevant intentions in a non-naturalistic way, and so conduce to outcomes not justifiable on facilitative grounds. They can therefore usefully be analysed in terms of the kinds of policy

---

[2] *Mussoorie Bank Ltd v Raynor* (1882) 7 App Cas 321.

considerations noted in the last chapter as cutting across the facilitative project.

We turn now to some of the most prominent of these rules and practices.

3.3 FAMILY PROVISION

The courts appear unusually ready to discover an intention to make a trust where the ensuing trust will make the kind of provision the alleged settlor ought to make for a member of his family.

In *Paul v Constance*,[3] a man had received some money in compensation for an accident which he had suffered, and had started a bank account with it, in his sole name. Later, he and his partner both won small sums at bingo, and these too were paid into the account. There were some vague conversational references to the money as being jointly owned. There was conceivably proof on the balance of probabilities that the man intended to make some sort of provision for his partner, but it is hard to say that there was such proof of an intention to make a trust. The court nevertheless held that the man had declared a trust of all the money in the account for himself and his partner.

The case arose after the man had died intestate. If he had been married to his partner, she would have inherited all his property. Their being unmarried meant that she got none of it,[4] and in fact it went to his estranged wife, from whom he had never been divorced. But the decision meant that his partner was entitled to half the money in the account after all.[5]

A keenness to find a trust in such circumstances is intelligible in terms of a communitarian policy, visible in the law since about the middle of the twentieth century, seeking to secure family obligations. We shall encounter it again in section 8.11, where we shall examine the constructive trusts which the law finds in respect of family property. These too are said to be based upon findings of intention, and we shall see that those findings show an optimism similar to that noted here.

Contrast the old case of *Jones v Lock*.[6] There, a man brought home a

---

[3] [1977] I WLR 527.

[4] Except possibly a reasonable amount for her maintenance, under the Inheritance (Provision for Family and Dependants) Act 1975.

[5] See too *Rowe v Prance* [1999] 2 FLR 787, where, on similarly weak evidence, a man was held to have created a trust for a woman with whom he had a lengthy relationship and from whom he had accepted substantial gifts, but whom he now neglected.

[6] (1865) LR I Ch App 25.

substantial cheque that he had received and announced that it was for his baby son, the child of his second marriage. He did so in rather vague terms, which the judge took to mean that he intended to provide for the child in an unspecified way.[7] After the man's death, leaving nothing to the child (but a good deal to the children of his first marriage) in his will, the court held that there was no trust for the baby. The judge insisted on intentions precisely identifiable with a trust on the part of the settlor: 'I think it would be of very dangerous example if loose conversations of this sort, in important transactions of this kind, should have the effect of declarations of trust.'[8] If anything, the approach was in terms of a standard of proof higher than the balance of probabilities. It did nothing to vindicate the duty that the man may be thought to have had to provide for the baby. Inclining against finding a trust, and specifically adding a demand for certainty, it tracks notions of economic utilitarianism. (As we saw in the last chapter, trusts are inimical to a free market in themselves, and any uncertainty over whether a piece of property is held on trust will only make matters worse, as clarifying the point will increase the transaction costs.) If the case arose today, we might expect it to proceed more like *Paul v Constance*.[9]

3.4 PRECATORY WORDS

Precatory words are those in which the alleged settlor exhorts the alleged trustee to use the property in a particular way, rather than expressly requiring him to: for instance, where I bequeath property to you 'in the confidence', or 'in the hope', or 'in the belief' that you will use it to take care of my child.

The use of hortatory language is not necessarily inconsistent with an intention to create a trust. It might have been employed merely out of politeness. But the law presumes that it does not denote such an intention. So where a person transfers property to another and expresses the confidence or similar that the latter will use it in a certain way, a trust, legally obliging the recipient so to use it, does not normally arise. Instead, the transfer is taken to be an absolute gift to the recipient, with at most a moral obligation on her regarding its use.

For example, in *Mussoorie Bank Ltd v Raynor*[10] a man's will leaving all his property to his wife 'feeling confident that she will act justly to our

---

[7] (1865) LR 1 Ch App 25, 29. [8] (1865) LR 1 Ch App 25, 29.
[9] [1977] 1 WLR 527. [10] (1882) 7 App Cas 321.

children in dividing the same when no longer required by her' was con-
strued as giving her the property absolutely, with merely a reminder of
her moral duty to the children, rather than as a trust. On the words of the
will and the circumstances of the case, that seems an uncontentious finding of the man's probable true intentions. However, there was more to it
than that. The previous attitude of the law had been that such precatory
language *did* normally indicate an intention to create a trust.[11] This attitude was displaced in favour of the opposite approach, found in *Mussoorie
Bank Ltd v Raynor*[12] and still the law today, by decisions in the nineteenth
century.[13]

In terms of the facilitative project, the current position is probably
more authentic than that which it replaced: the more natural interpretation of this kind of language probably is that no trust is intended.
However, the current position also resonates with arguments of rights
and of economic utility.

So far as economic utility is concerned, holding precatory words not to
create trusts has two main benefits. First, by producing absolute ownership of the property in question, it promotes the desideratum that property should be freely disposable, rather than tied up by incumbrances
restricting its alienation, such as trusts. Secondly, it helps minimize
transaction costs, by reducing uncertainty over whether property is held
on trust (which a facilitative approach would not especially do).[14] Both
effects are to the advantage of a free market.[15]

As to rights thinking, a rather specific concordance can be seen. Most

---

[11] Perhaps this was a manifestation of dynastic considerations, favouring the tying up of
property so as to keep it within the family: see sections 2.4 and 2.5. Alternatively, the
attitude may have arisen in the context of an old rule (against 'mortmain') whereby certain
trusts for religious foundations were illegal. To evade this ban, a would-be settlor of such a
trust might transfer the property in question to a friend and express the wish that the latter
should devote it to the foundation. To vindicate the ban, however, the courts may have been
inclined to construe such dispositions (to us, gifts with precatory words) as trusts after all.

[12] (1882) 7 App Cas 321.

[13] *Lambe v Eames* (1871) LR 6 Ch App 597; *Re Hutchinson and Tenant* (1878) 8 Ch D 540;
Mussoorie Bank Ltd v Raynor (1882) 7 App Cas 321; *Re Adams and the Kensington Vestry*
(1884) 27 Ch D 394; *Re Hamilton* [1895] 2 Ch 370; *Re Williams* [1897] 2 Ch 12.

[14] For attention to this, see especially *Re Williams* [1897] 2 Ch 12, 21.

[15] Some of the leading cases on precatory words arose in commercial contexts. Thus in
Mussoorie Bank Ltd v Raynor (1882) 7 App Cas 321 the widow, treating herself as the
absolute owner of the land left to her by her husband, mortgaged it to a bank, which now
sought to enforce its rights over it. If she had been a trustee of the land, the mortgage would
have been invalid, so the bank would have lost the value of its mortgage. The court decided
in favour of the bank by holding that the widow was absolute owner. *Re Hutchinson and
Tenant* (1878) 8 Ch D 540 and *Re Adams and the Kensington Vestry* (1884) 27 Ch D 394 are
similar.

of the important decisions establishing this rule involved husbands leaving property in their wills to their widows, on precatory terms as to the upbringing of their children, or some such;[16] and they date from the late nineteenth century. At that period there was a prevalent concern to enlarge married women's property rights, which the common law generally withheld. There emerged a series of statutes, the Married Women's Property Acts, from 1870 onwards.[17] At least at first, however, the approach was not straightforwardly to allow wives to enjoy absolute ownership of property. During their marriage, wives were still disabled from spending their capital, and confined to the income, by a restriction called the 'restraint upon anticipation'. This was acknowledged to be a curtailment of the right of married women to own their own property, but it was regarded as justified in order to protect them against being pressurized by their husbands.[18] But the restraint was lifted, and women became absolute owners of their property, on the termination of their marriage: notably, upon widowhood. And from 1882 the restraint was progressively retracted during marriage itself, giving the basic right still fuller expression.[19] In such a culture, the derogatory effect of trusts restricting widows to a life interest would have been particularly obtrusive. Thus it seems plausible to think of the decisions in which the courts disfavoured such arrangements, and secured that absolute ownership was conferred on the widow instead, as not only aligned with but even directly reflecting a rights perception in this vein.

3.5 PURPOSE TRUSTS

Our next rule of construction concerns purpose trusts: that is, cases where the settlor provides that the money should be spent on achieving some specified purpose, rather than paid out to beneficiaries, who can spend it how they like. The rule is that where achieving the purpose would benefit some person (as opposed, say, to maintaining the testator's cat), such a disposition is normally taken as conferring an absolute

[16] All the cases cited above are of this kind except *Re Hamilton* [1895] 2 Ch 370.

[17] For an account, see A Dicey *Law and Opinion in England during the Nineteenth Century* (1905) 369–93. For an instance of the Married Women's Property Acts being used to make a political argument outside their actual terms, see *Howes v Bishop* [1909] 2 KB 390, 394.

[18] See J Matthews *The Law Relating to Married Women* (1892) 101–2, though cf *Brandon v Robinson* (1811) 18 Ves 429, 434–5, where the idea of such a right in the wife is denied; without it, however, it becomes hard to identify the basis for promoting her interest at all.

[19] Married Women's Property Act 1882 s 1; Law Reform (Married Women and Tortfeasors) Act 1935 s 2; Married Women (Restraint upon Anticipation) Act 1949 s 1.

entitlement upon that person, with no requirement that the money be spent on the particular purpose after all. The reference to the purpose is regarded as merely an expression of the settlor's motive in making the disposition, rather than as a legally binding stipulation.

For example, in *Re Bowes*[20] a testator's will included this provision: 'I bequeath to my trustees the sum of £5,000 sterling upon trust to expend the same in planting trees for shelter on the Wemmergill estate'. It was physically possible to plant £5,000-worth of trees on the estate, but the owners of the estate did not want them. In their view, not only would the money be better spent on other things, but the land that this number of trees would occupy would be better devoted to other uses. So they sought to have the £5,000 instead of the trees. From the language used by the testator it seems clear that he intended to create a trust to plant the trees, rather than for the owners of the estate absolutely. Nevertheless, the owners' claim to have the money succeeded: the instructions about planting trees were taken as merely the motive with which an absolute entitlement to £5,000 was conferred on them, and as such were not binding on them.

In cases such as this, the language looks unequivocal enough, evincing an intention to create a purpose trust, but the rule of construction has it otherwise. Although couched in terms of the settlor's intention, the rule thus appears to push fidelity to facilitative ideas to the limit.[21] It does however make sense in terms of rights (regarding the beneficiary as in principle entitled to an absolute interest, from which the settlor would derogate in stipulating the purpose on which the money must be spent)[22] and of economic utility (the way the money is spent is opened to the market, rather than constrained by the limitations of the settlor's purpose).

These latter perspectives, moreover, illuminate the contrast between

---

[20] [1896] 1 Ch 507.

[21] It might be argued that the rule serves a facilitative end in validating trusts which would otherwise fail, in that (non-charitable) purpose trusts are generally invalid: section 14.3. In fact, however, it is only purpose trusts which are not beneficial to people that are generally invalid; those which benefit people are valid under *Re Denley's Trust Deed* [1969] 1 Ch 373. The rule discussed in the text applies (indeed, can by its nature apply) only to purpose trusts which benefit people. So it catches only such trusts as would *not* otherwise fail.

[22] Historically, the rule appears to be connected with that in *Lassence v Tierney* (1849) 1 Mac & G 551, that if a settlor first confers an absolute interest on a beneficiary he cannot then go on to qualify it: which idea seems certainly to revolve around rights. The connection is made in *Re Skinner* (1860) 1 J & H 102.

Re Andrew's Trust[23] and *Re Trusts of the Abbott Fund*.[24] In *Re Andrew's Trust*,[25] a fund was set up, and donations made to it, to provide for the education of the children of a deceased clergyman. The children had now reached adulthood, and their formal education was over, but there was still money left. The question was whether the children were absolutely entitled to the money in the fund, so that they should now have the rest of it too; or whether it was strictly for their education, so that the surplus should be returned to the donors. The usual rule of construction was followed, so the trust on which the donations were made was interpreted as one not for the purpose of the children's education but for the children as absolutely entitled beneficiaries. The children were therefore entitled to the surplus.[26]

Re Trusts of the Abbott Fund[27] went the other way. Two sisters, who were deaf and dumb and probably quite elderly, were left without means of support. Friends subscribed to a fund to provide for their maintenance. When in time both ladies died, some money remained in the fund. Again, the question was what was to happen to this money. If the money was treated as put into the fund for the ladies' absolute benefit, it should go to their estates now that they were dead. Whereas if it was treated as given for their maintenance alone, then that purpose came to an end with their deaths, so the remaining money had to be given back to the donors. It was held that the latter was the position. The usual rule whereby purpose trusts are read as conferring absolute entitlements was thus displaced, and at the same time it was assumed that at any rate a purpose trust such as this was valid.

The difference between the two decisions has been explained[28] on the ground that while it is reasonable to recognize an absolute entitlement for the named objects of a fund when they are still alive (as in *Re Andrew's Trust*[29]), it is going too far to deprive the donors of the surplus in favour of whoever is entitled to the objects' estate when they have died (as in *Re Trusts of the Abbott Fund*[30]). This idea is crude. Does the 'true construction' change, for example, if the objects are alive at the time of the hearing at first instance, but then die pending an appeal? There is a better

---

[23] [1905] 2 Ch 48. *Re Osoba* [1979] 1 WLR 247 is similar.　　　　[24] [1900] 2 Ch 326.
[25] [1905] 2 Ch 48.
[26] The decision was also put on a less general basis: that even if it was a purpose trust for the children's education, education is lifelong and all encompassing, and thus included anything on which they might have wanted to spend the money. This seems far-fetched.
[27] [1900] 2 Ch 326.
[28] *Re Osoba* [1978] 1 WLR 791, 795–6.　　　[29] [1905] 2 Ch 48.　　　[30] [1900] 2 Ch 326.

analysis. The effect of the usual rule is that people have full dominion over the money in question, rather than that it is spent on the designated purpose on their behalf. This is attractive in terms both of the rights thesis and of economic utility, as explained above. The attraction holds good, however, only where the people in question are of normal capability. If people of reduced capability are given full dominion over the money, their infirmity may lead to their being exploited. So it is appropriate that the rule should be disapplied, and the purpose trust allowed to stand, in these circumstances. The decision in *Re Trusts of the Abbott Fund*[31] makes good sense in these terms. At first sight, it might seem right to seek the same treatment of trusts for children, such as that in *Re Andrew's Trust*:[32] children too lack full capability and so need the protection of a trust. But children will eventually become fully capable adults (those in that case had done so by the time it came to court), and in the meantime it is safe to hold them absolutely entitled to the money, since they will still not be able to get their hands on the capital[33] until they reach majority.

3.6 CONTRACTS FOR THIRD PARTIES

If I make a contract with you, in which, say, I undertake to pay you £100, the benefit of that contract—the right to my payment—is a piece of property. As such, you can normally make a trust of it. If you make it clear that that is what you decide to do, there is no difficulty: a trust will arise. But sometimes it may be arguable that a contractual promisee is making a trust of an undertaking in this way without having so expressed himself.

This is the case especially where the contract is itself designed to benefit a third party. Say I make a contract with you in which I promise you that I shall pay £100 to your sister. My contract is with you, ie you are the promisee, but my performing it will mean my paying the money to her. Until it was recently heavily modified,[34] the English law of contract maintained a rule, known as 'privity', to the effect that only the promisee can sue on a contract.[35] So despite the fact that I was supposed to perform the contract in favour of your sister, privity prevented her from suing me if I did not. Only you could sue me, and if for any reason you chose not to, there was nothing she could do about it. This state of affairs attracted

---

[31] [1900] 2 Ch 326.   [32] [1905] 2 Ch 48.
[33] Under the rule in *Saunders v Vautier* (1841) 4 Beav 115, Cr & Ph 240: see section 12.4.
[34] By the Contracts (Rights of Third Parties) Act 1999.
[35] P Atiyah *Introduction to the Law of Contract* 5th edn (1995) ch 19.

much criticism. It was widely felt that someone in the position of your sister should be able to sue. So ways round the privity rule were sought. One possibility was a finding that you had made a trust of my promise in your sister's favour, even though you had given no positive indication to this effect. Then, your sister could insist (pointing to your duties to her under the trust) that you sue me if necessary to enforce my promise, and you would hold the ensuing damages on trust for her.

Such a finding requires discovery of the necessary intention on the promisee's part to make a trust of the contractual right for the third party. A practice of construction is often said to obtain in this area, in the shape of a judicial reluctance to find that intention unless compelled to by clear evidence.

In fact, there are some solid decisions in which trusts of contractual rights were found without clear evidence that they were intended. For example, where a partnership agreement provided that if one of the partners died, the other should pay his widow a pension, the court decided that this provision was held on trust for the widow.[36] Where the contract for the hire of a ship contained a promise by the shipowners to the hirers to pay a commission to the broker who had been their intermediary, it was found that the hirers held this promise on trust for the broker.[37] And where a man became a member of Lloyd's, the insurance market, and his father made a contract with the Lloyd's managing committee guaranteeing that he would meet any of his son's unpaid debts to his customers, it was found that the managing committee held this guarantee on trust for the son's customers.[38]

There is also material in support of the alleged practice, however. It is not strong (most of the best-known statements were *obiter*)[39] but it is certainly perceived as establishing that a trust of a contract is not to be found unless there is clear evidence that the promisee intended it. So in many modern cases of this kind, the possibility of a trust for the third party was not even argued.

On the face of it, a reluctance to find trusts in such cases is consonant with the precepts of economic utility. It could be said that free commerce is best promoted by affording contracting parties dominion over their own bargains; that is, by the original privity rule. According rights to

---

[36] *Re Flavell* (1883) 25 Ch D 89.
[37] *Les Affréteurs Réunis SA v Leopold Walford (London) Ltd* [1919] AC 801.
[38] *Lloyd's v Harper* (1880) 16 Ch D 290.
[39] eg *Re Empress Engineering Co* (1880) 16 Ch D 125, 129; *Re Stapleton-Bretherton* [1941] Ch 482, 485; *Re Schebsman* [1944] Ch 83, 89, 104; *Green v Russell* [1959] 2 QB 226, 241.

outsiders, as such a trust would do, would prevent the parties from dis-
solving their bargains and renegotiating them and trading their rights in
them. But although there is something in this view, it is not entirely
satisfactory. Economic utility may be better served by giving a right of
enforcement to the third party, as in the three cases mentioned earlier,
where trusts of promises were found.[40] In all of them, the point seems to
have been that the contract envisaged payment to the third party, and so
the trust had to be discovered in order to give efficacy to the bargain: a
copybook laissez-faire sentiment. Moreover, the discovery of the trust in
each of the cases played a positive part in fostering commerce: providing
for partners' widows' pensions facilitated the formation of partnerships;
providing for shipbrokers' commissions allowed them profitably to provide their service to shippers; and providing for underwriters' guarantees
promoted confidence, and hence trade, in the insurance market.

So in fact the opposing approaches are both intelligible in terms of
economic utility, the difference between them tracking competing read-
ings of the implications of that policy.[41] Although trusts of contracts
impede commerce, by tying the parties' hands, they also promote it by
effectuating the bargain as struck. It is quite possible to believe that the
latter consideration is of greater force than the former. That view appears
to be the foundation of the reforms which have now taken place to the
privity rule,[42] as a result of which a contract for the benefit of a third party
will often be enforceable against the promisor by the third party. As a
result of this reform,[43] it will now rarely be useful to inquire whether
a contractual promisee has impliedly declared a trust of the contract's
benefit for a third party.

3.7 GIFTS

If I transfer property to you (or pay another to do so), apparently as a gift,
the law will generally presume that I actually intend to make you trustee
of it, with myself as beneficiary (ie on 'resulting trust').[44] If however I am

---

[40] *Re Flavell* (1883) 25 Ch D 89; *Les Affréteurs Réunis SA v Leopold Walford (London) Ltd*
[1919] AC 801; *Lloyd's v Harper* (1880) 16 Ch D 290.

[41] See further P Atiyah *The Rise and Fall of Freedom of Contract* (1979) 412–14.

[42] Contracts (Rights of Third Parties) Act 1999.

[43] By s 1(1)(b), a non-party to a contract can enforce it if it 'purports to confer a benefit on
him', unless (s 1(2)) 'on a proper construction of the contract it appears that the parties did
not intend the term to be enforceable by the third party'.

[44] *Dyer v Dyer* (1788) 2 Cox 92; *The Venture* [1908] P 218; *Westdeutsche Landesbank
Girozentrale v Islington LBC* [1996] AC 669, 708.

your father, or stand *in loco parentis* to you, or am your husband, a converse presumption applies, confirming that the transaction is indeed a gift.[45]

The rules presuming these intentions (one in favour of a trust, the other against it) have ancient roots. They originated as a reflection of the commonest intention actually held by gratuitous transferors of land in the late Middle Ages.[46] They can be seen also as aligned with the dynastic project which endured until, but ended with, the classic period of the great family in the nineteenth century:[47] a resulting trust, tending against the alienation of property, helps ensure that it is passed down between generations of the family, while gifts from father to child are encouraged as setting the next generation up in life. The presumption of a gift from husband to wife tracks the policy which at one time prevailed of promoting the rights of married women, founded on rights considerations. The presumption against a gift can also be seen as a paternalistic measure, guarding transferors against easy alienation of their assets. None of these possible justifications can be regarded as compelling in the current age, however. At the same time, the presumptions offend facilitative logic, treating the transferor as intending a trust or a gift according to the circumstances, rather than attending to her true wishes. Unsurprisingly, therefore, the courts have tended to play down the strength of the presumptions, so that displacing them will now probably require only proof on a balance of probabilities;[48] and indeed to cast doubt on their continued existence.[49]

These presumptions are explored further in section 7.5, in the discussion of resulting trusts. It is on the face of it wrong to include in the present chapter the presumption which produces a resulting trust out of

---

[45] *Grey v Grey* (1677) 2 Sw 594; *Powys v Mansfield* (1835) 3 Myl & Cr 359; *Kingdon v Bridges* (1688) 2 Vern 67. Some Commonwealth jurisdictions recognize the presumption also where a mother gives to her child (eg *Brown v Brown* (1993) 31 NSWLR 582, Australia), but that is not English law (*Bennet v Bennet* (1879) 10 Ch D 474).

[46] A Simpson *A History of the Land Law* 2nd edn (1986) 177–9.

[47] See sections 2.4–2.5.

[48] *Fowkes v Pascoe* (1875) LR 10 Ch App 343; *Bennet v Bennet* (1879) 10 Ch D 474; *Standing v Bowring* (1885) 31 Ch D 282. But the presumptions can still determine outcomes where the evidence to rebut them cannot be adduced because it involves an illegality: *Tinsley v Milligan* [1994] 1 AC 340; *Tribe v Tribe* [1996] Ch 107. The unhappiness of this effect is the function as much of the illegality rules as of the presumptions, however.

[49] *Pettitt v Pettitt* [1970] AC 777, 793, 811, 824, regarding the presumption of advancement between husband and wife; *Tinsley v Milligan* [1994] 1 AC 340, 371 and *Lohia v Lohia* [2001] W & TLR 101, pointing to the Law of Property Act 1925 s 60(3) (also *Fowkes v Pascoe* (1875) LR 10 Ch App 343, 348), regarding the presumption against gifts where the property is land.

an apparent gift. This chapter is about finding the intentions which the law then effectuates in imposing an express trust, and the law distinguishes between express trusts and resulting trusts. But erection of a resulting trust on the basis of a presumed intention, in the manner under discussion,[50] necessarily puts pressure on that distinction. This is one of the several difficulties which mark the law on resulting trusts, as will be seen when we reach them.

3.8 THE OVERALL PICTURE

We have considered a number of rules and practices whereby the courts, deciding whether to find a settlor's intention in order to determine whether there is an express trust, depart from the ordinary standard of proof. The pattern we have discovered is uneven. Sometimes more than the balance of probabilities is demanded (so that the alleged trust or term is less likely to be found), sometimes less (so that it is more likely to be found). And although it is possible to justify each position taken in terms of one policy or another, there is no consistency in this respect either.

It would not be unreasonable to expect a purer line. The issue centrally at stake is the choice between the claims of the facilitative project, implying that trusts should be found on the basis of intention when, but only when, that intention is genuinely present; and the message of other considerations that allowing people complete, or at the extreme any, liberty to make or not make trusts is undesirable. At least some degree of acceptance of the latter position seems unavoidable. But the better vehicle for it is not the manipulation of the finding of intention, after the fashion of the rules described in this chapter. This is so above all because such rules will always be overridden by a sufficiently definite expression of the genuine intention: and today, when trusts are most often made with professional advice, intentions generally will be given sufficiently definite expression. The right vehicle to reflect a non-facilitative consideration is rather a positive rule, overriding any contrary intention: prohibiting a trust where one is not wanted, or generating a constructive trust in the opposite case.

---

[50] According to Lord Browne-Wilkinson in *Westdeutsche Landesbank Girozentrale v Islington LBC* [1996] AC 669, 708, all resulting trusts are based on some form of presumed intention. But this is dubious as regards resulting trusts other than those under discussion here: see section 7.6.

3.9 REPLACEMENT OF FAILED TRANSACTIONS

In the situations we have looked at so far, either outcome—finding or not finding the alleged intention—was possible, though in some cases credulity was strained. We now turn to a different sort of case. Say I try to make a gift to you, but for some reason am frustrated in that. My general plan was certainly to confer a benefit on you, and that would be achieved if I held the property in question on trust for you instead. It is clear that I did not intend to do so: my thoughts were purely about making you a gift. Might the courts nonetheless say that I did?

The point has not arisen in the material which we have considered hitherto in this chapter. There was no issue there of a trust, not intended in itself, being recognized so as to do substitute service in this way for some other concept which was intended. But at first sight, it seems unthinkable that the courts should recognize a trust in such circumstances. We are told that I had no intention to make the trust in question. Finding otherwise would therefore be contrary to the facilitative logic governing the creation of express trusts.

But this view assumes a particular conception of the facilitative project. It is that we should recognize an express trust when the alleged settlor intends to create that trust, but not otherwise. The 'not otherwise' is questionable, however. Perhaps the project is, or should be, not exclusively concerned with whether the alleged settlor had in mind precisely a trust, but prepared also to find a trust, or whatever other legal device may be most appropriate, to give effect to the alleged settlor's broad plan. By this way of thinking, the trust is 'intended', and so should be recognized, not only when the alleged settlor specifically intends to create a trust, but also where it is the best, or best available, legal match for that which she does intend.

On the whole, this wider view of the facilitative project seems preferable to its rival. Otherwise, the law in effect makes the establishment of an express trust depend on the successful negotiation of a conceptual obstacle course. It is clear that an express trust is created not only when the alleged settlor has that concept in mind by name, but also when she intends a set of arrangements equating with that which the law calls a trust.[51] But 'that which the law calls a trust' is a complicated concept, and to insist that the alleged settlor get every detail right is to expect a lot, and

---

[51] *Re Schebsman* [1944] Ch 83, 104.

in effect to limit the use of the concept to those who are well advised, or perhaps lucky.

Do the courts accept this view? There is evidence both ways. That evidence consists especially of the material in the two following sections.

3.10 TRANSFERS LACKING REQUIRED FORMALITIES

The degree of formality required for the full legal transfer of a piece of property is sometimes greater than that required to deal with the property in some other way: to make a trust of it, or a contract to transfer it. For example, a special kind of written document (a deed) is required to make a full legal transfer of land,[52] while a trust of it, or a contract to transfer it, requires only an ordinary signed written document.[53] So say the owner of some property means to transfer the legal ownership in it to another, but has used insufficient formality to achieve this. So far as formality goes, she may nonetheless have done enough validly to make herself trustee of the property for the intended transferee, or to contract with the intended transferee to pass the property to him, thus giving him the right to call for it. Will she be found to have done so? The wider view of the facilitative project suggests that she should; the narrower fastens on the fact that she undoubtedly had no idea of doing anything except make a complete transfer, and says that she should not.[54] What the law actually says depends on which of (apparently) three kinds of case is in play.

The first kind of case is where the intended transfer was to be a gift but the giver has not taken the correct steps to make it. The law will not readily discover an intention to create a trust in lieu[55] (and there is no

---

[52] This is in fact the old-fashioned rule (in the context of which most of the relevant case law was decided). Nowadays, for the most part, the crucial requirement is one of having the transfer entered on the official Land Register. The general point remains the same.

[53] For a trust, see Law of Property Act 1925 s 53(1)(b) (see section 5.4); for a contract, Law of Property (Miscellaneous Provisions) Act 1989 s 2.

[54] If she has in truth effectively entered into an alternative form of obligation pending the full legal transfer, there is no difficulty over recognizing and effectuating this. This was noted by Clarke LJ in *Pennington v Waine* [2002] 1 WLR 2075.

[55] *Milroy v Lord* (1862) 4 De GF & J 264; *Richards v Delbridge* (1874) LR 18 Eq 11. Cf *T Choithram International SA v Pagarini* [2001] 2 All ER 492, where a purported and ineffective gift to a foundation took effect as a declaration of trust, as the foundation was a trust (so any 'gift to it' would of necessity have taken the form of a transfer to its trustees on its trusts) and the putative donor was one of its trustees (so no *transfer to* its trustees was in fact required).

question of a contract in lieu, as a contract requires consideration). That is, the courts take the narrower view. The second kind of case is likewise where the intended transfer was to be a gift, but whilst the giver has taken the correct steps, other steps have to be taken by someone else (eg reregistration by a company of gifted shares in the name of the donee) before the transfer is complete. Here, adopting the wider view, the law will discover an intention to make a trust pending the completion of those steps.[56] The third kind of case is where the failed legal transfer was for consideration: that is, broadly, paid for. Here, the law treats the frustrated transferor as intending to contract with the purported transferee to transfer the property to him.[57] By relying on this contract, the putative transferee can claim the property after all. And, generally speaking, the law anticipates his doing so and treats him as if he had already got it, by regarding the transferor as holding it on a constructive trust for him in the meantime.[58] This manifests the wider view: the intention to contract is no more genuinely to be found in this case than the intention to hold on trust would be in the case of a failed gift.[59]

The pattern of these choices is aligned with economic utilitarian precepts. This policy favours the effectuation of commercial arrangements, ie those where consideration is involved, and so calls for the provision of substitute vehicles, even involving trusts, in their aid. Being generally offended by the creation of trusts, this policy is averse to their recognition in place of failed gifts. There is less difficulty where the fulfilment of the gift is merely delayed, for the offensive trust will soon disappear; and in the meantime a trust will allow the donee to act to an extent as though the property has become her own, which is preferable to the stagnation entailed by obliging her to await the full transfer.

---

[56] *Re Rose* [1952] Ch 499.

[57] *Parker v Taswell* (1858) 2 De G & J 559.

[58] See section 8.7.

[59] Note that, under appropriate circumstances, the law may alternatively effectuate any kind of intended but as yet ineffective transfer by saying that the transferor holds on *constructive* trust for the transferee: for which no finding of intention to create a trust is required. The constructive trust would most likely arise under the doctrine of proprietary estoppel: see section 8.10. In *Pennington v Waine* [2002] 1 WLR 2075, such a trust was found on the basis of 'unconscionability', but the discussion (at 2090–1) of what constituted the unconscionability, and why, is vestigial.

3.11 PAYMENTS TO CLUBS

People frequently want to make payments[60] to clubs and associations, whether by way of membership fee ('subscription'), gift, bequest, or purchase (eg of a raffle ticket). One would expect it to be quite straightforward to do so. But there is a problem. For the payment to be made, the payee must be capable of receiving it, ie of owning the money given. The law says that people can own property, but that organizations cannot, unless they are 'incorporated'. Trading companies are generally incorporated, and so are some clubs. Payments to these can therefore be validly made. But many clubs are not incorporated, so cannot own property: so no payments can be made to them.

In a clear example of the wider form of facilitative thinking, however, the judges have developed a practice of regarding apparent payments to unincorporated clubs as some other, valid, kind of disposition having an effect similar to the abortive direct payment. They use two principal approaches.

First, the purported gift to the club may be read as a trust for the club's purposes[61] (without this time treating that in turn as a gift to the club's members beneficially).[62] A trust to promote a charitable purpose is valid without more, as explained in Chapter 6; so a purported gift to a club with charitable objects will unproblematically be valid as a trust for those objects, and will always be taken thus.[63] A trust to promote a non-charitable purpose is valid if there are people benefited by, or perhaps otherwise interested in, its performance.[64] Most club members will be benefited by the performance of a trust for their club's purposes, and surely all, even if on the basis of altruism alone, will be interested in the performance of such a trust. Gifts read as trusts for the purposes of non-charitable clubs will thus normally achieve validity too.[65]

---

[60] Or occasionally to transfer some other form of property than money: the issues are the same.

[61] Some of the payments in *Re West Sussex Constabulary's Widows, Children and Benevolent (1930) Fund Trust* [1971] Ch 1 were treated in this way.

[62] Cf section 3.5. That further step was however taken (and the contractual analysis, below, then applied) in *Re Lipinski's Will Trusts* [1976] Ch 235.

[63] *Re Vernon's Will Trusts* [1972] Ch 300n; *Re Finger's Will Trusts* [1972] Ch 286.

[64] *Re Denley's Trust Deed* [1969] 1 Ch 373: see section 14.3.

[65] Thus in *Re West Sussex Constabulary's Widows, Children and Benevolent (1930) Fund Trust* [1971] Ch 1. Similar, though not identical, to the purpose trust approach is the suggestion in *Conservative and Unionist Central Office v Burrell* [1982] 1 WLR 522 that the payment be treated as to the club treasurer, with a mandate to spend it on the club's purposes. The latter analysis has not proved popular, perhaps partly because it is hard to see how it can apply to a purported *bequest* to a club.

Secondly, the purported gift to a non-charitable club may be read as a gift to its members.[66] A gift to the members merely in their personal capacity would be technically unproblematic,[67] but it would not be a close surrogate for the purported gift to the club. To achieve a better surrogate, the gift is taken as being to the members 'on behalf of the club'. Between the members of the club there will exist a contract, either express or implied: the club's rules. This contract will, again either expressly or impliedly, govern (amongst other things) the use which the members can make of any money which they own on the club's behalf: essentially, requiring them to spend it (only) on the club's purposes. Income regarded in this way will thus be owned by the members, but be caught by this contractual obligation.[68] This approach is often referred to as 'the contractual analysis'.

Sometimes the judges have no choice between the two approaches. A contract obliging me to make a payment 'to the club' can usually be read only as requiring a payment under the contractual analysis.[69] Say you sell me a £1 ticket for your club's raffle. In technical terms, this occurs under a contract, which obliges me to pay £1 in exchange for the ticket. I will not fulfil this obligation unless I give you the £1 absolutely. Settling £1 on trust for the club's purposes will not do. As the £1 then comes into your absolute ownership, it is caught by the club rules. The same goes for members' subscriptions. The contract under which they are demanded (in return for the benefits of membership) requires them to be paid, say to the treasurer, absolutely; they are then caught by the rules.

But in the case of donations voluntarily made, whether *inter vivos* or by will, the donor can choose the terms on which to make the payment, so

---

[66] Whether directly, or via a trust of which they are the beneficiaries. A gift to a club with charitable objects could not be read thus without itself becoming a non-charitable trust: conferring the property on the members makes it theirs (even if they have contracted to devote it to charity), and benefiting them is not a charitable purpose (see section 6.5). As the settlor surely intended a charitable trust, this construction is eschewed in favour of that in the previous paragraph.

[67] Unless for reasons of perpetuity (see section 2.5), if the gift is to members joining indefinitely into the future.

[68] *Re Recher's Will Trusts* [1972] Ch 526. Cases using this approach include *Re St Andrew's Allotment Association* [1969] 1 WLR 229; *Re West Sussex Constabulary's Widows, Children and Benevolent (1930) Fund Trust* [1971] Ch 1; *Re Sick and Funeral Society of St John's Sunday School, Golcar* [1973] Ch 51; *Re Buckinghamshire Constabulary Widows' and Orphans' Fund Friendly Society (No 2)* [1979] 1 WLR 936.

[69] Though a contract obliging me to pay money to a charitable club will presumably be taken to require a settlement on the club's trusts, so as not to produce a (non-charitable) payment to the members. Contracts obliging employers and employees to pay into pension schemes likewise require them to place the money on the scheme trusts.

both approaches are in principle viable.[70] We, however, are considering what happens if the donor has expressly chosen neither, but has purported to make a payment to the club, and the substitute analysis is being constructed by the court under the wider facilitative logic. It seems right to use the analysis which most closely reflects the failed intended disposition.

Under the purpose trust approach there is a trust obligation to spend the money on the club's purposes. The money in no sense belongs to the members, and they cannot claim it for themselves or otherwise change the purposes on which it will be spent from those (the club's existing purposes) regarded as designated by the donor.[71] Under the contractual analysis, however, the money belongs to the members. What stops them from taking it home as their own property, or otherwise spending it in a way different from that perhaps envisaged by the donor, is the relevant club rule. But this is a term of a contract made amongst themselves. As the sole parties to this contract, they can change its terms, or even terminate it, by mutual consent, allowing them after all to spend the money as they may wish. This is the main difference between the two approaches.[72] Some see the purpose trust approach's firmer adhesion to the original club purposes as an argument in favour of that approach, for being more faithful to the donor's intentions. But that is questionable. The donor, remember, sought to make a gift to the club. It is strongly arguable that in so doing she meant the members to settle the use of the money thereafter. (Just as if I give you some money as a present, I acknowledge that it is yours to spend, and that you are ultimately entitled to disregard whatever ideas I may have had about its use.) And the closer approximation to that is not the purpose trust approach, but the contractual analysis.

---

[70] The purpose trust approach is however doubtfully plausible for money placed in a collecting box. The small sum involved and the anonymity of the donor make it more realistic to see her as paying the money absolutely, ie under the contractual analysis. The essence of the point is taken, but its implications not made fully clear, in *Re West Sussex Constabulary's Widows, Children and Benevolent (1930) Fund Trust* [1971] Ch 1, 11–14.

[71] Though if the trustees were willing to misapply the money in some way that the members favoured, the members could bring that about by not enforcing the trust against them (unless the trust can be enforced by its settlor: cf *Carreras Rothmans Ltd v Freeman Mathews Treasure Ltd* [1985] Ch 207): see section 14.3. It would be possible to design a purpose trust whose purposes could validly be varied by the members, but this has apparently not been considered in respect of the purpose trusts which are found in lieu of purported gifts to clubs, as opposed to those made expressly.

[72] Cf *Re Lipinski's Will Trusts* [1976] Ch 235, where the judge did not notice that the two approaches have different consequences and treated them as interchangeable.

In practice, a judge impelled to use the contractual analysis regarding part of a club's income (notably the members' subscriptions) may well choose to use it also for the rest, for the sake of simplicity.[73] She is also likely to be swayed by the relative attractiveness of the results which the rival analyses would throw up in the circumstances which have emerged: often, upon the club's dissolution. If a gift is treated as made on a purpose trust, the failure of that purpose will (unless the giver has provided otherwise[74]) generate a resulting trust, requiring that the surviving amount be repaid to the giver.[75] Where the gift was small, or anonymous, or made some time previously by a person not since connected with the club, effecting such a repayment will be a difficult task. If a gift is treated as made under the contractual analysis, however, upon the club's dissolution it will (unless the contract, ie the club rules, original or as now amended, provides otherwise) be governed by an implied term requiring payment in equal shares to the members at the time of the dissolution.[76] This term will normally be easy to effectuate, especially in comparison with a resulting trust solution; it will thus be expedient to have adopted the contractual analysis in the first place.

---

[73] See eg *Re Buckinghamshire Constabulary Widows' and Orphans' Fund Friendly Society (No 2)* [1979] 1 WLR 936; but cf *Re West Sussex Constabulary's Widows, Children and Benevolent (1930) Fund Trust* [1971] Ch 1.

[74] By a stipulation in favour of a further object; or, if this be legally possible (assumed so in eg *Re West Sussex Constabulary's Widows, Children and Benevolent (1930) Fund Trust* [1971] Ch 1, but doubted by R Chambers *Resulting Trusts* (1997) 58–66, by an intention to leave the property ownerless, and thus, as *bona vacantia*, the property of the Crown. (According to *Air Jamaica Ltd v Charlton* [1999] 1 WLR 1399, 1412, even if it is possible to make the property ownerless an intention to do so cannot prevent a resulting trust from arising; but this both contradicts *Westdeutsche Landesbank Girozentrale v Islington LBC* [1996] AC 669, 708 and is wrong in principle: see section 7.7.)

[75] See section 7.5. In *Re Printers and Transferrers Amalgamated Trades Protection Society* [1899] 2 Ch 184, however, the 'resulting trust' was said to be for the members at the time of dissolution, notwithstanding that they were not the only settlors of the funds. Perhaps the neglected settlors were taken to have transferred their resulting trust interests to the members remaining at dissolution, though there was neither evidence of this nor the written documentation which ought to have been used (Law of Property Act 1925 s 53(1)(c): see section 5.7). Cf *Re Hobourn Aero Components Air Raid Distress Fund* [1946] Ch 86 and *Air Jamaica Ltd v Charlton* [1999] 1 WLR 1399, which use resulting trusts more conventionally.

[76] *Re Buckinghamshire Constabulary Widows' and Orphans' Fund Friendly Society (No 2)* [1979] 1 WLR 936.

4

Promises to make trusts

Except for trusts contained in their will, people generally want the trusts they make to come into effect immediately. In such cases, the settlor either transfers the property in question to trustees, or else keeps it and declares himself the trustee of it; and from then on it belongs to the trust.

But sometimes it is otherwise. A settlor may decide to make a trust, but despite being able to do so immediately, may not actually do so. Or he may not yet have the property which he plans to put on trust.[1] This will be the case, for example, if he plans to put on trust an inheritance which he expects to receive upon someone's death in the future. In these cases, until he makes the trust he has done nothing beyond conceive an idea about it in his mind, which has no legal effect. He can change his idea, or abandon it altogether, as he likes. In the case where he did not yet have the property in question, he can please himself whether he goes ahead and makes a trust of it, if and when he receives it.

Sometimes, however, a settlor might want to set up something more definite than this. Where he might have made a trust immediately but chose not to because the circumstances were not right, he might want to bind himself to make it if and when the circumstances are right. Or, in the case of property which he does not yet have, he might wish to establish a firm arrangement which will produce a trust if and when the property comes to him. This chapter looks at the ways in which settlors might go about making such commitments, and considers the effect that they have.

4.1 REVOCABLE UNDERTAKINGS

One possibility is for the settlor to have a document drawn up containing the terms of his intended trust and saying that the trust is to come into effect on receipt of the property in question, and then to arrange for the property, when it materializes, to be sent directly to the trustee. Going

---

[1] A trust can be made only of property which one already has: *Williams v Commissioner of Inland Revenue* [1965] NZLR 395.

this far does not bind the settlor. He can still change his mind about making the trust, and revoke the arrangements he has set up. But unless he does something positive to show that he has changed his mind before the property reaches the trustee (such as destroying the document, or cancelling the arrangement for the property to be sent to the trustee), it will generally then be taken that he still intends the trust. And when this presumed continuing intention comes together with the pre-established terms, and with the property now arriving in the trustee's hands under the arrangement, the trust will in fact be made.[2]

The advance that this approach makes over merely intending to make a trust is that instead of the settlor having to bestir himself into making the trust when he receives the property, the trust will automatically come into effect unless he actively prevents it. So it perhaps makes it more likely that the trust will eventually be made. Certainly, it looks more like a commitment than the case of pure intention, and so creates an effect which some people in some circumstances might find useful. Ultimately, however, such an arrangement is no more binding on the settlor than a pure intention.[3]

4.2 CONTRACTS TO MAKE TRUSTS

Sometimes, however, a would-be settlor may want positively to commit herself now to make a trust of property when she gets it in the future. She can in principle do so by making a contract to that effect.

This contract might be of the ordinary kind where both parties give consideration. For example, I might make a deal with my sister whereby she pays me a sum of money now in return for my undertaking to hold any inheritance I may later receive on trust for her children. Her consideration is paying me the money, and mine is the promise to make a trust of the inheritance for her children if and when I receive it. Alternatively, the contract might be of the special kind known as a covenant,

---

[2] *Re Bowden* [1936] Ch 71. The trust will not be made, however, if the property reaches the trustees not under an arrangement made by the settlor but adventitiously, eg because the trustee also happens to be the executor of a will under which the property in question is bequeathed to the settlor: *Re Brooks' Settlement Trusts* [1939] Ch 993. That seems right, as maintaining the primacy of the settlor's intention, but the contrary view was taken in *Re Ralli's Will Trusts* [1964] Ch 288, where *Re Brooks' Settlement Trusts* was not cited.

[3] Stipulating for a trust in one's will is a particular instance of this. On death, the property in question will go to the designated trustee and the trust will come into effect; but until then the will is revocable.

where the settlor uses a deed[4] to make his promise, and there need be no consideration in return. For example, if I want to undertake to give 2 per cent of my net income each year to a charitable trust, I might covenant to the charity's trustees to transfer the sum in question each year to their trust.

In former times, one common use of these contracts to make trusts was found in marriage settlements. These varied in details, but their basic outline was standard. When a woman married, her parents would put some money or other property into a trust, of which she was the beneficiary for her life, then her husband if he survived her, then their children if they had any, but otherwise her next-of-kin (remoter relatives such as nephews and nieces). This was an ordinary immediate trust, of property already in hand. But in addition, the woman signed a deed undertaking to the settlement's trustees that if she received further property during the marriage ('after-acquired property': an inheritance, for example), she would transfer it into this same trust.

This undertaking is clearly a covenant by the woman with the trustees (they did not normally give any consideration). But it is also a contract for consideration between her, on the one side, and on the other side her husband and any children of the marriage. The husband's consideration is the marriage itself, and the law regards this as extending also to their children: they are said to be 'within the marriage consideration'. The next-of-kin, however, are not parties to the covenant, as the trustees are; nor is there a contract between the woman and them in the way that there is between her and her husband and children, because the marriage consideration does not include them and they give no other consideration. Their position is purely that of potential beneficiaries of the trust which the woman has undertaken to make. As people who have given no consideration, they are called 'volunteers'.

4.3 THE ENFORCEABILITY OF CONTRACTS TO MAKE TRUSTS

These contracts to make trusts, whether for consideration or in the form of covenants, might be expected to behave just like contracts to do anything else. In principle they would be binding and enforceable. But in fact, as a result of the decisions that have emerged on the subject, the law

---

[4] A special formal document which, until recently, was characterized by a seal, but which now has only to proclaim itself a deed.

about contracts to make trusts has some peculiarities. To see the position, we need to separate three different scenarios.

First: where the beneficiary of the projected trust *has himself given consideration* for the settlor's undertaking to make it. (This is the position of the husband and children in the case of a marriage settlement.) Here, we would expect the contract to be enforceable by the beneficiary, as a party to it. And this is indeed the law.[5]

Secondly: where the beneficiary (such as a next-of-kin) does *not* give consideration, but the settlor makes her covenant not only with the prospective trustees *but also with the beneficiary himself* that she will make the trust, so that the beneficiary is not merely the designated object of the projected trust, but a party to the covenant itself. We would expect that the covenant can be enforced by the covenantees, both the trustees and the beneficiary. Again, this has been accepted in the case law.[6]

Those two positions are normal under the law of contract. Promisees under contracts, whether for consideration or in the form of a covenant, are able to enforce them. So far as these two scenarios are concerned, this goes for contracts to make trusts just as much as any other contract.

The difficulties set in with the third scenario: where the beneficiary (such as a next-of-kin) is a volunteer, ie does *not* give consideration, and the settlor makes a covenant promising the prospective trustees but, this time, *not the beneficiary* that she will make a trust for the beneficiary. Here, the situation is somewhat complex.

In the case of a covenant made before 11 May 2000, the old rules on privity of contract (changed on that date) will prevent the beneficiary from directly enforcing the covenant. Under the ordinary law of contract, however, we should expect the trustees, as covenantees, to be able to enforce. But the cases say that the trustees may not: that a covenant of this kind (one to create a trust in favour of a volunteer) is unenforceable.

In the case of a covenant made since 11 May 2000, the beneficiary is likely to have the benefit of the Contracts (Rights of Third Parties) Act 1999. Under this Act,[7] a contract may be enforced by someone who is not

---

[5] *Pullan v Koe* [1913] 1 Ch 9. Moreover, if the remedy of specific performance is available, then, because 'equity looks upon that as done which ought to be done', the settlor will hold the property on constructive trust pending compliance with the contract (see section 8.7): *ibid*.

[6] *Cannon v Hartley* [1949] Ch 213. There being no consideration, the remedy cannot be specific performance, so (cf n 5 above) there can be no constructive trust pending compliance.

[7] Section 1(1)(b).

a party to it (a 'third party') but on whom it purports to confer a benefit.[8] The Act probably applies to covenants as much as to contracts for consideration.[9] The third party's right to enforce is only, however, as strong as the right of the promisee, our prospective trustees: defences which the promisor can raise against the promisee can also be raised against the third party.[10] And as we have just seen, the law was already that the prospective trustees could not enforce the covenant against the covenantor. Under the 1999 Act, the beneficiary should therefore likewise be unable to enforce it.

Apparently, then, in the third scenario both pre- and post-1999 covenants are unenforceable either by the beneficiary or by the trustees. In the case of a beneficiary seeking to enforce a pre-1999 covenant, this is a result of the then rules regarding privity of contract, and is no surprise. But in the case of the prospective trustees seeking to enforce a pre-1999 covenant, or either the prospective trustees or a beneficiary seeking to enforce a post-1999 covenant, it follows from the cases declaring that covenants to make trusts for volunteers are unenforceable. We need to examine these cases.

4.4 THE UNENFORCEABILITY OF COVENANTS TO MAKE TRUSTS FOR VOLUNTEERS

The main decision holding covenants to make trusts for volunteers to be unenforceable is *Re Pryce*.[11]

The reasoning in the case begins by observing that a covenant of this kind is for the benefit of a volunteer beneficiary. Then it points out that a volunteer, such as this beneficiary, could not claim specific performance of the covenant, because specific performance is an equitable remedy and 'equity will not assist a volunteer'. And, it says, since the Judicature Act 1875, the rules of equity have been superimposed on the common law, so

---

[8] Unless on a proper construction of the contract it appears that the parties to it did not intend it to be enforceable by the third party (s 1(2)). A contract is also enforceable by a third party if it contains a term to that effect: s 1(1)(a).

[9] The Act itself does not make this clear, merely using the word 'contract'. The view in the text is suggested by the report proposing the Act: Law Commission Report No 242 *Privity of Contract: Contracts for the Benefit of Third Parties* (1996) para 6.4.

[10] Contracts (Rights of Third Parties) Act 1999 s 3(2).

[11] [1917] 1 Ch 234. Likewise *Re D'Angibau* (1880) 15 Ch D 228; *Re Plumptre's Marriage Settlement* [1910] 1 Ch 609; *Re Kay's Settlement Trusts* [1939] Ch 329; *Re Adlard* [1954] Ch 29. *Re Cook's Settlement Trusts* [1965] Ch 902 is often said to be similar, but must differ in denying that the covenant is held on trust: as explained below, the other decisions assume the contrary.

that the law as a whole will not now assist a volunteer: equity's embargo on specific performance for volunteers extends also to common law remedies such as the action to recover money promised under a covenant. Nor, the reasoning continues, will the law allow a volunteer to be assisted indirectly by someone else—the trustees—suing on his behalf. So the covenant is unenforceable.[12]

This reasoning, however, is erroneous.[13] Equity certainly withholds its remedy of specific performance from volunteers. Specific performance is a special remedy for the enforcement of contracts. The ordinary remedy is the common law right to monetary relief, either damages or debt. The latter is always available, but specific performance is not. It is given only when the common law remedy fails to do adequate justice to the plaintiff's claim, and in certain situations it will never be given. One of these situations is where the claimant has not given consideration (as with a promisee under a voluntary covenant). But that is as far as it goes. There is no foundation for the further idea that equity has a general antipathy towards volunteers, and that as a consequence not only are equitable remedies such as specific performance withheld from them, but also there is a ban on all other remedies that would benefit them, even common law remedies sought by other people (here, the prospective trustees).

Equity has no general antipathy towards volunteers. It does not even withhold all its own remedies from them. Although it denies them its remedy of specific performance of a contract, it allows, for example, beneficiaries of trusts to have injunctions, account, and so on even though (as is usually the case) they are volunteers. Again, it certainly does not insist that common law remedies be withheld from volunteers: no more since the Judicature Act 1875 than before.[14] If it did, ordinary covenan-

---

[12] It is sometimes pointed out that the question posed to the judge in *Re Pryce* [1917] 1 Ch 234 was 'must the trustees sue the settlor?', and the argument made that his statements to the effect that neither the trustees nor the beneficiaries could sue the settlor were therefore *obiter* (though they were adopted as part of the *ratio* in *Re Kay's Settlement Trusts* [1939] Ch 329). This is incorrect, however. The judge arrived at the answer that the trustees did not have to sue by observing (albeit fallaciously, as we shall see) that they could not sue even if they wanted to.

[13] The issue has provoked much discussion. See especially D Elliott (1960) 76 LQR 100; J Hornby (1962) 78 LQR 228; W Lee (1969) 85 LQR 213; J Barton (1975) 91 LQR 236; R Meagher and J Lehane (1976) 92 LQR 427.

[14] The 1875 Act lays down that equity's line prevails over that of the common law *if they are in conflict*. So if equity did disapprove of volunteers having common law remedies such as debt or damages, its view would prevail and these remedies would indeed be withdrawn. But that has never been equity's position. While withholding its own discretionary remedy of specific performance, it has always been perfectly content that volunteers should have the standard common law remedies.

tees, being volunteers, would be denied not only specific performance of the covenant in their favour, but also any common law remedy; so, there being no remedies at all for their enforcement, covenants would be so much waste paper; which they are plainly not.[15] Nor does equity place an embargo on volunteers being indirectly assisted, by someone else using the remedies to which he is entitled, equitable or legal, on their behalf (such as trustee-covenantees suing for the sake of a volunteer beneficiary). There is no such embargo even in respect of specific performance, which is where it might be most likely: in a case where one man contracted with another (himself not a volunteer) to pay money to a third party who was a volunteer, the House of Lords granted specific performance to the promisee to make the promisor perform this contract in favour of the third party.[16]

It is sometimes suggested that *Re Pryce*[17] can be circumvented, and a volunteer beneficiary enabled to sue after all, if we find that that the right of action—the right to sue the settlor on the covenant—was held by the trustees on trust for the beneficiary. That is incorrect, however. It is certainly possible for the right of action to be held on trust in this way.[18] And it is logical to think that it is indeed held by the trustees for the beneficiary, even without signs of a visible intention that it should be. For otherwise the trustees must either own it for their personal benefit (meaning that they can choose whether to sue and can keep the resulting damages if they do), or hold it for the settlor (meaning that she has these advantages). In the kind of case under discussion, where the settlor's goal was to confer benefits on the beneficiary, both these alternatives would be absurd, leaving the view that the trustees hold the right of action for the beneficiary as the only tenable possibility.[19] In fact, this view was taken, though not proclaimed, in *Re Pryce*[20] itself. Remember the assumption in

---

[15] *Cannon v Hartley* [1949] Ch 213 actually decided that a covenant with a volunteer prospective beneficiary was enforceable by him.

[16] *Beswick v Beswick* [1968] AC 58.

[17] [1917] 1 Ch 234.

[18] Though in *Re Cook's Settlement Trusts* [1965] Ch 902 it is said that whilst a covenant to settle a pre-determined amount can be held on trust, a covenant to settle an indefinite amount at an indefinite time in the future (as would normally be the case with a covenant to settle after-acquired property) cannot. There is, however, no known foundation for this view, which runs counter to the decision in a number of cases, including *Davenport v Bishopp* (1843) 2 Y & CCC 451, 1 Ph 698.

[19] Cf section 3.6, noting that in cases where it would not be absurd for the promisee to own the rights personally, clear signs of an intention to place them on trust are required before such a trust will be found.

[20] [1917] 1 Ch 234.

the reasoning of the case that, if the trustees were allowed to enforce such a covenant, it would assist the volunteer beneficiary. This was true only if the covenant was held on trust for the latter. Otherwise, ie if the covenant had belonged to the trustees themselves, their enforcement of it would have benefited not the beneficiary but themselves.

The right of action is thus rightly to be seen as held by the trustees for the beneficiary. But ultimately this does not help. For according to *Re Pryce*[21] the right of action is unenforceable: and there is no reason to think that placing an unenforceable right of action in a trust renders it enforceable. Contrast some older cases,[22] which likewise regarded the right of action on the settlor's covenant as held by the trustees for the volunteer beneficiary, but assumed (correctly: the contrary reasoning in *Re Pryce*[23] being fallacious, as we have seen) that the right was enforceable in the normal way. They concluded that the beneficiaries could enforce the covenant against the settlor, or more exactly could, by pointing to the trust of the right of action, force the trustees to enforce the covenant against the settlor to their benefit.

So the law says (albeit on the basis of fallacious reasoning) that a covenant to place property on trust for a volunteer beneficiary cannot be enforced. It should be noted however that if, despite its unenforceability against her, the settlor complies with the covenant and transfers the property to the trustees, that is nonetheless effective to constitute the trust.[24] There is no inconsistency in this: a promise to make a gift likewise cannot be enforced, but a gift once made is effective. One decision goes further (though another contradicts it),[25] telling us that the trust is also constituted if the trustees acquire the property not from the settlor but in some other way, eg because they are also executors of a will which leaves it to the settlor.[26] This latter position seems hard to defend. It attaches legal consequences to mere coincidence, rather than to the settlor's voluntary act, as where the settlor herself complies with the covenant. And it requires all trustees of more than one trust, such as banks, to check whether they hold property under one of their trusts for someone who

---

[21] [1917] 1 Ch 234.
[22] *Davenport v Bishopp* (1843) 2 Y & CCC 451, 1 Ph 698; *Fletcher v Fletcher* (1844) 4 Hare 67.
[23] [1917] 1 Ch 234.
[24] *Re Adlard* [1954] Ch 29.
[25] *Re Brooks' Settlement Trusts* [1939] 1 Ch 993.
[26] *Re Ralli's Will Trusts* [1964] Ch 288. *Re Brooks' Settlement Trusts* [1939] 1 Ch 993 was not cited.

has undertaken but cannot be forced to transfer it to them under another: an unrealistic expectation.

4.5 THE POLICY PERSPECTIVE

Although their reasoning is flawed, *Re Pryce*[27] and similar decisions do resonate with the relevant policy perspective of the period from which they begin to emerge, the late nineteenth century. At this time, perceptions about economic utility and married women's property rights became especially prominent considerations. Marriage settlements were problematic on both counts. By preventing a wife from getting her hands on her capital, and restricting her to the income, they tied the capital up, took it out of circulation in the market; and they infringed her right to control her own affairs. During the joint lives of the woman and her husband, and perhaps also if they had children, there were countervailing considerations. But if she were left a childless widow (the situation in which her covenant to settle after-acquired property on trust for her volunteer next-of-kin becomes relevant), the economic and rights arguments for restoring her absolute ownership of the capital possessed substantial power. The cases give her that absolute ownership.

There is an interesting contrast between *Re D'Angibau*,[28] a precursor to *Re Pryce*,[29] and *Lloyd's v Harper*,[30] a decision contemporaneous with it. The latter too involved a contract to pay money to volunteer third parties, but the context was this time not a marriage settlement, but trade. A father had given an undertaking to the managing committee of Lloyd's, the insurance market, to guarantee his son's debts when the latter became a member of it. This undertaking was for the benefit of the son's creditors, who were third party volunteers.[31] In terms of the law as it began to emerge in *Re D'Angibau*[32] and was later confirmed in *Re Pryce*,[33] this should have been fatal. But the court dealt with the case along the lines of the older authorities, deciding that the managing committee held the father's undertaking on trust for the creditors, who could insist on its enforcement. In this context there was nothing corresponding to the

---

[27] [1917] 1 Ch 234.   [28] (1880) 15 Ch D 228.   [29] [1917] 1 Ch 234.
[30] (1880) 16 Ch D 290.
[31] They did of course give consideration to the son (ie their premiums), but were volunteers so far as the father's undertaking was concerned. But although their bargain with the son was thus analytically an entirely separate matter, it rendered the context one of trade, which makes all the difference to the policy significance of the case.
[32] (1880) 15 Ch D 228.   [33] [1917] 1 Ch 234.

argument about married women's rights, and in terms of economic utility the arrangement was positively advantageous, for such guarantees were necessary to establish confidence, and so promote trade, in the insurance market. In these terms, then, it is quite consistent that this contract should have been held enforceable while those in marriage settlements were not.

But although the views taken in the cases were thus consistent with the dominant policy positions of the period in which they emerged, they strike few chords today. Confronted with the kind of arrangement under discussion, we should find it hard to find external policy reasons for wanting to see it enforced or otherwise. We should probably think simply that a covenant to make a trust ought (in the absence of the usual vitiating factors such as duress or misrepresentation) to be enforced, on the internal ground that that is what entering into a covenant means and demands.

We noted above that whilst the Contracts (Rights of Third Parties) Act 1999 allows a third party to enforce a contract, this will make no difference to this area of the law. The third party's action is made subject to the same defences as apply to an action brought by the promisee,[34] and as the law stands *Re Pryce*[35] tells us that the promisee has no action, since a covenant to make a trust for a volunteer is unenforceable. Nevertheless, the advent of the 1999 Act may provide the occasion for bringing this area of the law once more before the courts. Given that (as just suggested) to modern eyes there is little at stake in this kind of case beyond the normal impulse to uphold the covenant, the opportunity may well then be taken to leave behind the reasoning in *Re Pryce*,[36] whether expressly or by overlooking the difficulties and applying the Act.

There would in fact be problems about expressly overruling *Re Pryce*[37] in favour of a position that covenants to make trusts for volunteers are enforceable. Overruling a case declares that it always was wrong, and that the newly stated position has always has been the correct one. As explained in the previous section, there is no doubt that the prospective trustees hold the right of action under the covenant on trust for the beneficiary. If that right of action is enforceable, they are therefore under a duty to the beneficiary to use it. If *Re Pryce*[38] is overruled and the right of action declared enforceable, then, trustees who had relied on that case and not sought to enforce would therefore find themselves to have been, all along, in breach of their duty to the beneficiary.[39]

---

[34] Contracts (Rights of Third Parties) Act 1999 s 3(2).   [35] [1917] 1 Ch 234.
[36] [1917] 1 Ch 234   [37] [1917] 1 Ch 234.   [38] [1917] 1 Ch 234.
[39] Though relief might be available under the Trustee Act 1925 s 61: see section 12.2.

5

Formalities

In this chapter we shall look at the degree of formality which the law demands in the creation of trusts, and also in dealings with beneficial interests.

The law frequently requires that transactions which establish property interests should be marked with some formality: above all, it requires that the transaction should be embodied in a permanent form, such as writing. Traditionally, for example, changes of ownership of land had to be made by deed. Today, the important step is the recording of them in a government register; another kind of formality.

So far as making trusts is concerned, however, the basic rule is that no formalities are required. But there are two exceptions to this. First, when the trust is to come into effect on the settlor's death, it will be made through the medium of her will: and wills must be in writing, signed by the testator, and attested by two witnesses.[1] Secondly, where the subject matter of the trust is land, then even if it is to come into effect in the settlor's lifetime ('*inter vivos*'), it must be put in writing and signed by the settlor;[2] unless the trust is a resulting or constructive trust, when there is once again no formality requirement.[3]

There is a further formality rule in the trusts area, which concerns not the making of them but dispositions of the beneficial interests existing under them; for example, where a beneficiary transfers his interest to someone else. Such a disposition must be made in writing, and signed by the person making it.[4]

To assess these rules, we need to look first at the function of formality requirements in general.

---

[1] Wills Act 1837 s 9, as amended by Administration of Justice Act 1982 s 17.
[2] Law of Property Act 1925 s 53(1)(b).
[3] Law of Property Act 1925 s 53(2).
[4] Law of Property Act 1925 s 53(1)(c).

5.1 THE FUNCTION OF FORMALITY REQUIREMENTS

The principal function of formality requirements is to maximize certainty about the fact that a transaction took place at all, and about what it comprised.

This happens in two ways. One is obvious: having the fact that the transaction was made, and its details (eg exactly what was being transferred, and to whom, and on what terms), embodied in a permanent form makes them much less controvertible than if they had been left oral. The other is that having to write the transaction down will probably have the effect that those making it will concentrate on it more than if they were making it orally, so there is a better chance that they will deal with all the aspects of it of fully and coherently, rather than leaving gaps and loose ends. (This also has the benefit of making them consider more deeply whether they really want to make the transaction at all, so giving the formality requirement an additional 'cooling-off' effect.)

Making transactions as certain as possible is valuable at several levels. Most obviously, it is useful for the people actually involved in the transaction. It enables them to make it correspond with what they wanted to achieve. In this respect, then, formality serves the facilitative logic underpinning express trusts.

Beyond the people involved in the transaction itself, certainty is also important for others with whom they in turn deal. For instance, say I sell you a house. Later, you want to sell it to someone else, or to lease it to a tenant, or to offer it to your bank as security for a loan. You will need to establish that you really do own it; otherwise, these dispositions would all be ineffective. To do so, you need to point to the transaction by which you acquired it from me, and to that by which I myself acquired it before that, and so on down the chain into history. The ease with which you can do this, and so the marketability of your property, is a function of certainty, and that is promoted by formality.

The certainty provided by formality also allows transactions to be observed by state agencies, because it makes them more visible than if they were merely oral. This in turn allows the government to regulate both the transactions themselves and the state of ownership that results from them. A familiar illustration is registration of the ownership of motor vehicles, which enables taxes to be collected and traffic offenders to be traced. Similarly, traders are required to keep records so that their liability for value added tax can be checked. Another tax, stamp duty, has a particularly close relationship with formality rules. Stamp duty is levied on certain transfers of property, at a rate varying with the property's value. It is levied not on the transaction, with the formality just making matters more visible to the collectors, but on the formality, the written instrument embodying the transaction, itself. If the same transaction could be made without an instrument, the tax would not be payable. So the formality rules, determining when a transaction must be put in writing, *ipso facto* establish its susceptibility to stamp duty.

These, then, are some of the major advantages of maintaining formality rules in a general way. But there are also disadvantages. In particular, if the law disallows a transaction because it was made informally, it will fail to give effect to the intentions of the people involved in the transaction. That is disadvantageous in terms of facilitative thinking, the policy of allowing people to make whatever dispositions they like. Where, for example, someone has expressed himself perfectly clearly about what is to happen to his property after his death, but has failed to observe the formalities which the law requires for a will, facilitative policy will be affronted if the law says that no effect is to be given to his wishes. So in fact facilitative logic is ambivalent on the subject of formality requirements. They can both help, through getting people to make their meaning plain, and hinder, by disallowing clear but informal dispositions.

So when the law imposes a formality requirement, with the rider that non-compliance entails invalidity, it is not necessarily an unqualifiedly good idea to do so. The point may be rather that the arguments in favour of requiring formality outweigh those against. Deciding whether to require formality involves assessing the advantages and disadvantages either way, and comparing them, to see where the greater benefit lies. So, for example, in having the rule that any attempt to dispose of property on death other than by using the ordained formalities is a nullity, the law takes it that the balance lies in favour of such insistence; that the potential ineffectiveness of attempted informal dispositions is an acceptable price to pay for the advantages of minimizing uncertainty.

5.2 THE GENERAL POSITION IN TRUSTS

In principle, then, the question whether or not formalities should be required in the making of trusts involves a choice between two positions. One is to procure certainty by having a formality requirement, but at the expense of disallowing dispositions where the settlor omits to comply with it. The other is the converse: to accept as a valid trust every disposition that was meant as one, at the expense of having to accept uncertainty in at least some cases. In fact, the basic rule is along the latter lines: that no formality is required to make a trust. Ultimately, therefore, the desire not to frustrate settlors in the making of informal trusts is given precedence over the advantages of certainty.

But the absence of a formality rule does not mean that trusts are in practice often made informally. To a large extent, they are made in circumstances where a degree of formality will naturally tend to be present, even though the law does not require it. People who consciously make trusts will generally want to put beyond doubt that they have done so, and exactly what they have effected: and the natural way of doing this is to embody the transaction in a formal written document.

Not all settlors are as well organized as this, however. Some are quite vague about what they want, and do not use professional advice. The likelihood of informality is obviously greater in such cases. As we saw in section 3.1 however, the law is generally reluctant to recognize these vaguer dispositions as trusts anyway. In fact, in having as one of its bases (as we saw) the desire to avoid uncertainty over entitlements, this approach to recognition operates as a kind of surrogate for a formality requirement.

So these factors shaping the circumstances in which trusts are created, or are recognized by the law as created, mean that the absence of a general requirement of formality involves less of a sacrifice of certainty than might at first sight appear. But there can still be cases in which trusts do arise without formality. Evidently, the feeling is that the balance of advantage is in favour of accepting them as valid, in order to further the facilitative project, albeit at some cost in terms of convenience.

If this is so, however, why should there be the two exceptions to the basic absence of a formality requirement for the making of trusts, whereby testamentary trusts and *inter vivos* trusts of land must be made formally? Let us look at these in turn.

5.3 TESTAMENTARY TRUSTS

The rule for testamentary trusts is that they must be made in the form prescribed by the Wills Act: in writing, signed, and witnessed.[5] This is a general formalities rule for wills, rather than directed particularly at trusts within them, and so the perspective on the balance between the

---

[5] Wills Act 1837 s 9, as amended by Administration of Justice Act 1982 s 17.

advantages and disadvantages of the rule must be this more general one.

The advantages and disadvantages are the usual ones. The testator is served by knowing that effect will be given to the dispositions contained in his last will made in the proper form, and to these alone. The recipients and non-recipients of his property will know where they stand without contest. Title to the property in question is assured, easing subsequent trade in it. And having the dispositions encompassed in a single document which must be given official recognition (called 'probate') before it can be put into effect gives the revenue authorities a straight run at them for the collection of the relevant taxes. On the other hand, the rule will frustrate the wishes of anyone who attempts to dispose of his property on his death without using the proper form.

By requiring formalities for wills, the law takes it that the balance lies in favour of the advantages. This seems to be right. We all know that we are going to die, and it crosses our minds to make a will; almost all of us have also heard that the law imposes some formality requirements on the making of a will, even though we may not know exactly what they are; and we enjoy a literate and stable society in which finding out what the requirements are, and complying with them, is easy. So in this context, the problem of frustrating settlors ignorant of a certainty requirement is negligible, leaving very little to be said against the obvious advantages of imposing such a requirement: as the law does.

5.4 TRUSTS OF LAND

The other formality requirement in the making of trusts is that *inter vivos* trusts whose subject matter is land must be put in[6] writing and signed by the settlor. This rule is contained in the Law of Property Act 1925 section 53(1)(b).

Why should trusts of land be singled out in this way as the only *inter vivos* trusts for which formality is required?

Trusts of land are particularly likely to be made formally in practice. People making dispositions of land are especially likely to perceive that they are doing something important, and will almost certainly use professional advisers, who will always want to put important matters down on paper. So, as with wills, the danger of a requirement of formality

---

[6] Strictly, not 'put in' but 'manifested and proved by'.

frustrating settlors' intentions is slight, allowing the balance of advantage to come down in favour of its imposition.

Another consideration may be the protection of those who buy land from trusts. Someone buying property from a trust will want to acquire it as absolute owner, free from the trust obligations. If the trustees act properly in selling, that will be the result.[7] If they act improperly, however, the purchaser may find herself bound by the trust obligations. It will help her to guard against this outcome if she has the information that the sellers are trustees. Formality in the original making of the trust can provide this information. And trusts of land are special cases in this respect because of a rule, applying to them alone, that the sale will be improper unless the purchase money is paid to at least two trustees.[8]

5.5 RESULTING AND CONSTRUCTIVE TRUSTS OF LAND

There is, however, an exception to this formality requirement regarding trusts whose subject matter is land. By the Law of Property Act 1925 section 53(2), a resulting or constructive trust of land will be valid despite not being in writing.[9]

Purchasers of trust land are required to pay two trustees just as much where the trust is a resulting or constructive trust as where it is express, so it would be convenient for them if the formality requirement applied here too. But resulting and constructive trusts can arise without anyone giving any thought to the matter,[10] and so if formality were to be required for them to be valid, they would generally never come into existence at all. And that would frustrate the aims of the rules generating them in the first place.

The most common instance of a resulting or constructive trust of land arises where a family home is owned in the name of only one member of a couple, but the other has contributed to its acquisition. This topic is

---

[7] The trust obligations are 'overreached': see section 8.3.

[8] Law of Property Act 1925 s 27(2) (unless the trust has a corporate trustee, such as a bank, when payment to one suffices). Many cases reveal the adverse effect on a purchaser who does not comply with this rule, most notably *Williams & Glyn's Bank Ltd v Boland* [1981] AC 487.

[9] Strictly, the provision exempts 'resulting, implied or constructive trusts'. But 'implied' here seems to mean not 'express but not explicit', but 'imposed by the law for some other reason than to effectuate a settlor's wish', making it synonymous with 'constructive'.

[10] In the case of resulting trusts this statement is contrary to the position taken by Lord Browne-Wilkinson in *Westdeutsche Landesbank Girozentrale v Islington LBC* [1996] AC 669, 708, but follows the argument advanced in sections 7.6–7.7.

considered in detail in section 8.11. There are two features of it that concern us here. First, the fact that there is a trust will not be recorded in writing, or even, probably, be known to the couple themselves: the whole point is to deal with the situation where the couple themselves have not been organized enough to settle their own rights. So a purchaser will not have the usual warning that the house is trust property and that she therefore has to deal with two trustees. Secondly, there will in fact only be one trustee (ie the person in whose sole name the house is owned). So the purchaser will necessarily be dealing with only one trustee rather than two, and, as we have seen, that places her in jeopardy. There is quite a lot that she can do to protect himself—such as look to see who lives in the house, or require that all its residents sign a disclaimer—but, at the lowest, this kind of situation is one where the sale and purchase of trust property is not as streamlined as the law would normally want it to be. The trap of the rule requiring payment to two trustees exists without the formality requirement to signpost it. But to impose a formality require-ment would mean that virtually all of these trusts would be destroyed. So if they are to exist at all, it can only be on the basis that they are valid despite informality. Evidently, since the law does uphold them, it takes the view that the reasons for doing so outweigh the consequent difficulties.[11]

5.6 NON-COMPLIANCE WITH THE WILLS ACT AND SECTION 53(1)(B)

So we have looked at the two formality rules applicable to the making of trusts: that *inter vivos* trusts whose subject matter is land (except resulting and constructive trusts) must be in writing, and that all trusts on death must be in the form required by the Wills Act. Sometimes, of course, cases arise in which settlors have not complied with the relevant rule. We might expect the result to be that their trust therefore fails: after all, that is what the relevant statutes seem to say should happen. But this has not always been the outcome. The courts have sometimes given effect, direct or indirect, to the informal trusts.

In the testamentary context, the trusts given effect to are called 'secret

---

[11] Though the overall tenor of the cases concerning this area in fact shows considerable solicitude for the purchaser who is caught unawares by such a trust. She is often held not bound, on a number of grounds. See eg *Bristol & West Building Society v Henning* [1985] 1 WLR 778; *Abbey National Building Society v Cann* [1991] 1 AC 56; *Lloyds Bank plc v Rosset* [1989] Ch 350, [1991] AC 107.

trusts'. There are two kinds of secret trusts. The first is where the settlor makes a will leaving the property to the trustee and stipulating that the latter shall hold it on trust, but fixes the terms of the trust not in the will but in a private communication with the trustee. This is called a 'half-secret' trust, because the will does disclose that the legatee takes the property as trustee, but withholds the details of the trust. The second is where the settlor makes a will leaving the property to the trustee, as before, but this time without stipulating at all in the will that the property is given on trust, and settles both the fact that it is given on trust and what the terms of the trust are by private communication with the trustee. This is called a 'fully secret' trust, because the will omits not only the terms of the trust but also any mention of its very existence: it suggests that the legatee takes the property as absolute owner, for his own benefit. In both cases, notwithstanding the failure to comply with the Wills Act, the arrangement will have effect as a trust.

In the *inter vivos* context, if the owner of some land transfers it to someone else by a document which does not itself stipulate for a trust (as section 53(1)(b) requires), but arranges with the transferee orally that he will so hold the property, the law apparently gives effect to this arrangement as a trust too.[12]

The pivotal feature of all these cases is the fact that the settlor has consulted the intended trustee and obtained his agreement to, or at least acquiescence in, the projected trust in advance of the transfer to him.[13] (This is in contrast to the usual position. Although a person cannot be made to act as trustee of an express trust against her will, there is normally no requirement that her consent be sought in advance in this way: she may hear of her nomination as trustee only as she comes to receive the property—she is then at liberty to decline if she wishes.)[14] The principle in play is that if I transfer property to you after receiving your agreement to hold it on the trust terms proposed by me, it would be a 'fraud' for you

---

[12] *Rochefoucauld v Boustead* [1897] 1 Ch 196; *Bannister v Bannister* [1948] 2 All ER 133. In both cases, the stipulated beneficiary was also the transferor, so it is sometimes argued that the law, rather than effectuating the arrangement (as in a testamentary secret trust) merely restores the property to the transferor: cf J Feltham [1987] Conv 246; T Youdan [1988] Conv 267.

[13] In half-secret trusts, the English authorities say it must be earlier—before or contemporaneously with the settlor's making of the will (transfer occurs on the settlor's death): *Re Keen* [1937] Ch 236; *Re Bateman's Will Trusts* [1970] 1 WLR 1436. This complication may well be wrong (it is explicable in terms of a misplaced analogy with another doctrine, incorporation by reference); it is rejected in *Re Browne* [1944] Ir R 90, Ireland, and *Ledgerwood v Perpetual Trustee* (1997) 41 NSWLR 532, Australia.

[14] See section 13.1.

then to depart from those terms. The law reacts by requiring the recipient to adhere to the agreed trust. This view of the relevant law was established by the House of Lords in the leading case of *Blackwell v Blackwell*.[15]

Two points need to be absorbed about the meaning of 'fraud' used here. The first is that it does not necessarily imply deceit, as in other contexts. It is clear that a trust can arise under this principle as much where the recipient of the property agrees in good faith to hold it on the proposed trust as where he only pretends to agree. Nor does it necessarily imply that the recipient himself will gain if he is not held to his agreement. This point is crucial to the validity of half-secret trusts, for in their case (unlike fully secret trusts) there is no question of the trustee keeping the property for himself. The terms of the will establish that the bequest is made on trust, and if the proposed terms do not take effect, the trustee will hold the property on resulting trust for the testator's estate.

The second point is that ascribing these trusts to 'fraud' does not necessarily imply that the recipient of the property has broken his agreement with the settlor, or is proposing to do so. Some cases are indeed of that kind. But in others, the recipient is content or keen to comply with the agreement, but there are objections from other quarters to his doing so. Say, for example, that the trustee of a fully secret trust has become bankrupt. He wishes to go through with the agreement, but his creditors maintain that the agreement has no force, so that the property has come to him under the terms of the will alone: then, it would belong to him absolutely, and they could take it to pay off his debts to them. Or say that the trustee of a half-secret trust is willing to carry out the trust as agreed with the settlor, but the person entitled to the residue of the testator's estate argues that the agreement has no force, leaving only the terms of the will, with the result that the property would be held on resulting trust, to her benefit. It is clear that the agreed trusts arise in these cases just as much as they do where there is a breach or proposed breach of the agreement of the trustee's own volition. The law identifies what would be a fraud if it occurred, and proscribes it. Taking these two points together, it may be seen that the pejorative connotations which ordinarily attach to the idea of 'fraud' are not necessarily present in this context.[16]

---

[15] [1929] AC 318, 329, 334, 342. Likewise, regarding *inter vivos* trusts of land, *Bannister v Bannister* [1948] 2 All ER 133, 136.

[16] Fraud in its ordinary pejorative sense was sought in the early case of *McCormick v Grogan* (1869) LR 4 HL 82. By the time of *Rochefoucauld v Boustead* [1897] 1 Ch 196, 206, however, the meaning described in the text had been adopted.

These trusts based upon 'fraud' thus arise from the agreement between the settlor and the trustee, together with the settlor's having transferred the property to the trustee on the faith of that agreement. This dimension means that they are not on their face cases of a settlor doing informally that which the law says she may only do formally. So it is sometimes said that secret trusts operate 'outside—or *dehors*—the will'. That, however, does not explain why they are not caught by the formality rule.[17] In that secret trusts still appear to be trusts which come into effect on the settlor's death, why does the Wills Act not apply to them nevertheless? And if *inter vivos* trusts of land are effectuated under the same principle, why does section 53(1)(b) not apply to them nevertheless, in that they remain *inter vivos* trusts of land?

As regards secret trusts, the answer is sometimes suggested[18] to be that, on the contrary, the trust obligations arise at the point when the agreement is made, which is necessarily before the testator's death.[19] The agreement is thus *inter vivos*, and, runs the suggestion, this means that the secret trust emerging from it is *inter vivos* too, and is thus unaffected by the Wills Act. The equivalent reasoning as regards section 53(1)(b) would be that the trustee's obligations arise earlier than the transfer of the property, and so, since the trust cannot become operative until the property is transferred, do not add up to the 'making' of a trust of land. The crux of this argument is the idea that, although the transfer of the property 'constitutes' the trust, the earlier agreement (for which there is no formality requirement) amounts to a 'declaration' of it. That is a reasonable thing to say, if the word 'declaration' is being used in a non-technical sense. Unfortunately, in order to prove that the trust takes effect at the time of the agreement, the word must be used in its technical sense, as meaning 'creation' (normally, in the case where the settlor makes himself trustee).[20] The argument can then be seen to be unsustainable. As we saw in section 1.9, there cannot be a trust without property. Until the property reaches the trustee's hands upon the settlor's death, or under the *inter vivos* transfer of the land, the admittedly earlier agreement between the settlor and the trustee therefore cannot generate trust obligations

---

[17] P Critchley (1999) 115 LQR 631, 633–41.

[18] See especially J Martin *Hanbury and Martin Modern Equity* 16th edn (2001) 164–8.

[19] It is possible to some extent to communicate the terms of the trust after the required moment (by means of a sealed letter, placed in the trustee's hands, to be opened later), so long as the trustee has by the required time agreed to be bound by them no matter what they turn out to be. See *Re Boyes* (1884) 26 Ch D 531; *Re Keen* [1937] Ch 236.

[20] See section 1.4.

upon the latter.[21] It is possible that the agreement generates some other kind of obligation,[22] but it is clear that the entity for which we are trying to account here is indeed a trust. Although in part dependent upon the prior agreement, then, the trust takes effect at the time of the settlor's death, in the secret trust cases, or at the time of the transfer of the land, in the case to which section 53(1)(b) is relevant. So the applicability of the Wills Act or of that section cannot be negatived in this way. The trust must be effectuated despite the seemingly relevant formality rule for some other reason.

The explanation seems to lie in the fact that a trust of this kind arises not, as an ordinary express trust does, because the settlor wants it to. Instead, it arises because the law reacts to the (actual or potential) fraud of the trustee—in that he agreed to the settlor's terms, and on the faith of that the settlor transferred the property to him—by imposing a trust preventing such fraud. This trust is evidently a constructive trust.[23] The operation of section 53(1)(b) is expressly confined to express trusts: as we have seen, section 53(2) excludes constructive trusts from its ambit. The Wills Act is in effect so confined as well, applying as it does to testamentary dispositions. Though the Act does not define these, they appear to equate with the transfers that a testator asks the law to effectuate upon his death. When the law imposes a constructive trust on the legatee, it is countering her fraud, rather than effectuating the testator's requested transfer.

The argument is sometimes put in a different way.[24] On this view, the

---

[21] A secret trust whose effect pre-dated the testator's death was however found in *Re Gardner (No 2)* [1923] 2 Ch 230. This decision cannot be correct, for the reason given in the text.

[22] Possibly a contract, under which the settlor transfers the property in consideration for the transferee's promise to hold it on the agreed trusts. Under the Contracts (Rights of Third Parties) Act 1999, the beneficiaries could normally enforce such a contract, but this only gives them contractual rights against the trustee personally, not (as given by the rules under discussion) a beneficial entitlement arising from the moment the property reaches the trustee's hands. Such a beneficial entitlement would arise, however, if the beneficiaries' contractual rights allowed them to claim specific performance against the trustee of his obligation to hold the bequeathed property on trust; by the doctrine 'equity looks upon that as done which ought to be done' a constructive trust would be generated anticipating the trustee's compliance with this: see section 8.7.

[23] This is expressly stated in *Bannister v Bannister* [1948] 2 All ER 133, 136. *Rochefoucauld v Boustead* [1897] 1 Ch 196, 208 treats the trust as analogous to an express trust for limitation purposes (within the thinking developed in *Soar v Ashwell* [1893] 2 QB 390), but does not regard it as being an express trust. Section 8.8 discusses why the 'fraud' in play here should generate a constructive trust.

[24] See *McCormick v Grogan* (1868) LR 4 HL 82, 97; perhaps also *Rochefoucauld v Boustead* [1897] 1 Ch 196.

testator attempts to create a trust which the Wills Act or section 53(1)(b) invalidates, but in view of the circumstances (the agreement between settlor and trustee, and the settlor's consequent transfer to the trustee), to conclude that there is therefore no trust would be to permit a fraud by the trustee; and, because 'equity will not permit a statute to be an instrument of fraud', a constructive trust arises against the trustee. This is unnecessarily complicated, however. Both accounts agree that there would be fraud if, after the agreement and transfer, the trustee did not hold on trust. The constructive trust pre-empts that fraud. It is unnecessary (though not wrong) to add, as this alternative view does, that there would have been no such fraud if the statute had not invalidated the express trust, and that the constructive trust thus deals with that problem too.

Secret trusts, and the analogous trusts which may arise *inter vivos*, thus do not arise so as to uphold the express trust despite its informality. That would be impermissible. Rather, they arise as a reaction to the 'fraud' that would otherwise ensue as a result of the facts (notably, the trustee's undertaking) surrounding the making of the express trust. That is permissible. In practice, however, it is impossible to make such a clean distinction between the two projects. Remember that these constructive trusts arise as soon as the trustee has agreed to the settlor's terms and, on the faith of that, the settlor has transferred the property to the trustee. This state of affairs may easily be deliberately engineered by a settlor, at any rate with a trustee's collusion. A settlor who prefers not to comply with the formality rule therefore has a ready means of avoiding it. Indeed, the difference between bringing about the law's imposition of a 'fraud'-based constructive trust, and making an informal express trust to the same effect, is minimal. It consists in the securing of the trustee's prior agreement to the settlor's proposed trust. But to secure such agreement would in any event be no more than good manners, as well as prudent from the settlor's own point of view, so as not to nominate a trustee who would turn out to be unwilling to act. The upshot is that people may use these 'fraud'-based constructive trusts to opt out of the formality requirements whenever they choose. Is this acceptable? It seems unlikely that it is. As we saw earlier, there is a strong case for having the formality requirements. It seems however that in practice people do not exploit the loophole much. So far as one can judge from the reported case law, deliberately engineered 'fraud'-based trusts are more or less limited to two particular kinds of situation, both confined to the testamentary context. Our judgement about the justifiability of upholding such trusts depends on our feelings about these usages.

The first situation is where a testator wants to keep a bequest secret from the outside world. The main instance of this seems to be where a man wants to provide for his mistress or illegitimate child.[25] He would have no problem about complying with a formality requirement in itself, but probate, the process of having a will officially recognized as valid, involves placing it in the Public Record Office, where it can be looked at by anyone who so wishes. It is this publicity that the testator seeks to avoid.[26] So he leaves money in his will to someone to whom he might plausibly make a bequest—a close friend, say, or a brother—and privately gets the latter to hold it for the mistress or child. This arrangement then takes effect as a secret trust. (There is no corresponding difficulty if the testator wants surreptitiously to put land on trust for a mistress or illegitimate child during his lifetime, since instruments written in compliance with section 53(1)(b) do not become public documents in the way that wills do: they should in fact remain private.) So in allowing these secret trusts, the law seems to take it that the balance of advantage lies in favour of suspending the usual formality rule so as to permit people to make provision for their mistresses and illegitimate children in this way.

There might have been a case for this view in the past. But nowadays it seems implausible. A trust is really only apt for the posthumous preservation of the position of dependency in which the testator's illicit family would have existed in former times.[27] That position is surely not normally characteristic of mistresses and illegitimate children today. To the extent that mistresses and illegitimate children continue to feature in society (and developments in divorce and contraception have surely reduced that extent), they are likely to be financially less dependent on the man's generosity than previously, as a result of factors such as widespread women's employment, maintenance payments, and social security. So even if a man nowadays does want to make secret provision for his mistress or illegitimate child, it would be not only simpler but more in keeping with the nature of their relationship to do so not by establishing a (secret) trust

---

[25] See eg *Re Boyes* (1884) 26 Ch D 531; *Blackwell v Blackwell* [1929] AC 318; *Re Keen* [1937] Ch 236.

[26] The point was presumably as much to spare one's widow the embarrassment of a public declaration of one's infidelity, as to keep that infidelity a secret from her even after death; many wives surely knew of their husbands' mistresses and illegitimate children.

[27] During the testator's lifetime, indeed, his mistress and illegitimate children were dependent to the extent of having no legal rights against him at all. This state of affairs would be preserved after his death if he left property to (say) his brother absolutely, but with a moral obligation to care for his dependants. By adopting the trust device instead, with its legal rights, he in fact strengthened their position.

but by for example setting up a bank account in their name while he is still alive. It is therefore far from clear that there continues to be a public interest in favour of allowing the formality rule to be sidestepped.

The other main reason why people in the reported cases seem to want to avoid the formality rules is that they want to remain free to change their minds frequently about how to dispose of their property.[28] This again seems only to occur in the testamentary context. Since wills do not come into effect at the time we make them, but wait until our death, there is the opportunity for vacillation over their content; *inter vivos* dispositions are generally made so as to be immediately binding. Testators prone to vacillation could make a new will every time they had a new thought, but that would be tiresome, and expensive in solicitors' fees. So they make a will leaving some property to someone they are in close touch with, and then informally settle with the latter how they actually want the property disposed of, altering their instructions every time they have a new idea: and these arrangements will then be enforced despite their informality, as secret trusts.

We are talking here about people who are decisive but mercurial, rather than just vague. There will be plenty of the latter, but their thoughts will probably not be sufficiently organized to amount to trusts anyway; remember that incoherence in a disposition weighs against the finding that it was meant to be legally binding.[29] The decisive but mercurial testator is probably rather uncommon. Most people err on the side of infrequency in making provision for their own demise. So the point of in effect dispensing with the usual Wills Act formalities in this type of context would be to save the occasional testator of this kind the additional trouble and expense involved in making a series of wills to keep pace with his series of different ideas. It seems very hard to believe that this amounts to a sufficient justification.

5.7 DISPOSITIONS OF SUBSISTING BENEFICIAL INTERESTS

There is one further rule about formalities in the area of trusts that we need to look at. Unlike the rules that we have been looking at up to now, which concern the making of trusts, this one concerns dealings with trusts that already exist. By section 53(1)(c) of the Law of Property Act

---

[28] See eg *Re Snowden* [1979] Ch 528.

[29] See section 3.1 above; and *Re Snowden* [1979] Ch 528. *Ottaway v Norman* [1972] Ch 698 seems similar, though the point was not taken.

1925, a disposition of a subsisting—ie already existing—beneficial interest must be made in writing, and signed by the person making it (or, if it is to take effect on his death, placed in a valid will). This rule applies to trusts of any subject matter. So although no formality is needed to make *inter vivos* trusts of anything other than land, formality is required to make a disposition of the beneficial interests that arise under them whether they involve land or not.

Experience has shown that the apparently simple idea of a 'disposition of an existing beneficial interest' requires elucidation. Two questions need attention. First, as we are about to see, I can bring about such a transfer not only directly but also in certain indirect ways. Does the section apply to these too? Conversely, secondly, I can find myself transferring a beneficial interest not only as a self-contained exercise, as in the instance just given, but also as part of some transaction with other elements (eg a simultaneous transfer of the legal title). Is the section applicable under such circumstances? The statute itself does not help us with these questions. We have to look for answers in the decided cases.[30]

The first of our two questions was at issue in *Grey v IRC*.[31] In the case, a beneficiary under a trust wanted to transfer his interest to his grandchildren. If he had done so directly, the transfer would have been a straightforward 'disposition' and so would have had to be in writing, because of section 53(1)(c). But under the tax legislation then in force, that would have meant paying substantial stamp duty. He therefore decided to make the transfer instead by a roundabout route which did not involve a written instrument and so would not attract the tax. So he gave his trustees an oral instruction to hold in future for his grandchildren rather than himself. Giving such an instruction was accepted as being, upon some unspecified analysis, in principle an effective way of achieving the same result as transferring his interest to the grandchildren directly. But the question was whether it was likewise a disposition of a subsisting beneficial interest within section 53(1)(c), and had therefore to be made in writing. The court decided that, whatever the analysis upon which the manoeuvre was in principle effective, it amounted in reality to such a disposition. And that, the court decided, was the issue. In other words, section 53(1)(c) catches not only direct transfers of beneficial interests but also other transactions whose effect, regardless of the means employed, is the transfer of a beneficial interest.

To say that every 'effectual transfer' of a beneficial interest is caught by

---

[30] B Green (1984) 47 MLR 385.   [31] [1960] AC 1.

section 53(1)(c) would be over-inclusive, however. In the terms of the section, the transfer has always to be the product of a 'disposition'. 'Disposition' suggests the transferor having *set out to* make the transfer. So if the transfer occurs for reasons not connected with the transferor's wishes, it is not the product of a disposition, and is not caught by the section. Notably, if I own a beneficial interest and come under a constructive trust of it in your favour, the interest will be effectually transferred to you (since you gain an absolute right to it), but not as a result of a disposition on my part. As sections 1.3 and 7.1 explain, constructive trusts arise for reasons other than to vindicate a settlor's intention. (The ways in which they can arise are described in Chapter 8.) Lest the wording of section 53(1)(c) itself were not enough to exclude transfers occurring in this way, the point is put beyond doubt by section 53(2). The latter exempts constructive trusts from the application of section 53(1), and declares there to be no formality requirement regarding them: a sensible rule, as noted in section 5.5, since compliance with a formality requirement cannot realistically be expected on the part of someone who may not want, or indeed be aware of, the transaction in question, such as a constructive trustee. So in *Neville v Wilson*,[32] where people had contracted to transfer beneficial interests one to another, and, the contract being specifically enforceable, the law regarded the sellers as holding the shares on constructive trust for the buyers,[33] section 53(1)(c) was held not to apply notwithstanding that the interests were effectually transferred.

So long as the imposition of a constructive trust and the idea of a 'disposition' are mutually exclusive in this way, there is no difficulty. Unfortunately, this is not necessarily the case. If the owner of a beneficial interest deliberately engineers a constructive trust so as effectually to transfer his interest, he transfers the interest having set out to do so, and so makes a 'disposition' of it. In such a case, do we give precedence to the 'disposition' element, so as to require formality, or to the constructive trust, so as not to require it? On a literal reading of their terms, section 53(2), reacting to the constructive trust, seems to trump section 53(1)(c), reacting to the 'disposition', and exempts a transfer involving both from the formality requirement. But in *Oughtred v IRC*,[34] the judges took the opposite view. The pattern of facts in this case was essentially the same as that in *Neville v Wilson*,[35] except in the one respect which is crucial to the

---

[32] [1997] Ch 144.
[33] See section 8.7 for the principle generating constructive trusts in this way.
[34] [1960] AC 206.   [35] [1997] Ch 144.

point under discussion: that, so far as we know, it was only in *Oughtred v IRC*[36] that the parties deliberately engineered the facts generating the constructive trust, and so created a 'disposition' alongside the constructive trust. (They hoped that its effect in transferring the interest without writing would save them the stamp duty payable if the transfer were made in writing.) The court, by not wholly satisfactory reasoning, gave precedence to the 'disposition' element and so required compliance with section 53(1)(c). As a matter of principle, that seems the right choice (though it is inconsistent with the complaisance the courts show towards the engineering of constructive trusts in order to effectuate secret trusts). As explained above, the exemption of constructive trusts from the formality requirement is demanded because, and thus only to the extent that, the person responsible for its imposition cannot be expected to comply with the requirement. Exempting deliberately engineered constructive trusts would thus leave the requirement under-inclusive.

The second of our two questions was whether section 53(1)(c) applies to transfers of beneficial interests occurring within transactions with other elements. This was addressed in *Vandervell v IRC*.[37] Mr Vandervell was the beneficiary of a trust of some shares held by a bank. He decided to donate these shares to the Royal College of Surgeons. On his instructions, the bank transferred the legal title in the shares to the college. But he made no written transfer of his beneficial interest to the college. The court decided that he had nonetheless succeeded in giving the shares to the college (so that he did not on this account[38] have to continue paying income tax on the dividends on them). The ground for the decision seems to be that a beneficiary's transfer of her interest does not have to comply with the section unless the transferee becomes the beneficiary of a trust: Mr Vandervell's scheme was not merely to instal the college in his place as the beneficiary of the trust, but to terminate the trust by passing both the beneficial interest and the legal title to the college.

Together, then, these decisions tell us that section 53(1)(c) applies wherever a transaction in which someone sets out to transfer an existing beneficial interest (1) has the effect of transferring that interest, no matter by what means, and (2) substitutes the transferee for the transferor as the beneficiary of a trust. The merit of the first of these rules is easily understood: the law thus treats all similar transactions in the same way, rather

---

[36] [1960] AC 206.   [37] [1967] 2 AC 291.

[38] Though his retention of a beneficial interest in an option to repurchase the shares from the college made him liable to tax after all. See the discussion of *Re Vandervell's Trusts (No 2)* [1974] Ch 269 below.

than differentiating unmeritoriously on the basis of technical differences. The point of the second rule is perhaps less obvious. Lord Upjohn in *Vandervell v IRC*[39] offered an explanation. According to him, it is vital for a trustee to know who his beneficiaries are (ie to whom he owes his duties); if beneficial interests could be transferred—ie new beneficiaries substituted—without formality, the trustees might not get to know about it, or might not be sure what had been done; and section 53(1)(c) is aimed at preventing this difficulty. On this view, then, the section has application only where there is a trustee who might otherwise be deceived: ie where the transaction is aimed at replacing the transferee for the transferor as the trustee's beneficiary.[40]

Putting the two requirements and their explanations together, the purpose, and therefore the ambit, of section 53(1)(c) emerges as a means of informing trustees of changes in the identities of their beneficiaries, however those changes occur. There are two reasons, however, why this may not be a satisfactory justification for the section. First, there is nothing in the section to say that the required writing should be brought to the trustee's attention.[41] Secondly, the boon of informing trustees may not be so important as to merit a statutory requirement of formality, non-compliance with which makes a transaction ineffective. Compare the position as regards the establishment of a trust: an *inter vivos* trust of anything except land may be made informally. That too seems to create the possibility of mistakes about the identity of the beneficiaries (amongst other things, including whether there is a trust at all), but evidently the potential difficulties are accepted as tolerable. It is hard to see why the problem should be more widespread, or more serious, in the case of people acquiring interests under existing trusts than in the establishment of new trusts. For these reasons, then, section 53(1)(c) may be regarded as introducing into the law a rule which generates litigation and can defeat unobjectionable transactions, and as doing so for insufficient reason. If that is right, the section should be repealed.

A lack of judicial enthusiasm for the section is visible in *Re Vandervell's*

---

[39] [1967] 2 AC 291, 311.

[40] Though not quite always then. Accordingly to *Re Holt's Settlement* [1969] 1 Ch 590, s 53(1)(c) does not apply to transfers of beneficial interests made in the context of a variation of a trust under the Variation of Trusts Act 1958 (see section 12.5). Such a variation is necessarily recorded in a court order, which provides the trustee with all necessary information.

[41] Cf the Law of Property Act 1925 s 136, which requires that where a debt is assigned from the original creditor to a replacement, written notice must be given to the debtor: evidently, so that he can know to whom he owes his obligation.

Trusts (No 2).[42] The transaction here was apparently caught by all the rulings described above, but it was nonetheless declared immune from the section's operation. In donating the shares to the Royal College of Surgeons, Mr Vandervell had required the college to grant to his family trustees an option to repurchase the shares. This option was regarded as reaching the trustees in effect from Mr Vandervell himself, since he had made the donation dependent on it; and since the trustees necessarily held the option on trust, but Mr Vandervell had not indicated any beneficiary, they held it on resulting trust for Mr Vandervell.[43] Eventually, however, when Mr Vandervell discovered the loose end, he evinced his intention that the beneficiaries should be his children. But he failed to do this in writing, and the question was whether section 53(1)(c) therefore made the move ineffective. In that event, he would be liable to pay income tax on the share dividends which had been paid to the trustees, and used by them for the benefit of the children. The case seemed to fall squarely within the ambit given to section 53(1)(c) by the decisions already discussed. The transaction had the effect of transferring an existing beneficial interest; that is what Mr Vandervell sought to achieve by it; and it substituted the children for Mr Vandervell as the beneficiary of a trust. The court held, however, that the section did not apply.

By way of reasoning, the judges said that the transaction in favour of the children was not a disposition of a subsisting beneficial interest. Instead, it amounted to no more than a declaration of trust, which required no formality (the property not being land). In their view, the transaction consisted in the settlor's putting the finishing touch (the specification of beneficiaries) to the transaction which he had left unfinished earlier. For the settlor to specify the beneficiaries after an interval rather than at the outset did not change the transaction into a disposition of an interest under an existing trust. The resulting trust that arose in the interval was merely how the law filled the gap, rather than genuinely 'subsisting'; so it just died away when, the children being declared as beneficiaries, there was no longer a gap to be filled. This reasoning is hard to accept. A resulting trust may arise in order to fill a gap,[44] and the duties of its trustee may differ from those of other kinds of

---

[42] [1974] Ch 269.

[43] This was decided in *Vandervell v IRC* [1967] 2 AC 291 itself. As a result, the cast of the tax legislation made Mr Vandervell liable to pay income tax on the income which the Royal College of Surgeons received from the shares, notwithstanding his successful divestment of his beneficial interest.

[44] See section 7.5.

trustee,[45] but there is no authority other than this case for thinking that the beneficial interest arising under a resulting trust has a different nature from that arising under other kinds of trust. And the transfer of it to a new beneficiary poses the same issues for the trustees.

The judges' reasoning in *Re Vandervell's Trusts (No 2)*[46] thus fails satisfactorily to explain why, as they held, section 53(1)(c) did not apply. It is hard to resist the notion that the decision was instead driven by other considerations. If the section had applied, not only would Mr Vandervell's intended transaction have been ineffective, but also, as a result, he would have had to pay heavy income tax on the share dividends paid to the trustees for the children. That outcome would clearly have been unmeritorious in its disjuncture with the true nature and import of the circumstances. The fact that such distorted reasoning was required to circumvent section 53(1)(c) and to produce a more appropriate result confirms the sense that the law would do better without the section.

[45] See section 9.1.   [46] [1974] Ch 269.

6

Charitable trusts

Among the rules noted so far, we have seen that trusts are invalid if they infringe the rule against perpetuities,[1] or, in the view of some, if they do not have a legal person as beneficiary.[2] One type of trust is, however, treated differently, being exempt from any requirement of a beneficiary and from most aspects of the rule against perpetuities. This is a trust for a charitable purpose.

Trusts for charitable purposes attract certain other forms of special treatment. Some of these are unusual rules within the law of trusts, while others are not restricted to trusts, applying equally to other vehicles by which charitable purposes are promoted, especially charitable companies.[3]

A purpose is charitable if it is for the public benefit, in one of a long list of ways identified by the law. The kinds of purposes listed are, broadly speaking, not unfamiliar: most of them are catered to by the bodies which seek funds through public collecting boxes.

This chapter describes the special treatment, and explains which trusts qualify for it.

6.1 THE SPECIAL TREATMENT

There are four main aspects to the special treatment of charities.

First, special provision is made towards ensuring that charities are properly carried on. On top of the usual factors which tend to promote good performance on the part of trustees, which we shall look at in Chapter 13, for charities a body known as the Charity Commission, provided by the state at public expense,[4] gives general guidance (in the form

---

[1] See section 2.5.

[2] See section 1.5. The alleged need for a beneficiary, precluding trusts for purposes (other than charitable purposes) is examined further in sections 14.2–14.4.

[3] J Warburton [1999] Conv 20 argues that charities should no longer be thought of in conjunction with the ordinary law of trusts at all.

[4] Though under the Charities Act 1993 s 85, the Commission now charges for certain items of work.

of annual reports and pamphlets) and individual advice to trustees.[5] The Commission also offers help with the safeguarding and investment of charities' assets, in the shape of an Official Custodian for Charities and pooled investment and deposit funds.[6]

Secondly, special provision is also made for taking charities to court, if that seems to be called for. The normal way in which trustees' duties are enforced is by their being sued in court by some person interested in seeing the trust carried out, usually a beneficiary. But charities are exempt from any requirement of a beneficiary. This is the necessary corollary of the fundamental idea that they exist for the benefit of the public. That diffusion of benefit means, in turn, that very often no individual will be sufficiently moved to undergo all the trouble and expense involved in suing. So a substitute system for enforcement against charitable trustees is provided, again by the state, at public expense. Trustees who may have broken their duties can be brought to court by the Charity Commission.[7] So that the Commission can know when to intervene in this way, charities are required to register with it,[8] and to submit annual reports and accounts to it;[9] and the Commission may inquire into their affairs.[10] In some matters, moreover, the Commission can act in lieu of the court,[11] and it also has powers on its own initiative to change charities' trustees and freeze their assets.[12]

Thirdly, many taxes which would otherwise apply are wholly or partially lifted from charities. Broadly speaking, they are not liable to income tax, corporation tax, capital gains tax, and stamp duty, and they receive limited favourable treatment in respect of value added tax. They are exempt from 80 per cent (up to 100 per cent, at the discretion of the relevant local authority) of the rates on their premises. There are also major tax advantages in respect of gifts and bequests to charities.

Finally, there is a group of provisions whereby charitable trusts enjoy greater endurance than others. The fundamental idea that they are beneficial to society is taken to mean that if possible they should not be lost to it.

Partly this is achieved by exempting them from certain aspects of the

---

[5] Charities Act 1993 s 1.

[6] Charities Act 1993 ss 2, 21–5; Charities Act 1992 ss 29–30 (limiting the custodian's role to the holding of land).

[7] Charities Act 1993 s 32: alternatively, the proceedings may be brought by the Attorney-General or, exceptionally (s 33), by private individuals acting with the Commission's authority.

[8] Charities Act 1993 s 3.

[9] Charities Act 1993 ss 41–9.

[10] Charities Act 1993 ss 8–9.

[11] Charities Act 1993 s 16.

[12] Charities Act 1993 s 18.

rule against perpetuities, described in section 2.5. The branch of the rule known as 'the rule against remoteness of vesting' applies in the normal way to the commencement of a charitable trust: so any delay must be not longer than a life in being plus 21 years, or a named time up to 80 years. As we saw in section 2.5, this rule helps limit the duration of trusts for beneficiaries, by making it impossible to replace dying beneficiaries beyond the perpetuity period. But charitable trusts, having no beneficiaries, are immune from this effect. And while non-charitable purpose trusts are subject to 'the rule against inalienability', restricting their duration to (commonly) 21 years, charitable trusts are exempted from this. The result is that in principle they can endure forever.

This is not, however, to say that charitable trusts are by their nature necessarily immortal. They are prone to fail too, though in different ways from trusts for beneficiaries. For example, a charitable trust could simply run out of money, in the sense of no longer being able to afford to carry out its designated purpose. Or its purpose could become impossible or in some other way obsolete. Or it could be linked to some institution which ceases to exist, such as a trust for a particular orphanage, which closes down. So in pursuit of its desire to see charitable trusts endure, the law goes beyond exempting them from artificial termination through the perpetuity rules, and positively helps them to survive at least some of these more natural limits on their existence. It does this in two main ways.

The first concerns trusts which are attached to a particular institution, such as the trust for an orphanage instanced above. It might be thought that if the institution disappears, the trust fails. But the view is often taken that the institution is not essential to the trust, but is a dispensable mechanism for carrying the purpose out: so when it disappears, it merely has to be replaced, the trust itself carrying on. In one case,[13] for instance, a trust for the Sheffield Boys' Working Home was read as a trust for the purposes carried on at the Home, ie the care of poor boys in Sheffield. So the disappearance of the Home did not mean that the trust failed (there were still poor boys in Sheffield to be cared for); it merely necessitated a new mechanism to carry it out in the Home's place. This approach yields, however, if the institution was intended to be crucial to the trust—if, say, the settlor in this example had wanted only the Sheffield Boys' Working

---

[13] *Re Roberts* [1963] 1 WLR 406; see too *Re Finger's Will Trusts* [1972] Ch 286. A line of cases including *Re Faraker* [1912] 2 Ch 488 takes a slightly different approach, treating the money as on trust neither for the institution nor for that institution's current purpose alone, but for the purposes pursued by the institution, or any successor to it, as time goes on.

Home to carry out his trust.[14] In practice, it is usually unclear which interpretation is right on the facts of a particular case, and the choice depends on judicial attitude. To judge from the case law, at any rate some judges are evidently eager to see charitable trusts kept alive in this way.[15]

The second means of preserving charitable trusts from natural termination is a rule that if they do fail, the money does not go on a resulting trust, as would normally be the case, but is 'applied cy près',[16] ie allocated to some other charitable object, close to the original one. For example, if a trust for an orphanage in Leeds fails, the funds might be given over instead to an orphanage in Bradford. If the failure occurs after the original trust has come into effect ('subsequent failure'), application cy près follows automatically. However, if the failure prevents the trust from ever coming into effect ('initial failure'), application cy près follows only if the settlor had a 'general charitable intent': that is, if her overriding wish was to give money to charity, rather than exclusively to the particular object which she named. It is often unclear whether a settlor had such a general charitable intent, so again the matter becomes largely one of judicial attitude. The strength of the desire to prolong the endurance of charitable trusts is revealed in some decisions making cy près applications on the strength of unlikely findings of such intent.[17]

6.2 THE BASIS OF THE SPECIAL TREATMENT

All this special treatment has one factor in common. It is given at the expense of the state or the nation. Sometimes this is obvious, as with the provision of the Charity Commission and the tax relief. If less obvious, it is also true of the provisions extending the endurance of charitable trusts. As we saw in section 2.5, in non-charitable trusts the rule against perpetuities ensures that after a while the assets come into the hands of an absolute owner, and so become fully exposed to market forces, thereby playing their part in a process whereby (it is said) everyone becomes richer and happier. The provisions for prolonging the endurance of charitable trusts entail that the assets committed to such trusts may be at least partially withdrawn from the market indefinitely, and so will not participate so fully in this process. The withdrawal does not amount to complete isolation: normally, the capital will be invested, and the income expended

---

[14] *Re Rymer* [1895] 1 Ch 19; *Re Spence* [1979] Ch 483.
[15] This is especially visible in the judgment in *Re Roberts* [1963] 1 WLR 406.
[16] Pronounced 'see pray'; literally, 'near to it'.
[17] eg *Re Lysaght* [1966] Ch 191; *Re Woodhams* [1981] 1 WLR 493.

on the trusts' purposes. But the income will only be spent on the commodities required to effectuate the purposes, such as schooling or building; sometimes it will take the form of cash payments to people, usually the poor, but this has a similar effect, since by definition the poor will only spend the money on a limited range of commodities, the necessities of life. And the capital will be invested more conservatively than absolutely owned assets might be: as we shall see in section 9.4, trust money is generally invested less adventurously than non-trust money; and trustees of small charities are probably amongst the least adventurous investors. Overall, then, while the withdrawal of a charitable trust's assets from the market is certainly not total, it is substantial, and it is prolonged indefinitely by the provisions for increasing such trusts' endurance.

Why should charitable trusts be given special treatment at the expense of the state or nation in this way? It cannot be in order to assist the settlor's aims, for the treatment of non-charitable trusts has that aim, but does not possess the features under discussion. The latter seem to be explained rather by pointing to utilitarian and/or communitarian considerations[18] especially identifiable with charitable initiatives, ie those for the public benefit. In broad terms (we shall look at the rules defining 'public benefit' in a moment, and at the particular problem of matching 'public benefit' with the considerations under discussion in section 6.6), initiatives for the public benefit are by definition calculated to bring the nation a pronounced degree of good; and the altruism of their movers (settlors) can be seen as valuable in communitarian terms. It is the appeal of charitable initiatives to these considerations that seems to justify the expense which the state or nation suffers in treating them as it does.

6.3 CHARITABLE PURPOSES

What trusts count as charitable, so as to receive this special treatment? Broadly, charitable trusts are those whose object[19] is to provide benefit to

---

[18] See sections 2.4–2.5.

[19] A trust with mixed charitable and non-charitable objects does not qualify as charitable (*Chichester Diocesan Fund and Board of Finance v Simpson* [1944] AC 341; *IRC v Baddeley* [1955] AC 572) unless the two elements can be separated and treated as distinct trusts, the charitable of which alone will receive the special treatment (*Salusbury v Denton* (1857) 3 K & J 529); or the non-charitable element can be suppressed (*Re White* [1893] 2 Ch 41; Charitable Trusts (Validation) Act 1954), or be regarded as mere mechanism (*Re Coxen* [1948] Ch 747).

the public,[20] rather than to particular people. An instance of a straight-forward non-charitable trust might be '£100,000 for Adam': it benefits exclusively Adam. '£100,000 to assist the work of the National Health Service' would be a charitable trust: its benefit extends to the population at large.

Whether a trust or other putative charity qualifies as a charity is not, however, decided by an ad hoc judgement of its usefulness to the public. (There is an argument that it should be: this is considered in section 6.6.) Instead it is considered in terms of two main sets of rules. One set addresses what is required in terms of 'benefit'. The other says how widely the benefit must extend, ie explicates the idea that the trust should be beneficial to the 'public'. These rules are applied by the courts, or more usually by the Charity Commission, which in this matter has the role of a court.[21]

6.4 'BENEFIT'

The law maintains a catalogue of the kinds of benefits that count as charitable. In the main, this catalogue is one developed by the judges themselves, rather than statutory (though to some extent it is based upon a list of charitable purposes given in an old statute, now repealed: the Charitable Uses Act 1601). As is normal with judge-made law, there is no definitive articulation of the catalogue. It has to be gathered from the judges' decisions on the status, charitable or otherwise, of individual trusts, and the reasons they give for these decisions.

The most famous statement on the subject is a remark by Lord Macnaghten in *Income Tax Commissioners v Pemsel*.[22] He referred to three specific categories of charitable benefits—the relief of poverty, the advancement of education, and the advancement of religion[23]—and then

---

[20] Charity's legal conception in the utilitarian and/or communitarian terms of public benefit is different from its moral conception, which looks rather to altruistic motivation: J Gardner in C Mitchell and S Moody (eds) *Foundations of Charity Law* (2000) ch 1. The two often do coincide, but evidently need not.

[21] Charities Act 1993 ss 3, 4.

[22] [1891] AC 531, 581.

[23] Does this privileging of religions *vis-à-vis* philosophies not counted as religions infringe the prohibition (ECHR Art 14) on discrimination in respect of freedom of thought, conscience, and religion (Art 9), and so attract the Human Rights Act 1998? It is not in fact clear that philosophies not counted as religions receive less favourable treatment from the law, as they can be charitable in fostering the moral and spiritual welfare of mankind (below): *Re South Place Ethical Society* [1980] 1 WLR 1565.

a fourth, 'other purposes beneficial to the community not falling under any of the preceding heads'. On the face of it, this may suggest that beyond the first three categories the idea of 'beneficial' is left at large, rather than defined by law. But subsequent judicial statements have established that this is not the case: that the legal definition of the types of benefit recognized as charitable continues beyond Lord Macnaghten's first three categories, other purposes being charitable only if they are analogous to those mentioned in the 1601 Act or held charitable in a previous judicial decision,[24] or if they are established as such by statute.[25] So although there is no comprehensive canonical statement of the remainder of the catalogue comparable with Lord Macnaghten's statement of its first three items, it is possible, and for an accurate account necessary, to continue it by piecing together the precedents and statutes.

The following is a paraphrase of the list offered by one treatise:[26] relief of the aged; relief of disabled persons; relief of distress; promotion of public health; provision of public works and amenities; relief of rates and taxes; protection of human life and property; national or local defence and the preservation of public order;[27] promotion of agriculture, industry, and commerce; relief of unemployment; promotion of urban or rural regeneration; promotion of the arts; provision of public memorials, though perhaps only where this promotes some other charitable purpose;[28] the benefit of a locality;[29] conservation of the environment;[30]

---

[24] *Williams' Trustees v IRC* [1947] AC 447; *Scottish Burial Reform and Cremation Society v Glasgow Corp* [1968] AC 138.

[25] Notably the Recreational Charities Act 1958.

[26] P Luxton *The Law of Charities* (2001) 139–65.

[27] In a clear example of the law working via these historically derived categories, promoting good race relations is regarded as charitable not for its own sake but for the way it helps preserve public order: Charity Commission *Recognising New Charitable Purposes* (2001), www.charity-commission.gov.uk/rr1a/htm, Annexe B.

[28] eg a memorial to an act of bravery by lifeboat personnel may conduce to the future protection of human life and property by declaring a good example and assisting fundraising.

[29] A trust 'for the benefit of a locality' is read as one for purposes benefiting that locality in charitable ways: *Goodman v Mayor of Saltash* (1882) 7 App Cas 633, 642. This is recognized as anomalous, but remains the law: *Williams' Trustees v IRC* [1947] AC 447, 459–60; *A-G of the Cayman Islands v Even Wahr-Hansen* [2001] 1 AC 75, 82.

[30] The care of animals was once regarded as charitable only on the basis, and to the extent, that it furthered some other charitable end, eg that it promoted agriculture (*London University v Yarrow* (1857) 1 De G & J 72) or fostered the moral and spiritual welfare of mankind (*Re Wedgwood* [1915] 1 Ch 113; *Re Grove-Grady* [1929] 1 Ch 557). The conservation of the environment is now seen as publicly beneficial in its own right, probably as conducing to the long-term well-being of mankind: see Charity Commission *Preservation and Conservation* (2001), www.charity-commission.gov.uk/rr9.htm.

fostering the moral and spiritual welfare of mankind; promotion of sports and games;[31] provision for recreation.[32]

Each of these labels is only shorthand for the category it represents, and may not in itself convey a very accurate picture of what is regarded as charitable. Detailed answers are provided by further rules about what qualifies in the various areas: what exactly counts as 'relieving poverty', 'advancing education', 'advancing religion', and so on. These rules also come, in the main, from the case law. There are considerable numbers of such further rules, and of decisions exemplifying them. There is not space to cover them here; reference should be made to larger books.

It is sometimes said that, in order to qualify as charitable, a purpose must not only come within one of the recognized categories but also be beneficial as a matter of fact; but that purposes which relieve poverty, advance education, or advance religion are assumed to be beneficial unless proved otherwise.[33] The accuracy of this view is unclear. In reality, such further inquiry after factual benefit is rare, and not visibly commoner in the remaining categories than in the first three. But it can occur,[34] though sometimes only in the form of an inquiry whether the purpose is positively harmful.[35] Perhaps the most that can be said is that an inquiry into beneficial quality is always a possibility, but is not normally undertaken.

There is one other point about this question of what constitutes a

[31] On the basis that these promote other charitable purposes. Formerly, that was perceived to be so only in specialized ways (eg helping preserve public order, by improving the fitness of the police: *IRC v Glasgow Police Athletic Association* [1953] AC 380). Today, more broadly, by promoting public health (Charity Commission *Charitable Status and Sport* (2002), www.charity-commission.gov.uk/registeredcharities/pdfs/sport.pdf), or by 'encouraging participation and forging stronger communities' (Cabinet Office Strategy Unit *Private Action, Public Benefit: A Review of Charities and the Wider Not-For-Profit Sector* (2002), www.strategy-unit.gov.uk/2002/charity/report, para 4.35).

[32] Though only if calculated to promote public health (as in the case of recreation grounds: *Re Hadden* [1932] 1 Ch 133; *IRC v Baddeley* [1955] AC 572, 589), or 'in the interests of social welfare' in ways defined by the Recreational Charities Act 1958.

[33] *National Anti-Vivisection Society v IRC* [1948] AC 31, 65–6; Charity Commission *Recognising New Charitable Purposes* (2001), www.charity-commission.gov.uk/rr1a.htm, para 31.

[34] See eg *Royal Choral Society v IRC* [1943] 2 All ER 101; *Re Delius* [1957] Ch 299; *Re Pinion* [1965] Ch 85, considering whether various artistic works were of sufficient merit that their (educational) promulgation was charitable; *Anti-Vivisection Society v IRC* [1948] AC 31, whether the (moral welfare) gains of banning vivisection outweighed the (promotion of health) losses; *Gilmour v Coats* [1949] AC 426, whether a (religious) provision for intercessory prayer generated provable benefits.

[35] A trust advancing religion is valid even if trivial and ineffectual (*Re Watson* [1973] 1 WLR 1472, though cf *Gilmour v Coats* [1949] AC 426, above), and invalid only if 'adverse to the foundations of all religion or subversive of all morality' (*Thornton v Howe* (1862) 31 Beav 14).

'benefit'. If the purpose is 'political', it cannot be accepted as charitable even if it is of a kind that would otherwise qualify.[36] A purpose counts as 'political' in this way if it either advocates or opposes a change in the law or in government policy or in a particular government decision, either in the United Kingdom or abroad, or if it supports or opposes a political party.[37] So while a trust to relieve suffering and distress among prisoners of conscience would be charitable, one to do so by persuading governments to pardon them, or to repeal the laws creating the offences in question, or to alter their penal regimes, was held not charitable.[38] A judge who decided that, or even considered whether, the object of such a trust was 'beneficial' would, it was said, trespass upon the territory of the legislature or executive or stray into party politics. The government has now indicated a wish to see charities less discouraged from campaigning in their areas of expertise, while preserving the ban on party political activity.[39] But it is arguable that greater relaxation is appropriate. A trust to advance even a party-political position could be viewed as beneficial even without deciding on the merit of the position in question, on the basis that public debate is itself beneficial.[40]

6.5 'PUBLIC'

Given that the purpose in question is one recognized as a 'benefit', there is then the further requirement that the benefit must be to the 'public'. For example, setting up a trust to provide for the schooling of one's own child would certainly confer a benefit in the way of education, but only on

---

[36] *Bowman v Secular Society Ltd* [1917] AC 406, 442; *National Anti-Vivisection Society v IRC* [1948] AC 31.

[37] *McGovern v A-G* [1982] Ch. 321 (the discussion of politics, however, counts as education and is charitable: *Re Koeppler's Will Trusts* [1986] Ch 423). For a statement of what is allowable, see Charity Commission *Political Activities and Campaigning by Charities* (1999), www.charity-commission.gov.uk/cc9.htm.

[38] *McGovern v A-G* [1982] Ch 321.

[39] Cabinet Office Strategy Unit *Private Action, Public Benefit: A Review of Charities and the Wider Not-For-Profit Sector* (2002), www.strategy-unit.gov.uk/2002/charity/report, paras 4.49–56.

[40] Cf the acceptance of something like this argument as the basis for a defence in defamation (*Reynolds v Times Newspapers Ltd* [2001] 2 AC 127): see M Chesterman in C Mitchell and S Moody (eds) *Foundations of Charity Law* (2000) 261–9. Charity law's current rejection of the argument might be said to infringe the right to freedom of expression protected by ECHR Art 10, and so to require reversal under the Human Rights Act 1998. It may, however, be optimistic to think that the right is infringed by the non-conferment of the advantages of charitable status, any more than it would be by the imposition of VAT on books.

the child, not on the public. Further rules deal with this point, defining how widely the benefit needs to extend before a purpose is regarded as charitable.

Each of Lord Macnaghten's four categories has its own rule on this issue. (Indeed, since Lord Macnaghten's fourth category is really not a category at all, but merely a reference to a continuing list of other categories, there is no particular reason why they should all share a single rule in this respect; but it seems that they do.)

The notion of 'public' is strongest for purposes in the fourth category. The benefits must be open to anyone—or at least anyone in a particular area (such as the inhabitants of a certain town)—who is equipped and wants to take advantage of them. This does not mean that the facilities must be equally useful to everyone: providing a public recreation ground would qualify despite the fact that many people had no wish to use it. It means that no one who might want to use the facility in question may be *artificially* debarred, by limitations not inherent in the purpose itself. So a children's playground would be accepted, despite the fact that adults could not use it. But a trust to provide social and recreational facilities specifically for Methodists resident in West Ham and Leyton would not qualify,[41] because Methodists have no special need for such facilities and non-Methodists, who might want to use them just as much as Methodists, would be barred. (The fact that some selection is involved is not a problem so long as the competition is open in this way to all who could benefit. So a trust for the trustees to send, say, 12 disadvantaged children on holiday would qualify.)

The rule in the context of religion is similar: that the benefits should be available to any suitable person who wishes to take advantage of them. The fact that their availability is in practice confined to those of a religious disposition is not a problem. The same goes for confinement of the trust to an individual religion or denomination, to which only some people will in practice be drawn. A trust for the purposes of a cloistered order of Roman Catholic nuns was not accepted as charitable, however, despite the fact that in principle any woman might join the order.[42] Since joining the order required a formal vow of lifelong commitment and abandonment of the world, the proffered religious benefits were in effect restricted to a group narrower than those who might otherwise wish to take advantage of them. But this problem, and the similar one which arises where the benefits are limited to the members of a sect which does

[41] *IRC v Baddeley* [1955] AC 572.   [42] *Gilmour v Coats* [1949] AC 426.

not proclaim itself open to all who wish to adopt its creed, is removed if the recipients also mix with the rest of the population, so that the benefit of their religiosity becomes diffused amongst the public at large.[43] So a trust for an open, rather than cloistered, order should be accepted.

The rule for education is less stringent, in that some artificial restrictions are tolerated: that is, the benefits may validly be confined to a narrower class than all who are capable of taking advantage of them and wish to do so. So trusts providing scholarships for children defined by reference to their religion, nationality, or parents' occupation have been accepted, and a trust establishing a school for the children of Methodists resident in West Ham and Leyton would qualify. But the line is drawn at restrictions involving membership of a certain family,[44] or employment by a certain employer.[45] This is known as the 'nexus' rule. 'Nexus' means 'connection'. In fact, all designations involve a connection of some sort: in a trust to educate adherents to a particular religion, for example, the connection is the shared religious affiliation of those to be educated. So the rule is that the restriction of availability by reference to a relationship with a particular family or employer is not acceptable, while restriction by reference to other shared characteristics is acceptable. It is understandable that the former should not be accepted. As we have seen, charitable trusts are in effect subsidized by the state, and the educational provisions of families and companies are felt not to deserve this subsidy. It is less clear, however, why other artificial restrictions should be tolerated for education, when they are not for the fourth category and for religion: fundamentally, why the education of *any* restricted class is thought to confer the public benefit that is characteristic of charity.

In the area of poverty, there is no requirement of availability to the 'public' at all. Any artificial restriction is tolerated, without discrimination akin to the 'nexus' rule in education. So trusts to relieve poverty even amongst members of a particular family,[46] or amongst employees of a certain company,[47] or amongst Methodists resident in West Ham and Leyton, would all qualify as charitable. Why should this be? It is sometimes observed to be less unsatisfactory to give state subsidy to families' and companies' poverty trusts than to their educational trusts: alleviating their own members' poverty is presumably less attractive to them than providing for their own members' (children's) education, so any state

[43] *Neville Estates Ltd v Madden* [1962] Ch 832.   [44] *Re Compton* [1945] Ch 123.
[45] *Oppenheim v Tobacco Securities Trust Co Ltd* [1951] AC 297.
[46] *Re Scarisbrick* [1951] Ch 622.   [47] *Dingle v Turner* [1972] AC 601.

subsidy given to the former is unlikely to matter much in practice.[48] That, however, is at best an excuse rather than a justification for the rule. Historically, the justification seems to have been that relieving any class of the poor, however restricted, lifted the burden of doing so from the public generally, so benefiting the latter.[49] Such relief could also be seen as alleviating in its recipients the social ills associated with poverty, again to the benefit of the general community. This type of reasoning has found favour in other contexts too, such as the finding that a trust for a private hospital was charitable despite its artificial de facto restriction to those rich enough to afford the fees (unacceptable for a fourth-category purpose), among other reasons because it relieved pressure on the state hospitals.[50] The argument proves too much, however. One could as well argue that sending a family's children to private schools benefited the public generally by reducing the size of the classes those children would otherwise join in the state schools. That argument, with its consequence that such a purpose would be charitable after all, would presumably not be accepted; though in the last resort it is not clear what exactly is the flaw in it.

6.6 RULES VERSUS AN AD HOC APPROACH

It is sometimes proposed that the rules described in the last two sections should be abandoned, and an ad hoc approach substituted, in which a purpose's charitable status would depend on whether the Charity Commission and judges decide that it is 'for the public benefit'.[51] This thinking has found some,[52] though not general,[53] favour with the judges. The Charity Commission, regarding its role as to apply the traditional law, eschews the proposed alternative.[54]

---

[48] *Dingle v Turner* [1972] AC 601, 624–5, Lord Cross.

[49] *Re Compton* [1945] Ch 123, 139.

[50] *Re Resch's Will Trusts* [1969] 1 AC 514.

[51] See eg House of Commons Expenditure Committee *Charity Commissioners and their Accountability* (1975); Commission on the Future of the Voluntary Sector *Meeting the Challenge of Change: Voluntary Action in the 21st Century* (1996).

[52] *Dingle v Turner* [1972] AC 601; *Incorporated Council of Law Reporting for England and Wales v A-G* [1972] Ch 73; *A-G of the Cayman Islands v Even Wahr-Hansen* [2001] 1 AC 75, 82.

[53] Cf *Williams' Trustees v IRC* [1947] AC 447; *Scottish Burial Reform and Cremation Society v Glasgow Corp* [1968] AC 138; *Brisbane City Council v A-G for Queensland* [1979] AC 411, 422; *Re South Place Ethical Society* [1980] 1 WLR 1565.

[54] The Commission consistently refers to itself as applying the legal rules. See eg *The Review of the Register of Charities* (2001), www.charity-commission.gov.uk/rr1.htm, paras 6, 9, 11, 18, and A1.

How would an ad hoc approach work? There are two conceptions of such an approach. The first would require the court or Charity Commission to decide whether the proposed purpose is beneficial to the public, but take no account of the special treatment which charitable status would entail.[55] The second would require attention to that further dimension, and a decision whether the benefits to be had from the putative charity would outweigh the costs of the special treatment.[56] But although intelligible, and requiring less of a departure from the status quo, the first conception is unlikely to be stable. It would be difficult in practice to follow it and recognize as charitable a project judged beneficial but only marginally so, knowing that the consequence would be to secure it disproportionately generous treatment. The proposal for ad hoc thinking is thus best assessed in terms of the second conception, according to which that factor should be taken into account.

The assessment required to weigh a putative charity's benefits against its costs would not be straightforward. It would depend on the assignment of values to the costs and benefits; and these values would have to be expressed in comparable terms, so as not to have to test oranges against apples.

The cost of a putative charity's tax exemptions[57] can be easily quantified. The aggregate cost of financing the Charity Commission is also known,[58] though it is not clear how to compute an individual charity's due share of it. (Pro rata to size of endowment, perhaps? But would that not inequitably favour charities running largely on income?) Then there is the cost involved in the provisions extending the endurance of charitable trusts, allowing these trusts' partial but substantial withdrawal of their assets from the market to continue for longer than would normally be tolerated.[59] It is hard to put a figure on this part of the cost of recognizing a trust as charitable; no attempt seems ever to have been made.

Even if figures could be put on all these costs, moreover, they would

---

[55] This view was favoured by Lords Dilhorne, MacDermott, and Hodson in *Dingle v Turner* [1972] AC 601.

[56] Proposed by Lord Cross, with the agreement of Lord Simon, in *Dingle v Turner* [1972] AC 601 (though reckoning the costs almost exclusively in terms of the tax consequences: surely an underestimation of the significance of the others).

[57] In aggregate, they amount to over £2 billion per annum: HM Treasury *Review of Charity Taxation: Consultation Document* (1999) para 1.4.

[58] In 2000–1 the government's allocation to the Charity Commission was £21.3 million, which will rise to £26 million in 2003–4: Charity Commission *Annual Report 2000–1* (2001) 28.

[59] See section 6.2.

not mean much. They would be significant only when translated into terms of lost opportunities, such as how many new hospital beds and jobs there could have been but for the lost tax and other costs.

When we try to quantify a putative charity's benefits, the picture is more opaque still. Present-day political rhetoric commonly identifies a 'partnership' between the state and charities, which implies that the benefits of charitable activity can be measured in units recognizable by the state. On the simplest interpretation of this thinking, the units would have to be monetary. Then, a charity's benefit would be a matter of how much money its work saved the state. This approach to assessing benefit may have had some influence in the past,[60] and it is immanent in the way that the modern state relies on charities to provide aid which the state itself might otherwise have had to provide, enabling it to reduce public expenditure.[61] But it is probably too constricting, leaving out of account a number of other bases on which benefit might properly be found. For example, the state might be interested to see the venture go forward, but without itself taking primary responsibility for it. This could be the case with experimental types of welfare provision, in which it would be difficult for the state to conduct a selective pilot exercise, but easy for a charity. Or the idea could be that there is a merit in pluralism: so private education, medicine, social welfare, arts sponsorship, and so on could be valued for the very fact that they are not provided by the state. Or again, perhaps some activities which would never be undertaken by the state are nevertheless beneficial to society: religion, say. Or perhaps it is beneficial that citizens should undertake 'good works' in the sense that this makes them better people, irrespective of the objective value of the works themselves. All these ideas of benefit are plausible, though not unchallengeable, both in themselves and as positions which might be ascribed to the state.[62] But it is obviously hard to treat them quantitatively.

It would therefore not be straightforward to quantify either the benefits or the costs of granting charitable status in an individual case, certainly not in terms that allow them to be compared. The assessment could be

---

[60] M Chesterman *Charities, Trusts and Social Welfare* (1979), 18–19, 26–7.

[61] Note the Charity Commission's discussion of this phenomenon and of the difficulties it can cause: *The Independence of Charities from the State* (2001), www.charity-commission.gov.uk/rr7.htm.

[62] Benefits of these kinds are recognized in Cabinet Office Strategy Unit *Private Action, Public Benefit: A Review of Charities and the Wider Not-For-Profit Sector* (2002), www.strategy-unit.gov.uk/2002/charity/report, paras 3.14, 4.20; and HM Treasury *The Role of the Voluntary and Community Sector in Service Delivery* (2002), www.hm-treasury.gov.uk/mediastore/otherfiles/cross_cut_vol02.pdf.

performed only by making value judgements about their social worth. There is no other way of saying whether the kinds of benefits described above, in the measure that they would be delivered by a particular putative charity, are worth the loss of *n* jobs and hospital beds. Indeed, deciding to reckon the costs in jobs and hospital beds rather than some other currency itself involves a value judgement as to priorities.

Such value judgements would be far more numerous and profound than those found under the present law, which is calculated to limit the need for them. Take the adoption of Lord Macnaghten's classification[63] of charitable purposes into three defined categories, relief of poverty, advancement of education and of religion, and the insistence that his fourth category, 'other purposes beneficial to the community', is the umbrella title for a collection of further defined categories. This avoids the need for a live consideration of whether, for example, religion as such is for the public good. Instead, there is the much narrower question of whether a putative charity would 'advance religion', as defined more or less by the dictionary.[64] The need for ad hoc value judgements is not eliminated altogether: it must still be decided whether a purpose comes within or is analogous to one of the categories, and the courts will occasionally ask whether changes in perception (eg of what is educationally valuable, or what promotes good health) require adjustment of assumptions about what counts as charitable.[65] But it is significant that the alleged requirement (section 6.4) to examine putative charitable purposes for actual benefit, which would require value judgements, is generally honoured in the breach; cases in which the task is undertaken often show considerable discomfiture with it.[66] The rules about how wide a section of the public must be benefited likewise limit the need for value judgements, as does the rule that a political purpose cannot be charitable. Likewise too the structure of the jurisdiction to apply funds of

---

[63] *Income Tax Commissioners v Pemsel* [1891] AC 531, 581.

[64] 'Religion' is taken as any philosophy involving reverence of a higher being (*Bowman v Secular Society Ltd* [1917] AC 406; *Re South Place Ethical Society* [1980] 1 WLR 1565) and it is regarded as 'advanced' by any kind of support, however ineffectual and trivial (*Re Watson* [1973] 1 WLR 1472).

[65] *Anti-Vivisection Society v IRC* [1948] AC 31, 42, 74; *Scottish Burial Reform and Cremation Society Ltd v Glasgow Corp* [1968] AC 138, 154; *IRC v McMullen* [1981] AC 1, 15. Apparently in the same vein, the Charity Commission aims 'to act constructively and imaginatively' in applying the law: *The Review of the Register* (2001), www.charity-commission.gov.uk/rr1.htm, para A1.

[66] See eg *Anti-Vivisection Society v IRC* [1948] AC 31, holding the benefits of vivisection greater than the disbenefits; *Gilmour v Coats* [1949] AC 426, seeking but not finding a provable benefit from intercessory prayer.

charitable trusts cy près, which does not apply resources to a new purpose more valuable than the old[67] (which would require assessment of the relative value of the two), but awaits failure by way of sheer impossibility or unsuitability in terms of the settlor's intentions, and then applies the resources as closely as practicable to the settlor's original purpose.[68]

The difference between the proposed ad hoc approach and the current law thus lies in the extent of the social value judgements demanded of the judiciary and Charity Commission. This is probably the key to choosing between them. There is an important argument that courts, and therefore (because its role is modelled on that of the courts) the Charity Commission, should not make social value judgements. This is not because, as people, their personnel lack relevant ideas: they surely have as many as anyone else. But to require them to give official effect to those ideas, via decisions about charitable status, would (the argument goes) take them beyond their constitutional remit, and into the domain of governments and legislatures. According to one of the most celebrated versions of this thesis, the task of the courts is, and is only, to discern answers which are, or must be treated as, true.[69] Opinions can legitimately be made the basis of official actions only if they are, or can validly be represented as, the will of the majority of the population, discovered through the workings of democracy: normally, therefore, if they are the decisions of governments or legislatures.[70] The thesis underlying this argument is not necessarily easy to map on to reality. For example, the location of the crucial line between truth and opinion may itself be a matter of judgement; and there may be concerns over the adequacy of particular attempts at democracy. And it is beyond doubt that courts have on occasion breached the thesis, and presumably have at least sometimes thought it right to do so. But in

---

[67] As proposed by M Chesterman *Charities, Trusts and Social Welfare* (1979) 224–7.

[68] *Report of the Charity Commissioners for England and Wales for the year 1984* HC 394 (1984) paras 28–31.

[69] See especially R Dworkin *Law's Empire* (1986). The full thesis is of course subtler than the account given here.

[70] In deciding what counts as charitable, the Charity Commission takes account of public opinion: *The Review of the Register* (2001), www.charity-commission.gov.uk/rr1.htm, paras 23–4. This might be interpreted as an attempt to access the democratic credentials required to take a more judgemental role. In fact, however, the Commission clearly sees itself operating by reference to rules (ibid, paras 6, 9, 11, 18, and A1), and its attention to public opinion seems to be in connection with the task, required by such decisions as *National Anti-Vivisection Society v IRC* [1948] AC 31, of considering whether changes in perception (eg of what is educationally valuable, or what promotes good health) require adjustment of assumptions about what counts as charitable.

broad terms the thesis represents a view widely held among judges, politicians, and theorists.

Assessments of the benefit to be had from a putative charity, and of whether that benefit exceeds the costs of its special treatment, seem to involve opinions rather than truths. Since the ad hoc approach would require far more in this vein than the current law, from this point of view it would be the reverse of an improvement on the latter.[71]

According to this argument, however, the government or legislature is properly able to make the value judgements required. For example, the present arrangements could be replaced by ones under which a Minister, on the advice of civil servants, would grant or withhold charitable status and/or consequential special treatment based on an assessment of net benefit. But that suggestion is objectionable in a different way. It would entail a day-to-day privileging of the government's view of net benefit, when something less partisan, more catholic, may be thought appropriate. If change from the status quo is sought, therefore, the most promising approach would probably be for the legislature to establish new rules describing the incidence and consequences of charitable status: which new rules the Charity Commission, courts, and tax authorities would then apply as they do the current rules. This is certainly the approach taken by the most recent set of reform proposals. These, presented in a Government White Paper, expressly reject an ad hoc approach as too uncertain and prone to government interference,[72] and favour the enactment of a modernized list of charitable purposes.[73] A degree of confusion is introduced, however, by the inclusion, at the end of the list, of the category 'other purposes beneficial to the community'. According to the paper's own account of the latter,[74] applying it will involve ad hoc assessment of possible new charitable purposes.

---

[71] Another argument, differently based but in this instance leading to the same conclusion, stresses the value of certainty in the law. Requiring the courts and Charity Commission to judge putative charities ad hoc would reduce certainty. One consequence would be an increase in expenditure on litigating charitable status, which from many points of view is undesirable.

[72] Cabinet Office Strategy Unit *Private Action, Public Benefit: A Review of Charities and the Wider Not-For-Profit Sector* (2002), **www.strategy-unit.gov.uk/2002/charity/report**, para 4.17.

[73] Ibid, paras 4.12–14.

[74] Ibid, para 4.31: 'objects will be accepted over time by analogy to existing case law, *or based on evidence of public benefit from first principles*' (emphasis supplied). See too para 4.22.

7

Resulting and constructive trusts

So far, we have concentrated on express trusts. We turn now to the two other types of trust with which express trusts are customarily contrasted, namely resulting and constructive trusts.

7.1 THE NATURE OF CONSTRUCTIVE TRUSTS

Let us begin with constructive trusts, which in some ways are less problematic than resulting trusts. The essential difference between express and constructive trusts is easily stated. Remember the 'definition' of a trust that was offered in Chapter 1: 'A trust is a situation in which property is vested in someone (a trustee), who is under legally recognized obligations, at least some of which are of a proprietary kind, to handle it in a certain way, and to the exclusion of any personal interest. These obligations may arise either by conscious creation by the previous owner of the property (the settlor), or because some other legally significant circumstances are present.' In these terms, express trusts arise by the settlor's conscious creation, whilst constructive trusts arise because some other legally significant circumstances are present.

Contrast this way of expressing the distinction with two other, apparently similar, but in fact problematic formulations of it. According to one, express trusts are intended by a settlor, whereas constructive trusts are not. This is incorrect because some constructive trusts are intended: for example, those which effectuate secret trusts.[1] According to the other, express trusts arise because of the settlor's intention, whereas constructive trusts arise by operation of law. This deals with the point just made, but errs in contrasting the settlor's intention with the operation of law. All trusts arise by operation of law, in the sense that trusts involve legal obligations, and only the law can place legal obligations upon people. The question is rather why the law does so. In express trusts, its reason is to

---

[1] See section 5.6. As noted there, the fact that settlors can so easily engineer these constructive trusts generates the worry that they can in effect opt out of the Wills Act.

give effect to the settlor's wish;[2] while in constructive trusts it is something else. Hence the wording of the 'definition' referred to above.

This distinction between express and constructive trusts is important not only for a proper understanding of their bases. The law draws upon the distinction when it rules that the two kinds of trust shall be treated differently. In particular, by virtue of section 53(2) of the Law of Property Act 1925, constructive trusts[3] are exempted from the formality requirements of section 53(1), described in Chapter 5. A requirement of formality in making a trust can, in the nature of things, only be complied with by someone who knows that she is making a trust. That is the case with express trusts, since these are necessarily associated with a settlor's intention. But it is not the case with constructive trusts, which by definition may not be associated with such an intention and moreover, as we shall see, may arise in circumstances such that no one may realize a trust is at issue. If they applied to these trusts, therefore, the formality requirements would be very frequently not complied with, leading to the trusts' invalidity, so negating the law's concern that in the relevant circumstances such a trust should arise.

It ought to be unnecessary to stress that a situation cannot be a constructive trust unless it qualifies as a *trust*: ie, following our 'definition', property must be vested in the trustee, who must be under legally recognized obligations, at least some of which must be of a proprietary kind, to handle it in a certain way, to the exclusion of any personal interest. The expression 'constructive trust' has however been used to describe two kinds of situation which do not conform to this pattern, and which are not therefore properly trusts at all. In one of these I am required to compensate the trust's objects when I cause them damage.[4] My obligations do not require me to handle particular property in a particular way. They require me rather to pay the claimants the amount in question out of my general assets, ie they are personal rather than proprietary.[5] In the other I am required to honour a promise I made

[2] Ostensibly, at any rate. In fact, in some cases, a settlor's intention—and so an express trust—is 'found' less because it really exists than because the judge wishes there to be a trust for some other reason, which is tantamount to imposing a constructive trust: eg *Paul v Constance* [1977] 1 WLR 527: see section 3.3.

[3] Together with resulting and 'implied' trusts. 'Implied' here is normally read not as 'express but not clearly stated' (exempting such trusts would undermine the requirements in s 53(1) for express trusts) but as 'arising for reasons other than the settlor's conscious creation'. Implied trusts thus comprise nothing which would not be a constructive trust anyway.

[4] Thus especially 'dishonest assistance': see section 15.7.

[5] For this distinction, see sections 1.9, 14.1.

regarding my use of a particular piece of property, but my ob
neither of a proprietary kind nor to the exclusion of any inter\
property on my own part.[6] Since these situations are not proper
at all, many decline to see them as constructive trusts, and that is c   ..y
the approach we shall take.

Where the holder of some property has proprietary obligations arising
in the appropriate way to use it in a particular manner for another's
benefit, the term 'constructive trust' is correctly used. This does not
mean, however, that a constructive trust will arise whenever I owe you an
obligation and hold some property to which it might arguably be
attached. Sometimes the circumstances will call for a legal response, and
a constructive trust will be a candidate because a particular piece of
property is at issue, but the law will instead impose a personal liability.
Take the example of your accepting a bribe to neglect your duty to me.
Although it is now settled that you hold the bribe on constructive trust
for me, for a long time the rule was that you merely owe me the amount of
the bribe by way of a personal liability.[7] Or take the situation where you
are my agent and sell my goods. In some such cases, identified by reference to the precise arrangement between us, you will hold the proceeds
of the sale on trust for me; otherwise you will be able to take them into
your own funds and then have a personal liability to pay me the sum in
question from those funds.[8] The type of liability chosen, when either
is possible, matters above all because proprietary obligations give me
priority in your bankruptcy; personal obligations do not.[9] The law must
ensure that the circumstances in which constructive trusts arise (the
'other legally significant circumstances' of our 'definition') justify not
only some response, but also a response of a proprietary nature.

7.2 WHY DO CONSTRUCTIVE TRUSTS ARISE?

It is accurate to say that constructive trusts are generated by considerations other than a project of effectuating settlors' wishes, but so far we
have learnt nothing about what those considerations might be. In fact,
constructive trusts arise as a reaction to (on the face of it) a number of sets

---

[6] *Binions v Evans* [1972] Ch 359, 368–9; *Swiss Bank Corporation v Lloyds Bank Ltd* [1979]
Ch 548, 571; *Lyus v Prowsa Developments Ltd* [1982] 1 WLR 1044; *Ashburn Anstalt v Arnold*
[1989] Ch 1, 22–6: see section 8.8.
[7] *Lister & Co v Stubbs* (1890) 45 Ch D 1, disapproved in *A-G for Hong Kong v Reid* [1994]
1 AC 324.
[8] See section 8.4.   [9] See sections 1.9, 14.1.

of circumstances. They are detailed individually in the next chapter. It must be said, however, that the catalogue given there is probably not exhaustive. Indeed, it is probably impossible to give a complete list. There is nothing to prevent a court identifying for the law a new set of circumstances which, on reflection, seems to require the imposition of a constructive trust. It would be otherwise if the sets of circumstances in which constructive trusts arise all had a common factor, it being this that generates the constructive trust. No set of circumstances lacking that factor could then properly elicit such a trust.

Attempts have been made to identify such a common factor, but none has yet given a satisfactory account of the circumstances in which constructive trusts do in fact arise in English law. The most famous of these attempts asserts that constructive trusts exist solely to deprive the trustee of an unjust enrichment which she has received at the beneficiary's expense.[10] This view seems to be correct as regards the law of the United States,[11] but in other jurisdictions, whilst it is probably[12] correct to say that one of their bases may be the reversal of unjust enrichment, it is clear that constructive trusts arise also in other circumstances.[13] Other attempts at a general theory of constructive trusts seek exhaustively to describe these other circumstances. According to one view, constructive trusts also exist to deprive a person of property obtained in breach of a fiduciary duty;[14] another view adds an aim of perfecting incomplete dispositions.[15] Whatever their accuracy in accounting for some instances of

---

[10] D Waters *The Constructive Trust* (1964).

[11] A Scott and W Fratcher *The Law of Trusts* 4th edn (1989) vol V para 462.

[12] R Chambers *Resulting Trusts* (1997) denies this, ascribing the reversal of unjust enrichment exclusively to resulting trusts. But that thesis requires a view to be taken of resulting trusts at variance with that asserted in *Westdeutsche Landesbank Girozentrale v Islington LBC* [1996] AC 669 (see section 7.5). The constructive trust traditionally associated with the reversal of unjust enrichment is viewed by some as a remedial constructive trust (described in section 7.3), ie as mediated in its consequences by judicial discretion. The resulting trust argued for by Chambers is not commonly viewed as remedial, however. So at one level, Chambers' view can be seen as an attempt to remove discretionary judicial mediation from the proprietary reversal of unjust enrichment. That development would be welcomed by some but regretted by others: cf eg D Waters and P Birks in P Birks (ed) *The Frontiers of Liability Volume 2* (1994) chs 13, 16.

[13] In Canada, the United States view, previously held, was rejected in *Korkontzilas v Soulos* (1997) 146 DLR (4th) 214, 227–8.

[14] *Korkontzilas v Soulos* (1997) 146 DLR (4th) 214, 227–8, Canada.

[15] G Elias *Explaining Constructive Trusts* (1990). Elias also adds the project of securing reparation for loss wrongfully caused. But at least some of this work is carried on not by constructive trusts but by personal responses, such as 'dishonest assistance' (see section 15.7), albeit that these have sometimes been wrongly called 'constructive trusts': see section 7.1.

constructive trusts, however, these theses fail in their aim of exhausting the circumstances in which constructive trusts in fact occur. A major instance covered by none of them, for example, is the constructive trust which especially English law erects in certain cases regarding family property, which we shall look at in section 8.11. The discussion of constructive trusts in Chapter 8 in fact suggests that the trusts addressed there rest on essentially four kinds of basis.[16] But there is nothing about these to lead one to think that such trusts cannot, in principle, arise on any other basis. So far as producing a general theory goes, therefore, we can say only that constructive trusts arise in circumstances where, for whatever reason, it is right that the owner of some property should not enjoy it personally, but should hold it on trust for another.

All is sometimes swept together in an assertion that constructive trusts arise where good conscience so requires.[17] Such a formula, providing no information as to when good conscience does so require, does not effectively identify a common factor by reference to which the law imposes constructive trusts. Unlike the theses discussed in the last paragraph, however, it should not be read as attempting to do so. Instead, it stands for the proposition that a constructive trust will be found where the individual court, in its discretion, thinks fit. (The discretion need not be limitless, of course.) The view that constructive trusts depend on the explicit exercise of judicial discretion in this way refers to such trusts as 'remedial constructive trusts'.

7.3 REMEDIAL CONSTRUCTIVE TRUSTS

As will be seen in the next chapter, the use which English law normally makes of the constructive trust can be expressed in the form: 'if facts X and Y are present, a constructive trust will arise'. That is to say, the trust is regarded as arising if, but only if, the facts are of the kind stated; and as doing so automatically, and from the moment that those facts are present. A constructive trust of this pattern is sometimes referred to as

---

[16] Liberal property theory, via its predicates proprietary inertia and *nemo dat quod non habet*; a concern to reduce the disadvantages of agency, trust, and similar otherwise useful devices; a concern to protect someone who will otherwise have been irretrievably prejudiced by relying on another's word; and the implications of family relationships.

[17] eg *Beatty v Guggenheim Exploration Co* 122 NE 378 (1919) 380, United States: 'A constructive trust is the formula through which the conscience of equity finds expression. When property has been acquired in such circumstances that the holder of the legal title may not in good conscience retain the beneficial interest, equity converts him into a trustee'. See too *Korkontzilas v Soulos* (1997) 146 DLR (4th) 214, 225, Canada.

'institutional'. This is by way of contrast with the 'remedial' form of constructive trust, which, briefly, is one which arises if, when, and to the extent that a court chooses, in its discretion, to say so.

The degree of contrast between remedial and institutional constructive trusts should not be overstated. It may well be less than certain whether facts X and Y are present in an institutional constructive trust case, either because the evidence is unclear or because discovering these 'facts' requires the application of an evaluative concept, such as 'in good faith'.[18] Then, the court will in effect have a discretion whether to find an institutional constructive trust. But there remain differences between this and a remedial constructive trust. A court dealing with a remedial construct-ive trust will have a discretion even where the facts are clear. Even when the facts are unclear, the discretion in an institutional constructive trust case does not involve the overt consideration of the right outcome which is essential to thinking about a remedial constructive trust. And even where the recognition of an institutional constructive trust involves a discretion in this way, the court's choices will be only to find the trust to have arisen from the time of the facts, with all that that will entail, or to find it not to have arisen at all: whereas a court dealing with a remedial constructive trust can finesse the terms on which it is to be applied.

In its purest conception,[19] the jurisprudence of remedial constructive trusts has three main features of note. First, it is not limited in its applic-ability to a particular type or types of claim. It can be used in a case of any kind, though probably only where there is some 'causal connection' between the facts of which the claimant complains (eg the defendant's unjust enrichment at her expense) and the presence in the defend-ant's hands of the property at issue.[20] This feature, of course, makes sense only within an overall system whereby any remedy can in principle be matched with any cause of action. Thus, secondly, the court always has a discretion whether to impose a constructive trust, or to make some other award, such as an order for compensation. And thirdly, the court also has a discretion to say on what terms the constructive trust is awarded. This is

---

[18] On the face of it, a constructive trust arising wherever good conscience so requires seems an institutional constructive trust of this kind, contrary to the suggestion at the end of the last section that it is a remedial constructive trust. The matter is ultimately one of degree, but the suggestion is made on the basis that the good conscience formula has no other significance than to invite the court to exercise discretion.

[19] D Waters in P Birks (ed) *The Frontiers of Liability Volume 2* (1994) ch 13; D Wright *The Remedial Constructive Trust* (1998).

[20] The interpretation of 'causal connection' can, however, itself be highly discretionary. See *Peter v Beblow* (1993) 101 DLR (4th) 621, Canada.

especially important where third parties are involved. Say you own our family home in circumstances such that I deserve a share in it, but before I claim you mortgage the house to a bank. An institutional constructive trust arising on these facts[21] would give me an interest pre-dating, and thus commonly unaffected by, the bank's;[22] the mortgage takes effect only against the remainder of the property, which will be unwelcome news to the bank. A court deploying a remedial constructive trust would, however, have a discretion whether to award me my share free of the bank's interest, or subject to it.

The remedial constructive trust is undoubtedly recognized in some common law countries, being most highly developed in the United States and Canada.[23] It has not been recognized as part of English law.[24] Some have suggested that it may, and usefully could, be introduced into English law. A notable judicial statement[25] to this effect was made in the context of misgivings over the way that institutional constructive trusts automatically affect third parties, as just explained; replacing them with remedial constructive trusts would be a way of allowing third parties to be protected. Others have set themselves against the introduction of remedial constructive trusts into English law.[26] The leading judicial pronouncement of this point of view was made in a case where no institutional constructive trust appeared to be available, and it was being suggested that the court should nonetheless intervene by way of remedial constructive trust and moreover make that intervention effective against third parties whose rights pre-dated the order: ie in its discretion

---

[21] See section 8.11.   [22] *Williams & Glyn's Bank Ltd v Boland* [1981] AC 487.

[23] A Scott and W Fratcher *The Law of Trusts* 4th edn (1989) vol V para 462; D Waters *Law of Trusts in Canada* 2nd edn (1984) ch 11. The conception operating in those jurisdictions seems, however, to fall slightly short of the pure conception described in the text. There is authority, for example, that the trust automatically arises, with the discretion being merely whether to enforce the claimant's rights under it (*Knight Newspapers v Commissioner of Internal Revenue* 143 F 2d 1007 (1944), United States); and that whilst the imposition of a trust does lie in the court's discretion, the choice for the court is only between saying that there was such a trust from the time of the facts and saying that there is no trust at all (*Rawluk v Rawluk* (1990) 65 DLR (4th) 161, Canada).

[24] Though the English courts are currently and apparently happily operating the doctrine of proprietary estoppel in a way that seems to claim just as much discretion to award a transfer of property in situations, and on terms, defined only by the court making the award: *Sledmore v Dalby* (1996) 72 P & CR 196; *Gillett v Holt* [2001] Ch 210; *Jennings v Rice* [2002] EWCA Civ 159. It is hard to see how the law can be right simultaneously to proceed on these lines but not espouse the remedial constructive trust.

[25] *Westdeutsche Landesbank Girozentrale v Islington LBC* [1996] AC 669, 716. Note also *Metall und Rohstoff AG v Donaldson Lufkin & Jenrette Inc* [1990] 1 QB 391, 478–9.

[26] Especially P Birks in P Birks (ed) *The Frontiers of Liability Volume 2* (1994) ch 16, and (1998) 12 TLI 202.

retrospectively create a new proprietary right in the claimant's favour.[27] Each point of view is a very understandable reaction to its context and perspective, but neither can be regarded as a considered assessment of the full picture.

The principal stated objection to the remedial constructive trust is that it can produce departures from established property rights. Take the example above, regarding our family home. Say I currently have a claim to an institutional constructive trust. If the law decides to operate instead by remedial constructive trust, and my claim to a share in the family home is successful but not made effective against the bank, it can, as compared with the current position, be said that the proprietary quality of my right has in effect been confiscated. Equally, say I currently have no claim under an institutional constructive trust, but I persuade a court to award a remedial constructive trust against you. Again as compared with the current position, the court has confiscated rights from you. If it makes the award effective also against the bank, it has confiscated rights from the bank too.

But it is true to say that the remedial constructive trust produces departures from established property rights only so long as one regards the property rights as established before one admits the remedial constructive trust to the story. If the remedial constructive trust is seen as an original feature of the law, our understanding of property rights is necessarily that they may be affected by the use of the remedy, and so are more relative from the outset. Then, it is impossible to say that I suffer confiscation if my claim to a share in the family home is not made effective against the bank: the only right I have is one which reflects the possibility of this happening. Likewise, the very possibility of being affected by a remedial constructive trust in my favour means that your ownership of the home cannot be regarded as naturally absolute, and that the bank cannot assume its mortgage rights to be as you granted them.

So the question really is whether to approve or otherwise of the idea that the profiling of rights—the settling of their ambit, and their precedence amongst themselves—should lie in the discretion of judges, rather than being fixed by rules.[28] The first point to note is that the distinction

---

[27] *Re Polly Peck International plc (in administration) (No 2)* [1998] 3 All ER 812. The same situation obtained in *Re Goldcorp Exchange Ltd* [1995] 1 AC 74, 99, 104, where however the court was more receptive to the introduction of the remedial constructive trust, merely refusing to apply it in an unprincipled manner.

[28] R Dworkin *Taking Rights Seriously* (1977); D Galligan *Discretionary Powers* (1986); K Hawkins (ed) *The Uses of Discretion* (1992); S Gardner in P Birks (ed) *The Frontiers of Liability Volume 2* (1994) ch 14.

between rules and discretions is relative: propositions expressed as rules often, indeed normally or even inevitably, have latitude within them; while avowed discretions are normally operated according to discernible (though not necessarily desirable) patterns. Nevertheless, there remains a spectrum about the extent to which the law preordains its reaction to particular facts, and the terms 'rules' and 'discretions' can intelligibly be used to denote its two halves.

Rules, then, cater better than discretions to 'Rule of Law' values, notably the value that like cases should be treated alike (and unlike cases differently) and the value that those subject to the law should be able to know its impact on them so as to be able to conduct their affairs accordingly. Rules are also likely to be the product of more extended and circumspect reflection than discretionary determinations, and may make for more efficient disposal of disputes than discretionary techniques (though if the rules are complex and parties can appeal against alleged misapplications of them, the opposite may be true). Discretions, on the other hand, allow greater scope for the parties to a dispute to be involved in the process of its judicial resolution (though rules make it easier for them to negotiate out of court); in contexts where the appropriate position for the law depends on weighing the significance of a number of disparate factors, discretions better allow for the achievement of that position in individual cases; and discretions allow the law to feel its way towards the development of a rule when the right shape for that rule is not at first apparent.

It is apparent that neither approach is incontrovertibly preferable to the other in principle, but that one may seem more attractive than the other according to the degree of resonance that the considerations just outlined have in particular areas. For example, if the factors influencing one's view of the appropriate legal response are few and easily weighed, and an adverse legal outcome is especially damaging, the value that like cases should be treated alike may be overwhelmingly important. If the parties to a particular kind of dispute are typically adept at negotiating their own settlements, as for example shipping companies are, it will be most helpful for the law to give a clear statement of the starting point for those negotiations. If the parties typically need their negotiations to be moderated and if necessary shaped by an outsider such as a judge, though, that outsider needs to be given the authority to do this shaping. This may be characteristic of family breakdowns. The pure conception of remedial constructive trusts proposes them as candidates for application across the entire range of cases to which the law attends. Given what has just been said, however, their discretionary quality makes that candidacy appropriate in some areas but not in others. It would therefore be understandable for a legal system to adopt them, but eclectically.

A particular consideration arises in the cases where English law currently deploys constructive trusts, as described in the next chapter. The facts generating such trusts are in many cases unlikely to be apparent to those with whom the trustee continues to deal. When the existence of the trust eventually comes to light, therefore, it will confound the assumptions on which they conducted those dealings. For example, if our family home is in your sole name and you mortgage it, the bank will assume that the house's whole value is at your disposal as security for its loan, and will decide how much to lend you accordingly. If it emerges that I had a half-share in the house all along, under a constructive trust, that share's immunity to the bank's rights may mean that the value of the loan is greater than that of the security. Or if a company raises even unsecured loans to develop a site which is its only asset, its creditors will be dismayed to find that it holds that asset on constructive trust for another company for which it was a fiduciary.[29] It seems desirable to avoid such states of affairs. This has attracted some to the remedial constructive trust, with its facility to declare that any order shall not affect third parties. That technique, however, may be seen as essentially unjust to the claimant, who (as we currently see it) in principle merits rights which do affect third parties. So it is worth exploring whether other, more roundabout, strategies for balancing or reconciling the competing interests are possible. In some contexts it may make sense to require the beneficiary of a constructive trust to register the interest it gives her against the trustee's name or title to the property in question, so that others dealing with the trustee can know of it. In other contexts, eg that of family property, a rule requiring registration would be inept (as largely unknown or meaningless to those at whom it is directed), so a different approach is called for. This might, for instance, involve requiring banks to ensure that possible constructive trust claimants are alerted to and involved in any mortgage dealings, and to bear the risk (as the party best placed to spread the loss) of any cases that slip through the net. That is, in fact, largely the effect of the present law.[30]

---

[29] See sections 8.4–8.5.
[30] Land Registration Act 2002 Sch 3 para 2; *Williams & Glyn's Bank Ltd v Boland* [1981] AC 487; *Bristol and West Building Society v Henning* [1985] 1 WLR 778; *Barclays Bank plc v O'Brien* [1994] 1 AC 180.

7.4 RESULTING TRUSTS

Semantically, a 'resulting' trust is a trust whose beneficiary is also its settlor: a beneficial interest 'results', ie jumps back, to the person from whom the trustee acquired the trust property.[31] The term 'resulting trust' is not, however, usually used to describe every trust whose beneficiary is also its settlor. Normal usage of the term excludes the case where the trust for the settlor arises because of the settlor's own stipulation that it should, ie is an express trust to this effect.[32]

As we noted in section 7.1, the Law of Property Act 1925 section 53(2) exempts constructive trusts from the formality requirements imposed by section 53(1): and is right to do so because constructive trusts can arise, by definition, in circumstances such that no one may realize the fact, and so be in a position to comply with a formality requirement. Section 53(2) also exempts resulting trusts. It is right to do so only because resulting trusts are like constructive trusts in this respect. And they are like constructive trusts in this respect only because of the usage just referred to, confining the term 'resulting trust' to trusts whose settlor is also its beneficiary for reasons other than his own stipulation that he should be. If the term extended to the latter, it would include cases where the settlor could perfectly well comply with section 53(1).

It is tempting to conclude that a resulting trust is therefore any trust whose settlor is also its beneficiary, and which arises 'because some other legally significant circumstances are present', as our 'definition' has it. That is, that a resulting trust is any constructive trust whose settlor is also its beneficiary. But this is not the law. It differs in two respects from the view of resulting trusts taken by the House of Lords in *Westdeutsche Landesbank Girozentrale v Islington LBC*,[33] as expressed particularly by Lord Browne-Wilkinson. According to the latter view, resulting trusts arise only where someone intended (or is regarded as having intended) to make a trust in the first place; and they arise so as to give effect to the common intention of the settlor and the trustee. The next two sections explore these propositions.

---

[31] In *Re Printers and Transferrers Amalgamated Trades Protection Society* [1899] Ch 184 a trust in favour of persons other than the settlor was described as a 'resulting trust', but this usage is incorrect.

[32] Such as arises in the context of a pension fund trust, or of the arrangement under which the lender of money has the borrower hold it on trust for him, with a right or duty to expend it in a particular way (*Barclay's Bank Ltd v Quistclose Investments Ltd* [1970] AC 567).

[33] [1996] AC 669.

7.5 THE CASES IN WHICH RESULTING TRUSTS CAN ARISE

The first proposition is that a resulting trust cannot arise in my favour unless I intended (or am treated as having intended) to make a trust in the first place.[34] The effect of this rule is that resulting trusts can arise only in two classes of case.[35]

One is where I transfer property to you on express trust, but my stipulations do not determine what is to happen in at least some eventualities. I become the beneficiary to the extent of that omission. Say I transfer property to you, making it clear that you are to be its trustee, but continuing, 'I'll tell you later what to do with it': you hold it on trust for me.[36] Or say I transfer property to you on trust for Adam for his life, with no stipulation as to what should happen after his death: you hold it for Adam for life, and for me thereafter. Or say I transfer property to you on trust for my descendants, and the trust is to some extent invalid for perpetuity:[37] you hold for my descendants so far as that is permitted, and otherwise for me. Cases of this kind can be referred to as 'incomplete express trust' cases.

The other class of case in which a resulting trust can arise is where I transfer property to you apparently as a gift, ie gratuitously rather than by way of sale or loan, and you cannot establish that my transfer was indeed a gift.[38] A variant on this is the case where I pay a third party to transfer property to you, apparently as a gift to you on my part: again, if you cannot establish that I did indeed make you a gift, you hold the property on trust for me.[39] The common factor is that I am the provider of the property. These cases may be called 'apparent gift' cases. In them, I do not actually intend to make a trust, but the law presumes that I do so, ie treats me as so intending: which is enough to bring the case within the rule that a resulting trust can arise only where there is such an intention.

You can rebut this presumption that I intend you to hold an apparent gift on trust. You can do so either by evidence, or by invoking the

---

[34] *Westdeutsche Landesbank Girozentrale v Islington LBC* [1996] AC 669, 708. Likewise W Swadling (1996) 16 LS 133 and in P Birks and F Rose (eds) *Lessons of the Swaps Litigation* (2000) ch 9.

[35] Ibid.

[36] *Re Boyes* (1884) 26 Ch D 531; *Vandervell v IRC* [1967] 2 AC 291.

[37] See section 2.5.

[38] *Dyer v Dyer* (1788) 2 Cox Eq 92; *The Venture* [1908] P 218.

[39] If you and I each pay part of the price, the trust is for both of us, in proportion to our shares in the price.

'presumption of advancement', by which an apparent gift which you cannot otherwise prove to have been a gift is nonetheless taken as one if I am your father[40] or husband.[41] Both the presumption against a gift and the counter-presumption of advancement reflect a set of bygone social concerns, however, and today seem to operate largely in defiance of facilitative logic, according to which I should be free to make, or not make, transfers in whatever shape I please.[42] They are no longer regarded as strong, and the vast majority of cases are settled by ordinary evidence, including common sense inference,[43] as a result of which most apparent gifts will of course turn out to be gifts. The presumption of advancement has been disparaged by the courts,[44] and some believe that there is no longer a presumption against a gift where the property in question is land.[45] A strong case can be made for abolishing both presumptions altogether. A gratuitous transfer from me to you would then take effect as a gift unless I prove I intended you to take the property on trust. If I succeed in proving that, but have not identified the trust's objects, the trust would be an incomplete express trust and a resulting trust could arise on that footing.

Give or take such doubts about the place of the apparent gift class in today's law, these two classes of case are undoubtedly the major traditional instances of resulting trusts. But excluded by the rule under discussion, that a resulting trust can arise only if its settlor intended to make a trust in the first place, are situations of other kinds which previous authority had nonetheless treated as involving resulting trusts. These are situations where a person acquires property improperly, so that although she becomes its legal owner we reckon that she holds it on trust for the person deprived. The latter does not intend to create any trust, either because he is unaware that the property is being transferred at all, or

---

[40] *Grey v Grey* (1677) 2 Sw 594. Or if I stand *in loco parentis* to you: *Powys v Mansfield* (1835) 3 Myl & Cr 359. According to a number of Commonwealth cases also if I am your mother (eg *Brown v Brown* (1993) 31 NSWLR 582, Australia); but according to English law not in this case (*Bennet v Bennet* (1879) 10 Ch D 474), though the relationship will count as strong evidence in favour of a gift.

[41] *Kingdon v Bridges* (1688) 2 Vern 67.

[42] See section 3.7.

[43] *Fowkes v Pascoe* (1875) LR 10 Ch App 343; *Bennet v Bennet* (1879) 10 Ch D 474; *Standing v Bowring* (1885) 31 Ch D 282; *Vandervell v IRC* [1967] 2 AC 291, 312–13.

[44] See especially *Pettitt v Pettitt* [1970] AC 777, 793, 811, 824, regarding transfers from husband to wife.

[45] *Tinsley v Milligan* [1994] 1 AC 340; 371; *Lohia v Lohia* [2001] W & TLR 101, pointing to the Law of Property Act 1925 s 60(3). Note also *Fowkes v Pascoe* (1875) LR 10 Ch App 343, 348.

because he at the time intends to pass it fully to the transferee, and we come to reckon that the transferee must hold it on trust for him only when he later rescinds, ie backs out of, the transaction on account of the improper quality.[46] If these trusts cannot be resulting, they probably survive as constructive.[47] But their exclusion from the resulting category, where they were previously thought to belong, raises a query over the rule responsible for that exclusion. Lord Browne-Wilkinson unfortunately offers no justification for it.

7.6 THE BASIS OF RESULTING TRUSTS

The second of Lord Browne-Wilkinson's propositions about resulting trusts is that such trusts arise so as to give effect to the common intention of the settlor and the trustee.[48] This proposition differentiates resulting trusts radically from constructive trusts, of which it is certainly not true.[49]

We can assume that the intention which his Lordship demands is a presumed rather than an actual one. The settlors of trusts regarded as resulting do not commonly actually intend them, and neither do their trustees. And if actual intention was required, it would be hard to point to the differentiation which normal usage, and section 53 of the Law of Property Act 1925, assume to exist between resulting trusts and express trusts. Indeed, even reference to a presumed intention puts pressure on that differentiation. As we saw in Chapter 3, in a number of express trust cases the finding as to the settlor's intention is in fact based on a presumption, rather than naturalistic.

His Lordship does not explain the basis for presuming the required common intention that a trust arises for the settlor. The answer is

---

[46] *Ryall v Ryall* (1739) 1 Atk 59; *Lane v Dighton* (1762) Amb 409; *Agip (Africa) Ltd v Jackson* [1990] Ch 265, 290; *El Ajou v Dollar Land Holdings plc* [1993] 3 All ER 717, 734. It is possible to read some remarks in *Hodgson v Marks* [1971] Ch 892, 933 as in the same vein. More recently, too, note *Collings v Lee* [2001] 2 All ER 332, though the judgment asserts, at 336, 'whether the trust should be characterised as implied, resulting or constructive is a matter of no importance'.

[47] *Westdeutsche Landesbank Girozentrale v Islington LBC* [1996] AC 669, 716, so characterizing the trust which arises when you steal my coins and mix them with your own. As explained in section 8.1, this scenario is treated as one where you improperly take a transfer of the coins, and I necessarily have no intention to establish a trust.

[48] [1996] AC 669, 708.

[49] One type of constructive trust (ostensibly) requires the beneficiary and trustee to have had a certain common intention, but requires other things too, and does not operate simply to give effect to that common intention. See section 8.11. Accepting the radical differentiation from constructive trusts, Lord Browne-Wilkinson asserts that the latter are 'imposed by law against the intentions of the trustee', but this is inaccurate: see section 7.1.

probably that this intention is the one the settlor and trustee would have held in the relevant circumstances (ie the incomplete express trust and apparent gift scenarios), if they had thought about the matter. It follows that if the settlor and/or trustee would *not* have intended a trust for the settlor to arise, there will be no room for a presumed intention to the contrary, and so, on this reckoning, there cannot be a resulting trust. So if the courts have in fact found resulting trusts where the settlor and/or trustee would not have wanted them, the basis for these trusts cannot lie in a presumed common intention. And this appears to be the case.

Take first the assertion that a resulting trust arises partly because, and therefore only if, the person held to be its trustee would have intended it to. It is hard to see why this person would ever so intend. Since in the absence of a resulting trust she would retain the property for herself, there is every reason why she should not intend to hold it for the settlor. Reference to the intentions of the trustee is not to be found elsewhere, and no explanation for it is offered by Lord Browne-Wilkinson. Perhaps the demand is less for intention (implying concurrence) than for knowledge (with no such implication) on the trustee's part, for Lord Browne-Wilkinson, in the same decision,[50] asserted the latter to be essential to all trusts. In section 1.13, however, we doubted the latter view too.

It is at first sight more plausible that the settlor would want a resulting trust where she makes an apparent gift which is not proved to be a gift, or an incomplete express trust. But it is not always so. The settlor of an incomplete express trust would sometimes prefer a resulting trust not to arise. But, it was settled in *Vandervell v IRC*,[51] the law imposes one nonetheless. The claim that a resulting trust arose was made by the revenue authorities, seeking to recover the tax which the settlor owed if this claim was right; the settlor, seeking to escape paying the tax, argued *against* a resulting trust. The House of Lords held that a resulting trust arose. This decision is incompatible, therefore, with the proposition that a resulting trust arises because, and therefore only if, the settlor would have intended it to. As a decision of the House of Lords, Lord

---

[50] *Westdeutsche Landesbank Girozentrale v Islington LBC* [1996] AC 669, 705–6, 715.

[51] [1967] 2 AC 291 (*Re Gillingham Bus Disaster Fund* [1958] Ch 300 is to the same effect). Reflecting this decision, Megarry J in *Re Vandervell's Trusts (No 2)* [1974] Ch 269, 289 asserted that resulting trusts arise in apparent gift cases because of a presumed intention on the part of the settlor (though not also the trustee); but in incomplete express trust cases 'automatically', ie without need of any form of intention. Lord Browne-Wilkinson in *Westdeutsche Landesbank Girozentrale v Islington LBC* [1996] AC 669, 708 disapproves Megarry J's analysis, in favour of that discussed in the text, but does not explain how he avoids the reasons which led Megarry J to it.

Browne-Wilkinson would surely have had to make an explicit statement if he meant to depart from it. No such statement is to be found, however.

On reflection, therefore, it is impossible to say that resulting trusts are based on the presumed common intention of their settlor and trustee, or even on the presumed intention of their settlor alone. Given the authoritative status of Lord Browne-Wilkinson's view to the contrary, however, no other judicial account of the issue can be said to represent the law.[52] There appears to be a juridical vacuum on the subject, therefore.

7.7 AN ALTERNATIVE BASIS FOR RESULTING TRUSTS

How might that vacuum best be filled? It would be satisfying to explain all resulting trusts by a single account. Evidently, no account can explain all resulting trusts if it ascribes such trusts to the parties', or even only the settlor's, intentions. The obvious candidate is an account grounded in the second basis for trusts identified in our initial 'definition', namely the effect of 'other legally significant circumstances'. These circumstances must consist in the facts which the law treats as generating a resulting trust. And it must be shown why they predicate that effect.

The best account, it is suggested, runs as follows. The transferee of some property should hold it on trust for the transferor, aside from the case where the transferor so stipulates, whenever the transferor has not demonstrably chosen to give his property away and succeeded in doing so. That idea is in turn justified by the insight that whenever someone has not demonstrably chosen to give his property away and succeeded in doing so, he should remain its owner. Call the latter insight 'proprietary inertia'. It is rooted in a liberal vision of the institution of property. To give an owner maximal freedom in the disposition of his assets,[53] it is necessary maximally to treat them as for him alone to dispose of.[54]

---

[52] More recent statements in the Privy Council in *Air Jamaica Ltd v Charlton* [1999] 1 WLR 1399, 1412, and in the Court of Appeal in *Twinsectra Ltd v Yardley* [1999] Lloyd's Rep Bank 438, 457, took a different view, which is discussed below (n 65 below). These statements possess no authority, however, as they contain no reference to Lord Browne-Wilkinson's analysis.

[53] Cf section 2.2.

[54] If there were no rivals to this liberal theory, we would not accept the possibility of property being lost to its previous owner in any other way. But in the real world considerations ascribable to other theories call for this and are accepted. For example, we have to pay taxes even if we do not wish to, in causes broadly perceivable as utilitarian or communitarian.

Proprietary inertia operates in its simplest form where the owner in no sense loses his title: if you steal my pen, say, it merely remains mine. But the insight operates also in the more complex case, generated by the possibilities of the trust device, where the legal title has effectively been transferred, but its previous owner has neither (intentionally and effectively) conferred beneficial ownership on the transferee nor (likewise) alienated it in some other direction.[55] The logic of the insight is that in such a situation the previous owner should be treated as himself retaining beneficial ownership. That is achieved by saying that the transferee of the legal title holds it on trust for the previous owner.

The resulting trust which arises in the case of an incomplete express trust is readily explained in this way. If I transfer property to you on an incomplete express trust, there exists, to the extent of the incompleteness, a situation of my not intentionally and effectively having given my property away. The insight's corollary, that I should to that extent remain the owner, is achieved by the imposition of a resulting trust.[56]

The resulting trust arising in the apparent gift situation can likewise be explained in this way, if we view the presumption involved as saying merely that in making you an apparent gift, I do not intend you (or anyone else) to have the benefit of the property given.[57] The situation thus emerges as an incomplete express trust, the intention required for the generation of an express trust being established by the presumption. So once again I have not intentionally and effectively given my property away, and a resulting trust arises to secure that I remain its owner. (We might, however, regard the presumption as saying that in making you an apparent gift, I positively intend you to hold it on trust for me. On this view, as suggested already, it is hard to see why the trust for me is not simply an express trust, found on the basis of a presumed intention.)

The analysis thus offers a workable explanation of the trusts which

[55] The text says 'alienated it in some other direction', rather than simply 'conferred it on someone else', to allow for the possibility of a purpose trust, charitable or otherwise (see section 1.5). Subsequent statements of the proprietary inertia thesis should be read in the same way.

[56] Except where the express trust is charitable, when (unless the failure was initial and there was no general charitable intent) the property is instead applied cy près, ie to an analogous charitable purpose: see section 6.1. This departure from the liberally based proprietary inertia thesis can be explained on the utilitarian and/or communitarian grounds to which charitable trusts especially appeal: see section 6.2.

[57] Section 3.7 notes the argument that this presumption should be abandoned. If that occurred, you would hold an apparent gift on trust for me only if I proved that I expressly gave you the property on trust, either avowedly for myself or without completely stipulating for whom or for what.

Lord Browne-Wilkinson refers to as resulting trusts. It also, however, accounts for, and so demands that we regard as resulting trusts, certain other trusts which, as we saw in section 7.5, his Lordship refuses, contrary to earlier authority,[58] to accept as resulting trusts. These are the trusts which arise where you acquire my property improperly. Such cases are of two kinds. The first is where, although I did not intentionally transfer a legal title to you, the law treats me as having done so, while it is acknowledged that I did not intentionally and effectively confer the benefit of the property on you or in any other quarter. And the second is, where I did intentionally transfer property to you, but the improper quality of the transaction (say, your having deceived me as to its nature) allows me to 'rescind' the transfer, ie reverse its effects, and I do so: the legal title remains with you, but my rescission, reversing the effects of the transfer, requires the law to treat me as not having given you (or anyone else) the benefit of the property.[59] Take an example involving a case of the first kind. You steal my coins and mix them with your own. At any rate the traditional view is that, because of the impossibility of saying which of the coins now in your pocket came from me, I can no longer claim to be their owner: so you are.[60] I am thus treated as having transferred the legal title in them to you. It is agreed, however, that I did not intentionally and effectively confer the benefit of the coins on you or in any other quarter. The logic of proprietary inertia is that you, who now have the legal title to the coins, hold them (in the shape of a proportionate part of the mixture) on trust for me.

Reckoning those trusts predicated by proprietary inertia to be resulting, we should regard this as a resulting trust. But while Lord Browne-Wilkinson agrees that there should be a trust for me as described, he

[58] N 46 above.

[59] Prior to my rescission, it is true to say that I transferred the property to you with a flawed intention to confer it on you; and it might be argued that a flawed intention is not enough to separate me from my property, so that a resulting trust should arise. But the prevailing (though not unchallenged) judicial view is that there is no trust: see most recently *Twinsectra Ltd v Yardley* [2002] 2 WLR 802, 827, para 91. Further exploration of the issue is left to section 8.1, because the trust for which the argument contends would, following the ruling by Lord Browne-Wilkinson noted in section 7.5, be constructive rather than resulting.

[60] This is based on *Taylor v Plumer* (1815) 3 M & S 562. But this reading of the case is arguably wrong (L Smith *The Law of Tracing* (1997) 162–71), meaning that I can after all assert ownership, if not of the very coins taken, of a proportionate part of the mixture. The unintended 'transfer', which the trust corrects, would then not occur. If a different example therefore had to be sought, it might involve a transfer of land, unintended by the previous owner: when the transferee is registered as the land's new owner, that is conclusive that he has the legal title to it. Cf *Collings v Lee* [2001] 2 All ER 332.

insists, because of his view that resulting trusts can arise only in the incomplete express trust and apparent gift cases, that it is a constructive trust.[61] It is possible (and practically unproblematic, for the law generally treats resulting and constructive trusts alike) to divide trusts arising by reason of proprietary inertia into resulting and constructive categories in this way. But given what the present discussion suggests to be the common basis of these trusts, there is no reason to do so. Given his Lordship's insistence upon the division, however, the cases which he holds to involve constructive trusts will be returned to in the next chapter, which deals with such trusts.

The analysis proposed here was developed from two other suggestions as to the basis for resulting trusts. These other suggestions, however, have certain problems, which the proprietary inertia insight is designed to avoid.

The first of these other suggestions is the 'proprietary arithmetic' thesis. According to it, a resulting trust arises because a transferor of property necessarily (as a matter of arithmetic) retains so much of the beneficial entitlement to it as she has not given away (by giving it absolutely to the transferee, or by establishing a complete express trust of it).[62] Operating at the level of legal doctrine, this formulation is problematic in the way it presents a beneficial interest as existing in the settlor's hands even before the transfer, ie at the time when she was absolute legal owner. The contrary view, that beneficial interests exist only as the correlatives of trustees' duties[63] and so cannot exist before the transfer to the resulting trustee, is more generally favoured.[64] The proprietary inertia insight avoids this difficulty. Operating at the level of political theory, this insight merely observes that I should not be taken to have conferred benefits in

---

[61] *Westdeutsche Landesbank Girozentrale v Islington LBC* [1996] AC 669, 716. Lord Browne-Wilkinson does not deal explicitly with the second kind of improper acquisition trust, ie that arising after rescission; but he must regard it as likewise constructive, as arising in circumstances other than those which he regards as generating a resulting trust (section 7.5). It was however described as resulting in the earlier decision *El Ajou v Dollar Land Holdings plc* [1993] 3 All ER 717, 734.

[62] J Hackney *Understanding Equity and Trusts* (1987) 153–4. This seems to be the approach of the House of Lords in *Vandervell v IRC* [1967] 2 AC 291, 313–14, 329.

[63] See section 14.2.

[64] *Commissioner of Stamp Duties (Queensland) v Livingston* [1965] AC 694, 712; *Westdeutsche Landesbank Girozentrale v Islington LBC* [1996] AC 669, 706. So in *DKLR Holding Co (No 2) Pty Ltd v Commissioner of Stamp Duties* (1982) 40 ALR 1, Australia, where, unusually, it made a practical difference (for tax reasons) whether the resulting trust interest remained in the transferor throughout or arose by detraction from the transferee, the court held the latter.

other quarters except by voluntary disposition, and to the extent that I am not so taken, I should be treated as remaining owner myself. It is indifferent whether the legal rule aimed at achieving this conceives me as remaining beneficial owner throughout, or as newly becoming beneficial owner when the occasion arises.

The second suggestion portrays resulting trusts as generated by a lack of intention on the transferor's part that the transferee should have the benefit of the property transferred.[65] Thus, the settlor of an incomplete express trust does not intend the trustee to have the undisposed-of benefit, and the maker of an apparent gift which the recipient cannot prove to be a gift is taken not to intend the recipient to enjoy it beneficially. The similarity between this account and the proprietary inertia thesis is clear: the former talks of the owner not intending the transferee to have the benefit of the property, while the latter talks of the owner of property not voluntarily conferring the benefit of it in another quarter. The proprietary inertia thesis is presented here as preferable for two reasons. First, because it is more explicit about why this circumstance should generate a resulting trust (because to the extent that the owner has not conferred the benefit of the property elsewhere, it should remain his), and about the basis on which we should agree that in turn to be the case (the liberal vision of property). Secondly, because of its assertion that, when I transfer to you, a resulting trust is negatived by my intention to confer the benefit not only on you but also in any other quarter. It is this feature of the thesis that precludes a resulting trust where I transfer property to you as trustee of a complete express trust for some other person(s) or purpose(s). At face value, the second suggestion seems to demand a resulting trust even in that situation, for there too I transfer to you, not intending you to take beneficially. That position is unthinkable, of course; the second suggestion cannot but be amended accordingly.[66] Following the apparent position of the second suggestion, however, the Privy Council has asserted that there is a resulting trust for me wherever I transfer

---

[65] P Birks in S Goldstein (ed) *Equity and Contemporary Legal Developments* (1992) 335; R Chambers *Resulting Trusts* (1997). This view was adopted by the Privy Council in *Air Jamaica Ltd v Charlton* [1999] 1 WLR 1399, 1412, and by the Court of Appeal in *Twinsectra Ltd v Yardley* [1999] Lloyd's Rep Bank 438, 457, without however reference to the position taken by the House of Lords in *Westdeutsche Landesbank Girozentrale v Islington LBC* [1996] AC 669.

[66] Perhaps we should say that if I transfer property to you to hold on trust for some other person(s) or purpose(s), the beneficial entitlement is not part of that which I transfer to you, so it cannot result to me. But this approach seems to assume that the beneficial entitlement was separate from the legal title in my hands; a conception not generally favoured: see n 64 above.

property to you and do not intend you to have it, even despite an intention on my part to abandon my interest, ie to relinquish it as *bona vacantia* to the Crown.[67] Assuming that I am legally able to abandon my interest,[68] the proprietary inertia thesis produces the opposite conclusion: since I intended to confer the benefit in some other quarter,[69] there is no resulting trust.

---

[67] *Air Jamaica Ltd v Charlton* [1999] 1 WLR 1399, 1412. To justify its finding that the transferor had an interest under a resulting trust at the date of the claim, moreover, the Privy Council must also have assumed that such an interest cannot be given away after it has arisen. That assumption is contradicted by *Re Vandervell's Trusts (No 2)* [1974] Ch 269, where (though there was a difficulty about formality: see section 5.7) there was a successful disposition of an existing resulting trust interest.

[68] Authority (*Re West Sussex Constabulary's Widows, Children and Benevolent (1930) Fund Trusts* [1971] Ch 1) holds that I am, but R Chambers *Resulting Trusts* (1997) 58–66 contends that I am not. The Privy Council did not rely on the latter argument, however.

[69] Note that saying 'I intentionally and effectively confer the benefit in some other quarter; specifically, I abandon it' is not the same as saying 'I would not have wanted a resulting trust if I had thought about it'. The former precludes a resulting trust; the latter does not, either in law (*Re Gillingham Bus Disaster Fund* [1958] Ch 300; *Vandervell v IRC* [1967] 2 AC 291: see n 51 above) or in the terms of the proprietary inertia thesis. An inferred case of the former may however sometimes more truthfully consist in the latter: the intention to render the property ownerless in *Re West Sussex Constabulary's Widows, Children and Benevolent (1930) Fund Trusts* [1971] Ch 1 might be seen in this way.

8

Instances of constructive trusts

We turn now to consider a number of the situations in which a constructive trust occurs in English law, and the grounds on which it does so.

8.1 UNINTENDED TRANSFERS

Where the owner of some property transfers it to another (or is treated as doing so) without intending to do so, the transferee will hold it on constructive trust for the transferor, unless the unintended transfer is justified in some other way.

In particular contexts, the law may be justified in passing my property to another when I do not so intend. That is the case, for example, if my property has to be taken to pay my debts. Outside these contexts, however, the law adopts a liberal position, to the effect that you acquire my property when, but only when, I intend you to. If I give you a book as a present, I intend you to become owner of the book, and you do. But if you snatch my book from me, I do not intend you to become its owner, and you do not: it remains mine. We encountered this position in section 7.7, calling it 'proprietary inertia'.

In most cases where I do not intend to transfer my property to you (and which do not involve legitimate confiscation), the effect is simply that you do not in any sense acquire it: as where you snatch my book. Sometimes, though, the law says that you do become owner of the property, but gives expression to proprietary inertia instead by going on to say that you hold the property on trust for me. We should expect the law to treat all trusts ascribable to proprietary inertia alike. In fact, the prevailing law divides them into two classes. As section 7.7 also explained, those arising in the special situation where I intend to create a trust (or I am treated as so intending) are termed resulting trusts, while the remainder are termed constructive trusts.[1] This chapter being about constructive trusts, we shall avoid further allusion to the former class.

---

[1] *Westdeutsche Landesbank Girozentrale v Islington LBC* [1996] AC 669, 708, 716.

As further noted in section 7.7, trusts thus described as constructive arise on account of proprietary inertia in two situations.

One is where, although I did not intentionally transfer the legal title in the property to you, the law treats me as having done so, while nonetheless acknowledging that I did not mean you to have the property. Remember the case where you steal my coins and mix them with your own. As we saw, owing to the impossibility of saying which of the coins came from me, I can no longer claim to be their owner, so you are.[2] The result is a technical but unintended transfer. The law imposes a constructive trust, to the effect that you hold the mixture on trust for yourself and me in proportion to the value of our contributions to the mixture.[3] Or say you procure, without my knowledge, that my land is reregistered in your name. The register is conclusive as to ownership, so again there is a technical but unintended transfer. You hold the land on constructive trust for me.[4]

The other situation in which a constructive trust arises on account of proprietary inertia is where I transfer property to you intentionally, but in circumstances where my intention is flawed, say because I acted mistakenly.[5] The flawed quality of my intention is recognized by a rule allowing me to rescind the transfer, ie reverse its effects. If I do so, proprietary inertia logic becomes applicable, as the intention underpinning your acquisition of the property has now been removed. So although you for the moment still hold the legal title to the transferred property, you hold it on constructive trust for me. And that trust appears to operate retrospectively, so that you are treated as having held it on trust for me from the outset.[6]

Unless and until I rescind, however, the prevailing judicial view is that

---

[2] Though L Smith *The Law of Tracing* (1997) 162–71 argues that this reading of *Taylor v Plumer* (1815) 3 M & S 562 is wrong, and that I can after all assert ownership of a proportionate part of the mixture.

[3] *Westdeutsche Landesbank Girozentrale v Islington LBC* [1996] AC 669, 716.

[4] *Collings v Lee* [2001] 2 All ER 332. The previous owner was in fact duped into transferring the land into the transferee's name. The court treated this as showing that the previous owner lacked any intention to transfer to the transferee. That is defensible, but it would also have been possible to say that the transfer to the transferee was intended, but that that intention was flawed, making the case of the type discussed below.

[5] Or under duress or undue influence or in certain other similar circumstances.

[6] So, for example, I collect any profits you have meanwhile made from it (section 8.5), and can trace through any mixture you may have made with it (section 8.6): *El Ajou v Dollar Land Holdings plc* [1993] 3 All ER 717, 734. (The trust is there referred to as resulting, but that label cannot stand with the view taken of resulting trusts in *Westdeutsche Landesbank Girozentrale v Islington LBC* [1996] AC 669, 708.)

you do not hold the transferred property on trust for me.[7] An argument can be made that you should do so: that even without rescission, a flawed intention should be regarded as no intention, producing an unintended transfer and so, for reasons of proprietary inertia, a constructive trust.[8] The counter-argument, however, is that to impose a trust before rescission is to be over-draconian. Other things being equal, if you receive property from me in the kind of circumstances under discussion, you will have to repay me its value.[9] But that obligation is a merely personal one, not carrying the advantages for me (such as priority in your bankruptcy) of the proprietary obligations associated with trusts.[10] Those advantages are damaging to other parties, especially to your other creditors; saying that you hold the transferred asset on constructive trust withdraws it from the pool of your property available for distribution among the latter. The trust response, featuring those advantages, should therefore be reserved for the case where my claim is strongest, perhaps only the case where I have not even apparently made an intentional transfer of the property, though it would be little extension to add the case where I make the transfer under duress. Reflecting such considerations, the law imposes certain limitations on my right to rescind.[11] If any transfer made

---

[7] *Daly v Sydney Stock Exchange Ltd* (1986) 160 CLR 371, 387–90, Australia; *Guinness plc v Saunders* [1990] 2 AC 663, 698; *Lonrho plc v Fayed (No 2)* [1992] 1 WLR 1, 11–12; *Collings v Lee* [2001] 2 All ER 332, 337; *Twinsectra Ltd v Yardley* [2002] 2 WLR 802, 827 para 91. *Westdeutsche Landesbank Girozentrale v Islington LBC* [1996] AC 669, 689–90, 709, 718, 720, 738 appears to like effect. But at 714–15, Lord Browne-Wilkinson asserts that there is a constructive trust *from the time the transferee knows of the flaw in the transferor's intention*. His Lordship was discussing *Chase Manhattan Bank NA v Israel-British Bank (London) Ltd* [1981] Ch 105, which had found a trust in these circumstances, though without stating the recipient's knowledge to be crucial. The idea that it is appears to be a product of the general view taken in *Westdeutsche Landesbank Girozentrale v Islington LBC* [1996] AC 669, 705 — that one cannot become a trustee without knowing the facts generating the trust; that view was doubted in section 1.13. If the transferor's intention can indeed be negated by mistakes, etc., the logic of proprietary inertia should entail a trust regardless of the transferee's state of mind.

[8] P Birks in S Goldstein (ed) *Equity and Contemporary Legal Developments* (1992) 335; R Chambers *Resulting Trusts* (1997) chs 5 and 6 (addressing themselves to resulting trusts, however, for they do not accept the restriction of these to incomplete express trust and apparent gift cases; and using an analysis similar, though not identical, to proprietary inertia).

[9] On mistaken payments, see *Morgan v Ashcroft* [1938] 1 KB 49; *Barclays Bank Ltd v W J Simms (Southern) Ltd* [1980] QB 677; *Kleinwort Benson Ltd v Lincoln City Council* [1999] 2 AC 349.

[10] See sections 1.9, 14.1.

[11] For example, an unexercised right to rescind will lapse if the transferor, knowing of the flaw, concedes the transaction's effectiveness, or delays unacceptably ('is guilty of laches') in rescinding it. In some circumstances, it will not be exercisable if a court regards monetary redress to the transferor as adequate remedy (Misrepresentation Act 1967 s 2(2)). And it

on the basis of a flawed intention gave rise to a constructive trust, those limitations would be undermined.

There is however a suggestion in *Westdeutsche Landesbank Girozentrale v Islington LBC*[12] that a rule either way (ie that the transferee does, or does not, hold on trust in such circumstances) may be less attractive than one giving courts discretion to award the greater advantages of a trust in flawed intention cases where they are satisfied that all things considered this is the most appropriate response. The device contemplated here is a remedial constructive trust, as discussed in section 7.3.

8.2 TRANSFERS UPON HOMICIDE

If you acquire property from me by committing certain forms of homicide against me, you will hold that property on constructive trust.[13] The forms of homicide in question are all cases of murder, and some cases of manslaughter.[14] So if you are a legatee under my will, and so inherit on my death, you will in such a case hold your inheritance on constructive trust.[15] Similarly if you inherit as my intestate successor, ie the person who inherits my property if I leave no will.[16] The constructive trust will be for the person or persons who would inherit the property in question if you were overlooked. In the case of a bequest to you, then, the constructive trust would be in favour of the person entitled to the residue of my estate; in the case of intestate succession, to my next closest relative.

By committing homicide against me, you will have done me a wrong; and if you inherit as a result, you will have profited from that wrong. This

---

will be ineffective not only (like a constructive trust) against a bona fide purchaser for value of a legal interest in the property transferred, but (except if the property is registered land: Land Registration Act 2002 s 116) also against such a purchaser of an equitable right in it: *Phillips v Phillips* (1861) 4 De G F & J 208; *Latec Investments Ltd v Hotel Terrigal Pty Ltd* (1965) 113 CLR 265, Australia (cf D O'Sullivan (2002) 118 LQR 296).

[12] [1996] AC 669, 716.

[13] T Youdan (1973) 89 LQR 235.

[14] *Gray v Barr* [1971] 2 QB 554, 581 suggests that only more serious cases of manslaughter would attract a constructive trust, and the Forfeiture Act 1982 allows the court to disapply the trust in such cases of manslaughter as seem not to warrant it. (See eg *Re K (deceased)* [1986] Ch 180.) The contrasting rule as regards murder may infringe Art 1 of the First Protocol to the ECHR as redistributing property in a manner disproportionate (in its inflexibility, given the range of seriousness of murder cases too) to the public interest at stake.

[15] *In the estate of Crippen* [1911] P 108.

[16] *Re Sigsworth* [1935] 1 Ch 89. Likewise if you gain because you are a joint tenant with me, in which event my death necessarily vests the whole property in you: *Re K (deceased)* [1986] Ch 180.

might well be enough to make the law deprive you of that profit, but it does not obviously entail that you should hold the inheritance on constructive trust, as though it should not be yours at all. A constructive trust would make sense if, as in the previous section, the nature of your wrong meant I had no intention to pass you the property, or flawed my intention and I rescinded the transfer. In the case under discussion, I certainly intended to pass you the property: that is how you inherit at all. My intention does appear to be flawed, albeit in an unusual way: it can be assumed that a homicide victim would not, in retrospect, have chosen to leave property to her killer. Certainly, I cannot rescind now that I am dead, though it can, again, be assumed that I would have wished to do so. The fact that I no longer have the opportunity to rescind is not merely a coincidence, however, but the product of the wrong itself. That makes it right to treat it as your problem rather than mine, and so to treat the situation as though I had rescinded, leaving you holding the property in question on constructive trust.

8.3 RECIPIENTS OF TRUST PROPERTY

If I, a trustee for Adam, transfer my trust's assets to you, you in turn will generally hold them on constructive trust for Adam.[17] All trusts have some proprietary obligations, which affect all, such as you, who take the property to which those obligations relate.[18]

The basis of this trust is the reflection that I cannot give you more than I have myself.[19] This reflection is often put in the Latin form '*nemo dat quod non habet*'. If in my hands the assets have a set of obligations attached to them,[20] I cannot give them to you shorn of those obligations, because in that form the assets are not mine to give. The reflection is rooted in liberal property theory, to which we have already made reference.[21] The obligations attached to the assets reflect other interests

---

[17] According to Lord Browne-Wilkinson in *Westdeutsche Landesbank Girozentrale v Islington LBC* [1996] AC 669, 707, this situation is only to be termed a 'trust' if you are aware that I held the property on trust, but that view is generally rejected: see section 1.13. His Lordship accepts that a recipient lacking such awareness does not simply become absolute owner; in his view, in this (innominate) situation the recipient may not treat the property as his own, ie must give it up if called upon to do so.

[18] See section 14.1.

[19] *Re Nisbet and Potts' Contract* [1906] 1 Ch 386.

[20] Which is what it means to say that those obligations are proprietary: see sections 1.9, 14.1.

[21] See sections 2.2, 7.7.

existing in them. Letting me deal with the assets only to the extent that they are mine respects the monopoly over the disposal of those interests that the liberal vision of property accords *their* owner.

There are two situations in which the trust does not arise in this way. One is where the transfer to you was a legitimate one for me to make. Trustees legitimately transfer trust property all the time, as they treat their trust's assets as investments, selling them and buying others in their place. In those circumstances, the trust obligations are 'overreached', ie cease to attach to the property, at the moment of sale: so the property which reaches the transferee is no longer trust property. (Instead, the obligations attach to the money which the trustee receives in return.) But if, say, I sell trust property to you as if it were my own, in return for a payment into my private account, the transaction is unlawful and there will be no overreaching. Overreached obligations do not bind transferees because the transferring trustees are authorized to transfer the property without them. The second situation is where you are a bona fide purchaser of the property, for value, and without notice of its being trust property unlawfully transferred. Then, you cannot be affected by trust obligations relating to that property (and nor can anyone who takes the property after you).[22] Left vulnerable to the constructive trust are those who buy with notice[23] of their purchase's provenance; and those who take the property as a gift (sometimes called 'volunteers'), whether they have notice or not. But those who buy trust property innocently are protected. This rule is of course logically incompatible with the rule (in favour of a constructive trust) to which it is expressed as an exception. The fact that the transferee is a bona fide purchaser does not alter the transferring trustees' inability to transfer the property shorn of its proprietary obligations. It is explicable on the ground that the liberal vision underlying the usual rule can be overridden where more powerful considerations so require: and here a more powerful consideration, namely a desire to facilitate trade, does so require.

[22] *Wilkes v Spooner* [1911] 2 KB 473.

[23] The exact meaning of 'notice' varies between contexts. Possible meanings range from 'a situation in which a scrupulous purchaser would, by inquiry if necessary, have discovered the fact of the trust' to 'actual knowledge on the part of this individual purchaser'. The former was characteristically used where the property in question was land, though in land cases the use of notice has largely been supplanted by the rules in the Land Registration Acts 1925 and 2002. The latter meaning seems to be favoured in cases where the trust property is not land (*Polly Peck International plc v Nadir (No 2)* [1992] 4 All ER 769, 781–2), though it is evidence that this purchaser had the required knowledge that a reasonable person (though not an especially scrupulous one, nor after extensive inquiries) would have realized the property's provenance (*Eagle Trust plc v SBC Securities Ltd* [1993] 1 WLR 484, 493).

If the original trust was an express trust, is the trust under discussion really a constructive trust; or are you, the recipient, simply bound by the original express trust? Certainly, the reason you are a trustee is that when you acquired the property you incurred the obligation to hold it on trust, which obligation sprang from the original settlor's intention: to that extent, the trust against you can rightly be regarded as express. On the other hand, you do not simply substitute for me as trustee of the express trust. A legitimately substituted trustee of the original express trust would take over all the obligations which I previously had. That is, if (as is normal) I had an obligation to manage and invest the trust property, and if (as is very common) I had an obligation to exercise discretions,[24] a substituted trustee would take over those obligations, as well as the basic obligation to treat the property not as his own but as the trust's. In the context we are discussing, however, that would be an inappropriate out-turn, as you were not selected to undertake the trusteeship by reference to your suitability to carry out those obligations, as an express trustee, whether original or substitute, would be.[25] So it is thought that such obligations are personal, and that the proprietary obligations by which you are affected are only those of respecting the fact that the property is not beneficially your own and of keeping it safe pending the transfer to the beneficiaries or to freshly appointed trustees that you may be called upon to make.[26] Regarding the trust against you as constructive reflects this discontinuity with the original express trust.[27]

8.4 AUTHORIZED ACQUISITIONS BY FIDUCIARIES

A fiduciary who is authorized to receive property on her principal's behalf, and who does so, will hold it on constructive trust for the principal.

A fiduciary is someone whose role it is to serve the interests of another, the principal.[28] A trustee[29] is a fiduciary *vis-à-vis* the beneficiaries of his

---

[24] See Chs 9 and 11 respectively.   [25] Cf section 13.8.   [26] See section 9.1.

[27] Cf L Smith in P Birks and A Pretto (eds) *Breach of Trust* (2002) ch 5.

[28] A person may become a fiduciary by being appointed as such by her principal, or by purporting to act on behalf of another without being appointed to do so (*English v Dedham Vale Properties Ltd* [1978] 1 WLR 93), or simply by being in the necessary relationship even if involuntarily (eg the parent of a child, occasionally treated as a fiduciary).

[29] Certainly an express trustee. Constructive trustees are generally under fewer duties, but these seem always to include the duty not to treat the property as their own (see section 9.1), which appears, being aimed at serving another, to be of a fiduciary nature.

trust. A solicitor is a fiduciary for his client: the client relies upon the solicitor to safeguard and prosecute his interests for him. Similarly the relationships between a stockbroker and client, an employee and employer, an agent and principal, a company director and his company, and between business partners.[30]

A person who finds herself in the role of fiduciary incurs duties designed to put detail into the idea of 'serve the interests of another'. One of these duties dictates that where the fiduciary acquires property on behalf of her principal, she will hold it on trust for the latter.

There are two situations in which a fiduciary might, with authorization, acquire property on her principal's behalf. One is where she already holds property on trust for the principal (which many, though not all, fiduciaries do: trustees themselves, for example), and then some proceeds of that property come into her hands. She will hold those proceeds likewise on trust. Say the assets of a trust, held by the trustee, comprise some company shares. If a dividend is paid on those shares, it will come to the trustee as the holder of the shares; and he will hold it on trust in the same way. Or say the trustee sells the shares, something which trustees are normally authorized to do. The money he receives (and anything he spends it on, such as new shares) will likewise be held on trust. The original trust may have been express or constructive (a secret trust, for example), but the trust of the proceeds will be constructive. The trust arises not, like an express trust, because the person transferring the property to the trustee so intends (this may or may not be the case), but because of the fiduciary's obligation to receive the property for her principal.

The other situation of this kind is where the fiduciary is authorized to receive on her principal's behalf property which the principal would

---

[30] The classic work is P Finn *Fiduciary Obligations* (1977). See also A Oakley *Constructive Trusts* 3rd edn (1997) 85–110, and further references there; C Harpum, L Hoyano, L Smith, J Glover, D Hayton in P Birks (ed) *Privacy and Loyalty* (1997) chs 7–11. One major question is whether fiduciary relationships or duties are properly found in contexts where economic interests are not at stake (cf *McInerney v MacDonald* (1992) 93 DLR (4th) 415, Canada; *M (K) v M (H)* (1993) 96 DLR (4th) 289, Canada). Surely yes, in principle: there is nothing in the essential idea of service to indicate that the service must be aimed at promoting the principal's economic interests. Another major question is whether such relationships or duties are properly found as between parties dealing with one another on a commercial basis (cf *Hospital Products Ltd v United States Surgical Corp* (1984) 156 CLR 41, Australia; *United Dominion Corp v Brian* (1985) 157 CLR 1, Australia; *LAC Minerals Ltd v International Corona Resources Ltd* (1989) 61 DLR (4th) 14, Canada; *Re Goldcorp Exchange* [1995] 1 AC 74; *Banner Homes Group plc v Luff Developments Ltd* [2000] Ch 372 essentially raises the same issue). Again, surely yes, in principle: the real question is not whether the relationship is commercial, but whether it amounts to a joint venture.

otherwise have had to receive directly. An agent arranging the sale of her principal's goods will commonly be authorized also to receive the buyer's payment for them, for example. In some cases, the fiduciary's terms of engagement leave her to treat the incoming property as her own (and thus to mix it with her own property, eg by running a single bank account), with liability only to reimburse the principal its value, ie to 'account' for it. Because in this instance the fiduciary has no duties regarding the use of the particular property received on the principal's behalf, there is no trust of it.[31] In other cases, however, she will be required to treat the property as the principal's (and so, in particular, not to mix it with her own). Here she will have duties regarding the particular property, and a trust does arise. For example, say I sell my house. The purchase money normally comes not directly to me, but to my solicitor. The solicitor is expected not merely to account to me for the money, but to treat it as mine. So she will, after making certain deductions,[32] hold it on constructive trust for me.[33]

The ability to transact through an agent is valuable: by permitting us to deal otherwise than directly with the other party, it allows us to deal more distantly and frequently. The ability to establish a trust is also valuable, in allowing, to various ends,[34] the separation of title to and enjoyment of property. But using an agent leaves a principal more vulnerable than acting on his own behalf, and relying on a trustee leaves him more vulnerable than holding the property in question himself. One source of this vulnerability relates especially to the case under consideration, where an agency arrangement or trust leaves the fiduciary to receive newly arriving property which would otherwise have gone direct to the principal: the principal is exposed to the risk of potential difficulties in recovering it from the fiduciary, starting with the fact that the principal may not even know of the payment's existence. Unless corrected, this consideration would reduce the attractiveness of using agents and trusts. The law supplies correction so far as it can by ruling that, unless it is arranged otherwise, a payment reaching the fiduciary is immediately held by her on constructive trust for the principal.

---

[31] This will commonly be the sensible construction where incoming payments are expected to fund continued trading by the agent; saying that she holds them on trust would destroy the necessary liquidity: *King v Hutton* [1899] 2 QB 555, [1900] 2 QB 504.

[32] The sums needed to repay my outstanding mortgage, to meet her own and the estate agent's costs, and to pay for any house I am buying.

[33] *Brown v IRC* [1965] AC 244.

[34] See section 1.8.

8.5 UNAUTHORIZED ACQUISITIONS BY FIDUCIARIES

When a fiduciary acquires property in her personal capacity, she will usually keep it for herself: there will be nothing in her duties to say otherwise. Say my trustee also has a job as an accountant and is paid a salary for it: her duties to me do not assert that she should hold that salary on trust for me or indeed account to me for it. But a fiduciary's duties forbid her to make certain kinds of personal acquisitions. If she nonetheless does so, in breach of these duties, she will hold the acquisition on constructive trust for her principal.

The existence of duties forbidding fiduciaries to make certain personal acquisitions is a further product of the project, identified in the previous section, to counter the factors which would otherwise discourage the use of fiduciaries. Whenever I leave another to prosecute my interests, there is a risk that she will concentrate less firmly on my interests than I would have done if I had acted for myself. Against this, the law imposes on her a duty not to allow herself to be distracted from the service of my interest.[35] This unpacks to a collection of more specific duties, above all proscribing the fiduciary from acquiring for herself property which it is her duty to try to acquire for her principal, and from accepting bribes calculated to influence the way she performs her work for her principal. If she acquires property in breach of such a proscription, she holds the property on constructive trust for her principal.

So say I work for a property development company, my job being to seek out suitable sites for the company. In the course of my work, I find a site which the company might like. If I buy it for myself without first asking the company's permission, I will hold it on constructive trust for the company.[36] Or say I am a solicitor. Approaching on a client's behalf a company in which the client is invested, I learn something which suggests that a further investment in the company will be profitable. If I make such an investment with my own money, without asking permission of my client, I will hold the shares in question on constructive trust for my

---

[35] Judicial statements and exemplifying decisions are legion; the most celebrated include *Aberdeen Railway Co v Blaikie Bros* (1854) 1 Macq 461, Scotland; *Bray v Ford* [1896] AC 44, 51; *Regal (Hastings) Ltd v Gulliver* [1967] 2 AC 134n; *Boardman v Phipps* [1967] 2 AC 46; *Hospital Products Ltd v US Surgical Corp* (1984) 156 CLR 41, Australia. Section 13.10 details and examines this duty more fully, with particular reference to its application to trustees.

[36] *Industrial Development Consultants Ltd v Cooley* [1972] 1 WLR 443 is similar.

client.[37] Or say I am a senior government administrator. I allow you to bribe me to take decisions favourable to you. I hold the bribe on constructive trust for the Crown.[38]

If the fiduciary has a duty to her principal not to make personal acquisitions in cases like these, we can easily understand that on making such an acquisition she will be liable to disgorge it to the principal: it represents a gain which she has made at the principal's expense in the sense of via breach of a duty owed to the principal. Why, however, should the vehicle for disgorgement be a rule that the fiduciary holds the acquisition on constructive trust for the principal, rather than one requiring her to account to him for it?[39]

As with the case of fiduciaries' authorized acquisitions, considered in the last section, the explanation is probably that imposing only a requirement to account would be to reflect rather than redress the inherent weakness of the position which the principal otherwise occupies. It would entail his facing the risks of not discovering the acquisition and of encountering practical difficulties in securing its disgorgement. The constructive trust improves his position greatly, by making the acquisition his from the outset.

At first sight, the argument seems weaker in the unauthorized case than in the authorized case. Principals contemplating the employment of a fiduciary are less likely to think about, and so hesitate over, the problems of recovering unauthorized acquisitions than those of recovering authorized acquisitions. But they are likely to feel concern about the prospect of the fiduciary being distracted from the service of their interests. The rules against distraction constitute the law's effort to counter this concern. And the strength of this effort is enhanced by the choice of the constructive trust as the response to breach, for this provides the strongest enforcement for the rules, so enhancing the chances of their succeeding in keeping the fiduciary from distraction. It is however arguable that

---

[37] *Boardman v Phipps* [1967] 2 AC 46 is similar.

[38] *A-G for Hong Kong v Reid* [1994] 1 AC 324 (not following *Lister & Co v Stubbs* (1890) 45 Ch D 1, which required the fiduciary only to account for bribes). In *Reading v A-G* [1951] AC 507, the doctrine was applied to an army sergeant who took bribes to assist smuggling. It is unclear that a fiduciary relationship truly existed here. But even if many of the usual facets of such a relationship were absent, government officials and military personnel are surely under the crucial obligation not to accept bribes influencing their conduct when actually or apparently carrying out their duties.

[39] Reasoning directed at the bribe case is offered by the Privy Council in *A-G for Hong Kong v Reid* [1994] 1 AC 324, but it is incoherent: S Gardner [1995] CLJ 60.

the rules against distraction are themselves too hard on fiduciaries,[40] and that they may even do a disservice to principals, in preventing a useful alignment between principal's interest and the fiduciary's self-interest.[41] If this is the case, the constructive trust presumably makes matters worse.

8.6 UNAUTHORIZED EXCHANGES AND MIXTURES

Say someone holds property on trust for certain objects, and, without authorization to do so, exchanges that property for other assets ('exchange products'): for example, by using the trust's money to make a personal purchase. The law rules that she holds the exchange products on trust for the same objects.[42] Or say someone holds property on trust for certain objects, and, without authorization, mixes that property with other property in such a way that it cannot be separated again: for example, by combining the trust's money and her own in a single bank account. The law rules that she holds an appropriate part of the mixture on trust (or, sometimes, subject to a charge) for those objects.

By acting without authorization, the trustee in these cases breaks her duty to keep the trust property safe,[43] and will of course be liable to pay compensation for any resulting loss. The law could have halted there, treating the trust property as lost and requiring compensation for its value. (As it does when a trustee carelessly allows trust property to be stolen, or indeed embezzles it herself and neither trades it for a tangible exchange product nor incorporates it into a surviving mixture: say, spends it on a holiday.) But the law does not halt there. Instead, it subjects the exchange product or mixture itself to a constructive trust, or sometimes a charge, in the objects' favour.

The justification for its doing so is the same as that for the rules discussed in the previous two sections. The fact that a trustee has legal title to, and usually custody of, the trust assets but no personal stake in

[40] Cf *Boardman v Phipps* [1967] 2 AC 46, 124, where Lord Upjohn dissented from a decision that a solicitor had broken his duty to avoid distraction by his own interests, wishing to limit the duty to cases of a 'real sensible possibility of conflict' between the fiduciary's interests and her principal's.

[41] W Bishop and D Prentice (1983) 46 MLR 289.

[42] Arguably also when she makes the purchase on credit, and uses trust money to repay the debt: L Smith [1995] CLJ 290; but English law has not fully accepted this argument: *Bishopsgate Investment Management Ltd v Homan* [1995] Ch 211, 217, 221–2; *Foskett v McKeown* [1998] Ch 265, 283–4, 289, 296.

[43] See section 9.2. The trustee may be a constructive trustee; the duty to keep the property safe applies equally to such a person, and so do the tracing rules, discussed below.

their proper treatment is a source of vulnerability for the objects. The practical possibility it generates of the trustee improperly exchanging or mixing the trust assets is a central instance of that vulnerability. The strength of the trust device (whether as used by settlors or by the law) is enhanced if the degree of the vulnerability can be lessened. Rules subjecting unauthorized exchange products and mixtures to a trust or charge have that effect. They bolster the duty to keep the trust property safe in the same way as the constructive trust considered in the previous section bolsters the duty not to make acquisitions in distracting circumstances. That is, they seek as far as possible to prevent the trustee from gaining from a breach.

The constructive trust or charge is thus applied (only) to those assets which the trustee gains as a result of the breach.[44] In the present context, however, it is not altogether easy to identify these gains. This is especially true in the case of a breach by wrongfully mixing the trust property: how much of the mixture is property which the trustee acquires by wrongfully destroying the separate identity of the original trust property, and how much of it is acquired from the other contributor to the mixture? The remainder of this section discusses the difficulties, and the ideas the law has evolved in response to them. These ideas are embodied in rules making the required identification. The business of making the required identification, by applying these rules, is known as 'tracing'.[45] The tracing rules are sometimes depicted as founded on an assessment of which assets now in the trustee's hands 'represent' the assets which she held on the trust before her breach.[46] This view portrays the business of identification as something we can think about in naturalistic terms. The idea of one asset 'representing' another cannot be more than a metaphor, however. The suggestion here is that the reality for which the metaphor stands is the normative phenomenon of isolating the assets over which the wronged trust shall have a claim of the kind under discussion, by a set of rules owing less to nature than to the considerations relevant to that kind of claim. On this account, then, the question is ultimately not whether some asset in the trustee's hands 'represents' an asset which she previously held on trust, but whether, if not subjected to a constructive trust

---

[44] A more generous position was taken in *Space Investments Ltd v Canadian Imperial Bank of Commerce Trust Co (Bahamas) Ltd* [1986] 1 WLR 1072, 1074, but this departure was in effect disapproved in *Re Goldcorp Exchange Ltd* [1995] 1 AC 74, 108–10.

[45] See generally L Smith *The Law of Tracing* (1997). Smith's account is broadly adopted in *Foskett v McKeown* [2001] 1 AC 102.

[46] Thus in *Foskett v McKeown* [2001] 1 AC 102, 108–9. Further statements at 115, 127 may be founded on the same view, but are less assertive of it.

or charge, we ought to regard it as a gain to the trustee as a result of her breach. In speaking of the overall operation of making the identification and then imposing the constructive trust or charge over the assets so identified, however, we often say, without inaccuracy, that the law treats the assets in question as belonging to the trust.

Let us begin with the case of unauthorized exchange, where the imposition of the constructive trust requires identification of the exchange products. This is a comparatively simple matter. Say I, who am trustee for you, improperly spend £500 of trust assets on a painting. The trust assets' exchange product is the painting, so I now hold the painting on constructive trust for you. Likewise, if I resell the painting for £5,000, I hold the £5,000 on constructive trust for you.[47] Or say, in a slightly more complex case, that I buy the painting with £500 of trust assets and £1,000 of my own money (in separate lots), before again reselling the painting for £5,000. Here, the exchange product of the trust's £500 is that proportion of the painting and so of the £5,000 which the £500 was of the original price, ie one-third. So I hold the £5,000 on constructive trust one-third for the trust and two-thirds for myself.[48] If in either scenario you could claim only the £500, allowing me to keep the profit, I would have an incentive to misuse trust property. Treating the relevant proportion of the painting as trust property bolsters my duty not to do so, and so strengthens the duty's correction of your vulnerability, by removing that incentive. If however I can resell the painting only for £5, I hold that £5 on trust for you, but as to the remaining £495 which I improperly spent you will have to sue me for compensation: there is no asset in my hands to which the tracing rules direct a constructive trust.

As regards mixtures of trust assets with others, matters are more complicated. To prevent the trustee gaining by having wrongfully made the mixture, the law subjects an appropriate part of the mixture and its proceeds to a trust, or sometimes imposes a charge. The rules detailing what is an 'appropriate part', and whether there arises a trust or a charge, are intricate. They differ especially between two cases.

In one case, the sources of the mixture are the assets of the trust and of another innocent party, commonly another trust. The trustee has put no assets of her own into the mixture. So, to prevent her gaining from the breach, the law must and does impose a constructive trust over *all* the

---

[47] *Re Hallett's Estate* (1879) 13 Ch D 696, 709.

[48] *Foskett v McKeown* [2001] 1 AC 102, 130–1, disapproving a contrary statement (that the trust's share is only the amount of its initial contribution, ie £500) in *Re Hallett's Estate* (1879) 13 Ch D 696, 709.

assets now in or emanating from the mixture. The only issue is the secondary one of ensuring that, in the way that they allocate the subsisting assets and any profits and losses as compared with the original assets, the rules operate even-handedly as between the two innocent parties to the mixture. As we shall see in a moment, however, this issue is not quite as simple as it sounds, and the law's treatment of it has if anything exaggerated its complexity. In the other case, the sources of the mixture are the assets of the trust and of the breaching trustee herself. Here, the assets now in or emanating from the mixture cannot necessarily (to put it no higher) *all* be regarded as gains that the trustee has made from the breach and so apt to attract a constructive trust in correction of that. At least some of them should probably be ascribed to the trustee's own contribution to the mixture. So the task is to sort the assets now in or emanating from the mixture as between these two possibilities. But since the project is to strip a wrongdoing trustee of any gains resulting from her breach, the law's approach to that task is not even-handed. Where it is doubtful whether an asset should be seen as such a gain or ascribed to the trustee's own contribution, the law broadly resolves the doubt against the trustee. So, especially, if the mixture and its proceeds have suffered any loss in value, that normally has to be borne by the trustee: the trustee's gain, over which the constructive trust or charge is imposed, is regarded as consisting in the value which survives. The rules used in this operation are especially complex, and are detailed later in this section.

We take first, then, the case in which the sources of the mixture are the assets of the trust and of another innocent party. As we noted above, in stripping the trustee of the mixed assets and their proceeds by imposing a constructive trust in these innocent contributors' favour, the law should and does seek to be even-handed as between the contributors.

The most natural way of producing an even-handed allocation is to divide the assets between the contributors in the same proportions as (*pro rata* with) their contributions to the original total. This approach is known as '*pari passu*'. Imagine that I take £500 that I hold on trust for you, and £1,000 that I hold on trust for Adam, and mix the two sums by placing them in a savings account. If I spend £500 from the mixture on a holiday, *pari passu* reckoning allocates that loss to the two trusts to the extent of £167 (one-third of £500) to your trust, £333 (two-thirds of £500) to Adam's trust. So I likewise hold the remaining £1,000 as to £333 for your trust, £667 for Adam's. If I spend £500 on a painting and sell it again for £5,000, the £5,000 belongs £1,667 to your trust, £3,333 to Adam's, and the unspent £1,000 as before.

That is how the law will handle a case involving just those facts. But certain changes in the pattern of facts will unexpectedly entail a different approach.

Imagine an example similar to the above, but slightly more complex. Say I place £500 from your trust and £1,000 from Adam's trust into a savings account, then later add £1,000 from Briony's trust. Between the mixing of the original £500 and £1,000 and the addition of the money from Briony's trust, I spend £500 from the mixture on a painting which I resell for £5,000. In principle, in applying the *pari passu* rule the law should regard withdrawals from the mixture as made up of the contributing funds in the same proportions as the mixture itself *as the mixture stood immediately before the withdrawal*. Briony's trust contributed to the mixture only after the withdrawal, the profits arising from which we are seeking to allocate. It should therefore be left aside, and the allocation made only amongst those—your trust, and Adam's—who in fact contributed to the mixture from which the withdrawal was made. So I should again hold the £5,000 realized by selling the painting as to £1,667 for your trust, and as to £3,333 for Adam's. Of the £2,000 left in the mixture, £1,000 remains Briony's trust's untouched contribution, while £333 is your trust's, and £667 is Adam's trust's.

Although as a matter of principle it seems clearly correct that the *pari passu* technique should be operated in this way (known as 'rolling *pari passu*'), the English courts have sometimes refused to do so. They have declared that if rolling *pari passu* is difficult to administer,[49] they will instead proceed on the fictitious basis that all the contributions to the mixture were put into it simultaneously, and immediately before the likewise simultaneous withdrawals.[50] This version has no acknowledged name, but call it 'static *pari passu*'. Applying it to the example in the last paragraph, we find that the £5,000 realized by selling the painting belongs £1,000 to your trust, £2,000 to Adam's, and £2,000 to Briony's; and that the £2,000 remaining in the mixture belongs £400 to your trust, £800 to Adam's, and £800 to Briony's. Briony's trust is thus made to share in the expenditure of £500, and given a proportion of the gain resulting from the purchase of the painting, despite forming no part of the mixture at the time when these transactions occurred.

More dubiously still, in one very common variation on our example

---

[49] Notably, it seems, where there are many payments into and withdrawals from the mixture. Given computerized bank records, however, applying a rolling *pari passu* treatment to such facts ought to give rise to no particular difficulty.

[50] *Barlow Clowes International Ltd v Vaughan* [1992] 4 All ER 22.

the law uses neither version of the *pari passu* technique. Instead, it uses a technique which is also even-handed, but in a different, and less satisfactory, way. The scenario in question is that where I mix the money by paying the different contributions *sequentially into an ordinary current bank account*. When I then make withdrawals from this mixture, the law regards the contributions as withdrawn in the order in which they were paid into the account: 'first in, first out'.[51] Assume, then, that I place £500 from your trust in a current account, and then pay £500 from Adam's trust into the same account. If my only transaction after this is to spend £500 on a painting worth £5,000, I hold this painting for you, and the remaining £500 in the account still for Adam. But if my only transaction is to spend £500 on a holiday, although I again hold the remaining £500 for Adam, I no longer hold anything on trust for you. This approach is even-handed in the same way as a game of Russian roulette is: the law does not itself favour one contributor over another, but it allows uneven outturns. It has been much criticized,[52] and has now been held not to apply (so that the *pari passu* technique does) where the contributors can be taken to have intended it not to.[53]

Now let us turn to the other type of case of a mixture: that where the sources of the mixture are the assets of the trust and of the breaching trustee herself. Remember that, whilst the law's essential project is to strip the trustee of any gains resulting from her breach, the difficulty is to say which of the assets now in or emanating from the mixture are such gains, and which are the proceeds of the trustee's own contribution. We need to see how the law deals with this difficulty.

A number of situations require attention. But assume, as the basis for all of them, that I, trustee for you, mix £500 of trust money with £1,000 of my own. Then, in situation (a), I spend the mixed £1,500 on a painting which proves to be worth £5,000. The rule is that I hold the painting in the same proportions as the contributions to the mixture, ie one-third for the trust and two-thirds for myself.[54] You are not restricted to

---

[51] *Re Stenning* [1895] 2 Ch 433; *Re Diplock's Estate* [1948] Ch 465. The 'first in, first out' technique is also known as the rule in *Clayton's case* (1817) 1 Mer 572, but the latter was not concerned with tracing.

[52] See especially *Barlow Clowes International Ltd v Vaughan* [1992] 4 All ER 22, 43–6.

[53] *Barlow Clowes International Ltd v Vaughan* [1992] 4 All ER 22: the contributors there knew that their funds were to be pooled, so were taken to have chosen the *pari passu* approach. At 39, it is suggested that the 'first in, first out' approach should also be disapplied if it is inconvenient or unjust. It is never inconvenient, for it is easy to apply, but always unjust, for the reason given in the text.

[54] *Foskett v McKeown* [2001] 1 AC 102, 130–1.

£500-worth of the eventual assets. It is reasonably easy to see that, if you were, I should retain some of the gain I made from my breach. I should have been stripped of the £500, but not of the profit which I made by using it.

In situation (b), I make not a profit but a loss. I squander £500 of the mixed £1,500, say by spending it on a holiday. The rule is that the remaining £1,000 belongs £500 to the trust, £500 to myself.[55] Why is the trust not restricted to one-third of the subsisting assets, ie £333, in the same way as it could claim one-third of the £5,000 in (a)? Because it is arguable that, if I can retain £667 rather than only £500, I have gained from my wrongful appropriation of the trust assets: I have saved part of my own contribution to the mixture by using part of the trust's to buy my holiday. And because I am a wrongdoing trustee, that arguable view is upheld against me.[56]

In situation (c), I again make a loss. I reduce the mixed £1,500 to £300 by squandering £1,200 it. But then I replenish the mixed fund with a further £600 of my own money. The £900 now in the fund belongs £300 to the trust, £600 to myself.[57] This is known as the 'lowest intermediate balance' rule, £300 being the lowest figure to which the fund *as comprising the mixed assets* fell. You cannot claim more than the £300, notably £500 as in (b), because the remaining £600 is not a gain which I have made as a result of my breach: only my retention of the £300 remaining of your trust's £500 can be described in that way. That said, the fact that you can claim £300 at all, rather than just £100, is explained in the same way as in (b).

Your right to claim £500 in situation (b), and £300 in situation (c), takes the form of a charge over the remaining £1,000 in (b), or the remaining £300 in (c), for £500.[58] Like some trust rights, a charge is a proprietary right, meaning that it can affect transferees of the assets

---

[55] *Re Hallett's Estate* (1879) 13 Ch D 696; *Re Oatway* [1903] 2 Ch 356.

[56] In *Re Hallett's Estate* (1879) 13 Ch D 696, 727, the rule in situation (b) is presented in a different, and problematic, way. The trust is said to be able to claim £500 from the remaining £1,000 because the trustee is presumed to withdraw her own money from the mixture first. But if the facts are reversed—say the £500 first withdrawn was spent on a painting, and the remaining £1,000 squandered—this explanation gives the wrong answer. It would enable the trustee to retain an asset (the painting) which is arguably a gain resulting from her breach, and of which she ought therefore to be stripped. Focusing on the latter issue directly, as in the text, is therefore preferable.

[57] *James Roscoe (Bolton) Ltd v Winder* [1915] 1 Ch 62; *Bishopsgate Investment Management Ltd v Homan* [1995] Ch 211, 220 (if I declare a trust of the replenishment in your favour, you can of course have it).

[58] *Re Hallett's Estate* (1879) 13 Ch D 696, 709; *Re Oatway* [1903] 2 Ch 356, 360-1. See too *Foskett v McKeown* [2001] 1 AC 102, 131 (the charge is there referred to as a lien).

charged, and that it will take priority in their owner's bankruptcy. But a trust has to be attached to a specific item of property, and the value of your claim under it will vary with the standing of that item of property. So it is a suitable vehicle for your claim to the trustee's gain where the gain in question is a particular asset which has maintained or risen in its value: such as the claim to one-third of the £5,000 painting, rather than simply £500, in situation (a).[59] By the same token, however, it is an unsuitable vehicle for a claim to the trustee's gain where that gain takes the form of the trust assets' very presence in the mixture, albeit that the particular assets comprising the mixture and its proceeds have overall lost value: such as the claim to the £500 rather than £333 in situation (b), and the £300 rather than £100 in situation (c). A charge, on the other hand, is a right that the assets in question shall be used to meet a liability that the owner of the assets owes to the owner of the charge: and its value is fixed at the quantum of the liability.[60] In the context under discussion, the liability that is secured by the charge is my liability to compensate you for the loss resulting from my breaking my duty to keep the trust property safe. I am liable to you in this way for the £500 that I embezzled from your trust: so a charge for £500 arises in your favour over the £1,000 (or, in situation (c), £300) still in my hands. A charge thus gives the tool for stripping the trustee of one kind of gain that we can discern where she wrongfully mixes trust assets with her own, but which a constructive trust cannot capture.

8.7 ANTICIPATED TRANSFERS

When the owner of certain kinds of property, especially land, contracts to sell it to a buyer, and the buyer has paid the money for it[61] but the title has not yet been formally transferred to him, the seller holds it on

---

[59] Also for all the claims arising in the case, discussed earlier in this section, where the trustee mixes assets belonging to the trust and some other innocent party. There, as we saw, losses as well as profits are distributed even-handedly among the contributors.

[60] A mortgage is a familiar form of charge. The householder, having borrowed from the bank, is liable to repay a certain sum. The house is subjected to a charge, meaning that, if necessary, the bank can insist that the house is sold (after 'repossession') in order to provide that sum. 'Negative equity' is the case where the sum is larger than the house's value.

[61] Some of the effects of a trust arise earlier in the transaction that this, but the further back one goes the more qualified the purchaser's interest becomes (*Lysaght v Edwards* (1876) 2 Ch D 499), and hesitation arises over calling the vendor's obligations exactly a 'constructive *trust*': A Oakley *Constructive Trusts* 3rd edn (1997) ch 6.

constructive trust for the buyer.[62] Similarly where the seller does not have the property at the time of the contract, ie contracts to transfer 'after-acquired' property: when she acquires it, she immediately holds it on constructive trust for the buyer.[63]

This means, for example, that if a seller of land goes bankrupt before the formal transfer takes place, the land is not seized as part of her assets to pay her debts. Or if the seller gives the land to someone else, the buyer's entitlement goes with it and can be enforced against the new owner. Likewise if a seller of after-acquired property goes bankrupt after acquiring the property, or transfers it to a third party.

This constructive trust springs from the doctrine 'equity looks upon that as done which ought to be done'.[64] The seller ought, under the circumstances, to transfer the land to the buyer. We know this because a court would order specific performance of the contract to transfer,[65] ie would force the seller actually to transfer the land in question to the buyer. But for the moment the transferor is still in fact the owner of it. The legal device for treating the land as transferred to the buyer at the same time as it is still owned by the seller is to say that the seller holds it on trust for the buyer. To the extent provided by the trust, the contract is thus made to perform itself.

To point to the doctrine just mentioned does not provide a satisfying account of the reason for such trusts, however. We are left wanting to know why equity should look upon as done that which ought to be done. Instead of making the contract perform itself, why does it not leave the seller as absolute owner until she makes the actual transfer to the buyer, allowing the buyer to sue her if she does not? The constructive trust is more advantageous to a buyer than a mere right to enforce the contract (which would not give the buyer priority in the seller's bankruptcy, or allow him to retrieve the property from a third party): but why should the law extend such advantages?

---

[62] Where the contract is for the grant of a proprietary interest less than ownership (eg a lease), the law again anticipates the formal grant of the interest (regarding the prospective lessee as already having a lease): *Walsh v Lonsdale* (1881) 21 Ch D 9. But since in such cases the grantor is to retain an interest in the land or other asset in question (eg as landlord), the upshot is not a *trust* for the grantee.

[63] *Holroyd v Marshall* (1860) 10 HLC 191; *Tailby v Official Receiver* (1888) 13 App Cas 523; *Pullan v Koe* [1913] 1 Ch 9; *Re Lind* [1915] 2 Ch 345.

[64] Also known as 'conversion', though that term also has other meanings.

[65] Implying that if for any reason the court would or could not order specific performance, the trust will not arise. The role of this factor is however variable and controversial: S Gardner (1987) 7 OJLS 60.

The historically correct explanation seems to be as follows. At the time when the constructive trust rule was invented, the remedies for breach of contract remained under-developed. A buyer of property other than land, to whom the property had not yet been delivered, was able to claim it because he was nonetheless regarded as its owner: the law treated the contract itself as effecting the transfer. The law could not however treat the contract itself as effecting the transfer of land, for land could be transferred only by a physical act ('livery of seisin'). This left the buyer of land without an effective claim. Something like a transfer without livery of seisin could however be brought about, and was, by ruling that the seller held the land on constructive trust[66] for the buyer.[67]

This class of constructive trust cannot be justified on this basis today, however, for in the meantime the law's remedies for breach of contract have been more fully developed, and the constructive trust is no longer needed so as to give the buyer any claim at all. We are seeking a justification for the trust's effect of giving the buyer rights superior to those which he would enjoy if confined to his ordinary contractual claim.

The justification seems to be similar to that encountered in the previous three sections. There, we saw how the law uses constructive trusts to counter some of the disadvantages which would otherwise attend the otherwise valuable devices of agency and trust. We see a not dissimilar sort of problem in the present context. In some kinds of transactions, especially those involving land, progress towards formal transfer is typically slow and to some extent outside the parties' control.[68] The buyer remains more vulnerable than his counterpart in the case of a simple sale because he cannot take the purchased property immediately in hand: he is forced to rely on the seller's behaving properly towards him until he can. A buyer of after-acquired property is similarly vulnerable as having to rely on the seller for a potentially substantial period before he can take the property: until the property is ultimately transferred (and even when the seller does acquire the property, the buyer will not necessarily know of this so as to move to claim it), the seller may encounter temptations to

---

[66] At the time in question, the term was 'use'.

[67] S Gardner (1987) 7 OJLS 60, 74–81. Thus 'specific performance' of a sale of land was not an order to a seller to perform his contract, so much as an order to a trustee to transfer the trust's subject matter to the beneficiary. The largely automatic availability of the latter kind of order explains why specific performance is nowadays routinely available to enforce a contract to buy land, when it is only exceptionally available to enforce other kinds of contract.

[68] The completion of a land sale, for example, will wait on steps to be taken by the parties' lawyers and perhaps financiers and by the state land registry.

repent of her contract with the buyer, or otherwise, most obviously through bankruptcy, become a less reliable trading partner than the buyer had reason to think her when the contract was made. The constructive trust rule can be justified as being an effort on the law's part to reduce the buyer's vulnerability in such cases, and so to render such transactions more commercially attractive.[69]

8.8 TRANSFER SUBJECT TO AN UNDERTAKING

Where you transfer property to me on the faith of an undertaking I give you to hold it on a certain trust, a constructive trust arises against me in the shape of that trust, thus holding me to my undertaking. This is certainly true of the case where you transfer the property to me on your death; the trust which I undertake to observe, and which arises against me under this rule, is the 'secret trust' discussed in section 5.6. The rule may also apply if your transfer to me is *inter vivos*, though on the authority as it stands the law's response in this case may be not to hold me to my undertaking, but to require me to restore the property to you.[70]

Why does this pattern of facts merit the imposition of a constructive trust? According to the traditional account,[71] the trust arises in order to prevent 'fraud'. Where I agree to take the property and hold it on trust, and you transfer the property to me on the faith of that agreement, it would be fraud for me then to renege and not hold it on the agreed trust. But this account leaves us wondering exactly what features in the facts produce the fraud, and why a constructive trust is the appropriate response to those features.

Probably the best explanation runs as follows. The law is concerned to prevent the transferor being prejudiced, ie made worse off than he was initially, by believing in the transferee's promise. Such a principle is discernible also in other areas of the law.[72] In the abstract, the law's response is not to hold the promisor to her promise without demur (the

[69] Note that the parties can agree to exclude the trust or certain of its implications. In particular, the trust shifts the risk (eg of the bought house being burned down) from seller to buyer. This effect is not nowadays practically favoured (Law Commission Report No 191 *Transfer of Land: Risk of Damage after Contract for Sale* (1990)), and is normally excluded by the terms of the contract.

[70] J Feltham [1987] Conv 246; T Youdan [1988] Conv 267.

[71] See section 5.6. That section rejects the alternative thesis that I place myself under an express trust at the time I give you my undertaking.

[72] Especially promissory estoppel: *Central London Property Trust Ltd v High Trees House Ltd* [1947] KB 130.

normal bases for doing that being by definition absent), but to hold her to
it to the extent that that is necessary if the promisee is not to be worse off,
when it is not fulfilled, by having relied on it.[73] In the area under discussion, if the undertaking does not take effect, the transferor will be prejudiced by relying on the transferee's undertaking if he has meanwhile lost
his opportunity to make his intended disposition by way of an effective
express trust. The transferee should therefore be allowed to go back on
her undertaking to the extent that it is possible to recreate that opportunity.
To the extent that it is not, the law should hold her to her undertaking.

It is important to be precise about what 'that opportunity' means.
First, it means the opportunity to establish the trust with effect from the
date on which it was originally intended to arise. Secondly, it does not
mean the opportunity for the transferor to change his mind and instead
make no trust or a different one. He has lost this opportunity equally if
the transferee honours her undertaking, and in fact lost it by trying to
make the disposition at all. It seems in fact not to be possible to recreate
the opportunity, so defined. In particular, it cannot be recreated by literally revesting the property in the transferor and leaving him to subject it
to an express trust in accordance with his intentions. That response
would meet neither of the above points, and moreover it would be futile
in the situation, as in all testamentary cases and some *inter vivos* ones,
where the transferor has died in the meantime. As it is thus not possible
to restore to the transferor the opportunity effectively to make his trust
which he had before he relied on the transferee's undertaking, he will
have been prejudiced, if the undertaking is not fulfilled, by his reliance
upon it. To negate that prejudice, the law must enforce the undertaking,
ie must regard the transferee as holding the property on a (constructive)
trust in the terms which she agreed with the transferor.

The rule under discussion also has a wider application, but one that is
dubiously proper. If I undertake that I will accept some property from
you on certain terms *which do not themselves amount to my holding it on
trust*, and you transfer the property to me on the faith of that undertaking, a constructive trust again arises, obliging me to keep to the agreed
terms. Say I own a large estate, and allow an old lady to live in one of its
cottages for the rest of her life. I sell the estate. The lady's right to stay in
the cottage does not in itself bind the purchaser, because it is merely a
contract between her and me, which the doctrine of privity of contract
prevents from affecting others. In his dealings with me, however, the

---

[73] *Tool Metal Manufacturing Co Ltd v Tungsten Electric Co Ltd* [1955] 1 WLR 766.

purchaser undertakes to honour the old lady's position. That is not an undertaking to hold the land on trust for her, but a constructive trust will arise obliging him to honour it.[74]

It is in keeping with the principle just discussed that such a purchaser should be held to his undertaking. (By transferring the estate to him in reliance on his promise to honour the old lady's position, I have lost the opportunity to protect her in some other way, so I shall be prejudiced unless the promise is enforced.) But where, as here, the undertaking was not itself one to hold on trust, holding the purchaser to his undertaking should not involve imposing a trust on him. Referring to it as a trust is inaccurate in two respects. First, we saw in section 1.10 that it is part of the nature of trusts that the trustee, whilst holding the legal title to the trust property, is subject to duties which leave no room for a personal interest. But in the doctrine under discussion, the purchaser's obligation is simply to use the property in the specified way: to allow the old lady to remain in the cottage, for example. In all other respects, he owes no duties as to his use of the property, and so can enjoy it as his own. In particular, if he were to sell the property, the proceeds would be his. So he evidently has a personal interest in the trust property. Secondly, as we saw in section 1.9, trust obligations are proprietary, ie are attached to the property and so affect it in the hands of a recipient from the original trustee. If a trust arises in the situation under discussion, therefore, the duty owed to the beneficiary (in the example, the duty to allow the old lady to stay in the cottage) should be proprietary. Yet while I was her landlord, her rights were merely personal ones against me. It is odd that a person's rights should change their quality in this way, by virtue of a transaction, the transfer of the property to the purchaser upon the faith of his promise, to which that person is not even a party.[75] And it has now in fact been

---

[74] *Binions v Evans* [1972] Ch 359, 368–9; *Swiss Bank Corporation v Lloyds Bank Ltd* [1979] Ch 548, 571; *Lyus v Prowsa Developments Ltd* [1982] 1 WLR 1044; *Ashburn Anstalt v Arnold* [1989] Ch 1, 22–6. The example given involves a contract between the transferor and the person who becomes beneficiary of the constructive trust, and that feature is to be found in these cases. But it seems unnecessary. Say I sell the estate to you after taking a promise from you that you will allow my elderly mother to move into and remain in the cottage. There is no contract between her and me, but in terms of the doctrine under discussion it would seem nonetheless a fraud by you not to adhere to that promise.

[75] At one time, this oddity in fact led the courts to decide that someone in the position of the old lady (a contractual licensee) must have had proprietary, rather than personal (merely contractual), rights all along, even in her original relationship with me. See *DHN Food Distributors Ltd v Tower Hamlets LBC* [1976] 1 WLR 852; *Re Sharpe (a bankrupt)* [1980] 1 WLR 219. This view was disapproved, albeit without advertence to the difficulty which had caused it, in *Ashburn Anstalt v Arnold* [1989] Ch 1.

decided that no such change occurs, and that the obligations upon the purchaser are personal.[76]

So although it is right that an obligation should arise on the basis under discussion against someone who acquires property having undertaken to use it in a certain way, that obligation should only be a 'trust' if the undertaking was to hold on trust.

8.9 MUTUAL WILLS

A further rule in a similar mould (generating a constructive trust where the owner of some property undertakes to give another person a claim on it) is that of mutual wills.

Say you and I agree to make wills aimed at ultimately leaving some property to Adam, and agree also not to resile from that (as the revocability of wills, before death, would normally permit). Say then that I die before you, having complied with this agreement. The upshot is that any property of yours to which the agreement applies is held by you, from the moment of my death, on constructive trust for Adam. Usually, the agreement is that I shall leave some property to you, and that you in turn will leave it to Adam. But this feature is not necessary, and the arrangement may simply be that we shall each leave property to Adam.[77]

The doctrine of mutual wills fits the principle explained in the previous section.[78] Relying on your promise to leave the property to Adam, I die leaving my will in a particular form (bequeathing the property to you or otherwise). I have thus lost my opportunity to provide for Adam in some other way, which I might have wished to do if we had not had our agreement. I shall therefore be worse off if you resile from the agreement than if we had never made it. In order to prevent that (for it would be 'fraud'), the law holds you to the agreement. And since the agreement obliges you to make Adam the owner of property in your hands, we can correctly say that you hold the property on (constructive) trust for Adam.[79]

---

[76] *Chattey v Farndale Holdings Inc* (1996) 75 P & CR 298, 313–17.

[77] *Re Dale (deceased)* [1994] Ch 31.

[78] The common basis with secret trusts is noted in *Re Cleaver (deceased)* [1981] 1 WLR 939.

[79] Sometimes, because this is the nature of the agreement, you will hold the property on trust for yourself and Adam; and sometimes again the size of the two shares will be for you to decide (with limits or otherwise). The latter arrangement seems to involve a power of appointment in your own favour, though other, more problematic, concepts are sometimes invoked. See *Birmingham v Renfrew* (1937) 57 CLR 666, Australia; *Re Cleaver (deceased)* [1981] 1 WLR 939; *Re Goodchild (deceased)* [1996] 1 WLR 694; also *Ottaway v Norman* [1972] Ch 698, a secret trust case on similar lines.

8.10 PROPRIETARY ESTOPPEL

In the doctrines described in the preceding two sections, a constructive trust arises if the (present or future) owner of some property undertakes to hold it for or transfer it to someone else, and the recipient of the undertaking acts in reliance on that undertaking in such a way, or in such circumstances, that she will be worse off than she originally was if the undertaking is now broken. A further doctrine which on the face of it could be a member of the same family is that of 'proprietary estoppel'. One way of presenting this doctrine is to say that if the owner of some property undertakes to allow someone else rights over it, and the latter[80] acts in reliance on that undertaking, the owner must normally keep to the undertaking. If the content of the agreement equates with the nature of a trust (it sometimes will,[81] but sometimes will not[82]), the upshot can be described as a constructive trust arising against the owner,[83] though in fact the expression is not commonly used in the proprietary estoppel context.

Say I am elderly. I would like you, my daughter, to come and live close by me. I buy the house next door to mine and ask you to come and live there, promising that if you do I will make you the owner of it. Relying on my promise, you move into the house, and perhaps also look after me and make some improvements to the house. But I never quite get round to transferring the legal title in it to you. The law will probably make me do so.[84] Moreover, it will say that pending my doing so you have rights tantamount to ownership against me. So, for example, if, before transferring the house to you, I mortgage the house to a bank, without your permission, to raise money to pay my debts, your right to it will not be damaged.[85] If we wish we can say that in the period before the transfer I hold the house on constructive trust for you.

---

[80] So it is a two-party arrangement. Secret trusts and mutual wills are three-party arrangements, since the promisee is seeking to secure a benefit to a third party after his own death; but this feature is inessential to the principle we are invoking, as can be seen in the case where I transfer land to you to hold on trust not for a third party but for myself (without, as I should, declaring the trust in writing): eg *Bannister v Bannister* [1948] 2 All ER 133.

[81] Especially where the claimant is entitled to become the owner of the property, as in *Dillwyn v Llewelyn* (1862) 4 De GF & J 517; *Re Basham (deceased)* [1986] 1 WLR 1498.

[82] As where the claimant is entitled only to occupy the property, or to traverse it, as in *Inwards v Baker* [1965] 2 QB 29; *Crabb v Arun DC* [1976] Ch 179.

[83] As in *Giumelli v Giumelli* [1999] HCA 10, Australia.

[84] *Re Basham (deceased)* [1986] 1 WLR 1498.

[85] In the case of registered land in England, this is made clear by the Land Registration

Remember that, under the principle which explains the secret trust and mutual wills doctrines, a promise is enforced against its maker only when the promisee has so relied on it that, if it is not kept, she will be worse off than originally. Promises are always enforced by those doctrines because, in their contexts, the promisee is always in that situation. That is not obviously true of proprietary estoppel, however. In the example just given, moving next door to me might (if I do not keep my promise) have made you worse off than you were before, as perhaps if you gave up other, especially advantageous, accommodation in order to do so, or forewent the chance of 'getting on to the housing ladder' in your own right. But equally, it might not, as where you already owned a house and simply let it out so as to live next door to me. Your expenditure of money and labour (looking after me, improving your home) will have left you worse off, but that can be rectified without holding me to my promise, by making me reimburse you. Where you are thus not irretrievably prejudiced if I resile from my promise, the principle we have been using offers no warrant for insisting that I keep it, by giving you the house and meanwhile holding it on constructive trust for you.

The uneven way in which the facts of proprietary estoppel cases thus interact with our principle may help to explain the resistance judges have shown to precisely defining either the facts essential to a proprietary estoppel claim[86] or the effects of enjoying such a claim.[87] The problem is that the class of facts to which *some* response is required, even if only reimbursement for the expenditure in reliance, is wider than the class in which enforcement of the understanding will be appropriate. There are probably other problems too, however. It is possible that a particular type of response can arise for more than one reason, and so from more than one kind of facts. The judges might award the claimant the defendant's house, for example, not only on the basis of the principle we have been using and so only in cases whose facts fit that principle (ie show that the defendant so promised and that the claimant will have been irretrievably

---

Act 2002 s 116. The rule outside that context is controversial, but the bulk of authority is to like effect: eg *Williams v Staite* [1979] Ch 291; *Pascoe v Turner* [1979] 1 WLR 431.

[86] *Taylors Fashions v Liverpool Victoria Friendly Society* [1981] QB 133; *Gillett v Holt* [2001] Ch 210.

[87] *Sledmore v Dalby* (1996) 72 P & CR 196; *Jennings v Rice* [2002] EWCA Civ 159. Especially striking are the leading Australian cases (*Waltons Stores (Interstate) v Maher* (1988) 164 CLR 387; *Commonwealth of Australia v Verwayen* (1990) 170 CLR 394), which emphasize an outcome of reimbursement in their rhetoric but in fact uphold the promise. *Giumelli v Giumelli* [1999] HCA 10 has now reinterpreted the rhetoric in the latter direction.

prejudiced if that promise is broken); but also on the basis that such a response is merited for some other reason. This may have happened in *Pascoe v Turner*,[88] where the 'some other reason' was perhaps a concern on the court's part to achieve a clean break from the parties' decayed relationship. In noticing this we are touching on a different kind of basis for constructive trusts, which will receive fuller treatment in the following section.

8.11 FAMILY PROPERTY

Say I am the owner of a house, and live in it with you on a family footing.[89] If you and I have a common intention that a share in it should belong to you, and you act in reliance on that, you are entitled to that share. That is, I will hold the house on constructive trust for you and myself in the proportions we intended.[90] (If we intend that it should belong entirely to you, I will hold it on constructive trust for you alone.)

On the face of it, this class of constructive trust arises once more under the principle we have already used whereby a promise can be enforced where this is necessary to prevent the promisee suffering irretrievable detriment by relying on it. In the family context, moreover, that will almost always be the case. Relying on my undertaking to give you a share in the assets at my disposal, you have thrown in your lot with me in the entire way that constitutes being a 'family' with me. As a result, you have foregone the opportunity you would otherwise have had (by establishing our relationship on a different footing, by entering a different relationship, or by remaining single) to secure your material interests. That opportunity cannot be restored, so you will be prejudiced unless I am held to our agreement.[91]

To the extent that these cases involve a genuine common intention, this explanation of the constructive trust which emerges is all that is needed. The complication, however, is that the courts find the required common intention in an artificial way. The artificiality is of two kinds.

---

[88] [1979] 1 WLR 431.

[89] Whether married or unmarried, same sex or otherwise, as sexual partners or otherwise.

[90] *Gissing v Gissing* [1971] AC 886; *Lloyds Bank plc v Rosset* [1991] 1 AC 107. An earlier decision of the House of Lords, *Pettitt v Pettitt* [1970] AC 777, sheds little light.

[91] Some cases have noted the similarity with proprietary estoppel: eg *Grant v Edwards* [1986] Ch 638, 656; *Lloyds Bank plc v Rosset* [1991] 1 AC 107, 132–3. The similarity is however inexact since, as we saw above, the application of the principle in the estoppel context neither requires nor elicits enforcement of the promise in the virtually automatic way that is required and occurs in the family property context.

First, if they are seeking to find an implied rather than express common intention, the only evidence to which they will resort is 'direct contributions to the purchase price by the partner who is not the legal owner, whether initially or by payment of mortgage instalments'.[92] So it is good evidence of an implied common intention if the claimant pays her own money to the bank or building society in order to help repay the mortgage. Presumably likewise if the couple pool their incomes into a joint bank account, out of which the mortgage is paid by a direct debit. But these are apparently the only facts that will suffice. Excluded from consideration are indirect financial contributions, as where the couple keep separate accounts but each takes care of certain expenses on behalf of both of them, the title owner paying the mortgage, and the claimant the household bills; the claimant's payment of the household expenses, by allowing the title owner to concentrate entirely on the mortgage costs, indirectly helps pay the mortgage. Similarly excluded, whether or not it is possible to view them as indirect financial contributions, are activities such as redecorating the house, looking after the children, cleaning the house, cooking the meals, and doing the washing.[93]

In evidential terms, the division between direct financial contributions and others is a strange one. It is hard to see why (say) housekeeping work *cannot* provide evidence of an implied common intention that the claimant should have a share in the house. In truth, the rule embodies a value judgment as between the various kinds of possible contribution. The content of this value judgment gives cause for concern. In that women more often undertake unpaid work in the home than men, a woman is less likely to satisfy the rule than a man, so the rule discriminates on gender grounds. The rule also discriminates in favour of family members who undertake paid work, against those who work in the home; yet it seems likely that the former are more likely to be able to look after their own interests (notably, by having their names included in the formal title to the house), while the latter need the law's protection.[94]

---

[92] *Lloyds Bank plc v Rosset* [1991] 1 AC 107, 133. The judgment actually asserts that it is 'at least extremely doubtful' that any other form of evidence will suffice, but it is generally read as establishing a firm rule that no other form of evidence will suffice. This reading was rejected, however, in *Le Foe v Le Foe* [2001] FLR 970.

[93] *Burns v Burns* [1984] Ch 317.

[94] It may be asked whether these discriminations attract the operation of the Human Rights Act 1998, if that Act affects rights as between private individuals. Article 14 of the European Convention forbids discrimination on grounds 'such as' sex and property, but only as regards the enjoyment of other Convention rights. Possibly relevant to the matter under discussion is the right in Art 8, ie the right to respect for family life and the home.

This first artificiality, then, is that the courts will sometimes not find the required common intention when the evidence, taken as such, might support such a finding. The second artificiality is that at other times, the courts will find common intention regardless of whether the evidence supports such a finding.[95] This routinely happens when the claimant has made a direct financial contribution. The courts do not treat this merely as evidence, continuing to inquire whether or not she has proved the common intention which she alleges. Instead, they proceed directly from the fact of the contribution to the imposition of a constructive trust. It has also happened in some cases where the claimant had made no direct financial contribution, so the court could not impose a trust on that basis, but the court purported to discover an express common intention which in truth the evidence did not reveal, and imposed a trust on that basis. In some of these cases the evidence was merely opaque, and it could not be more than guesswork whether the parties ever reached an express common intention, but the court reached this conclusion.[96] Sometimes the evidence positively pointed away from there having been an express common intention, but one was found nonetheless. An example is the decision in *Grant v Edwards*.[97] A man refused to have a house put into the joint names of himself and his partner. He told her that this was because she was going through divorce proceedings with her previous husband, and he was concerned that any share she had in the new house might be taken away in those proceedings. This was found to be an excuse (ie, the man had no belief that such a thing could happen) rather than a valid reason for denying her a share. The court treated this as disclosing an express common intention between the couple that the woman should have a share. According to the judges, the fact that the man made such an excuse showed that he really agreed to the woman having a share. This is

---

Some cases have declared this Article applicable to questions of property rights: *Marckx v Belgium* (1979) 2 EHRR 330 para 52; *X, Y and Z v UK* (1997) 24 EHRR 143 paras 48–9. The discriminatory nature of the rule described in the text might not, however, fall foul of Art 14 in any event, as the cases have so far declined to extend the Article to instances of indirect discrimination: see *Belgian Linguistic Case (No 2)* (1968) 1 EHRR 252; *Abdulaziz, Cabales and Balkandali v UK* (1985) 7 EHRR 471; though perhaps the real thrust of those cases was that the discriminations therein were justifiable, which might not be true of that under discussion here.

[95] Despite a ruling in *Gissing v Gissing* [1971] AC 886, 904 that the required common intention must be found to have been genuinely present.

[96] *Hammond v Mitchell* [1991] 1 WLR 1127; *Stokes v Anderson* [1991] 1 FLR 391.

[97] [1986] Ch 638. The facts and majority reasoning in *Eves v Eves* [1975] 1 WLR 1338 are similar.

most doubtful, however. An excuse is not a way of saying 'yes'; it is a softened way of saying 'no'.[98]

As regards the size of the interest, indeed, the courts have said that it is not necessary to find a genuine common intention. A genuine common intention will presumably be respected, but in its absence the court will impute to the parties such an intention as it thinks appropriate. This was decided in *Midland Bank plc v Cooke*.[99] Mrs Cooke had made a direct financial contribution amounting to less than 7 per cent of the value of the house which had been bought in her husband's name. This permitted the inference of a common intention that she should have a share in the house. Having heard the parties state that no discussion as to the size of their shares ever took place, the court imputed to them an intention that Mrs Cooke should have a 50 per cent share, and imposed a constructive trust accordingly.

Given especially this second artificiality, the constructive trust cannot arise on the basis of enforcing the owner's promise as the only means of preventing the irretrievable detriment that the claimant will otherwise suffer from her reliance on that promise: for in the material we have discussed there was no promise, and no reliance on it. What is the trust's basis, then? It seems to be the ethical implications of the parties' relationship itself.[100]

This is most visible in *Midland Bank plc v Cooke*.[101] The court declared itself moved to impute the common intention for 50 per cent shares by the reflection that, being a married couple, the parties had committed themselves to the goal of sharing their lives, including the material gains and losses which came their way; and that the parties' conduct over the years had, taken in the round, evinced their continuing commitment to this goal: Mrs Cooke's interrupted career pattern and efforts in the home being taken as having a significance equal to that of Mr Cooke's more

---

[98] The existence of a common intention must be judged through the eyes of a reasonable bystander (*Gissing v Gissing* [1971] AC 886, 906); but this makes no difference. A reasonable bystander hearing me say 'I'd love to come to your party, but I'm busy that night', and knowing that I will not be busy at all, could not conclude that I am in fact agreeing to attend: rather, than I have no wish to, but prefer not to say so.

[99] [1995] 4 All ER 562.

[100] Various alternative bases for imposing a constructive trust in family property cases have been asserted in Canada, Australia, and New Zealand. The leading cases are respectively *Pettkus v Becker* (1980) 117 DLR (3d) 259, *Baumgartner v Baumgartner* (1987) 164 CLR 137, and *Gillies v Keogh* [1989] 2 NZLR 327. Despite their articulated reasoning, the courts operating these doctrines seem in reality likewise to treat the ethic of the parties' relationship as a basis for imposing a constructive trust: S Gardner (1993) 109 LQR 263.

[101] [1995] 4 All ER 562.

heavily financial contributions.[102] Likewise, the true significance of the excuse in *Grant v Edwards*,[103] discussed above, was its disclosure of a realization on the man's part that, given the nature of the parties' relationship, when he said 'no' he *ought to have* said 'yes': a view which the judges shared, in finding for the woman.

Is the law right thus to erect a constructive trust on the basis of the nature of the parties' relationship, as well as of a project to reverse otherwise irretrievable detriment incurred in reliance on a genuine assurance? Imagine an argument that it is wrong, and that it should react only to arrangements which the parties have negotiated. That sort of argument, resting on a liberal foundation, has broad currency so far as dealings between businesses are concerned. It is less appropriately, indeed inappropriately, applied to family members. The latter cannot realistically be expected to negotiate their own arrangements: any leaning to do so would be inhibited as contrary to the register of normal family discourse, and also by lack of expertise as to the issues. The register of normal family discourse, with its inhibiting effect on businesslike negotiation, reflects the ethic of the family relationship. People entering into, or finding themselves in, family relationships are essentially required to trust and collaborate with each other: that is what 'being in a family' means. This ethic of trust and collaboration entails (among other things) the duty to act on behalf of family partners as well as oneself, and equitably to share the burdens and benefits associated with shared life. Where one party's role in the relationship has been to amass the family's assets while the other's has lain in family work of a kind that does not bring material advantage, such as bringing up children, the implication is that those assets should be shared, ordinarily equally. It seems reasonable to regard this insight as justifying the imposition of a constructive trust by reference to the relationship itself, as occurs in family property cases lacking relevant genuine intentions.[104]

---

[102] Cf *Drake v Whipp* [1996] 1 FLR 826. There, so far as financial issues went, an unmarried couple's relationship was seen as directed more towards the purchase and refurbishment of a particular property than towards the establishment of an entire shared life. The claimant emerged with a 30 per cent share.

[103] [1986] Ch 638.

[104] S Gardner (1993) 109 LQR 263. The insight certainly appears to inform the statutory provision (Matrimonial Causes Act 1973 s 24) which governs the particular issue of distributing a family's assets in the event of separation or divorce. The doctrine described in the text applies on the dissolution of family relationships other than marriages; and, in all types of families, to the discovery of interests before dissolution—so as, for example, to know whether a wife has an interest opposable against a bank to which her husband, in whose sole name the title is vested, has mortgaged the house without her knowledge: cf *Williams & Glyn's Bank Ltd v Boland* [1981] AC 487.

Since the insight proposes the imposition of a constructive trust on the basis of the implications of the parties' relationship, care must be taken to attend sufficiently sensitively to the implications of the particular relationship in question. Some relationships are so organized that, while they possess an ethic of trust and collaboration, it is not all encompassing. In these cases, the law's response should respect the extent to which the parties have chosen to keep their affairs separate as much as that to which they have chosen to share.[105] Other relationships again will have no 'family' characteristics at all. Here the law will not be justified in responding on the present basis. Making these kinds of distinctions can be practically difficult, however. Take an unmarried heterosexual relationship. Are the parties to be seen as 'married in all but name', or, despite appearing in many ways as an established unit, have they chosen not to marry as a symbol that they do not wish to assume the kind of responsibility for one another that is associated with marriage? How does one read a relationship where marriage is not an option: same-sex couples, for example, and non-sexual relationships, such as between the elderly and an adult child who cares for them, or between siblings or platonic companions who set up house together? Moreover, the parties' own perceptions of the nature of their relationship may be prone to fluctuation and misunderstanding. For such reasons, it is perhaps unsurprising that, whilst there may in practice be a focus on the ethic of the parties' relationship, the law has been slow explicitly to align itself with this approach.[106]

---

[105] Hence the different outcomes in *Midland Bank plc v Cooke* [1995] 4 All ER 562 and *Drake v Whipp* [1996] 1 FLR 826: see nn 101, 102 above.

[106] Apart from some exploration by Lord Denning MR in the 1960s and 1970s (see eg his judgment in *Eves v Eves* [1975] 1 WLR 1338), explicit reference to the nature of the relationship rather than an ostensible search for a genuine common intention came only with *Midland Bank plc v Cooke* [1995] 4 All ER 562. The variety of relationships and consequently of their implications has led the Law Commission, unsurprisingly, to recommend against treating them all alike: Report No 278 *Sharing Homes: A Discussion Paper* (2002).

9

Stewardship

We turn now to look at trustees' duties: ie what is actually required of trustees.

9.1 TRUSTEES' DUTIES GENERALLY

The most basic duty on a trustee is to respect the fact that the property is not beneficially her own. So, where the trust has beneficiaries, she must respect the beneficiaries' rights. This duty consists only in a requirement that, if the trustee still has the trust property, she shall transfer it if asked to do so to the beneficiaries if they have immediate rights to it, or to fresh trustees. This duty is found in all trust situations.[1]

Express trusts, however, generally ask far more of their trustees, in two main ways. They normally call for the payment out of money (to the beneficiaries, or on the usually charitable purpose), not as a simple immediate transfer but in a more complex manner. Complex duties of payment are examined in the following two chapters. They also normally require the safe-keeping and management of the trust property pending payment out. This interim stewardship is needed because settlors do not generally stipulate that the entire trust property should be immediately paid out, but instead provide for the trust to endure for a time; there would generally be little point in establishing a trust to do the work of a simple gift. The implications of this duty of stewardship are the topic of the present chapter.

These calls on trustees are onerous, and their satisfactory performance cannot be taken for granted. Chapter 13 is devoted to the range of techniques, some of them involving further, adjectival, duties, calculated to promote such performance. Allowing settlors to demand so much also poses problems when essentially well-meaning trustees fall short of what

[1] And Lord Browne-Wilkinson in *Westdeutsche Landesbank Girozentrale v Islington LBC* [1996] AC 669, 705–7, accepts its application to the situation, generally regarded as but not in his view a 'trust' (see section 1.13), where someone unwittingly holds property received from true trustees (see section 8.1).

is required, or when the settlor's scheme offends the objects' desires, or otherwise over time comes to appear ill conceived. The law accordingly has rules allowing for trustees' duties to be modified. That is the topic for Chapter 12.

Trustees of resulting and constructive trusts are subject to the basic duty of respect for the trust with which this section began. They will also incur some duties of stewardship. But there these trusts probably (authoritative exemplification of the contention is scant)[2] diverge from express trusts. Where they call, as they often do, only for the entire property to be transferred to a particular person, by a single act and without delay, their trustees' duties of stewardship are less numerous and complex than those upon express trustees. There will be the duties of keeping the trust property safe described in section 9.2, but not the duties regarding management and investment, nor those regarding disposition, considered in the remainder of this and the following two chapters. The provisions for securing the satisfactory performance of those duties and for modifying them, explained thereafter, are also probably only patchily applicable to such trusts. Some resulting and constructive trusts call for more, however. Where a resulting trust arises as part of (because of the incompleteness of) a complex express trust,[3] the trustees should not differentiate their behaviour as between it and the express trust. The same is true where a constructive trust arises in respect of an express trustee's authorized acquisition.[4] And where a resulting or constructive trust is destined to last some time, as one for a child or involving family property, its trustees should manage the property accordingly.[5] These statements, which are moreover founded on principle rather than firm authority, do not amount to a precise statement of the duties in constructive and resulting trusts. In principle this is unsatisfactory, but few problems seem to arise in practice.

---

[2] And the contrary seems to have been assumed in *Lord Napier and Ettrick v Hunter* [1993] AC 713, 738, 744, 752.

[3] See section 7.5.

[4] See section 8.4.

[5] In particular, the statements in the Trusts of Land and Appointment of Trustees Act 1996 of trustees' duties regarding land held on trust do not generally differentiate between express trusts and the constructive and resulting trusts on which much land is in fact held (not least all land purportedly vested in more than one owner: Law of Property Act 1925 ss 34, 36).

9.2 SAFEGUARDING THE TRUST PROPERTY

If trust property does not survive, it cannot be transferred to the objects. Trustees accordingly have duties to safeguard it. One of these is a duty not to divert the property to anyone not entitled to it, including themselves. Another requires them not to mix it with other property (the danger being that it will prove impossible to retrieve from the mixture). A third requires them, if the trust property is not already in their own hands, to seek without delay to have it vested in themselves[6] or in their nominees or custodians.[7] Once there, a further duty requires them to endeavour to keep it safe.[8] In the case of a piece of land, for example, that might mean providing sensible security, and taking steps against any trespassers.

A trustee is probably[9] not required to safeguard the property come what may. She will be liable for failing to do so only if she knows, or should know, the property to be trust property. If she loses the trust property before realizing it to be trust property, she thus commits no wrong. And she is required not to guarantee the property's safety, but to exercise reasonable care and skill to safeguard it (though this does yield a strict duty not voluntarily to divert the property to someone not entitled to it).

The Trustee Act 2000 has introduced a new formulation of the duty of care incumbent on trustees in respect of certain of their duties. Subject to exclusion by the settlor,[10] a trustee 'must exercise such care and skill as is reasonable in the circumstances, having regard in particular—(a) to any special knowledge or experience that he has or holds himself out as having, and (b) if he acts as trustee in the course of a business or profession, to any special knowledge or experience that it is reasonable to expect of a person acting in the course of that kind of business or profession'.[11] Very arguably, 'the circumstances' include a particular trustee's *lack of* professed knowledge or experience, meaning that only a reduced level of care and skill can be demanded of him. This formulation is however applied

---

[6] *Wyman v Paterson* [1900] AC 271.

[7] Trustee Act 2000 ss 16, 17.

[8] *Speight v Gaunt* (1883) 9 App Cas 1.

[9] R Chambers *Resulting Trusts* (1997) 201–12; C Harpum in P Birks and F Rose (eds) *Restitution and Equity Volume One, Resulting Trusts and Equitable Compensation* (2000) 165–7. But the contrary seems to be assumed in *Westdeutsche Landesbank Girozentrale v Islington LBC* [1996] AC 669, 690, 703.

[10] Trustee Act 2000 Sch 1 para 7.

[11] Trustee Act 2000 s 1(1).

only to those trustees' functions listed in the Act,[12] and these do not include the duty to take care of the trust property. This, therefore, seems still to be governed by the previous formulation, namely that (again, subject to exclusion by the settlor)[13] a trustee should emulate an ordinary prudent man of business looking after the interests of others,[14] it being less clear than in the new formulation that the standard rises for professionals[15] and drops for avowed amateurs.

One would think that the general duty of keeping the property safe would commonly entail a duty to insure it. Curiously, this has never been authoritatively confirmed in England,[16] though it is clear that trustees can spend trust funds on the purpose.[17] In respect of details such as the choice of policy, trustees must use reasonable care and skill, as formulated in the 2000 Act.[18]

9.3 GENERAL MANAGEMENT

Pending the ultimate transfer of the trust property, especially where substantial time is to elapse before this (so especially, but not exclusively, in express trusts), trustees also have a number of more active management functions. One of them, the investment of the trust assets, is singled out and dealt with separately in the next section. Some others are considered here. They are, broadly, matters of housekeeping. They might include setting up, and where appropriate changing, bank accounts; deciding whether to employ an accountant, and if so choosing one; deciding whether and how to try to recoup from a solicitor loss caused to the trust by her bad advice, and implementing the decision taken; and so on, down to buying the postage stamps needed to communicate with the beneficiaries.

In respect of these matters, the law does not require trustees to take what hindsight reveals to be, or a judge might later think, the 'right'

---

[12] Sch 1.

[13] *Armitage v Nurse* [1998] Ch 241, 253.

[14] *Re Whiteley* (1886) 33 Ch D 347, *Learoyd v Whiteley* (1887) 12 App Cas 727. On the traditional rule see generally J Getzler in P Birks and A Pretto (eds) *Breach of Trust* (2002) ch 2.

[15] It was said to do so in *Re Waterman's Will Trusts* [1952] 2 All ER 1054, 1055, and *Bartlett v Barclay's Bank Trust Co Ltd* [1980] Ch 515, 534; but no such statement was made, where it would have been relevant, in *Nestlé v National Westminster Bank plc* [1993] 1 WLR 1260.

[16] Indeed, the old case *Bailey v Gould* (1840) 4 Y & C Ex 221 denied any duty; but one was accepted in *Pateman v Heyen* (1993) 33 NSWLR 188, Australia.

[17] Trustee Act 1925 s 19, substituted by Trustee Act 2000 s 34.

[18] Sch 1 para 5.

course.[19] So turning down an out-of-court settlement and instead suing the solicitor for her bad advice, only to lose the case completely, will not necessarily be a breach of their duty. Instead, the law leaves trustees[20] to exercise judgement as to whether something should be done, and if so what. It does, however, require them, in the way they exercise their judgement, to pursue an appropriate end; to adopt an appropriate philosophy; and to display an appropriate level of care and skill.

The end at which trustees must aim is the promotion of the interests of the trust's beneficiaries or purposes, to the exclusion of all else.[21] The philosophy with which they must pursue that end is (subject to exclusion by the settlor)[22] that of an ordinary prudent man of business looking after the interests of others.[23] That is, in seeking to promote the interests of the beneficiaries, they should generally be cautious and responsible rather than venturesome and idiosyncratic. Neither of these matters is affected by the Trustee Act 2000. The required level of care and skill is that described in the Act,[24] in relation to functions to which the Act applies it,[25] and otherwise that contained in the previous formulation:[26] both formulations were given in the last section.[27] As regards the quarrel with the trust's solicitor, therefore, the trustees should aim at looking after the trust's interests, rather than say at venting personal spite; should be cautious and responsible in deciding whether to pursue litigation, or accept an out-of-court settlement, or indeed cut their (the trust's) losses by admitting defeat; and should display the 2000 Act's standard of care and skill in pursuing whatever course they decide upon.[28]

[19] *Tempest v Lord Camoys* (1882) 21 Ch D 571.
[20] A settlor can stipulate for the trustees' choices to be subject to veto by some other person, or entrust such choices to such other person. The other person is nowadays often termed a 'protector', and may well be introduced into the trust to represent a particular interest, especially that of a particular beneficiary or the settlor. In that event, the protector (and hence the administration of the trust) may be free from the duties described in the following text. See D Waters in A Oakley (ed) *Trends in Contemporary Trust Law* (1996) ch 4.
[21] *Cowan v Scargill* [1985] Ch 270, 286. See further section 9.5. This requirement cannot be excluded: *Armitage v Nurse* [1998] Ch 241, 253-4.
[22] *Armitage v Nurse* [1998] Ch 241, 253.
[23] *Re Whiteley* (1886) 33 Ch D 347, *Learoyd v Whiteley* (1887) 12 App Cas 727. This statement of the required philosophy was thus combined with the old formulation of the required level of care and skill.
[24] Section 1.
[25] Sch 1.
[26] *Re Whiteley* (1886) 33 Ch D 347, *Learoyd v Whiteley* (1887) 12 App Cas 727.
[27] At nn 11, 14 above.
[28] This function being one to which the Act applies: Sch 1 para 4.

Much of the general management of a trust is not naturally attended to by the trustees themselves, but is given over to professional agents: clerks, bankers, solicitors, stockbrokers, and the like (unless the trustee is a trust corporation, such as a bank, when everything might be done under its own umbrella). Subject to certain safeguards regarding what functions are entrusted to whom and how, the law allows trustees to use agents and other kinds of representatives in this way.[29] Subject to exclusion by the settlor, the accustomed position follows. In deciding whether to use an agent, the trustees must follow the usual aim of acting in the trust's interests, and the usual philosophy of a prudent businessman looking after the interests of others. Especially the latter entails that if one of the trustees' functions is normally performed only by someone with special-ist expertise, and they lack that expertise, they should recruit someone who has it. Likewise, they should review the continuing satisfactoriness of any delegation.[30] Then, if a decision to delegate is made, the Trustee Act 2000 applies its statement of the necessary level of care and skill to the implementation of that decision[31] and to the required review of continuing satisfactoriness.[32]

9.4 INVESTMENT

The idea of investment is to produce a periodic return, or to preserve or increase the real value of the capital sum, or both. So investing trust property will help provide for the payments out to the beneficiaries. Say that a settlor settles £100,000, and stipulates for the income to be paid to you for your life, and then the capital to me. If the £100,000 were left in a non-interest-bearing bank account, there would be no income to pay to you, and the capital would still be £100,000 when, on your death, it had to be paid over to me. That would be displeasing if the worth of £100,000 had meanwhile been eroded by inflation. By investing the money, how-ever, it should be possible to do better. A return can be produced for payment to you. Everyday investments like bank deposit accounts and building society accounts provide this; company shares generally do too—'dividends'—but there is no guarantee: how much, if anything, they yield depends on how well the company is doing. It should also be possible to increase the value of the capital. Bank deposit accounts and

---

[29] Trustee Act 2000 Part IV. The facility can however be limited or excluded by the settlor: s 26.

[30] Ss 21, 22.   [31] Sch 1 para 3.   [32] Ss 21–3, Sch 1 para 3.

building society accounts do not have this feature of capital appreciation, but company shares generally do, because their value is a reflection of the actual worth of the undertaking, and if all goes well this will rise as part of the general growth of the economy; though again, there is no guarantee: the company could fade and then its shares will lose value. Land, too, can produce both an income return (eg if it is rented out) and capital appreciation.

Unsurprisingly, therefore, trustees[33] normally have the power[34] to invest the trust property (and to change investments from time to time). Even if there is no express duty to invest, as there often is (especially in unit trusts, of which it is the whole point), the general duty to act in the interests of the beneficiaries will normally require investment, so as to get the best financial return for them.[35] The trustees in the example above could hardly, given this requirement, receive the £100,000 and keep it as cash, providing no income for you and only £100,000, devalued by inflation, for me. But investing so as to seek the best financial return for the beneficiaries is not necessarily a simple matter. Before even approaching the selection of a particular investment, trustees seeking such a return must deal with two dilemmas of principle.

First, an investment's possible gains have to be weighed against its risks. Generally speaking, more speculative investments have the greater potential for large gains, but also for heavy losses (eg shares in a new company intending to prospect for gold, which might either make a fortune or fail completely). On the other hand excessive caution can equally result in loss, albeit by attrition rather than collapse (eg a basic savings account, which maintains its nominal capital value while inflation erodes its actual worth). Seeking the 'best' financial return involves striking a balance between these considerations. Secondly, different types of investment will affect different beneficiaries in different ways. There is an economic trade-off between maximizing income and preserving or

---

[33] Trustees may (Trustee Act 2000 s 11), and commonly will, delegate their investment function to an agent. The agent may be appointed on its own terms (s 14); only where this is 'reasonably necessary', but market conditions mean that it often will be. Subject to that, the agent must (s 13) broadly speaking follow the same precepts as to the conduct of the function as would have applied to the trustee. The settlor may also introduce a protector, see n 20 above, in respect of investment.

[34] Individual settlors may impose an express duty, as does the law itself in certain cases (eg Trustee Act 1925 s 31: where income that would otherwise be payable to an infant beneficiary is instead retained and added to the trust capital, it must be invested).

[35] *Cowan v Scargill* [1985] Ch 270, 286. See section 9.5 for the question whether a different approach is ever called for.

increasing capital value. Investments which are good for one tend to be relatively poor for the other. So an investment which is advantageous for objects entitled in the present (like you in the example above) would be disadvantageous for those entitled in the future (like me), and vice versa. Again, a balance has to be struck. The law controls the way in which trustees strike these balances, and the choices of investments that they then go on to make.

To control the balances struck, the law uses the familiar technique of a requirement as to philosophy. The Trustee Act 2000 requires trustees to appraise possible investments in terms of their 'suitability to the trust'.[36] The traditional formulations were more explicit and may continue to give guidance. As regards the balance between risk and caution, the approved philosophy was the familiar one of an ordinary prudent businessman acting on behalf of others.[37] For the balance between income (for present beneficiaries) and capital (for future beneficiaries), the requirement was of even-handedness,[38] more recently expressed as fairness.[39] Especially operating together, these ideas tended, and would still tend, to produce a relatively conservative approach to investment. A prudent businessman investing on behalf of others and trying to be fair as amongst them would, in particular, not wish to place the capital at significant risk.[40]

The trustees must then select a particular investment from among those 'suitable'.[41] In this, they must, unless the settlor negates this, exercise

---

[36] S 4(3)(a). This duty is apparently not excludable by a settlor.

[37] *Re Whiteley* (1886) 33 Ch D 347, *Learoyd v Whiteley* (1887) 12 App Cas 727.

[38] *Raby v Ridehalgh* (1855) 7 De GM & G 104. As regards certain scenarios, the law translates this requirement into detailed rules, especially that in *Howe v Earl of Dartmouth* (1802) 7 Ves 137. The complexity and patchiness of these rules is problematic, however, and their abolition (leaving the more abstract requirement of even-handedness) has been recommended: Law Reform Committee 23rd Report *The powers and duties of trustees* Cmnd 8733 (1982) Part III.

[39] *Nestlé v National Westminster Bank plc* [1993] 1 WLR 1260. The change may be one of substance: trustees are now said (ibid, 1279) to be permitted, for example, to seek income at the expense of capital value so as to favour a poor beneficiary over a rich one, or a close relative of the settlor over a distant one. Presumably this conversion of the discretion from administrative to dispositive (cf section 11.1) is ascribable to the settlor's intentions.

[40] *Nestlé v National Westminster Bank plc* [1993] 1 WLR 1260, 1284–5. As the unreported first instance judgment in the case asserted, however, the correct approach is not to view each investment in isolation, but to consider the exposure of the portfolio as a whole.

[41] They may consult the beneficiaries as to their wishes, so long as they do not surrender their own ultimate discretion: *Fraser v Murdoch* (1881) 6 App Cas 855, Scotland. According to *X v A* [2000] 1 All ER 490, they *must* so consult, but this is unlikely, if only for impracticability. Where the trust is of land, however, they must (unless the settlor ordains otherwise) consult the beneficiaries and give effect to their majority wish, 'so far as consistent with the general interest of the trust': Trusts of Land and Appointment of Trustees Act 1996 s 11.

the level of care and skill described by the 2000 Act, noted above.[42] This requirement is partly explicated by rules that trustees must have regard to the need to diversify the trust's investments, so far as is appropriate to its circumstances;[43] and that they must obtain and consider the advice of a person qualified to give it, unless they reasonably consider it unnecessary in the circumstances to do so.[44] Although phrases such as 'have regard to' and 'obtain and consider', and the possibility of not seeking advice at all, make these latter rules rather loose, the desirability of staying clearly within them nevertheless exerts a degree of pressure. Oddly, whilst the requirement to exercise the usual standard of care and skill can be negated by the settlor,[45] these latter rules apparently cannot.

Investment choices complying with these requirements as to philosophy and care and skill will not be interfered with on the basis that a judge thinks them nonetheless inappropriate.[46] It is, however, possible to deny trustees certain choices altogether. Rules to this effect were once an important feature of the law. Before 1961, they broadly speaking allowed trustees to invest only in government securities, not in company shares ('equities'). Prior to the late nineteenth century, this was an intelligible position. Equities were not then a credible form of responsible investment. The law regulating companies' conduct *vis-à-vis* their shareholders was comparatively primitive, and, following such earlier debacles as the South Sea Bubble, from 1825 to 1866 there was a series of roughly decennial financial catastrophes. People were still lured into such investments, but there was a clear sense that they were foolish.[47] From the late nineteenth century on, the modern, more favourable, view of equity investment emerged, but the law did not fully reflect this shift until the Trustee Investments Act 1961 allowed trustees to invest in shares. This new facility extended only to half of the trust's property, however, and was subject to certain other restrictions. These limitations too were soon found unduly restrictive. They were removed by the Trustee Act 2000, which allows trustees to invest trust property in any way that would be open to

---

[42] Trustee Act 2000 s 1 (see at n 11 above), Sch 1 para 1.

[43] Trustee Act 2000 s 4(3)(b).

[44] Trustee Act 2000 s 5. The exception could apply to very small trusts and to trustees (including corporate trustees) who are themselves qualified to give the advice.

[45] Trustee Act 2000 Sch 1 para 7.

[46] *Tempest v Lord Camoys* (1882) 21 Ch D 571.

[47] See Charles Dickens's *Little Dorrit* (1855–7), where Mr Clennam invests partnership (ie trust) money in Mr Merdle's undertakings, and is mortified as they then collapse. For the background, see Dickens's 1857 Preface, and N Russell *The Novelist and Mammon* (1986).

them if they were its absolute owners,[48] and controls their decisions only in the manner described above.

The investment of the assets of pension fund trusts and unit trusts is generally not subject to the regime of the 2000 Act.[49] Pension fund trusts are, however, in this respect governed by some essentially similar provisions of the Pensions Act 1995,[50] while the investment arrangements of unit trusts are governed by those trusts' own defining instruments, backed by financial services regulations.[51]

9.5 THE PRIMACY OF THE OBJECTS' (FINANCIAL) INTERESTS

It was stated above that trustees must act in the trust's best interests.[52] Various court rulings have assumed that this obliges trustees to seek the best financial return for the objects, both in the matter of investment and in managing the trust generally. Trustees selling trust property must allow gazumping, ie must renege on an informal agreement to accept a certain price if they later receive a higher offer.[53] They must take possession of the property which the settlor has placed in trust, even if it is in the hands of the beneficiaries' relatives and to insist on retrieving it from them will damage family relationships.[54] And they must choose investments with an eye to financial return rather than to the moral or political positions held by some of their beneficiaries, or argued (ultimately unverifiably) to be implicit in their charitable purposes.[55]

This equation between a duty to promote the objects' interests and one to maximize the financial benefit to them is not inevitable, however. Whilst the former cannot be excluded,[56] the latter certainly can be. An express or implied stipulation by the settlor can achieve this: as where say paintings, furniture, or jewellery are placed on trust for use as such,

---

[48] S 3. The range of permitted investments can however be limited by the settlor: s 6. A settlor might for example insist on investment only in ethical funds.

[49] Trustee Act 2000 ss 36, 37.

[50] Ss 34–6. The duty of care and skill (which remains defined by the traditional formulation) cannot be excluded: s 33.

[51] Again, the duty of care and skill cannot be excluded: Financial Services Act 1986 s 84.

[52] *Cowan v Scargill* [1985] Ch 270, 286.

[53] *Buttle v Saunders* [1950] 2 All ER 193.

[54] *Re Brogden* (1888) 38 Ch D 546.

[55] *Cowan v Scargill* [1985] Ch 270; *Harries v Church Commissioners for England* [1992] 1 WLR 1241.

[56] *Armitage v Nurse* [1998] Ch 241, 253–4.

rather than to be sold and the proceeds invested for a yield;[57] or where a potential investment (eg in a tobacco company) would be indisputably antagonistic to the trust's purposes (prevention of heart disease).[58] Likewise an express or implied preference on the part of the beneficiaries themselves: a position held by all a trust's beneficiaries (say, against the drinking of alcohol) takes precedence over contradictory financial considerations (indicating, say, investment in a brewery).[59] If a sufficiently uncontroversial alternative conception of benefit could be identified, it might also in principle be possible for trustees to take a non-financial view of their beneficiaries' benefit, unless the settlor insisted otherwise. But in our culture it is questionable whether such a conception can be identified, though in another context the courts have found benefit for beneficiaries, outweighing financial loss, in various kinds of family well-being.[60]

Is it possible to go further, and suggest that trustees need not necessarily act in their objects' best (financial or non-financial) interests at all? The duty to do so has been said to be fundamental to the very idea of a trust,[61] and as already noted is therefore not excludable even by the settlor,[62] though beneficiaries could presumably condone a breach of it.[63] Derived from this duty is the rule that trustees must not promote their own values over the objects' interests, where the two conflict.[64] (The argument that particular people or institutions are appointed trustees for their individual qualities, and so should not be required to disregard their own values,[65] is not detectable in the material on trustees' management duties.) So long as the effect is not to exclude all obligation to serve the objects, however, the law itself can instruct trustees to give priority to some competing goal of public policy. Various goals might be promoted at the expense of the objects' interests in this way. Given the vast amount of

---

[57] A very familiar instance is the holding of stately homes and their contents by charities such as the National Trust, but provisions for use by beneficiaries are also common in family trusts.

[58] *Harries v Church Commissioners for England* [1992] 1 WLR 1241, 1246–7.

[59] *Cowan v Scargill* [1985] Ch 270, 288.

[60] *Re T* [1964] Ch 158; *Re Weston's Settlements* [1969] 1 Ch 223; *Re CL* [1969] 1 Ch 587; *Re Remnant's Settlement Trusts* [1970] Ch 560: all dealing with the variation of trusts (section 12.5).

[61] *Armitage v Nurse* [1998] Ch 241, 253–4.

[62] Ibid. It was held that a clause requiring trustees only to act 'honestly' would exclude all but this duty; but a trustee (or perhaps only an especially qualified trustee, such as a solicitor) acts 'honestly' only if his actions can *reasonably* be viewed as in the beneficiaries' interests: *Walker v Stones* [2001] QB 902, 939.

[63] See section 12.3.

[64] *Cowan v Scargill* [1985] Ch 270, 286–8.

[65] Cf section 1.6.

wealth that is tied up in trusts, a prominent concern might be the good of the economy. As we saw in section 2.5, economic liberalism is chary of trusts, because (at the lowest)[66] the caution associated with serving the interests of others militates against full exposure of the trust property to the market and so the maximization of wealth and happiness. To counteract that, trustees would need, in managing their trusts, to forget that they are trustees. At one point, the law briefly experimented with a rule ordering them to do so. Before it came to refer to the prudent businessman looking after the interests of others,[67] the formulation of the required philosophy instructed trustees to emulate an ordinary prudent man of business *acting on his own behalf.*[68] This approach was dropped presumably because it was felt to go too far in subordinating the objects' interests. Another impediment to the maximization of wealth is sometimes said to be the phenomenon of 'short-termism', whereby money is invested so as to produce an advantageous return in the short term, rather than for the long-term benefit of the economy. During the 1980s there was accordingly a proposal that the law should conscript a proportion of the assets of institutional investors, including large trusts, away from the service of their objects' interests to the financing of a national investment bank, whose remit would be the promotion of domestic industrial development; but this proposal was never implemented.[69]

At first sight, the fundamental necessity for trustees to serve their objects' interests seems to conflict with some rules that trustees may buy land for a beneficiary's occupation or 'for any other reason',[70] and that a beneficiary may, under certain circumstances, claim trust land for his occupation.[71] The occupying beneficiary can be regarded as choosing to enjoy his interest in a non-financial form. But as the assets concerned are

---

[66] The ability to make any kind of investment available to an absolute owner (Trustee Act 2000 s 3(1)) now means that the problem is no worse than that; previously the law itself placed some forms of investment to some extent out of bounds for trusts. See section 9.4.

[67] *Re Whiteley* (1886) 33 Ch D 347, *Learoyd v Whiteley* (1887) 12 App Cas 727.

[68] *Speight v Gaunt* (1883) 22 Ch D 727, 9 App Cas 1.

[69] The idea was a minority recommendation in the *Report of the Committee to Review the Functioning of Financial Institutions* Cmnd 7937 (1980) ch 20, and was Labour Party policy for the 1983 and 1987 elections. An attempt by the National Union of Mineworkers to have the National Coal Board's pension fund invested along such lines (ahead of legislation) was the background to *Cowan v Scargill* [1985] Ch 270, which reaffirmed trustees' duty to secure the best financial return for their beneficiaries.

[70] Trustee Act 2000 s 8(1). The power can be excluded by the settlor: s 9(b).

[71] Trusts of Land and Appointment of Trustees Act 1996 ss 12, 13.

in no way used for the benefit of the non-occupying beneficiaries,[72] the rules appear to exclude the duty to serve their interests. Perhaps, however, the idea is that trustees are given a discretion, to the extent of these rules, to suspend or destroy beneficiaries' interests: in which case those interests would not exist to be served. (Discretions to adjust beneficial interests are considered in Chapter 11.) But if all the beneficiaries' interests were destroyed in this way for the sake of 'any other reason', no trust would remain. The rules may not be fully supportable, therefore.

[72] The occupying beneficiary may (but not must) be charged rent (s 13(6)), but this is paid only to other beneficiaries who might have occupied the same land, and thus does not equate to an investment return for all the other beneficiaries to whom such a return would otherwise have been payable. In some cases family comity may be served, but there is nothing to restrict the application of the rules to such cases.

10

Operating fixed trusts

The point of an express trust is to confer benefits upon the objects. Sometimes this will be by the transfer of some or all of the capital; more often, at least for a period, the capital is held and invested to produce an income, as we saw in the last chapter, and this income is paid to the objects. The essence of the operation, payment out according to the settlor's stipulations, is the same either way. In this chapter and the next we shall look at what this operation involves.

On the face of it, payment out would seem a straightforward exercise. If the trust provides for the money to go to such-and-such a person, that seems to be the long and short of it: the trustees have to pay that person, no more and no less. There are none of the questions of judgement which we found as regards management. In some trusts, in fact, matters are not so simple, because the settlor leaves the trustees to decide such questions as who shall be paid, how much, and when: this is the case in discretionary trusts, and in powers of appointment, maintenance, and advancement. Here the actual business of payment is preceded by these discretionary activities on the part of the trustees, and the law's attitude to the conduct of the latter is a matter of interest in its own right. We shall look at that in the next chapter. In the present chapter, we shall confine ourselves to the kind of trust, known as a 'fixed trust', where there is no such complication: the beneficiaries' entitlements are established by the settlor.

So, for example, '£1,000 to Adam', '£2,000 each to Adam and Briony', '£3,000 to be divided equally between Adam, Briony, and Caitlin' would all be fixed trusts. But '£4,000 to be divided as my trustees think right between Adam, Briony, and Caitlin' would be a discretionary trust, which we are leaving for the moment.

10.1 DISTRIBUTION IN FIXED TRUSTS

The duty to pay the trust's objects is known as the 'duty to distribute'. The trustees must pay the correct amount to the designated object(s), and refrain from paying anyone else.

In some cases, the trustees have simply to follow the settlor's stipulation. In '£1,000 to Adam', for example, they have to pay Adam his £1,000, and not pay it to anyone other than Adam. Similarly with '£2,000 each to Adam and Briony': they have to pay Adam and Briony (and no one else) their £2,000 each. In cases of this kind the payment to each individual beneficiary is independent, and carrying it out requires no reference to any surrounding dispositions. In '£1,000 to Adam' this is obvious: Adam is the only beneficiary. '£2,000 each to Adam and Briony' takes a moment's thought, but the point is that it consists of two dispositions, each of £2,000, one to Adam and one to Briony: it could equally well be expressed in the form '£2,000 to Adam; £2,000 to Briony'. A problem with one of the dispositions need have no repercussions on the other. So if there is no such person as Briony, it makes no difference to the position regarding Adam: he still gets his £2,000, no more and no less.

In other cases, there is an additional stage. Before the trustees come to make the actual payment, they need to calculate each beneficiary's entitlement: '£3,000 to be divided equally between Adam, Briony, and Caitlin' is a case of this kind. To know how much they have to pay each object, the trustees have to divide the total amount available (£3,000) by the number of objects (three). Such a trust is still fixed: the amounts of the beneficiaries' entitlements do not depend on the trustees' discretion. But its terms stipulate not the actual amount to be paid to each individual beneficiary, as in the cases covered in the last paragraph, but the arithmetical formula by which that amount is to be calculated. The trustees have to perform the calculation in order to arrive at a concrete figure. And in contrast to those cases, the figure arrived at will vary with the circumstances. We saw a moment ago how the non-existence of Briony made no difference to Adam: he still got his own £2,000, no more and no less. But if there is no such person as Caitlin (say she has already died), Adam and Briony will each get £1,500 from the £3,000 which was to have been divided equally between the three, but now only two, of them.

10.2 THE NEED FOR CERTAINTY

According to the law's classical position (which we shall examine further in section 14.6), a disposition can be accepted as a valid trust only if it is guaranteed to be capable of enforcement.[1] That is, the trustees'

---

[1] *Morice v Bishop of Durham* (1804) 9 Ves 399, (1805) 10 Ves 522.

duties—such as those just described—must be capable of performance by them, and this performance must be susceptible to judicial scrutiny and if necessary enforcement and correction. This requirement seems to stem from the provision of trusts as facilitative devices: in offering them to settlors as vehicles for giving effect to their wishes, the law has to ensure that they can be relied upon to do just that.

So say a settlor required her trustees 'to pay most of the income to my nicest grandchild, the rest to the others'. This instruction would be invalid, because the trustees and the court could not say how much (what is 'most'?) should be paid to whom (who is the 'nicest' grandchild?). The example shows how imprecision in the instructions to the trustees can entail the invalidity of the trust, because it can mean that the trustees' duties cannot be performed or supervised in the required way. Precision sufficient to the duty in question is needed—and in the example is lacking—both as to the amount of money to be paid ('certainty of subject matter') and as to the identity of the person to whom, or purpose upon which, it must be paid ('certainty of object').

10.3 CERTAINTY OF SUBJECT MATTER

So the subject matter must be well enough identified that the trustees and the court can know what it is.[2] Where different provisions are made for different objects of the trust, the trustees and the court must also be able to say what property is dedicated to each provision.

References to particular assets, such as 'my house', will normally be sufficiently precise, unless there is a difficulty such as ambiguity (eg if I have two houses). But a problem seems to arise if the reference is to *part of* an asset or collection of assets. Say I declare a trust (ie create a trust with myself as trustee) of £1,000, or of 100 of my 1,000 shares in X Co, in your favour. How are we to know which £1,000 amongst the £20,000 that I in fact have, or which 100 of the 1,000 shares, are the subject matter of the trust, to be distributed to you? We might need to know this if, for example, I subsequently gamble away £10,000 of the money or 500 of the shares in my possession. Do my losses include the £1,000 or 100 shares of which I declared myself trustee for you, or do they extend only to the assets which I retained as my own?

The courts have not allowed this problem to invalidate such trusts,

---

[2] The property so identified must also exist. So a trust of 'the contents of my deposit account', when I have no deposit account, would have no effect: *MacJordan Construction Ltd v Brookmount Erostin Ltd* [1992] BCLC 350; *Re Goldcorp Exchange Ltd* [1995] 1 AC 74.

however.[3] If the trust is valid, I (as trustee) incur duties to safeguard the trust property; notably, the duty to bring about that it stands in my hands in a form unmixed with other assets.[4] If I perform this duty, the £1,000 or 100 shares which will belong to the trust will thenceforth be separately identified, and it will be possible to say whether a later transaction on my part, such as a gambling loss, affects them or only my own property. If on the other hand I do not perform this duty, so that the £1,000 or 100 shares remain unseparated from my own assets, I have in effect wrongfully mixed them with the latter. The tracing rules, aimed at allocating the assets emerging from and remaining in wrongful mixtures, will then say whether my gambling losses comprise the trust assets as well as my own.[5] By this reasoning, the problem we initially identified falls away, and there remains no difficulty about regarding such dispositions as valid trusts.

But since this approach relies on the trustee to separate the trust assets out from the surrounding pool, there is a further difficulty if the assets in the pool are not all the same. Each £1 in my £20,000 is the same as any other, and all my shares in X Co are (let us say) of the same kind. So it does not matter which £1,000, or which 100 shares, I separate out. But if I purport to declare myself trustee of, say, '10 hectares of my land', or '20 cases from my stock of wine', the question 'which 10 hectares or 20 cases are the trust's?' cannot be so simply answered 'whichever 10 hectares or 20 cases the trustee separates out', because some of my land and wine will be different from (better than) the rest. The presence of this additional difficulty in such cases has led the courts to rule that purported trusts of part of a collection of heterogeneous assets are invalid for uncertainty.[6] This position is not inevitable, however. It will sometimes, though not always,[7] be possible to think that the settlor has given the trustee the further duty of choosing which of the heterogeneous assets shall be held for the specified object(s), and which shall remain the settlor's: ie that the settlor has created a trust which is to this extent discretionary.[8] Given such a duty, there is no reason why the trust should not succeed, so long

---

[3] *Hunter v Moss* [1994] 1 WLR 452.

[4] See section 9.2.

[5] See section 8.6. On the facts as given, the trust's £1,000 or 100 shares would be regarded as part of the remaining assets.

[6] *Re London Wine Co (Shippers) Ltd* [1986] PCC 121.

[7] Sometimes it will not make sense to think that the trustee can favour one object over another in this way: eg where the trustee is a dealer holding a bulk store of a heterogeneous commodity for its customers, as between whom it should be neutral. *Re London Wine Co (Shippers) Ltd* [1986] PCC 121 was a case of this kind. [8] Cf Ch 11.

as there is sufficient identification of the overall collection of assets from which the choice is to be made.[9]

Finally, contrast expressions such as '£1,000', or '100 of my 1,000 shares in X Co', or '10 hectares of my land', or '20 cases from my stock of wine' with others such as 'most of my land', or 'the bulk of my money'. The latter suffer from yet a further difficulty. As well as not saying *which* among the relevant collection of assets shall be held on the trust, the settlor has not even said *how much* of it shall be. The courts have accordingly held trusts of this latter kind invalid.[10] But an apparently imprecise expression will be acceptable if the identification is supplied in some other way. 'Income' sounds vague, in that the income from an asset can vary over time, as for example interest rates change. But a trust to hold £1,000 on trust and pay the income as it arises to Adam will be valid, as by the time the trustee has to pay each instalment of income to Adam the amount of that instalment will necessarily have been established. Likewise, it is common for a testator to leave the 'residue' of her estate on trust: that is, the property left in her estate after the payment of particular legacies. 'Residue' sounds vague, but when the testator dies and her estate is reckoned up, which is the time from which the trust will come into effect, it will necessarily be possible to say precisely what constitutes the residue. So such a trust will be valid. A trust to pay a beneficiary 'a reasonable income' has also been held valid on the basis that 'a reasonable income' can be objectively determined,[11] but this may be thought optimistic. Beyond such cases, too, it should once again sometimes be possible to read a trust of this kind as requiring the trustee to decide how much of the property in question the designated object(s) shall have, ie as a valid discretionary trust.[12]

---

[9] Note too that a trust giving you some part of a collection of assets can be valid as a trust of the collection for both of us as 'co-owners'. Then, neither of us is entitled to any particular part of the collection: it remains a single entity, held for us together, in proportion to our shares. A declaration in your favour of a trust of 'half of my land' might well be read thus. But it seems that a declaration of a trust of '10 hectares', when I in fact possess 20 hectares, will not (but rather in the manner, and with the problems, discussed in the text). Arguably, the law ought to be readier to salvage such dispositions by adopting such a reading, by analogy with the devices regarding certainty of objects discussed in section 10.5.

[10] *Sprange v Barnard* (1789) 2 Bro CC 585; *Palmer v Simmonds* (1854) 2 Drew 221.

[11] *Re Golay* [1965] 1 WLR 969.

[12] Cf Ch 11.

10.4 CERTAINTY OF OBJECTS

The trust's beneficiaries,[13] too, must be identified well enough for the performance of the duty to distribute.

Consider a perfect distribution, ie one in which the designated objects are correctly paid, period. Consider then its implications in terms of the identification of the beneficiaries. (In a moment we shall see that the law, deterred by the difficulty of the latter, does not in fact demand a perfect distribution, but this theoretically ideal position is the right place to start.) To pay the right people, the trustees need to know who the beneficiaries are and to be able to locate them. To avoid paying the wrong people, they need to be able to tell whether any given person is or is not a beneficiary. When the trust involves the further operation of quantifying the beneficiaries' entitlements, they also need to know how many beneficiaries there are, because this information will always figure in the calculation. Remember our example of '£3,000 to be divided equally between Adam, Briony, and Caitlin'. To know whether Adam should be paid £1,000 or £1,500 or £3,000, they need to know whether the £3,000 has to be shared equally with two other people (Briony and Caitlin), or one (Briony or Caitlin), or none.

There are in fact four different kinds of information involved in all this, and it will be helpful to separate them.[14]

To be able to know who is a beneficiary and who is not, so as not to pay the wrong people, would require two kinds. First, that the description of beneficiaries used in the trust should be precise enough that one could say in principle (ie assuming that the facts are clear) whether someone matched it or not. This quality is called 'conceptual[15] certainty'. So something like 'Adam Smith, of [his address]', or 'my husband', will normally be valid. But 'my old friends', for example, will not. We might have no doubt about people's relations with the settlor, but not know whether or not they fitted the description because we are unsure what kind, degree, or duration of amity the description requires. Secondly, given conceptual certainty, it would need to be possible to determine whether someone matched the description on the facts. This requirement is called 'evidential[16] certainty'. For example, the description might be 'the former employees of X Co'. As a description, this seems perfectly clear, but if the

---

[13] Or purposes: essentially the same considerations will apply.
[14] See generally C Emery (1982) 98 LQR 551.
[15] Or 'semantic', or 'linguistic', or 'definitional'. [16] Or 'factual'.

company's premises have been burnt down and some of the former employees have lost their old payslips and so on, it might be impossible for the trustees to know whether they fit it or not.

Thirdly, in those cases where quantification is needed as a prelude to distribution, the trustees would need to be able to know the total number of beneficiaries. Conceptual and evidential certainty alone, equipping the trustees to say whether people are beneficiaries *when they claim*, would not suffice for this.[17] To perform the calculations required to quantify the beneficiaries' shares, the trustees would need to know the number of beneficiaries: and to do so even if the beneficiaries do not come forward to claim. In the instance '£3,000 to be divided equally between Adam, Briony, and Caitlin', for example, in order to know whether to pay Adam £1,000, or £1,500, or £3,000, the trustees would need to know whether Adam is the only extant beneficiary or whether he has to share the £3,000 with one or with two others, ie whether Briony and Caitlin exist: and they must be able to know this even if no one claiming to be Briony or Caitlin presents herself. (As in this example, the usual way of knowing the number is to identify—though not necessarily locate—those entitled, and so the requirement is often referred to as one for a 'complete list' of beneficiaries. But in principle the crucial information is the number.) A description which might be deficient in this respect is 'all the descendants of Y'. If a settlor created a trust to divide £10,000 between 'all the descendants of Y', there might be no conceptual or (given DNA testing) evidential uncertainty, ie no obstacle to deciding on the entitlement of anyone who claimed, but the trustees might well not be able to discover the total number involved, so as to put a figure on the individual entitlements.

Fourthly, a perfect performance of the duty to distribute would involve not just knowing who are the right people and who are not, and sometimes working out the size of the right people's entitlements, but also actually paying them. To do this, the trustees would need to be able to find them. This goes further even than the requirement which we have just discussed. That did not involve the trustees actually being able to find the beneficiaries; just being able to know how many they were, so as to calculate their shares. Physically to pay money over to someone, it is necessary to locate them.

In short, then, for a perfect performance of the duty to distribute in a

---

[17] Some accounts use the expression 'evidential certainty' to refer, without distinction, to the two issues which the text insists on separating, namely (reactive) evidential certainty and (proactive) enumerability.

fixed trust, there would need to be conceptual and evidential certainty as to the identity of the beneficiaries, and knowledge of their whereabouts. In cases where the trustees have to quantify the beneficiaries' shares, they would also need to be able to know of their existence; but in fact this does not demand anything extra, because it is subsumed within the ability to locate them.

This position would be extremely exigent. The possibility, for example, that the trustees might not be able to perform their duty actually to pay out to the beneficiaries would apparently invalidate a purported trust. Such a possibility would be almost inevitable, for a beneficiary might disappear at any moment. The implication is that valid trusts would be rare. That would pose a problem for the facilitative project. Trusts are supposed to offer a legal facility by which people can make certain kinds of dispositions. There would be little point in offering such a facility if people had to meet such impossible certainty requirements in order to take advantage of it.

The problem arises from the nature of the operations that appear to be required of trustees. As we have seen, a perfect distribution requires trustees to clear a number of practical hurdles, and the certainty requirements have to anticipate the difficulties inherent in these. To enable the certainty requirements to be relaxed, so allowing sensible access to the facility after all, therefore, the law does not in fact seek a perfect distribution. There are several rules which require less of trustees.

10.5 DILUTING THE REQUIRED DISTRIBUTION

These rules exist in respect of each of the four aspects of certainty that we considered above.

Take first the need to be able to locate the beneficiaries, so as to pay them their entitlements.

The problem is that a beneficiary might disappear at any time, making it impossible to guarantee that this duty can be performed. The law's solution has been to allow trustees to discharge their duty to pay out the money without it necessarily reaching the hands of the designated objects. If a beneficiary cannot be found, his share can be paid into court, whence he can claim it if and when he turns up. Moreover, in certain relatively safe cases a missing beneficiary's share can be paid to other beneficiaries instead. If either there is evidence that a beneficiary is dead, or he is presumed to be, as having disappeared for seven years, or if he has failed to respond to advertisements placed in newspapers, the trustees can[18] obtain a court order permitting them to administer the trust in disregard of his claim.[19] Thus, if he is an object of a trust requiring money to be shared between a number of objects, the trustees can divide his share amongst the other objects. Relaxing the duty to pay out to the designated objects in these ways, then, means that there is no need to be able to locate them after all: so this requirement is in effect removed.

The difficulty of knowing the total number of beneficiaries, so as to quantify their shares in trusts where that is necessary, has been eased by placing special meanings on some of the most frequently used descriptions, so as to confine them to groups whose numbers are likely to be easily discoverable. 'My relatives', for example, could be troublesome. Meaning all those connected with the settlor by blood, it is conceptually certain, and let us assume that there is no problem with evidential certainty, but trustees might well find it hard to know the number of such people off their own bat. So the law presumes that 'my relatives' means instead only the settlor's statutory next-of-kin, which is likely to be a much tighter class, with a much better prospect of enumerability.[20] This device is, however, obviously useful only in certain cases, rather than across the board. A more generalized palliative seems not to have been devised.[21]

---

[18] Arguably, not 'can' but 'should'. Since trustees' options must be exercised in the best interests of all their beneficiaries, and since a decision to exclude would surely contravene that rule, as palpably not in the interests of the missing beneficiaries, the facility surely cannot viably exist as an *option*. Whereas a *duty* to exclude could comprise a recognition that the facility sacrifices the interests of missing beneficiaries, together with a judgment on the law's part that it is right to do so.

[19] *Re Benjamin* [1902] 1 Ch 723; Trustee Act 1925 s 27 (though the latter does not apply to all kinds of trust). These devices do not immediately destroy the unpaid beneficiary's entitlement. If, up to six years later, he turns up after all, he can reclaim his share from those to whom it has been paid over. But they absolve the trustees from the breach of their duty to pay the beneficiary which they would otherwise have committed, and for which they would have been obliged to compensate him. A different approach is for the trustees to accept the risk of being in breach, but to buy (at the trust's expense) 'missing beneficiary insurance' to cover their liability if the missing beneficiary reappears and claims against them.

[20] This presumption operates only as a palliative to difficulties of enumerability; in cases where such difficulties do not arise, 'relatives' is given its more natural wider meaning of all blood relations: *Re Poulton's Will Trusts* [1987] 1 WLR 795. In the discretionary trust case *Re Baden's Deed Trusts (No 2)* [1973] Ch 9, Stamp LJ (at 27–9), in a minority on this point, used the device so as to allow the listing of beneficiaries (if not complete, then close to it) which he wrongly thought to be required in that context.

[21] It may however be suggested that a generalized device could be found, by extension of existing 'class-closing rules'. Where trustees are to distribute to a class which at the moment is open ended, eg 'my grandchildren' (some of whom may not yet have been born), these rules allow the class to be closed off on to those members who already exist. The calculations and distribution are then made solely on this basis: a future-born grandchild cannot

Evidential certainty is in principle necessary so as to distribute to the true beneficiaries, and to no one else. It is the ability to know whether, on the facts, any given person is or is not entitled to payment. The problem is that there is always quite a strong chance that the answer might be unclear. This time the response is to say that it is up to the putative beneficiary to prove, on a balance of probabilities, that she fits the trust's description of its beneficiaries. If she cannot prove that she does, then it is taken that she does not.[22] So as far as evidential matters are concerned, then, the trustees' apparent duty to pay the right people and not the wrong people becomes instead one of paying those, but only those, who can prove themselves entitled. The requirement of evidential certainty is thus virtually eliminated: so long as the description used is of a nature that it is not impossible for people to show that they fit it, which is hardly likely, potential evidential difficulties will not be a reason for invalidity.

The same technique is also used to reduce difficulties of conceptual certainty. Again, it is up to the claimant to show on a balance of probabilities that she is within the description—but this time in the sense that the meaning of the description used is such as to embrace her. So a description will be sufficiently certain so long as it is possible for a claimant to do that: that is, so long as the description is not devoid of any clear meaning at all. Take the description 'my old friends'. Although this has a large grey area in which it is hard to say whether a person qualifies, it also has a recognizable core meaning (we could think of at least one 'old friend', even if only hypothetically). So it is valid; and actual claimants are then left to show that it covers someone like them. This approach was originally taken in *Re Allen*.[23] In *Re Gulbenkian's Settlement Trusts*,[24] however, it was disapproved in favour of the purist view, deduced in section

---

claim a share back from those thus paid. The idea is that the settlor's intention for (say) his existing grandchildren to have some money is higher than his wish to benefit all his grandchildren. As it stands, this device does not help in the case where, amongst the beneficiaries who *already* exist, there may be some whom the trustees do not know about. But could not a similar approach be used to allow the trustees to divide the fund only between those beneficiaries who are known to them? It would mean attributing to the settlor the higher intention of saving his trust from invalidity; which seems not less plausible than the higher intention which supports the present form of the class-closing rules, or than the special meaning given, where helpful, to the word 'relatives'.

[22] *Re Baden's Deed Trusts (No 2)* [1973] Ch 9, 19–20, Sachs LJ; the remaining judges do not address the issue. The case deals with discretionary trusts, but it should apply equally to the fixed trusts under discussion here, as the relevant duty—paying (only) objects—is the same in both.

[23] [1953] Ch 810.

[24] [1970] AC 508; followed for discretionary trusts in *McPhail v Doulton* [1971] AC 424.

10.4, whereby the terms of the description must allow one to say definitely whether or not any given person fits it. This decision concerned powers of appointment rather than fixed trusts, but the requirement of conceptual certainty is aimed at the duty of not paying the wrong people, which is common to all types of disposition, and so ought to be the same across the board. However, in the context of fixed trusts *Re Gulbenkian's Settlement Trusts*[25] has not been followed: the approach in *Re Allen*[26] was taken up again in *Re Barlow's Will Trusts*,[27] and that is the present position.

10.6 DUTIES, CERTAINTY, AND THE FACILITATIVE PROJECT

In short, then, the theoretically ideal notion of distribution under a fixed trust is that payment should be made to all those, and only those, designated by the settlor. But a trust has to be guaranteed operable in order to be valid, and a duty to distribute in this form would demand so much in the way of certainty that in all probability no trust would ever be valid. In reality, the certainty requirements for fixed trusts are less daunting.

We have examined the devices used to produce these lower certainty requirements. They are various in their juridical nature. Some, for example, are put in terms of an interpretation of the words used, others in terms of burdens of proof. But essentially, they all address what is required by way of distribution. In place of the ideal of paying all those, and only those, designated by the settlor, they imply a qualified duty, which requires less certainty. Trustees must pay people who can show on a balance of probabilities that they fit the settlor's description, conceptually and evidentially, and not those who cannot; and if they cannot find a particular person whom they are supposed to pay, they can generally administer the trust in disregard of her entitlement, or pay the money into court. Where trustees need first to quantify the beneficiaries' shares, and so need to know the entire number of beneficiaries, they are instructed to take a narrower view of who the beneficiaries are.[28]

At first sight, such dilution of what is required in respect of distribution arguably means that the law fails to respect the settlor's wishes, and

---

[25] [1970] AC 508.   [26] [1953] Ch 810.   [27] [1979] 1 WLR 278.

[28] Settlors often also insert provisions exempting trustees from liability in respect of honest but unsuccessful attempts to distribute as the law requires. These, however, do not alter what is required by way of distribution in the manner of the rules described in the text, as conscious reliance on them would not be honest.

so loses sight of its facilitative mission. The settlor might well want payment to all those, and only those, whom he has designated. He might say, for example, that by the expression 'my relatives' he really does mean all his blood relatives, and not just his statutory next-of-kin.

But when we introduce the consideration of certainty requirements, it seems likely that the settlor would change his view. Distribution in accordance with the ideal can never take place because the law, seeking only to offer the trust facility where it can ensure performance,[29] and realizing that it cannot do so if the performance has to be in accordance with the ideal, will not allow the trust to come into effect. For the settlor to persist in demanding the ideal would then be quixotic. He would probably accept the diluted arrangements for distribution, for the sake of their more easily satisfied certainty requirements. It is plausible, then, that the package deal which the law has devised, involving a qualified form of the duty of distribution and a lower certainty requirement, is the best compromise: the most convincing overall representation of what settlors want, and so, in fact, facilitatively the best response after all.

[29] *Morice v Bishop of Durham* (1804) 9 Ves 399, (1805) 10 Ves 522.

I I

Operating dispositive discretions

In Chapter 10 we looked at fixed trusts, ie those in which the settlor tells the trustees whom to pay, how much, and when. Sometimes, however, a settlor will give her trustees the task or option of deciding such matters for themselves. Such a task or option is a 'dispositive discretion'. In the present chapter, we look at the questions that arise when trustees are given a dispositive discretion.

I I.I FIXED STIPULATIONS AND ADMINISTRATIVE AND DISPOSITIVE DISCRETIONS

The characteristic of a fixed trust, as we noted in the previous chapter, is that the settlor stipulates the objects of the trust and their entitlements (either concretely, or by laying down an arithmetical formula for arriving at a concrete result). We have seen[1] how the law in fact replaces the settlor's specification with a more subtle and qualified one calculated to make the trustees' task more practicable. But this substitute is still essentially fixed. The trustees have to use their judgement at certain points. For example, they have to decide whether a putative claimant has demonstrated on a balance of probabilities that he is entitled. This is a matter for their judgement in the sense that there will sometimes be no clear answer. But they are supposed to approach it in an objective spirit. They are not asked or entitled to make active choices whether or not to pay somebody some money.

But the law also allows settlors to provide that their trustees should make such active choices: that is, to exercise discretion. Trustees very commonly avail themselves of this option. It is a valuable one at several levels. At the lowest, it would be inefficient for a settlor to stipulate in fixed terms every step his trustees must take: as regards many matters, there will be little danger in leaving trustees to work things out for

[1] See section 10.5.

themselves, and it will be a waste of time to give them detailed instructions. It would be absurd, for example, for a settlor to prescribe the brand of stationery his trustees should buy. Then, a settlor who stipulates everything in fixed terms, according to what seems advisable at the time of creating the trust, will leave his trust vulnerable to changes in circumstances over the time of its existence, which can be long. He can solve the problem by giving the trustees discretion to decide how to proceed. For instance, a settlor who prescribed the exact investments his trustees were to make would very likely prevent them from using more appropriate alternatives at some stage, even if not at the outset. Especially the latter point is true not only as regards matters of management but also of the trust's very beneficial interests (or purposes). A settlor, realizing that his original configuration of those interests may turn out to be inappropriate (as, for instance, if a beneficiary proves in an unforeseen way unworthy of his beneficence), can give his trustees discretion to alter that configuration, by deciding afresh whom to pay, and/or how much, and/or when. Such a discretion is especially used to deal with foreseeably but unpredictably changing needs, such as the requirements of growing children or elderly persons. Indeed, the settlor can even leave the trustees to configure the beneficial interests from the outset (with or without the option of changing them thereafter), which is especially helpful if the interests are not to come into effect immediately, or as a means of effectuating a wish that beneficial interests shall reflect degrees of need or desert.

Trustees' discretions are commonly sorted into two types, 'administrative' and 'dispositive'. Dispositive discretions are intended to allow a structuring or restructuring of the beneficiaries' interests, whilst administrative discretions are not. The significance of the distinction[2] is that (it follows) trustees with an administrative discretion must exercise it evenhandedly as between the beneficiaries:[3] whereas trustees given a dispositive discretion are on the contrary expected to make the sort of choices, which will often involve favouring one possible object at the expense of another, that a settlor would otherwise make.[4]

Discretions in which trustees are explicitly or implicitly asked to make choices of the latter kind are thus inevitably classed as dispositive. Discretions in which they are told not to make such choices can only be administrative. Some, however, neither require nor rule out such choices.

---

[2] *Pearson v IRC* [1981] AC 753, 785.
[3] *Raby v Ridehalgh* (1855) 7 De GM & G 104; *Learoyd v Whiteley* (1886) 33 Ch D 347, (1887) 12 App Cas 727.
[4] *Edge v Pensions Ombudsman* [2000] Ch 602, 618–21, 627.

A discretion of this kind could fall into either class: in principle it is for the settlor (though in practice usually for the judges) to say whether or not the trustees are to act even-handedly in exercising it. Traditionally, the discretions found in the management of trusts (described in Chapter 9) were normally taken as administrative. In particular, the discretion to select investments for the trust assets was regarded thus, meaning that choices had to be made which did not, in particular, favour capital growth (and so future beneficiaries) at the expense of current income (and so present beneficiaries), or vice versa.[5] But recently, and perhaps controversially, this discretion has been described as dispositive, permitting trustees to angle their choices so as (say) to favour a poor beneficiary over a rich one, or a close relative of the settlor over a distant one.[6]

Can allowing trustees the option of creating especially dispositive discretions be understood in terms of facilitative logic? Certainly, in recognizing such discretions, the law goes beyond the idea of 'giving effect to a settlor's wishes' in the sense required to explain the recognition of fixed trusts. Instead, it fulfils the wishes of those settlors who choose to operate by leaving the crystallization of their project to at least some extent to others. This extension can be understood in terms of the thinking developed in section 2.2, where the facilitative thesis was rooted in the liberal argument that people should be accorded the largest possible degree of autonomy regarding their actions. According (therefore) the owner of some property the greatest possible freedom as to how he deals with it means effectuating not only his fixed stipulations regarding it, but also such arrangements as he may wish to make whereby it is controlled by the decisions of others.[7] It should also be noted, though it is not essential to this argument, that trustees operating such discretions are commonly, and it seems properly,[8] guided by what they understand of the settlor's own views regarding the issue, or kind of issue, facing them.

We looked at the operation of the principal administrative discretions regarding management in Chapter 9. The remainder of this chapter

---

[5] *Raby v Ridehalgh* (1855) 7 De GM & G 104; *Learoyd v Whiteley* (1886) 33 Ch D 347, (1887) 12 App Cas 727.

[6] *Nestlé v National Westminster Bank plc* [1993] 1 WLR 1260, 1279.

[7] *Re Beatty* [1990] 1 WLR 1503 explicitly considers whether dispositive discretions can be reconciled with the facilitative nature of testamentary trusts in particular, and answers in the affirmative.

[8] *Breadner v Granville-Grossman* [2001] Ch 523, 532 paras 20–2. Trustees given a discretion must not however cede judgement entirely to the settlor (or anyone else): *Turner v Turner* [1984] Ch 100 (see section 11.5).

concerns the nature of, and the problems presented by, the main instances of dispositive discretion.

11.2 VARIETIES OF DISPOSITIVE DISCRETIONS

We shall look particularly at five of the most important types of dispositive discretion: discretionary trusts; powers of appointment; powers of accumulation; powers of maintenance; and powers of advancement.

In a *discretionary trust*,[9] the settlor defines a class of people—such as the members of a family, or the employees of a company—and stipulates that the available property has to be distributed to members of this class, but leaves it to the trustees to decide what, if (normally) anything,[10] each particular individual in the class will receive. Dispositions such as '£10,000 to be divided as my trustees shall decide amongst my children' and '£50,000 to be divided as my trustees think best among the employees of X Co' would be discretionary trusts.

Discretionary trusts were at one time commonly used in family contexts to avoid certain tax liabilities. The fact that the beneficiaries' entitlements lay in the trustees' discretion left them insufficiently concrete to attract the fiscal rules as these were then framed.[11] Also in family contexts, and more enduringly, the discretion provides the flexibility to respond to changing circumstances: the needs of the children, for example, as their lives take shape and move in one direction or another, or those of an elderly person who may begin to find difficulty in managing her own affairs and meeting the expense of special medical or residential requirements. A particular instance of this is the 'protective trust',[12] where a beneficiary is given a fixed interest until (broadly) such time as he goes bankrupt, whereupon he loses that interest and instead becomes one of a number of beneficiaries of a discretionary trust. This device enables his entitlement to be kept out of the hands of his creditors (it may be thought surprising that the law should allow this),[13] while allowing him to continue in practice to be provided for.

Discretionary trusts are also extensively used to confer benefits on deserving cases amongst large constituencies, in the same way as

---

[9] Or 'trust power', though that expression is, confusingly, also used with other meanings.

[10] Though trustees might, for example, be asked to decide which of two beneficiaries shall enjoy each of two houses.

[11] For the lack of concreteness of interests under a discretionary trust generally, see *Gartside v IRC* [1968] AC 553 (see section 14.3).

[12] A standard form is provided in the Trustee Act 1925 s 33.

[13] Cf section 2.5.

charitable trusts, but without the charitable status. For example, such trusts often provide for payments amongst the employees of a company or their dependants. A trust for such a constituency will not normally be charitable;[14] providing essentially private fringe benefits to the employees rather than a public benefit, it does not merit the special treatment (especially tax exemption) given to charities. But just as might occur in a similar charitable trust, a discretion is given so as to avoid the difficulty of defining 'a deserving case' in advance; and so as to allow the amount paid to reflect the degree of desert, for which it would be hard to stipulate in a fixed formula.

Powers of appointment are quite similar to discretionary trusts. Again, there is provision for assets to be distributed to members of a class, the selection of the actual recipients and the fixing of the amounts they are each to receive being left to the trustees. (Or sometimes these are left to other 'appointors', though the trust within which the power is located continues to be in trustees' hands.)[15] The difference is that whereas in discretionary trusts the trustees are required to pay out all the available property to members of the class, in powers of appointment they are not. Any property that they do not pay to members of the class—which might even be all of it—goes instead to people known as the 'takers in default of appointment' (because they take the property if the trustees do not exercise their power to 'appoint' it to members of the class). So an example of a power of appointment would be '£10,000 for my children so far as my trustees may think fit, but otherwise to my widow absolutely'. The children are the objects of the power; the widow is the taker in default.[16]

Traditionally, such dispositions were seen as primarily trusts for the takers in default, but with an option for the trustees to give the property

---

[14] See section 6.5; *Oppenheim v Tobacco Securities Trust Co Ltd* [1951] AC 297; cf *Dingle v Turner* [1972] AC 601.

[15] Trustees or other appointors can apparently be potential recipients themselves: eg a trust of property on trust for the trustee and another beneficiary in whatever proportions the trustee chooses (*Birmingham v Renfrew* (1937) 57 CLR 666; *Ottaway v Norman* [1972] Ch 698; *Re Cleaver (deceased)* [1981] 1 WLR 939; *Re Goodchild (deceased)* [1996] 1 WLR 694), or a trust of two houses, 'one chosen by Adam for himself, the other for Briony' (cf *Boyce v Boyce* (1849) 16 Sim 476). But note the problem in such a situation of the appointor's self-interest: cf n 41 below.

[16] Two types of power arrangement may be confusing at first sight. First, the objects of the power and the takers in default may be the same people: eg '£10,000 for my children so far as my trustees may think fit, but otherwise to be divided between my children equally'. Secondly, where the terms make it clear that (unlike in a discretionary trust) the trustees do not have to pay all the available money out to the members of the class, but do not specify who is the taker in default; the answer being the settlor herself, under a resulting trust: eg '£10,000 from which my trustees may, if they think fit, make payments to my children'.

to other people, the objects of the power, if they felt it right to do so.[17] On this view, the objects of the power were Cinderellas, the passive recipients of fortuitous bounty if the trustees happened to exercise the power in their favour, rather than having any real entitlement: that was the monopoly of the takers in default.[18] So although the legal effect is the same either way, the real flavour is better sensed if the wording of the example is reversed: if instead of '£10,000 for my children so far as my trustees may think fit, but otherwise to my widow absolutely', we put it in the form '£10,000 for my widow absolutely, except to the extent (if any) that my trustees think fit to appoint to my children instead'. This perception reflects the traditional use of such arrangements in family contexts, their primary provision being a fixed stipulation for the taker(s) in default, the power to appoint differently being inserted so as to allow for the unforeseen.

At one point, powers of appointment came to be used in order to minimize tax liability. This usage traded on the idea, just explained, that the interests of a power's objects were not entitlements but merely hopes of having the power exercised in one's favour. But whilst that idea genuinely reflected the conception of powers of appointment as traditionally used, it did not correspond to the reality of these arrangements aimed at avoiding tax. In the latter, it was understood that in practice the money would be paid to at least some objects of the power (generally members of the settlor's family), and not left for the takers in default. So (certain of) the objects of the power were the true centre of attention; the takers in default were decoys. In time, this new conception of the realities of powers of appointment was reflected in a new construction of their legal nature, which obtains today under the name of a 'fiduciary power'.[19]

---

[17] *Re Somes* [1896] 1 Ch 250, 255; *Vatcher v Paull* [1915] AC 372, 379; *Re Greaves* [1954] Ch 434, 446.

[18] It seems to follow that, unlike objects of trusts, objects of powers of appointment were not required to be people at all; since they had no rights even if they were, they could just as well be animals or non-charitable purposes. *Re Douglas* (1887) 35 Ch D 472, sometimes cited in support, does not deal explicitly with the issue, and is equivocal in what it appears to assume about it. But the thesis may be accepted in *Re Harpur's Will Trusts* [1962] Ch 78, 91, and is assumed correct by the Ontario Perpetuities Act 1966 s 16 and similar statutory provisions, reconstructing failed purpose trusts as valid purpose powers. *Barclays Bank Ltd v Quistclose Investments Ltd* [1970] AC 567 and analogous cases are said to feature a purpose power (*Twinsectra Ltd v Yardley* [2002] 2 WLR 802, 806 para 13, cf 824–30 paras 77–100), but always to date one for the benefit of certain persons, and so analogous to the type of purpose trust validated by *Re Denley's Trust Deed* [1969] 1 Ch 373 (see section 14.3).

[19] The development is visible especially in *Re Gestetner Settlement* [1953] Ch 672, 688; *Re Gulbenkian's Settlement Trusts* [1970] AC 508, 518 (but cf 521, 524–5); *McPhail v Doulton* [1971] AC 424, 449; *Re Manisty's Settlement* [1974] Ch 17, 25–6; *Re Hay's Settlement Trusts*

Although the development may not be quite complete,[20] the essential idea is that appointing under the power and sending the money over in default are equipollent options, the trustees having an even choice as between them, and the objects of the power having rights as powerful as those of the takers in default. (The old conception continues to apply to 'non-fiduciary' powers.[21] But a judge commonly has scope to characterize a power either way, and the burgeoning of the fiduciary category reveals the current attraction of the latter. It is sometimes said that a non-fiduciary power may be more readily found in a family trust,[22] but the cases in which fiduciary powers have been developed do not obviously bear this out. There may, however, be a tendency against finding a power to be fiduciary where the appointor is not otherwise a trustee.)[23]

A *power of accumulation* is like a power of appointment in involving a trust, for the taker(s) in default of accumulation, which the trustees may override by choosing to exercise their power. Here, the overriding takes the form of keeping back income from the trust's investments, which would otherwise be payable to the taker(s) in default, and adding it to the assets invested—that is, turning it into capital. Trustees exercising the power will thus benefit beneficiaries entitled in the future, as they will receive more (whether the enlarged capital itself or the increased income flowing from the enlarged capital), at the expense of those entitled in the present.[24] Like powers of appointment, powers of accumulation came to be used in an attempt to minimize tax liability, as the theoretical emphasis remained on the trust in default of accumulation while the real expectation was that there would be an accumulation. But, also in parallel with

---

[1982] 1 WLR 202, 209–10; *Mettoy Pension Trustees Ltd v Evans* [1990] 1 WLR 1587, 1614, 1617–18; *Breadner v Granville-Grossman* [2001] Ch 523, 540 para 49.

[20] There remains no remedy if trustees wrongfully fail to consider exercising a fiduciary power within the time allowed: *Re Allen-Meyrick's Will Trusts* [1966] 1 WLR 499, 505; *Breadner v Granville-Grossman* [2001] Ch 523, 540–1 paras 52–3.

[21] *Mettoy Pension Trustees Ltd v Evans* [1990] 1 WLR 1587, 1613–14.

[22] *Imperial Group Pension Trust Ltd v Imperial Tobacco Ltd* [1991] 1 WLR 589, 597; *Mettoy Pension Trustees Ltd v Evans* [1990] 1 WLR 1587, 1618.

[23] A traditional possibility, but in modern times, especially in 'off-shore' jurisdictions, such an appointor may be referred to as a 'protector'. One form of protector is a person or group of people whose role is to introduce the settlor's thinking into the operation of the trust, and who may well have little or no legal responsibility. See D Waters in A Oakley (ed) *Trends in Contemporary Trust Law* (1996) ch 4.

[24] Contrast a *duty* to accumulate, ie a situation where the settlor stipulates that the trustees must (subject to any powers to do otherwise) add income as it arises to the trust's capital. (This is possible only for a limited period: see section 2.5.) Here, there is no otherwise-entitled beneficiary whose interests are harmed by the accumulation in the way that there is in the case of a *power* to accumulate.

the story regarding fiduciary powers of appointment, just noted, the courts came to realign their perception of the theoretical with the practical, regarding the possibility of accumulation and the trust in default of it as options of equal validity, between which trustees have an even choice.[25]

A *power of maintenance* allows trustees to pay out trust income for an infant beneficiary's upbringing, schooling, etc., when otherwise they would have to accumulate it. A paternalistically cautious regime normally governs the position of beneficiaries who are children. They are not generally trusted simply to receive the trust income as cash in the way that they would if they were adults. The income which would otherwise have been payable to them is accumulated into the capital. But a power of maintenance enables trustees to devote some or all of the income to (what adults regard as) their infant beneficiaries' proper expenses. The usual version of this power, which is set out in section 31 of the Trustee Act 1925, gives trustees discretion to apply the available income for an infant beneficiary's 'maintenance, education, or benefit'. Unless the settlor stipulates otherwise,[26] the section automatically implies this provision for accumulation and maintenance into all trusts where income would otherwise have been payable to an infant beneficiary. A power of maintenance is much narrower than a discretionary trust or power of advancement or accumulation. It merely provides for the accelerated expenditure on the beneficiary in question of money which was ultimately to go to her anyway. That money is not taken from other beneficiaries.[27]

A *power of advancement* applies where a beneficiary is due to become entitled to trust capital—not just income—at some time in the future, and allows the trustees to anticipate his entitlement by paying him some or all of the capital to which he will eventually succeed. Just as it may be a good idea to spend income to provide for children's education and so on ahead of their unfettered entitlement to it, it is felt sensible sometimes

---

[25] *Pearson v IRC* [1981] AC 753, deciding that a beneficiary under the trust in default of accumulation does not have an 'interest in possession': given the possibility of deprivation by accumulation, her interest is too unstable to be so described. The result was that tax was payable which would otherwise have been avoided.

[26] Trustee Act 1925 s 69(2).

[27] Other rules commonly found in association with the power of maintenance can have the latter effect, however. By these rules, income is sometimes treated as payable to a beneficiary (and so, if she is a child, accumulated into a beneficiary's capital and/or applied to her maintenance) even if her interest lies in the future, and therefore is uncertain ever to come into effect: eg if she is to gain an interest only if and when she reaches the age of 18, or marries. Details of these rules, which are complex, may be found in larger works.

also to be able to pay over capital to a beneficiary early: say, if he needs to buy a house. Section 32 of the Trustee Act 1925 gives the standard version of the power, which is again implied unless the settlor indicates otherwise:[28] it allows for such anticipatory payments for the beneficiary's 'advancement or benefit'. But note that trustees, making such an advancement, are not simply paying the beneficiary money which is ultimately certain to be his. Unlike a power of maintenance, a power of advancement can affect other beneficiaries too, in two ways. First, since the advanced beneficiary's normal entitlement lies in the future, he may never arrive at it, if for no other reason because he may die first. In that case, the money advanced to him would have been payable to someone else: and the latter will now have lost it. (It cannot be reclaimed from the advanced beneficiary's estate: otherwise the advanced beneficiary would be unable safely to spend it, so defeating the usefulness of the advancement.) As a partial safeguard, section 32 provides that not more than half the anticipated entitlement can be advanced, though settlors sometimes override this and allow for advancement of the whole sum. Exercise of the power on especially the latter terms amounts to a substantial adjustment by the trustees of the trust's beneficial interests. Secondly, the money to be advanced may be capital from which another beneficiary currently derives income. Section 32 stipulates that in these circumstances the advancement requires the latter's consent.

11.3 DUTIES AND CERTAINTY REQUIREMENTS IN TRUSTS INVOLVING DISPOSITIVE DISCRETIONS

These, then, are the principal kinds of dispositive discretions. Now we need to think about what duties arise in performing trusts involving such discretions. There are two main ones. The first is basic, and shared with fixed trusts: remaining within the terms of the disposition as laid down by the settlor (above all, paying only the right people). The other, though, is distinctive to discretionary dispositions: handling the exercise of the discretion in a proper way. We shall look at these in turn.

Then there is the question of certainty. We saw in the last chapter how a need for certainty arises from the principle that a trust must be capable of performance by its trustees, and if necessary, supervision and performance

---

[28] Trustee Act 1925 s 69(2).

by the court.[29] As we look at each of the duties, therefore, we shall also need to think about what it requires in this respect.

11.4 REMAINING WITHIN THE TERMS OF THE DISPOSITION

First, then, we look at the duty to remain within the terms of the disposition as laid down by the settlor.

Any action that the trustees, in their discretion, decide to take must be an action that is authorized by the terms of the trust. For example, trustees do not validly exercise a power of accumulation if they embezzle the money in question for themselves, or a power of maintenance or advancement if they spend the money on something not beneficial to the relevant beneficiary.[30] Most especially, if they decide to pay out money to someone as a beneficiary, that person must indeed be a beneficiary. In the case of a power of maintenance or advancement, this person is fixed by the settlor himself; as we have seen, the discretion is to accelerate the payment which the beneficiary should ultimately receive. In discretionary trusts and powers of appointment, on the other hand, the trustees choose whom to pay. But they may make a choice only within the range defined by the settlor. So in a discretionary trust '£50,000 to be divided as my trustees think best among the employees of X Co' they can choose and pay no one other than such employees. And in a power of appointment '£10,000 for my children so far as my trustees may think fit, but otherwise to my widow absolutely', they can select and pay only the settlor's children (and in default, must pay the settlor's widow).

This duty is essentially the same as the duty not to pay anyone other than the designated objects in fixed trusts, examined in the last chapter.[31] So we should expect that in this context too the duty would be diluted to one of paying only people who seem on a balance of probabilities to fit the stipulation. Just as with fixed trusts, this would dispense with the apparent need for conceptual and evidential certainty—ie for it to be possible to say definitely whether any given person is or is not an object—and would instead demand merely that the settlor's designation must not be meaningless.

---

[29] *Morice v Bishop of Durham* (1804) 9 Ves 399, (1805) 10 Ves 522.

[30] 'Maintenance', 'education', and 'advancement' alone are more restrictive, but as regards both kinds of power the Trustee Act 1925 (ss 31 and 32) adds 'or benefit'. Even this wider formulation has limits, however, some of which were examined in *Pilkington v IRC* [1964] AC 612.

[31] See section 10.1.

As regards powers of maintenance and advancement, where the people in whose favour the power can be exercised are fixed by the settlor anyway, there is no reason to doubt that this is the rule. However, as to discretionary trusts and powers of appointment the courts have decided that the position developed in the fixed trust context is only partially applicable. It obtains so far as evidential considerations are concerned.[32] But on the conceptual side, the duty remains the full one of paying only someone who is definitely within the stipulation, and the certainty requirement is correspondingly that of being able to say whether any given person is or is not within it.[33] So while, as we have seen, a fixed trust '£10 to each of my old friends' would be valid,[34] a discretionary trust '£1,000 to be divided as my trustees think best among my old friends' would not. It cannot be said whether *any given person* is or is not an 'old friend' (although it can be said one way or the other of *some* people), because this description has a grey area in which the answer could be unclear. This discrepancy between fixed trusts and discretionary trusts and powers of appointment is unsatisfactory. Not paying the wrong people is the same operation in discretionary trusts and powers of appointment as it is in fixed trusts, so the legal duty and concomitant certainty requirement should also be the same. And there is a strong case[35] that it should be at the lower level, currently confined to fixed trusts; as we saw in section 10.6, this may well offer the better reading of the facilitative thesis.

Once the trustees have decided to exercise a discretion in a certain way (in favour of certain objects of a discretionary trust, for example), the money has to be paid over accordingly. In the context of fixed trusts, we saw how in principle this could create difficulties, because the trustees

---

[32] *Re Baden's Deed Trusts (No 2)* [1973] Ch 9, 19–20, Sachs LJ (the issue is not addressed by the remaining members of the court).

[33] *Re Gulbenkian's Settlement Trusts* [1970] AC 508 (powers of appointment); *McPhail v Doulton* [1971] AC 424 (discretionary trusts).

[34] *Re Barlow's Will Trusts* [1979] 1 WLR 278: see section 10.5. A trust '£1,000 to be divided equally between my old friends', however, would fail, because the fact that it requires the trustees to quantify the beneficiaries' entitlements makes it additionally necessary to be able to know the overall number of beneficiaries; and this description is too vague for that.

[35] Some judges have indeed taken this position. See *Re Gibbard's Will Trusts* [1967] 1 WLR 42, and the Court of Appeal in *Re Gulbenkian's Settlement Trusts* [1968] Ch 126: both overruled in favour of the 'is or is not' test by the House of Lords, [1970] AC 508. A variant on the suggested position was also advocated by Megaw LJ in *Re Baden's Deed Trusts (No 2)* [1973] Ch 9, 24, requiring it to be possible to think of a 'substantial number' of people who definitely fit the description, rather than just one.

might seem to be under a duty to pay someone who had disappeared, but that these difficulties are dispelled by measures such as payment into court. It is improbable that this question would arise in the present context, because trustees are unlikely to exercise their discretion in favour of an object of whose whereabouts or existence they are unsure. But if it did, it would presumably be dealt with by the same measures.

A discretionary payment will be within the terms of a particular disposition only if it consists of the money (or other property) which the trust permits to be distributed in this way. In the case of a discretionary trust, indeed, the discretionary payments must distribute all the assets available for them. The money (or other property) available for distribution under the discretion must therefore be sufficiently defined: ie there must be appropriate certainty of subject matter. This issue was discussed in section 10.3, in the context of fixed trusts. *Mutatis mutandis*, what was said there applies here too. Remember however that a problem of uncertain subject matter in a fixed trust can sometimes be solved if the trust is instead regarded as discretionary. So an invalid fixed trust of '20 cases of my wine' in your favour could, for example, be a valid trust of all my wine, the trustee having the duty to choose 20 cases and allocate them to you, while holding the remainder for me.

11.5 THE CONDUCT OF THE DISCRETION

The trustees' other kind of duty in respect of dispositive discretions concerns the exercise of the discretion itself. If there were no requirements as to the trustees' behaviour in this regard, they would be left to make decisions as arbitrarily and whimsically as they liked. In fact, the law demands certain standards of them.

Trustees' duties in this respect are probably essentially the same for each of the five principal types of dispositive discretion described above, though the implications may differ from one type to another. Excepted from this are non-fiduciary powers of appointment, which adhere to the old conception of the power as primarily a trust for the takers in default, the trustees having an option to divert money to the objects of the power instead, but the latter having no rights in the matter. Those holding such a power have duties to behave properly only so far as a failure to do so will injure the takers in default. There is thus no such thing as a wrongful non-exercise of such a power,[36] because that would injure only the objects of the power.

---

[36] *Re Somes* [1896] 1 Ch 250; *Re Greaves* [1954] Ch 434.

Put shortly, the law requires that trustees should give proper consideration to their discretion, and neither exercise it nor refrain from exercising it without such proper consideration. (Breach of these duties is sometimes called a 'fraud', but breach is not confined to cases of dishonesty in the way that that word might suggest.)[37]

Most basically in this, trustees are required to think about whether to exercise their discretion at all. So they are at fault if they refrain from making an advancement, say, without even thinking about whether they should; or, conversely, if they do make it, without thinking about whether they should not.[38] For example, there is a failure in this respect if the trustees merely follow instructions which they receive from the settlor, without exercising any judgement of their own;[39] or indeed if they simply do not realize, or forget, that they have a discretion to exercise, and do nothing about it. This requirement seems to make no demands in the way of certainty; it does not need the settlor to supply any information for the trustees to be able to know that they have to think.

But the law requires trustees not simply to think, but also to think properly: to take all relevant matters into account, and leave irrelevant ones out of account.[40] There are two aspects to this. The first concerns the bases on which trustees should make their decisions: the kinds of considerations that should and should not influence them. The second concerns the lengths to which they need to go in providing themselves with information relevant to those considerations before making their decision. We shall take these two aspects in turn.

11.6 THE PROPER BASES FOR A DECISION

There are some matters to which trustees must not attend. For example, it will not normally be right for a trustee to take account of his own

---

[37] *Vatcher v Paull* [1915] AC 372, 378.

[38] *Wilson v Turner* (1883) 22 Ch D 521.

[39] *Re Locker's Settlement Trusts* [1977] 1 WLR 1323; *Turner v Turner* [1984] Ch 100. Though they must not be automatically followed, the settlor's wishes are nevertheless a relevant consideration: *Breadner v Granville-Grossman* [2001] Ch 523, 532 paras 20–2.

[40] Some old decisions required trustees merely to act in good faith (eg *Gisborne v Gisborne* (1877) 2 App Cas 300, 305). Others added that a discretion must be exercised only for a, or the, purpose for which it was given (eg *Duke of Portland v Lady Topham* (1864) 11 HLC 32, 54, 55–6). The formulation given in the text reflects *Re Beloved Wilkes' Charity* (1851) 3 Mac & G 440, 448 and especially *Re Hastings-Bass* [1975] Ch 25, 41; *Mettoy Pension Trustees Ltd v Evans* [1990] 1 WLR 1587, 1621–5; *Scott v National Trust for Places of Historic Interest or Natural Beauty* [1998] 2 All ER 705, 717–18; *Edge v Pensions Ombudsman* [2000] Ch 602, 627–36; *Breadner v Granville-Grossman* [2001] Ch 523, 542–3 paras 58–63.

personal interests.[41] So it will be wrong, say, for a trustee having a power of appointment, of which he himself is not an object, to exercise it in a particular person's favour in return for a percentage of the sum appointed.[42] Again, the trustee's unreasoned feelings about the beneficiary ought not to come into the matter. So refusing to make an advancement out of personal dislike of the beneficiary would be wrong.[43] The objection, however, is to a reliance on mere prejudice, not to the formation of a personal but reasonable opinion: the trustee's very role is to bring such an opinion to bear on the discretion, and commonly he will have been appointed trustee because the settlor likes (among other things) his set of values.[44]

Beyond such basic matters, what factors are relevant and irrelevant depends on the particular discretion, or at any rate kind of discretion, involved. As regards a power of maintenance under the statutory formula, for instance, the objective has to be the child's 'maintenance, education or benefit'; and for the corresponding power of advancement it must be the beneficiary's 'advancement or benefit'. These formulae are broad, but they nevertheless set limits to the bases upon which the trustees may act. Maintenance, for example, must not be given in order to benefit the child's father[45] (though it is recognized that benefiting children will usually help their parents too), nor withheld out of disapproval of him.[46]

For discretionary trusts and powers of appointment and accumulation, there is no such standard formula, and the proper bases for the exercise of the discretion will vary from one trust to the next. In theory, settlors could write into the terms of the trust itself a catalogue of the matters to

---

[41] Problems evidently arise if the persons in whose favour the discretion can be exercised are expressed to include the trustee. This often occurs in pension fund trusts, the trustees including representatives of the pensioners, employees, and employer, all of whom may be benefited by the discretions ordinarily given. After earlier misgivings, the courts came to accept self-interested decisions by such trustees as not *ipso facto* invalid (*Re Drexel Burnham Lambert UK Pension Plan* [1995] 1 WLR 32), and to regard the overall balance of the board of trustees (*Edge v Pensions Ombudsman* [2000] Ch 602, 630, 633) and the employer's duty of good faith towards its employees (*British Coal Corp v British Coal Staff Superannuation Scheme Trustees Ltd* [1995] 1 All ER 912, 923–8) as substitute guarantees of fairness. A statutory provision (Pensions Act 1995 s 39) covers some of the same ground.

[42] *Vatcher v Paull* [1915] AC 372, 378.

[43] *Klug v Klug* [1918] 2 Ch 67.

[44] *Edge v Pensions Ombudsman* [2000] Ch 602, 630.

[45] *Wilson v Turner* (1883) 22 Ch D 521: the trustees paid all the available money over to the father, without considering whether it was actually needed for the child's maintenance.

[46] *Re Lofthouse* (1885) 29 Ch D 921, 925–6: the trustees withheld maintenance apparently from disapproval of the child's father having become a town councillor (for the wrong party?); the judge at first instance found a breach, but the case was compromised on appeal.

which their trustees should attend. In practice, they rarely do so explicitly, though they may give implicit pointers. (They may and often do give guidance to the trustees outside the terms of the trust, either alongside making the trust or as time goes by, but such guidance cannot be binding on the trustees.)[47] There is some confusion as to whether such a lack of direction presents a problem.

The leading case on discretionary trusts asserts that the potential objects of a discretionary trust must amount to 'something like a class'.[48] 'All the residents of Greater London' was said to be objectionable in this regard, and discretionary trusts for the inhabitants of West Yorkshire,[49] and for the whole world except a few specified people,[50] have subsequently been regarded as objectionable on this score. This assertion has puzzled commentators.[51] But from the surrounding context it seems to have been intended as a certainty requirement: a demand that, for a discretionary trust to be valid, the information needed to secure its 'administrative workability',[52] ie to perform it and to control that performance, must be present. In these terms, a discretionary trust for 'all the residents of Greater London', without more, is apparently bad because there is nothing in its terms to provide information about the proper bases for the exercise of the discretion. (The requirement has been said not to apply to powers of appointment,[53] though this may be less because they are relevantly different[54] than because of a reluctance to disturb a traditional understanding that powers can be made in favour of such classes.)

On the other hand, it is more usually thought that the bases for the

---

[47] *Turner v Turner* [1984] Ch 100.   [48] *McPhail v Doulton* [1971] AC 424, 457.

[49] *R v District Auditor, ex p West Yorkshire Metropolitan County Council* [1986] RVR 24.

[50] *Re Hay's Settlement Trusts* [1982] 1 WLR 202, 213–14.

[51] See eg L McKay (1974) 38 Conv 269; Y Grbich (1974) 37 MLR 643; I Hardcastle [1990] Conv 24.

[52] *McPhail v Doulton* [1971] AC 424, 457.

[53] *Re Manisty's Settlement* [1974] Ch 17; *Re Hay's Settlement Trusts* [1982] 1 WLR 202. The same is assumed in *Re Beatty* [1990] 1 WLR 1503.

[54] One suggested explanation for the requirement of a 'class', however, is that 'the residents of Greater London' are too multitudinous to be permitted to enforce against the trustees the rights to a proper exercise of discretion enjoyed by potential objects of a discretionary trust (I Hardingham and R Baxt *Discretionary Trusts* 2nd edn (1984) 37–41). If that is right (which it may not be), the different rule in powers might be explained on the ground that the potential objects of powers traditionally had no rights against the trustees (*Re Hay's Settlement Trusts* [1982] 1 WLR 202, 213–14). Nowadays, however, the rights of potential objects in this respect are the same in powers as in discretionary trusts (*Mettoy Pension Trustees Ltd v Evans* [1990] 1 WLR 1587), suggesting that the 'class' requirement should apply to powers too.

exercise of discretion need not be indicated by the settlor, but can be left to be devised by the trustees themselves. (So long as they do not relinquish their own discretion, they can, though they need not,[55] invite suggestions from others, notably the settlor and beneficiaries.)[56] The trustees are required only to avoid acting 'capriciously', as one judge put it, discussing a power of appointment: on the basis of factors which are 'irrational, perverse or irrelevant to any sensible expectation of the settlor; for example, if they chose a beneficiary by height or complexion or by the irrelevant fact that he was a resident of Greater London'.[57] Take, say, a discretionary trust in favour of the employees of a company. The trustees might adopt criteria such as loyalty, need, contribution to the firm; they could not look at matters such as race or religion. This approach of leaving trustees to establish their own bases, so long as these are not capricious, demands little in the way of certainty. It implies that a trust or power will be valid so long as it is not impossible for its trustees themselves to arrive at a reasonable notion of a basis upon which to exercise it: which should not normally be any problem at all. In one case[58] it was suggested that a power to appoint amongst 'the residents of Greater London' would fail because such a designation would be inconsistent with the adoption of sensible criteria by the trustees in this way. But that suggestion is hard to accept in principle, and indeed the same case went on to hold a power in favour of the entire world, minus a few specified people, to be valid.[59]

11.7 ASSEMBLING INFORMATION

The other issue regarding the duty to take relevant and not irrelevant matters into account concerns the depth of information with which trustees are required to equip themselves before making their decision. Given some suitable criterion, to what lengths should trustees go in acquainting themselves with the claims of potential objects in terms of it?

Trustees who, on the basis of some criterion, are minded to exercise a discretion in favour of a particular person must of course take steps to check that that person is indeed deserving in terms of the criterion. For

---

[55] Except perhaps from a beneficiary whom they have hitherto favoured, if they are contemplating a change of approach such as to cut that beneficiary off: *Scott v National Trust for Places of Historic Interest or Natural Beauty* [1998] 2 All ER 705, 718.

[56] *Hartigan Nominees Pty Ltd v Rydge* (1992) 29 NSWLR 405, 431, Australia.

[57] *Re Manisty's Settlement* [1974] Ch 17, 26.

[58] *Re Manisty's Settlement* [1974] Ch 17, 27.

[59] Likewise *Re Hay's Settlement Trusts* [1982] 1 WLR 202.

example, they would be wrong to exercise a power of advancement on the ground that the beneficiary to be advanced needed the money to buy a house without at least asking the beneficiary to provide some substantiation of this assertion.[60]

Must trustees also take stock of the standing, relative to their criteria, of those whom they propose not to benefit? They need not invite representations from any beneficiary,[61] though they may do so, and they must listen to any they do receive.[62] But before making their selection, they must themselves to some extent consider the claims in respect of their chosen criteria of all the potential objects of the discretion.

The latter requirement, however, takes the form of a duty to make only such a survey of potential recipients as seems sensible in regard to the size of the class in question. In the case of a discretion as between the settlor's living children, for example, the trustees probably have to think about the claims of each child individually; there is no difficulty about their doing so.[63] At the other extreme, in the case of a discretion amongst a very large class, such as a company's employees, the trustees are not expected to give individual consideration to every member of the class. The requirement here is known, rather opaquely, as 'inquiry or ascertainment'. With the criteria for the exercise of the discretion in mind, they are expected to examine the field, by class and category; possibly to make diligent and careful inquiries, depending on the amount of money and the means available, as to the composition and needs of particular categories and of individuals within them; to decide on priorities or proportions, and then to select actual individuals to receive the money.[64] So in a discretionary trust for company employees, for instance, where they have adopted criteria of need and/or loyalty, they might decide to look primarily at those on low salaries, those who had recently taken maternity leave, those approaching retirement, and those who had served the firm for upwards of ten years, and then perhaps work on some sort of points system to

---

[60] *Nestlé v National Westminster Bank plc* [1993] 1 WLR 1260, 1279 (duty to check whether a beneficiary is poor before setting the trust's investment policy so as especially to benefit him on that ground).

[61] *Karger v Paul* [1984] VR 161, Australia.

[62] *Re Manisty's Settlement* [1974] Ch 17, 26. The courts will assist a beneficiary with a potentially strong case to make such a representation, by if necessary ordering disclosure of the trustees' names and addresses: *Re Murphy's Settlements* [1999] 1 WLR 282.

[63] According to the decision on the facts in *Karger v Paul* [1984] VR 161, Australia, but questionably, a very superficial appreciation of the different individuals' claims is enough.

[64] *McPhail v Doulton* [1971] AC 424 (discretionary trusts); *Re Hay's Settlement Trusts* [1982] 1 WLR 202 (powers of appointment).

arrive at a provisional allocation, before doing a final detailed check on the circumstances of the names arrived at and finally paying out.

Once again, for the disposition to be valid any information necessary for this exercise must be present. Where trustees have to inform themselves about one or more specific individuals, therefore, they must be able to identify who those individuals are. Identifying the person in whose favour a power of maintenance or advancement might be exercised should require only such information as is already required by the duty ultimately to pay her anyway. In the case of a discretionary trust or power of appointment, in order to identify the members of a small class (such as the settlor's children) so as to think about them all individually, it must be possible to compile a complete list of the members. As regards a large class such as the employees of a substantial company, however, the business of 'inquiry or ascertainment' does not require a complete list, nor obviously involve any requirements in the way of information. The ability to devise categories, for example, seems to need imagination rather than information; and the eventual narrow field of actual individuals will supply itself, rather than needing to be defined from the start. One proposed explanation for the demand (discussed in the previous section) that the potential objects of a discretionary trust amount to 'something like a class' suggests that the trustees might not be able satisfactorily to make 'inquiry or ascertainment' across a group the size of 'the residents of Greater London'.[65] But given what has just been said, there seems no foundation for this view.

---

[65] *Re Hay's Settlement Trusts* [1982] 1 WLR 202, 213, adding that powers of appointment are exempt from the requirement because the duty of inquiry or ascertainment is less stringent in them (itself a questionable view, assuming that the set of potential objects is the same in both: any difference in duty should be less a question of trust or power than a reflection of the size of that set).

12

Modification

We have spent the last three chapters looking at some of the main duties that trustees have in regard to the performance of express trusts. One point we noticed, especially when we were dealing with fixed trusts in Chapter 10, was how these duties are sometimes not what one might at first expect: they are more qualified. For example, the trustees' apparent absolute duty of paying a beneficiary her entitlement is replaced by a more dilute, but more practicable, duty. So instead of having to pay the designated objects, and no one else, and to do so come what may, the trustees are required to try to pay the people who can show that they are probably the designated objects, and not anyone who cannot, and if they cannot find them to pay the money in some circumstances to certain other people, and otherwise into court.[1]

With these dilutions, the idea is not that the duties were once absolute but are then relaxed, or that an imperfect performance of them is tolerated. It is their very definition that is diluted. Say, for example, a claimant showed that he was probably, though not definitely, the designated beneficiary, but the trustees still refused to pay him. He could sue the trustees, because they would be in breach of their duty to pay the money over to him. There never was any absolute duty only to pay genuinely designated beneficiaries: it was a theoretical mirage, which turns out to be this more tractable duty when properly examined.

Thus diluted or otherwise, however, the forms of the duties we have examined are default configurations. The law maintains a number of provisions whereby these default configurations can be modified. This chapter sets out to consider these provisions.

12.1 EXCLUSION CLAUSES

Express trustees' duties are in practice often modified by exclusion clauses inserted in the terms on which the trust is established. Depending

---

[1] See section 10.5.

on their particular wording, exclusion clauses operate either to adjust the duty itself, or, leaving the duty itself unchanged, to adjust the liability that the trustees would otherwise incur upon breaching the duty. It normally makes no difference which approach is taken.

The courts have allowed the exclusion of all duties except that of honestly acting in the beneficiaries' best interests.[2] It can be asked whether this is not too generous; English law controls exclusion clauses in contracts,[3] and many common law jurisdictions control them also in trusts.[4] In attempting to answer this question, it is important to understand that trust exclusion clauses probably make little difference to the way in which trustees aim to perform their role. Trustees having the benefit of a clause excluding liability for everything except dishonesty, for example, will not normally set out to act all-but-dishonestly. Rather, such clauses are commonly part of a deal that the settlor offers her intended trustees, against the background that without the exclusion of liability the trustees would or might decline to act, or would raise the fees they demand in order to cover the cost of insuring against the greater chance of liability to which they would thus be exposed. Such clauses help to secure the supply of trustees, and to keep their fees down; as explained in section 13.2, they thus contribute to the project of promoting the satisfactory performance of trusts. But their positive effect in these terms must be set against the negative consideration that they reduce the compensation obtainable if the trustees do go wrong. It might be possible to strike a better balance between these considerations if trustees could exclude liability for honest and reasonable breaches, but remained liable, and carried insurance, for the remainder. Unfortunately, however, discovering

---

[2] *Armitage v Nurse* [1998] Ch 241; interpreted in *Walker v Stones* [2001] QB 902, 939, as requiring (though perhaps of only specially qualified trustees) a performance reasonably perceivable as in the beneficiaries' best interests. The duty of care and skill regarding investment cannot be excluded in unit trusts or pension fund trusts: Financial Services Act 1986 s 84, Pensions Act 1995 s 33. See generally J Penner in P Birks and A Pretto (eds) *Breach of Trust* (2002) ch 8.

[3] Unfair Contract Terms Act 1977; Unfair Terms in Consumer Contract Regulations 1999 SI No 2083. Trust exclusion clauses are thought not normally part of a contract, so do not attract these provisions. But could not the 'deal' described below be analyzed as an offer by the settlor to the trustees to allow them to serve as trustees (especially if they are to be remunerated for doing so: after all, corporate trustees act for profit), which they accept by agreeing to serve, either before or after the institution of the trust?

[4] Cf eg *Robertson v Howden* (1892) 10 NZLR 609, New Zealand; *Re Poche* (1984) 6 DLR (4th) 40, Canada; Trusts (Jersey) Law 1984 Art 26(9). The general tendency is to allow exclusion of liability for ordinary negligence, but not for anything worse. The Law Commission is currently considering the case for legislation on these or other lines in England and Wales: Consultation Paper No 171 *Trustee Exemption Clauses* (2003).

the applicability of such an exclusion in individual cases might require costly litigation, upon which the trustees' insurers might insist.

12.2 TRUSTEE ACT 1925 SECTION 61

Section 61 of the Trustee Act 1925[5] provides that where trustees have breached their duty, but in doing so they acted honestly and reasonably, the court can negative their liability (entirely or partially) if it thinks it fair to do so. Many of the cases in which this provision has been applied have involved a misunderstanding by the trustees of their duty (eg by misinterpreting the terms of the trust),[6] though it can also be used where trustees make no mistake about what they are supposed to do, but fall down in actually doing it.

Discussion of this provision by the courts usually centres around the requirement that the misunderstanding or default must have been a reasonable one. When the duty breached is one to use care and skill in the management of the trust, there might be thought no scope to find the breach 'reasonable', for such a duty demands no more than reasonable behaviour in any event;[7] though it would be rash to press this point too hard, for 'reasonable' could have at least slightly different connotations in the two contexts. The inquiry whether a breach is reasonable really comes into its own, however, in respect of duties with which a strict compliance is on the face of things demanded, as especially the duty to act in accordance with the terms of the trust. Many kinds of factors could come into the reckoning in this inquiry, but in practice two are especially important. One is whether the trustees misunderstood their duty in a way with which the court can sympathize.[8] The other is whether the trustees have taken what the court regards as appropriate procedural steps in an effort to perform the trust properly.[9] In particular, their error will not be regarded as reasonable if they should have sought instructions from the

---

[5] L Sheridan (1955) 19 Conv 420; J Lowry and R Edmunds in P Birks and A Pretto (eds) *Breach of Trust* (2002) ch 9. S 61 was originally enacted as the Judicial Trustees Act 1896 s 3, and many of the reported cases concern the latter.

[6] Expressly recognized as a proper case for the section's application in *Re Allsop* [1914] 1 Ch 1.

[7] In respect of such duties, trustees are required to 'exercise such care and skill as is reasonable in the circumstances': Trustee Act 2000 s 1(1). (Previously, to emulate an ordinary prudent man of business looking after the interests of others: *Re Whiteley* (1886) 33 Ch D 347, *Learoyd v Whiteley* (1887) 12 App Cas 727.) See section 9.3.

[8] *Re Grindey* [1898] 2 Ch 593; *Re Allsop* [1914] 1 Ch 1.

[9] *Re Windsor Steam Coal Co (1901) Ltd* [1929] 1 Ch 151.

court (a consideration mentioned by the section itself), or consulted a lawyer or some other appropriate professional, but did not. Trustees who act confidently upon a pardonable misunderstanding, however, cannot be blamed for failure to seek advice; and where they are expected to do so they are not required to go to the same lengths in every case: what reasonableness demands varies with the amount of money at stake.[10] Only in case of substantial amounts are the trustees likely to be expected to incur the expense of going to court or taking counsel's opinion (ie the advice of a barrister specializing in the field) in order to be said to have acted reasonably; in trusts of more moderate dimensions, they will probably have acted reasonably if they consulted their normal solicitors; and in the smallest ones, it may well be reasonable for them not to have taken professional advice at all.

With section 61 the law is not saying (as it does when it dilutes an apparently absolute duty into a more practicable one, or allows the trustees' duty itself to be modified) that it was actually correct for the trustees to act as they did.[11] In the cases to which the section applies, the trustees were still supposed to perform their duty in its unmodified form, but the law thinks it right to exonerate them when, in pardonable circumstances, they did not. This idea is a familiar one in the criminal law, in its division of defences into 'justifications' (where the behaviour is regarded as desirable: eg use of reasonable force in prevention of crime) and 'excuses' (where the behaviour is regarded as undesirable, but pardonable: eg use of such force under duress). Using this terminology, the defence provided by section 61 is an excuse, rather than a justification. This is secured by three features of it.

The first is the fact that the section only applies to breaches that have already occurred, and does not provide for the court to authorize them in advance.[12] The second is the requirement that the trustees should have acted honestly, as well as reasonably. This means that they should have been trying to observe their duty, and not doing something, however reasonable, deliberately contrary to it.[13] And the third is statements by the courts that relief under the section will depend on all the circumstances

---

[10] *Re Grindey* [1898] 2 Ch 593, 602–3; *Re Allsop* [1914] 1 Ch 1, 13, 21; *Marsden v Regan* [1954] 1 WLR 423, 435.

[11] *Re Stuart* [1897] 2 Ch 583, 590. But note *Perrins v Bellamy* [1899] 1 Ch 797, where the court, exonerating trustees for an unauthorized investment, seems to comment that they were right to make it.

[12] *Re Tollemache* [1903] 1 Ch 457; *Re Rosenthal* [1972] 1 WLR 1273.

[13] But cf *Perrins v Bellamy* [1899] 1 Ch 797, n 11 above.

of the individual case.[14] These statements seem to be principally aimed at preventing the judges' hands from becoming tied by precedent, but they also prevent other trustees from interpreting the grant of relief in a previous case as the green light for them to commit a similar breach (though since the judges exercise the jurisdiction in a regular rather than capricious fashion, trustees may not be taken in by this, especially if they take professional advice).

But there is a fundamental difficulty about providing an excusatory defence in a civil law context. A trustee's liability for breach is not like criminal liability. Excusing a transgressor in the criminal context has no repercussions for anyone else (or only remotely, in terms of its effect on the law's future deterrence). By contrast, in our context the liability is to compensate the beneficiaries for the damage that the breach has done them: so relief of the trustee means non-compensation of the beneficiaries, a two-sided matter which does not arise in the criminal law.

Section 61 seeks to absorb this difficulty by leaving it to the court to decide in the individual case whether, on top of the breach being honest and reasonable, it is 'fair' to give relief. But in many of the decisions under the section, the court has missed the significance of this element, and gone straight from finding honesty and reasonableness to granting relief. The point is sometimes taken, however. In one case, the court decided that there was no unfairness in leaving a trust corporation, which acted for payment, to bear its own liability.[15] The argument cannot be that a higher standard of performance is expected of such a trustee,[16] for that would tell us that the breach was not a 'reasonable' one, rather than that the breach was reasonable but the trustee ought not fairly to bear it. It is perhaps that a commercial entity such as the trust corporation was better placed to bear and spread the loss than private individual trustees would have been, and certainly than the beneficiaries were.[17]

The jurisdiction in section 61 is referred to much less frequently nowadays than it was in the first years after its original enactment at the end of the nineteenth century.[18] This decline matches a similar decline, over

---

[14] *Re Turner* [1897] 1 Ch 536, 542; *Re Kay* [1897] 2 Ch 518, 524.

[15] *National Trustees Co of Australasia Ltd v General Finance Co of Australasia Ltd* [1905] AC 373; see too *Re Windsor Steam Coal Co (1901) Ltd* [1929] 1 Ch 151.

[16] Though that is true, at any rate in today's law: Trustee Act 2000 s 1(1)(b).

[17] The fairness requirement also received attention in *Re Evans* [1999] 2 All ER 777, but the reasoning concentrates on keeping the trustee from bearing too much of the loss (given her position) rather than on why it was right to make the beneficiary suffer any of it.

[18] As the Judicial Trustees Act 1896 s 3.

the same period, in the number of reported cases of possible breach of trust. (For a quick if unscientific measure, compare the two, occasionally three, volumes per year in the 'Chancery' series of the Law Reports towards 1900 with the generally one volume today.) One explanation might be that trustees' standards of performance have risen, especially as professional trustees have become more common and the creation of small family trusts with lay trustees has declined. Another suggestion might be that the standards required of trustees have fallen, but this is less easy to substantiate: formally, at any rate, the law has remained much the same over the period. A third, certainly plausible, is that cases of unsatisfactory performance have come to be dealt with in some other way, especially by the invocation of an exemption clause so as to negative the breach or its consequences—the increased use of such clauses being itself associated with the increased use of professional trustees, who commonly insist upon them.

12.3 THE CONSENT PRINCIPLE

Trustees incur no liability for breach of trust if they act with their beneficiaries' consent.[19]

Beneficiaries who consent to a breach and continue to approve of it will of course not wish to sue anyway. The consent principle attains practical importance where consenting beneficiaries regret what occurs. So, for example, if the beneficiaries agree to an investment outside the terms of the trust, thinking it advantageous, but in the event it fails, the trustees commit no breach and so cannot be sued for the loss. The beneficiaries' consent also prevents an interested third party, who might otherwise have been able to sue the trustees,[20] from doing so.[21]

'Consent'[22] can involve instigating the trustees to commit the breach, or expressly concurring in their proposal to do so, or tacitly acquiescing in it; and can be given before the breach, or after it. The beneficiary's consent can count as such despite at any rate some degree of misunderstanding of what is afoot, including a failure to realize that a breach is involved (eg agreeing to a particular investment, assuming it to be authorized, when in fact it is unauthorized). That is not to say, however,

---

[19] J Payne in P Birks and A Pretto (eds) *Breach of Trust* (2002) ch 10.
[20] *Re Denley's Trust Deed* [1969] 1 Ch 373: see section 14.3.
[21] *Shaw v Lawless* (1838) 5 Cl & Fin 129, 155–6.
[22] *Walker v Symonds* (1818) 3 Swans 1, 64; *Re Pauling's Settlement Trusts* [1962] 1 WLR 86, 106–8 (not discussed on appeal, [1964] Ch 303).

that consent will be found in every case falling within the terms of this pattern. It will be found only if the overall nature of the circumstances makes it 'fair and equitable' that the trustee should not be liable. So consent might well not be found, and the trustee would remain liable, if, say, the beneficiary learns of the breach only as a fait accompli, does not fully understand what has occurred, and concurs only to the extent of not objecting. There is no consent if the beneficiary acts under undue influence,[23] or is under 18 or disqualified on grounds of mental infirmity.

The judges seem not to regard the beneficiary's consent as a reason to approve of the breach, ie to regard it as justified. In some situations (especially where the beneficiary has positively pressed the trustees to commit it), they may regard the breach as excused, but more generally they take the line that the trustees should have adhered to their duty, but a beneficiary who consents to the breach should not be allowed to blow hot and cold by then suing for it.[24] The trustees' duties are thus modified only to the extent that they cannot be sued for departing from them. This conception of the consent principle is intelligible in terms of facilitative logic, for it means that the principle poses no real challenge to the primacy of the settlor's instructions. But it fails to capture the reality that, in many consent cases, the beneficiaries actively desire a departure from the settlor's instructions, and the breach occurs in response to that desire. In such cases, the beneficiaries in effect ask (invoking the thinking explained in section 2.6) to be recognized as having the right to enjoy the trust property as they wish, and that that right be given precedence over the effectuation of the settlor's intentions. Accepting that view means treating the breach as not merely not actionable, perhaps excused, but justified: that is, regarding the trustees' original duties as replaced by those preferred by the beneficiaries. Although this conception is not visible in the judges' statements of the consent principle, it seems central to a narrower rule based on the beneficiaries' consent, to which we now turn: the rule in *Saunders v Vautier*.[25]

---

[23] The central instance of undue influence is pressure, but it extends more widely, especially to cases where there is a prima facie possibility that pressure might have been exerted and the contrary is not proved: see generally *Royal Bank of Scotland plc v Etridge (No 2)* [2002] 2 AL 773.

[24] See especially *Re Pauling's Settlement Trusts* [1962] 1 WLR 86, [1964] Ch 303.

[25] (1841) 4 Beav 115, Cr & Ph 240.

12.4 *SAUNDERS v VAUTIER*

According to the rule in *Saunders v Vautier*,[26] if all the beneficiaries of a trust are adult and not under incapacity, and they agree to do so, they can wind the trust up entirely. If they want to modify rather than dismantle their trust, they can do so by settling the capital again on whatever new terms they please (and even use the same trustees, if the latter are amenable).[27] It is clear that the trustees are not merely excused, or the beneficiaries prevented from suing: the trustees are required to do as the beneficiaries ask. Their departure from the settlor's trust is thus regarded as justified, ie as preferable to adherence to the settlor's intentions.

The techniques of diluting trustees' prima facie duties that we examined in section 10.5 and alluded to at the start of this chapter are at least reconcilable with the law's general facilitative aim of effectuating the settlor's intentions, and may in fact offer the best available way of promoting it: for they allow trusts to go forward in a looser but more practicable form when they would otherwise fail for potential impossibility.[28] The jurisdiction to excuse a breach in section 61 of the Trustee Act 1925 allows trustees to depart from the settlor's terms without liability, but as we saw it is calculated not to encourage departure. The consent principle too is expressed in terms emphasizing the trustees' duty to adhere to the terms of the trust. In *Saunders v Vautier*,[29] however, the beneficiaries' wishes are given precedence over the settlor's. And that seems a clear product of the thesis, described in section 2.6, that the beneficiaries, as recipients of the property, should be able to enjoy it absolutely rather than on the settlor's terms.[30]

One facet of the rule is especially revealing in this vein. Where a

---

[26] (1841) 4 Beav 115, Cr & Ph 240.

[27] The latter procedure can have bad tax consequences, however, and in one respect, the replacement (in certain cases) of the trustees, the law allows beneficiaries to alter the trust without dismantling and resettling: Trusts of Land and Appointment of Trustees Act 1996 s 19.

[28] See section 10.6.

[29] (1841) 4 Beav 115, Cr & Ph 240.

[30] In fact, applications of *Saunders v Vautier* (1841) 4 Beav 115, Cr & Ph 240—or its derivative, the Variation of Trusts Act 1958, which we come to in a moment—are often aimed at reducing tax liabilities, and in these cases it is often unreal to think in terms of the settlor's wishes being overridden. Many settlors have tax avoidance as one of their main concerns in making their trust, and will be happy to see the beneficiaries further streamlining it. In these cases, *Saunders v Vautier* is better seen and judged as a part of the facility which the law offers the settlor: a device by which he can have his disposition fine-tuned as circumstances develop.

beneficiary is given an absolute interest but only upon some condition such as his reaching a certain age—eg 'for Adam once he reaches the age of 25'—the condition can be disregarded. So Adam could invoke the rule, and take the property, as soon as he is 18, despite the fact that the trust appears to stipulate that he shall have no interest at all until seven years later. It is said that in giving him an absolute interest but delaying it until he is 25 the trust contradicts itself: so the contradiction is removed by dispensing with the age requirement.[31] But there is only a contradiction if we assume his interest is absolute in the first place: which, given the condition of his reaching 25, it is not. The assumption, then, seems to be tendentious, based less on the settlor's actual disposition than on the objectives of the rights argument itself.[32]

12.5 THE VARIATION OF TRUSTS ACT 1958

The rule in *Saunders v Vautier*[33] allows the trust to be dismantled only if all the beneficiaries are adult and not affected by incapacity, and agree to the initiative. The rule is therefore unavailable in many cases. For example, the beneficiaries may include children, or people not yet born, or adult beneficiaries who are incapacitated by mental illness or who cannot be found. But the law goes on, in the Variation of Trusts Act 1958,[34] to provide that in various cases of this kind trusts may be modified or dissolved, on the strength of a judge's supplying such people's agreement on their behalf.[35]

The Act details the kinds of people for whom a judge can give consent in this way.[36] They are those under 18 (including the unborn), those incapacitated, (roughly speaking) those who might become beneficiaries

---

[31] *Gosling v Gosling* (1859) John 265, 272 (adopted as the classic exposition of the doctrine in *Wharton v Masterman* [1895] AC 186, 192–3).

[32] The rule was rejected for the United States in *Claflin v Claflin* 149 Mass 19 (1889) and following cases, allowing what is there termed the settlor's 'dead hand' to prevail over what the English rule treats as the beneficiary's right to unencumbered enjoyment. See G Alexander (1985) 37 Stanford LR 1189.

[33] (1841) 4 Beav 115, Cr & Ph 240.

[34] J Harris *Variation of Trusts* (1975).

[35] Alternatively, and avoiding the need to go to court, the settlor may have given one or more people the power to reconfigure the trust's beneficial arrangements. These might be the trustees, or some or all of the adult beneficiaries of full capacity, or an outsider; in the latter two cases perhaps referred to as 'protector(s)'. See D Waters in A Oakley (ed) *Trends in Contemporary Trust Law* (1996) ch 4.

[36] S 1(1).

in the future,[37] and the beneficiaries under the discretionary element of a protective trust,[38] where that element has not yet come into effect. There is thus no power under the Act to supply the consent of a beneficiary simply on the grounds that her whereabouts are not known, or that she, however inconveniently, refuses to consent to what is proposed. In most trusts, there is a mixture of people covered by the Act and others. A modification can then occur only if the judge supplies consent on behalf of the former, and the rest give their own consent.[39]

The Act is not designed simply to remove obstacles from the path of those who are able to consent for themselves. A judge can normally supply consent on a person's behalf only if the proposed variation is to that person's benefit.[40] In most cases, the proposed variation will bring financial gain to that person, and the judge has no difficulty in seeing this as the necessary benefit. (Sometimes chances are involved, but the judges will then take an actuarial approach to finding financial gain.)[41] But the Act requires benefit as a proxy for a more nebulous but essentially correct inquiry whether the person in question would have wanted the modification to which his consent is being supplied, if he had been adult, of full capacity, etc.[42] In one case the judge, posing himself the latter question, found benefit to an elderly, mentally incapacitated beneficiary in a variation which deprived her of a small amount of income which she did not need, but which saved large sums in tax for her presumable heirs.[43] Other decisions too have departed from a strictly financial view of benefit. Perhaps as a result of not focusing on the question just referred to, they can

[37] S 1(1)(b): eg the person a beneficiary may at some time marry, or the people who will be a beneficiary's next-of-kin when she dies: *Knocker v Youle* [1986] 1 WLR 934.

[38] See section 11.2.

[39] There is an inelegancy here. The Act allows consent to be supplied in the cause of 'varying or revoking' the trust (s 1(1)), which has been held to exclude the complete restructuring of it (*Re T's Settlement Trusts* [1964] Ch 158, 162; *Re Holt's Settlement* [1969] 1 Ch 100). *Saunders v Vautier* (1841) 4 Beav 115, Cr & Ph 240 however allows only the revocation of the trust, after which there can be a resettlement amounting either to a varying or a complete restructuring of the original trust. There is thus a mismatch in what can be achieved, and the procedure to be used for achieving it, as between those relying on *Saunders v Vautier* and those for whom the Act is invoked.

[40] S 1(1). Benefit is not required in the case of a beneficiary under the discretionary element of a protective trust which has not yet come into effect: perhaps because such a person's role in the trust is viewed (cynically, but correctly) as to lend colour to a device aimed at protecting the principal beneficiary's entitlement against the effects of bankruptcy (see section 11.2).

[41] *Re Cohen's Will Trusts* [1959] 1 WLR 865; *Re Holt's Settlement* [1969] 1 Ch 100, 122; *Goulding v James* [1997] 2 All ER 239, 242.

[42] *Re Van Gruisen's Will Trusts* [1964] 1 WLR 449.

[43] *Re CL* [1969] 1 Ch 587.

however be criticized, as impositions of the judge's own values. Thus judges have perceived benefit in a proposed variation which, though likely to be financially detrimental to infant beneficiaries, was calculated to secure family amity;[44] and in a variation postponing from 21 to 30 the age at which infant beneficiaries would come into their interests, so as to improve their moral fibre.[45] Conversely, and most strikingly of all, they have found a proposed variation not to children's benefit when, although to their financial advantage, it would have involved their moving to Jersey.[46]

The Act provides that, given benefit in the cases where it is required, the court 'may if it thinks fit' supply consent 'on behalf of' a person who cannot give it for herself.[47] These words introduce an element of discretion. They allow the judge, asking the familiar question 'would a beneficiary able to consent for himself agree to this?', to consent on a beneficiary's behalf only if she thinks the proposed modification offers the beneficiary *enough* benefit.[48] They also allow the judge to refuse consent on a beneficiary's behalf if that question deserves a negative answer on grounds other than the beneficiary's self-interest.[49] But given a positive answer to the question, the judge should use the discretion against giving consent only if to consent would involve the court in an illegality.[50] By contrast, involvement in legal tax avoidance is not regarded as a problem,[51] and indeed this is the nature of most applications under the Act. Nor is there an objection to departure from the settlor's wishes: the rule

---

[44] *Re Remnant's Settlement Trusts* [1970] 1 Ch 560. But in *Re Tinker's Settlement* [1960] 1 WLR 1011, on similar facts, the judge refused to find benefit.

[45] *Re Holt's Settlement* [1969] 1 Ch 100. The judge also held that even if the postponement was a detriment, it was outweighed by other aspects of the variation which gave these beneficiaries more money. See too *Re T's Settlement Trusts* [1964] Ch 158.

[46] *Re Weston's Settlements* [1969] 1 Ch 223. Although the judgment lauds an upbringing in England, the objection was perhaps less to an upbringing in Jersey than to a life organized around financial considerations. General adoption of the latter perspective would of course be fatal to large numbers of proposals for variation which are in fact accepted.

[47] S 1(1).

[48] *Re Van Gruisen's Will Trusts* [1964] 1 WLR 449. A beneficiary able to consent for himself might not consent to a proposed modification giving him some benefit if he can stick out for more: the discretion enables the judge to do the same on behalf of a beneficiary not able to consent for himself.

[49] *Re Steed's Will Trusts* [1960] Ch 407, where the beneficiary's very role in the trust was to prevent its becoming the arrangement proposed.

[50] Such as a fraud on a power (*Re Robertson's Will Trusts* [1960] 1 WLR 1050), or, presumably, the creation of new provisions impermissible under the law of trusts (eg on grounds of perpetuity).

[51] *Re Sainsbury's Settlement* [1967] 1 WLR 476; *Fitzwilliam v IRC* [1993] 1 WLR 1189, 1197 (but cf 1222, and *Re Weston's Settlements* [1969] 1 Ch 223, n 46 above).

in *Saunders v Vautier*[52] allows departure on the part of beneficiaries who are able to consent for themselves, and the Act operates to extend that rule to those not able to consent for themselves.[53]

12.6 OTHER MODIFICATION RULES

The law contains a number of other rules under which trustees' duties can be modified, of less general importance than those dealt with so far.

These include[54] (justificatory) provisions allowing the court to enlarge the trustees' management powers in an emergency,[55] or where this is 'expedient',[56] or in certain trusts involving land, where the modification would be to the benefit of the land or the beneficiaries.[57] (These are of less importance given the wide investment powers now conferred by the Trustee Act 2000.)[58] The latter provision also allows modification of the beneficial interests. Under all these provisions, the court can authorize the modification without need of consent even from those beneficiaries able to give it. In practice, however, the provisions are mostly[59] used to vindicate the beneficiaries' interest in having the trust operated as they wish, in much the same vein as *Saunders v Vautier*[60] and the Variation of Trusts Act 1958.

Also of note is the cy près jurisdiction, described in section 6.1. Where a trust to promote a charitable object fails, it is commonly restructured into a new form in which it can carry on, ie its trustees are given new duties, by application cy près. The jurisdiction as currently understood promotes utility in keeping charitable provisions alive, for the benefit of society, in circumstances where a non-charitable trust would terminate. But it reconciles this with a close adherence to the settlor's wishes by defining the occasion for cy près application, 'failure', very much in terms of the impossibility of effectuating the settlor's wishes,[61] and by a practice

---

[52] (1841) 4 Beav 115, Cr & Ph 240.
[53] *Goulding v James* [1997] 2 All ER 239.
[54] See also *Chapman v Chapman* [1954] AC 429.
[55] *Re New* [1901] 2 Ch 534.
[56] Trustee Act 1925 s 57.
[57] Settled Land Act 1925 s 64.
[58] See section 9.4.
[59] Cf *Hambro v Duke of Marlborough* [1994] Ch 158, holding that the Settled Land Act 1925 s 64 can be used to diminish a beneficiary's interest against his wishes, the objective there being fundamentally facilitative: to preserve the essence of the settlement against depredation.
[60] (1841) 4 Beav 115, Cr & Ph 240.
[61] Failure is defined in the Charities Act 1993 s 13. The widest cases are those in s 13(1)(a)(ii) ('where the original purposes . . . cannot be carried out . . . according to the directions given and to the spirit of the gift'), and in s 13(1)(e)(iii) ('where the original purposes . . . have . . . ceased . . . to provide a suitable and effective method of using the property . . . regard being had to the spirit of the gift').

of ensuring that the cy près application is very close to the settlor's original purpose. (It is easy to follow both policies at once in this area as a charitable settlor by definition wishes to provide something of public utility.) Some[62] however have suggested that utility should predominate: that the jurisdiction should be used to modify charitable trusts whenever a better use can be found for the money involved, so as to apply the money to that use, regardless of the settlor's wishes. It can be argued that this is right in principle: the special treatment of charitable trusts entails a price for society, so society should get its money's worth. But the off-putting effect such an approach might have on prospective charitable settlors, and also the cost of administering it, might render it counterproductive in terms of its own utilitarian aspirations. And the approach would apparently mean the law breaching faith with settlors: inducing them, facilitatively, to think they could safely entrust it with the effectuation of their intentions, before in fact putting their money to ends of its own.

---

[62] Notably M Chesterman *Charities, Trusts and Social Welfare* (1979) 224–7.

13

Securing performance

The law advertises the express trust device as a means by which settlors can achieve their intentions. But the mere fact of making a trust—placing the property with trustees, and putting them under a legal obligation to carry out those intentions—does not guarantee that outcome. There exist, however, a number of mechanisms that help to ensure its delivery.[1] We shall consider the main ones in this chapter.

First we shall look at mechanisms calculated to ensure that trusts are performed *at all*. Then we shall look at mechanisms calculated to see that they are performed *properly*.

13.1 THE PRESENCE OF TRUSTEES

We saw in section 1.6 that a trustee is essential to the concept of a trust, because a trust consists in duties to handle the trust property in a certain way, and duties are propositions about what people ought to do. The point can also be put more pragmatically. A trust stipulating for property to rest undisturbed for all eternity, if not pointless, would certainly be illegal.[2] Valid and realistic trusts require certain acts to be done: above all, money to be invested and paid out to objects. These things cannot do themselves: someone is required to do them. Ensuring the presence of such a someone, ie a trustee, is the most fundamentally useful way in which the law can promote the performance of trusts.

The settlor will normally name people as trustees; if he does not, the court will make the appointment.[3] But it cannot be taken for granted that someone nominated as a trustee will be available, either initially or for the trust's duration. She might die or disappear. Or she might be unwilling to act. In the latter case it would be unwise to insist that she does, because of the consequent danger of her doing so badly. So the law allows people to

---

[1] On the relationship between extra-legal ideas of 'trust' and the law's visions regarding the satisfactory performance of its 'trusts', see R Cotterrell (1993) CLP 75.

[2] See section 2.5.   [3] *Dodkin v Brunt* (1868) LR 6 Eq 580.

opt out of being trustees, either by disclaiming a trusteeship for which they have been named before they have embarked on it, or, later, by retiring from it.[4] All this would be a source of vulnerability for trusts if it were not for rules allowing for the appointment of new trustees.[5] The details of these rules are complex, and left to larger works. The effect of all these provisions is encapsulated in the idea that trusts will not be allowed to fail for want of a trustee.

13.2 ENSURING THE SUPPLY OF TRUSTEES

But such provisions are not a panacea for ensuring that there are trustees to operate trusts. There must also be an adequate supply of people willing to serve as trustees.

By and large, it seems that the law does not need to do anything positive to induce people to act as trustees. People are generally willing in principle to serve as trustees, out of family loyalty, friendship, and the like, to oblige the settlor and/or the prospective objects, to whom or which they are in some way devoted. And the supply is augmented by the existence of those offering to serve as trustees on a commercial basis, in return for payment: such as solicitors, accountants, banks. So human goodwill and the profit motive between them can be relied upon to produce a supply of people prima facie willing to be trustees. What the law needs to do is essentially conservative: to see that these people are not put off when they find out more about what trusteeship involves: that the position of a trustee is not so unattractive as to make them think better of their original willingness to act.

In particular, the law needs to ensure that the demands made of trustees—their duties—are kept within tolerable bounds. In our survey of the main kinds of trustees' duties, in Chapters 9–11, we noticed how the law does this. We saw in section 10.5, for example, how instead of the apparent duty in a fixed trust to pay the money to the true designated object, and to no one else, come what may, the trustees are actually required to try to pay the person who shows that he is probably the true designated object (and not anyone who does not), and failing that to pay the money in some circumstances to certain other people, or otherwise into court:

---

[4] Especially under the Trustee Act 1925 s 39.
[5] Particularly the Trustee Act 1925 ss 36 and 41. A settlor can however stipulate that the original trustee shall not be replaced, or that only persons with particular characteristics shall be trustees: *Re Rymer* [1895] 1 Ch 19. If a replacement is required and is blocked by such stipulations, the trust will fail.

which is much more practicable. And we saw in sections 9.2–9.4 that the general requirement in regard to managing the trust and investing its assets is only to exercise such care and skill as is reasonable in the circumstances,[6] not to ensure success come what may. So the demands made of trustees are much less off-putting than might have been the case. The trend has not been unqualified, however. There remain some stringent, and so off-putting, duties: especially those aimed at keeping trustees from distraction from the trust's interests, described in section 13.10. As noted there, and unsurprisingly in view of our present preoccupation, the strictness of these duties has been criticized by both judges and commentators.

Further in this vein of ensuring that trusteeship is not too unattractive, the law also maintains a safety-net provision whereby, when trustees have in fact broken their duty but acted honestly and reasonably in doing so, the courts have discretion to relieve them from liability. This is section 61 of the Trustee Act 1925, which we looked at in section 12.2. This provision was originally enacted in 1896,[7] upon the recommendation of the House of Commons Select Committee Report on the Administration of Trusts, 1895.[8] Members of the committee, and its witnesses, felt that there was a shortage of people willing to be trustees, and ascribed this to the excessive onerousness of trustees' duties. So the committee recommended reducing the duties to a more reasonable level, via this jurisdiction to exonerate trustees who had broken their duty but acted pardonably. In fact, this provision was ill adapted to reassuring trustees that nothing unreasonable was expected of them, because, as we have seen, it makes no promises as to the kinds of situations in which relief will be given, and the courts have made none in applying it. Moreover, to our eyes, the courts had already taken the point and pitched the duties at not too off-putting a level:[9] it is unclear why in 1895 this development was thought insufficient.

The law also allows for the exclusion of trustees' liabilities by the terms of the trust itself, and this is frequently done.[10] Those otherwise prepared to serve as trustees may be unwilling to do so without such an exclusion, and to that extent the practice makes a contribution to keeping up the supply of trustees. In practice, however, the mechanism is probably subtler than that. Exclusions allow professional and corporate trustees, in

---

[6] Trustee Act 2000 s 1(1).   [7] Judicial Trustees Act 1896 s 3.   [8] HC 248.
[9] *Speight v Gaunt* (1883) 22 Ch D 727, 9 App Cas 1; *Re Whiteley* (1886) 33 Ch D 347, *Learoyd v Whiteley* (1887) 12 App Cas 727.
[10] See section 12.1.

particular, to keep down their costs, by removing or reducing the need for insurance and expert advice; such trustees' costs work through into their charges; and the lower their charges, the more likely settlors and beneficiaries are to employ them.

The law's main efforts in the direction of ensuring the supply of trustees thus take the form of ensuring that the demands of trusteeship are not too off-putting. But there is a longstop, in the form of a corporate trustee provided by the state: the Public Trustee. This facility, established by the Public Trustee Act 1906, also flowed from the 1895 Select Committee report. Nowadays, the need for such a longstop is quantitatively much less than it was perceived to be then. This is especially because of the rise of the commercial corporate trustees (banks, etc, whose undertaking of trust work was eased by a change in the law in 1920),[11] and because trusts are nowadays much less commonly made in family situations than they were a century ago. The number of trusts in the office's hands climbed sharply in the decade or so immediately after its establishment, and continued rising to peak at over 20,000 in the 1940s, but has fallen steadily since. The need for such a longstop is not just quantitative, however: despite the small numbers involved, the Trustee is still apparently regarded as a worthwhile provision for those few cases where, for one reason or another, settlors cannot find ordinary trustees that suit them.

13.3 SECURING AN ACCEPTABLE PERFORMANCE

So far, we have been thinking about the basic, though essential, matter of seeing that trusts are performed at all, by ensuring that they have trustees to perform them. Now, we shall progress to a higher-level matter: ensuring that the performance rendered is acceptably good.

It is important for the law's facilitative objective that trustees should achieve reasonably good standards of performance. Moreover, it is more desirable that trustees should perform their trusts satisfactorily in the first place than that they should fail but then have to pay compensation. This is self-evident so far as the trustees themselves are concerned, but it is also true from the objects' point of view, because recovering such compensation involves time, effort, expense, and unpleasantness, and may ultimately not succeed anyway, if the trustee is a private individual whose own resources do not cover the amounts for which he is responsible (though it is common nowadays for trustees to be covered by insurance).

---

[11] Administration of Justice Act 1920 s 17.

The remainder of this chapter will be devoted to the mechanisms which help secure a successful performance. First, we shall look at some relatively direct measures, which operate by pointing trustees in the right direction. Then we shall go on to other factors, which work more indirectly, by establishing a culture in which trustees can normally be relied upon to do their job satisfactorily. Finally we shall encounter a further factor: exclusions apart, the legal liability facing trustees who fail in their duties.

13.4 THE STANDARDS REQUIRED OF TRUSTEES

The first of these mechanisms is the most obvious: the standards which the law sets for trustees. On the face of it, it might seem that the higher they are, the better. But that would be wrong.

If the duties were too stringent, trustees, seeking to avoid liability, would err on the side of caution: making for a less satisfactory performance than if they were left more room to manoeuvre. For example, if there were an absolute duty to pay the persons designated by the settlor, the trustees would spend time and money making as sure as possible of the identity and whereabouts of these persons before paying out. And if they were required never to allow the trust's capital to diminish in value, they would confine themselves to the sorts of financial products which in practice would probably serve the beneficiaries less well than more speculative ones. So the setting of trustees' duties at more practicable levels also serves this objective of achieving a decent performance. Because the need for such defensive measures is reduced or eliminated, the trust can be performed, perhaps not perfectly, but at least acceptably, and certainly more expeditiously.

Clauses excluding trustees' liability can be viewed in the same light. It has been held permissible to exclude all duties except that of honestly acting in the beneficiaries' best interests.[12] Exclusions on these lines are common, either from a desire by settlors to remove the worry of legal liability from the relatives and friends whom they appoint as trustees, or because professional or corporate trustees refuse to act without such an exclusion. Such exclusions likewise mean that the trustees need not

---

[12] *Armitage v Nurse* [1998] Ch 241; interpreted in *Walker v Stones* [2001] QB 902, 939, as requiring (though perhaps of only specially qualified trustees) a performance reasonably perceivable as in the beneficiaries' best interests. The duty of care and skill regarding investment cannot be excluded in unit trusts or pension fund trusts: Financial Services Act 1986 s 84, Pensions Act 1995 s 33.

spend excessive time and money watching their step. But do they go too far? As regards levels of performance in practice, probably not. Although they permit not only acceptable and expeditious, but also positively poor, performance, they do not promote the latter: trustees normally want to perform satisfactorily, for reasons considered below. As explained in section 12.1, however, they may be more problematic from other perspectives.

13.5 THE LAW'S ACCOUNTS OF TRUSTEES' DUTIES

A statement, for example, that trustees should in relation to management duties 'exercise such care and skill as is reasonable in the circumstances'[13] is less conducive to a good performance than a statement telling trustees more exactly what is expected of them. Faced with the uncertainty inherent in the more abstract statement, they might err on the side of caution, impeding their performance of the trust as much as if perfection were demanded. Or they might underestimate what is required of them, and fail to provide an acceptable performance.

To some extent the law addresses this problem. It sometimes translates abstract standards such as these into more concrete terms, spelling out what they mean in practice. So, for example, the management duty just referred to is explicated into such specific measures as the diversification of investments[14] and the taking of appropriate advice.[15] Similarly, in the business of payment under a fixed trust, the law stipulates such measures as the placing of advertisements, after which, if the beneficiary does not appear, the trustees should deal with his money on the basis that he is dead.[16] Especially in regard to management duties, however, the law has over time tended away from such explication. In particular, after at one time proscribing most forms of investment altogether from use by trustees, the law progressively gave wider scope, the current rule allowing a trustee to 'make any kind of investment that he could make if he were absolutely entitled to the assets of the trust'.[17] From today's perspective, the greater transparency of the previous approach cost too much in terms of substantive restrictiveness.

In the case of charities, trustees' duties are explicated in a

---

[13] Trustee Act 2000 s 1(1): see section 9.2.   [14] Trustee Act 2000 s 4(2)(b).
[15] S 5.   [16] See section 10.5.
[17] Trustee Act 2000 s 3(1). See section 9.4.

semi-authoritative way (and at public expense) by the Charity Commission and promulgated through its publications, website,[18] and programme of seminars and presentations.

13.6 ELUCIDATION OF TRUSTEES' DUTIES IN INDIVIDUAL CASES

As the law thus tends not to explicate its general statements of trustees' duties, situations can arise in which trustees remain unsure what is required of them. They can commonly obtain the necessary guidance from their solicitors and other professional advisers. As well as a good understanding of trustees' duties in the abstract, these advisers will have access to information about specific precedents: similar situations that have arisen in the past, where one course of action or another was taken, which a court either approved or disapproved on subsequent litigation.

The law provides a further means of elucidating, and thus helping to secure the good performance of, trustees' duties. Trustees can go to court[19] (at the trust's expense) and have a judge tell them what would be a proper course for them to follow. They can use this procedure, for example, if they are unsure whether a putative beneficiary fits the settlor's definition. For instance, in the case of a trust 'for Adam, on condition that he is a practising Christian', when he holds Christian beliefs but attends church only for the annual carol service, they can ask the court to say definitively whether he is entitled.

There are strong incentives for trustees to take advice in these ways. Doing so will almost certainly bring them within the terms of any exclusion they may have: reckless indifference to the beneficiaries' interests is not covered by a term limiting liability to 'dishonesty',[20] and might be shown by failure to take advice. Even where there is no such exclusion, moreover, trustees who take advice are likely to be safe from liability. This is certainly the case when the advice is that of a judge: this counts as a definitive statement of the trustees' duty, so they are completely protected when they act upon it.[21] Taking appropriate advice about investment, and other management matters, may be the best way of showing

---

[18] www.charity-commission.gov.uk.

[19] Or in the case of a charity, to the Charity Commission, either formally or via its helplines and surgeries.

[20] *Armitage v Nurse* [1998] Ch 241, 250.

[21] Charity trustees taking formal advice from the Charity Commission are similarly protected: Charities Act 1993 s 29(2).

that they have taken the required degree of care. And trustees who have broken their duty on the strength of professional advice are much more likely to be relieved from liability under section 61 of the Trustee Act 1925[22] than those who acted in a similar way on their own initiative.[23] To have taken advice is thus in trustees' interests if the advice turns out to be bad: but more usually it will be good, so encouraging trustees to take it again helps towards securing a satisfactory performance from them.

13.7 BACKGROUND FACTORS PROMOTING SATISFACTORY PERFORMANCE

Now we move to factors lying more in the background, which operate by establishing a culture in which satisfactory performance is more likely than it would otherwise be. Here we shall look at three of the most important: the characteristics of those made trustees in the first place; the ability of beneficiaries to scrutinize the trustees' activities, and so criticize them; and a rule, or set of rules, whereby trustees must not allow themselves to be distracted by factors which might lead them to neglect their duty to serve the trust.

13.8 TRUSTEES' CHARACTERISTICS

Perhaps the most important of all the factors promoting the successful performance of trusts is the nature of those who are trustees.[24]

Children cannot be appointed trustees.[25] People convicted of crimes of dishonesty, and bankrupts, cannot normally be trustees of charities,[26] and are liable to be removed from other trusts as 'unfit to act'.[27] Those incapacitated by illness are liable to be removed, and a trustee who remains out of the UK for more than a year may also be removed.[28]

Beyond that, the choice of trustees is a matter for settlors themselves, though there is further provision for removing trustees who turn out to neglect the trust's interests[29] or whom the beneficiaries wish to see

---

[22] See section 12.2.   [23] *Re Allsop* [1914] 1 Ch 1, 13.

[24] For recognition of the relationship between this factor and the judicial approach to the maintenance of standards, see *Edge v Pensions Ombudsman* [2000] Ch 602, 630, 633.

[25] Law of Property Act 1925 s 20.

[26] Charities Act 1993 s 72. The lack of ongoing scrutiny by charitable settlors, and the absence of particular beneficiaries, increases the risk of malversation.

[27] Trustee Act 1925 s 36(1).

[28] Ibid.

[29] *Letterstedt v Broers* (1884) 9 App Cas 371; *Clarke v Heathfield (No 2)* [1985] ICR 606.

removed[30] or who prove unsuitable to administer a charity.[31] A settlor will generally choose people in whom she has confidence, and who seem to her suitable for the kind of trust in question. Assuming that settlors' judgement is mostly good (sometimes, of course, it is unfortunately not), those whom they select can generally be relied upon to make a decent job of their task.

There are some specific characteristics that those chosen as trustees are likely to have, which also affect the prospects of a satisfactory performance. Two main types of trustee are commonly used, and they have different kinds of motivation towards performing their trust well, and different strengths and weaknesses affecting their likelihood of doing so.

One type of person frequently appointed trustee is someone closely connected with the settlor herself and/or the objects of the trust. In a family trust, for example, it might be a relative or friend or colleague of the settlor. In a trust for company employees, representatives of the workforce and the board would probably feature largely. The motivation of trustees of this kind towards performing the trust well arises from a sense of loyalty to the settlor and/or the objects.

The alternative is a professional trustee: a person or entity prepared to act as a trustee as part of their work. A professional trustee may be an individual, eg a solicitor or accountant, or a corporation, commonly a bank (which of course in practice operates through individual officers). Professional trustees' services will normally have to be paid for. Their principal motivation to perform the trust well is a desire to do a good job, but they are also encouraged by commercial and professional factors.

The commercial encouragement comes from competition with other professional trustees (and with lay trustees too, for that matter), settlors seeking the best buy amongst them. This is not a complete recipe for securing a good performance from them, however, because the market is an imperfect one. Although their prices can be compared, from their published tariffs, it is more difficult to judge their quality. In particular, people who appoint trustees at all must rarely do so more than once in their lifetime, and so are ill placed to make comparisons about performance. The deficiency is, however, to a large extent made up by such trustees' professional standards. Banks, for example, have training, rule books, and procedures for their staff, designed to ensure a good performance. They are also subject to the control of the Financial Services

---

[30] Trusts of Land and Appointment of Trustees Act 1996 s 19.
[31] Charities Act 1993 s 18.

Authority,[32] with its systems of authorization, training, and discipline, and the Financial Ombudsman Service.[33] There are parallel regulatory arrangements for solicitors, accountants, and so on.

The strength of lay trustees such as family friends is their intimate understanding of the settlor's wishes and the beneficiaries' situations, which makes especially for a refined handling of a trust's dispositive discretions. On the other hand lay trustees are likely to be relatively weak on matters such as investment, and their closeness to the settlor and objects may also make them susceptible to pressure, so that they go wrong: for example, they may be persuaded into exercising a power of maintenance or advancement not for the benefit of the child, but so as to help its parents out of some financial difficulties. The strengths and weaknesses of professional trustees are generally the reverse of these. They should be adept at the managerial aspects of the trust. Being more remote, they will lack the intimate understandings shown by their lay counterparts, but this should make them better able to resist improper pressures.[34] So the two types of trustees are complementary to one another, and the best approach is often to combine the two: to have at least one trustee of each kind.

It is wrong to view the ideal performance as that given by a trustee uninfluenced by settlor or objects: trustees may consult and attend to input from both,[35] so long as they do not allow themselves to be dictated to.[36] Trustees are often selected precisely because of their likely receptiveness to such input. They may indeed be selected because they can supply the input themselves, usually through being also settlor or beneficiary. The appointment of such 'stakeholder' trustees is common. In pension fund trusts some of the trustees must be drawn from the scheme's members,[37] and others will usually represent the employer: the overall mix being explicitly seen as a factor promoting appropriate

---

[32] www.fsa.gov.uk.　　　　　　[33] www.financial-ombudsman.org.uk.

[34] But note *Nestlé v National Westminster Bank plc* [1993] 1 WLR 1260 and *Re Pauling's Settlement Trusts* [1964] Ch 303, notorious cases where bank trustees fell short of such expectations.

[35] *Fraser v Murdoch* (1881) 6 App Cas 855, Scotland; *Re Manisty's Settlement* [1974] Ch 17, 26; *Hartigan Nominees Pty Ltd v Rydge* (1992) 29 NSWLR 405, Australia; *Breadner v Granville-Grossman* [2001] Ch 523, 532 paras 20–2. (Sometimes they *must* consult, and in this case give effect to their majority wish, 'so far as consistent with the general interest of the trust': Trusts of Land and Appointment of Trustees Act 1996 s 11. See too *X v A* [2000] 1 All ER 490.)

[36] *Re Pauling's Settlement Trusts* [1964] Ch 303; *Re Locker's Settlement Trusts* [1977] 1 WLR 1323; *Turner v Turner* [1984] Ch 100.

[37] Pensions Act 1995 s 16.

performance.[38] Charity trustees often include 'consumers' of the charity's activities.[39] In certain family private trusts of land, the law used to give the principal beneficiary (the 'tenant for life') most of the trustees' powers,[40] and it remains common for such a person to be a trustee or to be delegated trustees' powers.[41]

While the trustees' characteristics are a factor promoting good performance, they can be a source of weakness. The law contains some provisions calculated to check that possibility. In case the appointed trustees lack the professional expertise needed to carry out the trust's administrative functions, they can delegate these.[42] (But they cannot delegate their dispositive functions: this would be a case of failure to exercise their own discretion.) Against the possibility of ineptitude or dishonesty, the settlor, court, Charity Commission (in case of charity),[43] or trustees themselves[44] can appoint a custodian, ie a bank or similar whose sole function is to hold the trust assets safely; and trustees must act in not less than a pair to receive purchase money when selling land (though it is unclear why that should be a case of special danger).[45] Presumably as a corrective to idiosyncrasy,[46] except in charities[47] and pension trusts[48] (the justification for these exceptions probably lying in the larger number of trustees such trusts often have) they must be unanimous in choosing their courses of action.[49]

A settlor may not be content to rely on her trustees' characteristics. Especially in 'offshore' jurisdictions, she is increasingly likely to introduce a 'protector' into the trust arrangements. The protector is a person,

---

[38] *Edge v Pensions Ombudsman* [2000] Ch 602, 630, 633. Having representation from one constituency but not the other, however, can cause distortion: M Milner [1997] Conv 89.

[39] Charity Commission *Users on board: users who become trustees* (2000), www.charity-commission.gov.uk/publications/cc24.asp.

[40] Settled Land Act 1925 Part II.

[41] Trusts of Land and Appointment of Trustees Act 1996 s 9.

[42] Trustee Act 2000 s 11, and Part IV generally. The rules for charities are slightly different: ibid. In choosing a delegate, etc, trustees are required to 'exercise such care and skill as is reasonable in the circumstances' (Sch 1 para 3). The decision whether to delegate at all is probably controlled by the traditional requirement to act as a prudent businessman looking after others' interests.

[43] Charities Act 1993 s 18.

[44] Trustee Act 2000 s 19; Part IV generally, and Sch 1 para 3.

[45] Law of Property Act 1925 s 27(2).

[46] J Jaconelli [1991] Conv 30.

[47] *Re Whiteley* [1910] 1 Ch 600, 608.

[48] Pensions Act 1995 s 32.

[49] *Luke v South Kensington Hotel* (1879) 11 Ch D 121, 125. The rule in default of a choice to do otherwise can thus be important, and if inappropriate can produce odd results: *Re Mayo* [1943] Ch 302.

or group of people, given power to veto the trustees' proposed actions, or indeed to instruct the trustees to take a particular course, whether in administrative or dispositive matters; and possibly having few or no legal responsibilities.[50] The settlor will choose as protector a person likely to represent her own thinking regarding the operation of the trust; or that of a particular beneficiary or class of beneficiaries whom she wishes especially to protect.[51] The use of a protector, thus selected for his characteristics, will conduce to a good performance of the trust from the perspective of the person or people represented. Evidently, however, there may be a price to be paid from other perspectives.

13.9 DISCLOSURE AND SCRUTINY OF TRUSTEES' ACTIVITIES

The second of our background factors is the visibility of trustees' activities to those interested. Even if such scrutiny were not the prelude to suing or prosecuting the trustees, it would disclose anything questionable in their operation of the trust, and so create a source of pressure and assistance towards a good performance.

A beneficiary is entitled to see the documents constituting the trust,[52] and also (unless she has only a remote chance of being favoured under a discretion) to know the names and addresses of the trustees.[53] She can also see the accounts which trustees must keep,[54] recording both the state of the trust's investments and the payments out to the objects; and can insist that the accounts be audited.[55]

Beyond this, however, there is little that trustees are required to disclose about their running of the trust, at any rate as a matter of routine. In particular, they do not have to make available the agendas and minutes of their meetings, nor their correspondence with different beneficiaries, in which might be revealed, say, the thinking leading up to their exercise of a power of appointment or suchlike: why, for instance, they decided to give a sister a larger amount of money than her brother. One would have thought, given human nature, that people would have sought very

---

[50] D Waters in A Oakley (ed) *Trends in Contemporary Trust Law* (1996) ch 4.

[51] The protector may indeed be the favoured beneficiary or beneficiaries; possibly even the settlor, though in this case the settlor's lack of detachment from the trust assets may leave her enduringly liable to tax upon them, normally a prohibitive consideration.

[52] *Re Londonderry's Settlement* [1965] Ch 918.

[53] *Re Murphy's Settlements* [1999] 1 WLR 282.

[54] *Pearse v Green* (1819) 1 Jac & W 135, 140.   [55] Public Trustee Act 1906 s 13.

regularly to have access to material of this kind. But the rule was comprehensively asserted only in 1964, in *Re Londonderry's Settlement*.[56] Equally curiously, especially since the judgments in that case were far from models of clarity, and left much scope for further probing, the rule has been little tested in the English courts since.[57] The rule was derived from an old decision taking a similar line regarding a charity,[58] notwithstanding the public interest in charities; and it has been applied in the context of a pension fund trust,[59] notwithstanding the argument that the members of the pension scheme deserved greater access because of their contractual rights in it. There is however extensive provision for the disclosure of more formal kinds of information about such trusts,[60] and in the case of pension schemes the mandatory presence of scheme members among the trustees[61] may make it likely that trustees will choose to go further.

One basis for the absence of a general disclosure requirement is a notion that trustees have no duty to think, or to abstain from thinking, in a particular way (other than in good faith, which is assumed unless clearly disproved): making information as to their thoughts irrelevant.[62] That is not, however, the current law regarding trustees' duties. In particular, they are required to take account of proper considerations and not of improper ones.[63] Information as to their thoughts seems fully relevant to the question whether they have done so.

Might the non-disclosure rule be justified nonetheless? It is sometimes said that the questioning and disputation consequent upon revealing their thinking might render the trustees' role so invidious as to deter people from agreeing to undertake it in the first place, so endangering the supply of trustees: the preoccupation with which we began this chapter.[64] Another suggestion is that having to disclose their thinking might lead trustees to exercise their discretion one way rather than another with an

---

[56] [1965] Ch 918.

[57] But see *Hartigan Nominees Pty Ltd v Rydge* (1992) 29 NSWLR 405, Australia, and other cases there cited.

[58] *Re Beloved Wilkes' Charity* (1851) 3 Mac & G 440

[59] *Wilson v Law Debenture Trust Corp plc* [1995] 2 All ER 337.

[60] Charities Act 1993 Part VI (trustees of charities must make their accounts available to the public, and where the annual turnover exceeds £10,000 must each year submit accounts and a report to the Charity Commission); Occupational Pension Schemes (Disclosure of Information) Regulations 1996 SI No 1655.

[61] Pensions Act 1995 s 16.

[62] *Re Londonderry's Settlement* [1965] Ch 918, 936–7; *Hartigan Nominees Pty Ltd v Rydge* (1992) 29 NSWLR 405, 412–13, 441, Australia.

[63] See sections 11.5–11.6.   [64] *Re Londonderry's Settlement* [1965] Ch 918, 937.

eye to minimizing the ensuing dissension, rather than according to what they see as the real merits: so that protecting them in this way conduces to a more satisfactory performance of their function. A third is that to compel disclosure would be to injure the private quality which appropriately characterizes (at any rate family) trusts.[65] One can see the sense in these perceptions. On the other hand, such problems will surely arise from the trustees' very decisions, eg the simple fact that the sister received more than the brother. To explain the thinking behind the decisions is unlikely to make matters worse, and might help. Moreover, one cannot satisfactorily note only the drawbacks of disclosure, and overlook the arguments in its favour, such as its promotion of good performance and of a sense of 'ownership' on the beneficiaries' part.

Information not otherwise available can sometimes be elicited in the event of litigation, either by an order for disclosure or by the questioning of a witness. A beneficiary who sues the trustees, therefore, might force them to disclose their thinking.[66] While in theory this is possible only once the beneficiary has an arguable case for alleging breach of trust on the basis of other evidence,[67] in practice that case might rest on inferences, the trustees being forced into disclosure in order to dispel these.

13.10 PROVISIONS AGAINST DISTRACTION

We have noted the requirement that trustees must normally attend to the trust objects' interests and not any others, such as their own.[68] The third background factor promoting a satisfactory performance of their duties is a rule against entering upon certain obvious situations in which they might do otherwise. This is the rule that trustees must not pursue other interests (especially their own, but also those of others, such as another trust), where these might conflict with those of the trust's objects.[69]

The rule is often portrayed in terms of a collection of more specific sub-rules and sub-sub-rules. The differences between them reflect the different ways in which trustees might be called upon to serve the objects' best interests, and in which they might be distracted from doing so. This

---

[65] See section 2.4.

[66] *Scott v National Trust for Places of Historic Interest or Natural Beauty* [1998] 2 All ER 705, 719.

[67] *Hartigan Nominees Pty Ltd v Rydge* (1992) 29 NSWLR 405, 437, Australia.

[68] See section 9.5.

[69] This duty applies not only to trustees but also to other fiduciaries. The constructive trust arising where property is acquired in breach of it is discussed in section 8.5.

disaggregation of the main rule is helpful in focusing its implications, but carries the danger of sight being lost of its essential point.

There are three principal sub-rules. One, the most general, prohibits trustees from entering into arrangements (most obviously, but not necessarily, taking bribes) calculated to influence their conduct of the trust.[70] The second is that a trustee must not purchase property from her trust.[71] The duty of a trustee selling trust property is to obtain as high a price as possible for it. A trustee purchasing it for herself would wish to pay as low a price as possible. To obviate the danger that the latter consideration might eclipse the former, trustees are barred from buying trust property.[72] The third sub-rule is that a trustee must not extract profit from her position as trustee. This in turn yields perhaps three sub-sub-rules. One prohibits a trustee from making an acquisition for herself which it was her duty to strive to make for the trust: a trustee contemplating the possibility of gaining for herself might neglect that duty.[73] The second requires trustees not to use the trust's shares to vote themselves into directorships of companies in which the trust is invested.[74] Their interest in the resulting fees might distract them from their duty to cast the trust's votes for the most promising directors, so as best to promote its interests. The third prohibits trustees from paying themselves from the trust assets: if they could, their self-interest might lead them to maximize the extent of their work and so their charges, cutting across their duties to use their best judgement in deciding what work the trust needs, and normally to maximize the financial benefit to the objects.[75]

All these rules can be modified or excluded by the settlor,[76] by the

---

[70] *Vatcher v Paull* [1915] AC 372, 379; *Re Smith* [1896] 1 Ch 71.

[71] This is sometimes linked with a rule that trustees' purchases from their beneficiaries are the subject of suspicion. But that rule is not calculated to obviate distraction from the trustees' duties *in carrying out the trust*. Rather, it restates the fact that undue influence is presumed between trustee and beneficiary (*Re Brocklehurst* [1978] 1 All ER 767, 785), so that such a purchase is invalid unless that presumption is rebutted.

[72] *Campbell v Walker* (1800) 5 Ves 678; *ex p Lacey* (1802) 6 Ves 625; *ex p James* (1803) 8 Ves 337. It is irrelevant whether the purchase is profitable for the trustee: that is why this rule does not merge with the next.

[73] *Keech v Sandford* (1726) Sel Cas t King 61.

[74] *Re Macadam* [1946] Ch 73; cf *Re Gee* [1948] Ch 284.

[75] *Robinson v Pett* (1734) 3 P Wms 249.

[76] This seems to be the basis of *Edge v Pensions Ombudsman* [2000] Ch 602: the trust being structured so as to have beneficiary trustees, they were able to make a discretionary decision in their own favour. (Note also Pensions Act 1995 s 39.) While the duties under discussion are excludable, that which they are calculated to promote, the duty to serve the beneficiaries' interests, is not: *Armitage v Nurse* [1998] Ch 241.

consent of the beneficiaries,[77] or by the leave of the court.[78] The last of them, concerning the payment of trustees, has also attracted a collection of provisions negativing it, at first in narrow situations where there was inherently no danger of abuse[79] but latterly by way of a general regime whereby professional trustees and trust corporations can obtain 'reasonable remuneration' for their work.[80] Behind this erosion of the rule against payment lies a realization that those having some kinds of expertise needed to perform the trust well will not be prepared to act for nothing. Though conceived as a means of promoting good performance, therefore, the rule had become injurious to that aim.

There is controversy also over the rules' zeal in other respects. This is especially true of the rule preventing a trustee from making for herself an acquisition which she ought to seek for the trust.[81] In what tend to be regarded as the classic cases, the judges have regarded acquisitions as being of this kind even when there was little chance of their being obtained for the trust.[82] For example, in *Keech v Sandford*[83] a lease was held on trust. As the lease approached its end, the trustee tried to persuade the landlord to renew it in the trust's favour. When, for firm reasons, the landlord was unwilling, the trustee secured a renewal in his own favour. It was held that he should not have done: presumably because there might have been some chance of the landlord's reluctance being overcome by sufficient persuasion on the trustee's part.[84] And in *Boardman v Phipps*[85] a trust's solicitor, treated as caught by the same

---

[77] In the case of contractually hired fiduciaries, such consent is commonly given by an express or implied term of the contract: *Kelly v Cooper* [1993] AC 205.

[78] *Re Duke of Norfolk's Settlement Trusts* [1982] Ch 61 (trustees' remuneration); *Re Drexel Burnham Lambert UK Pension Plan* [1995] 1 WLR 32 (extracting a profit).

[79] *Cradock v Piper* (1850) 1 Mac & G 664.

[80] Trustee Act 2000 ss 29, 30. These provisions were preceded by narrower ones: Judicial Trustees Act 1896 s 1(5), Public Trustee Act 1906 ss 4(3) and 9, Trustee Act 1925 s 42.

[81] See too *Holder v Holder* [1968] Ch 353 and *Hillsdown Holdings plc v Pensions Ombudsman* [1997] 1 All ER 862, 895–9 (purchase of trust property); *Re Keeler's Settlement Trusts* [1981] 1 All ER 888 (directorships).

[82] This leaning is sometimes facilitated by invoking the parent rule against a trustee extracting profit 'from her position as trustee': that phrase begs the question when put under pressure.

[83] (1726) Sel Cas t King 61.

[84] Likewise *Regal (Hastings) Ltd v Gulliver* [1967] 2 AC 134n; *Industrial Development Consultants Ltd v Cooley* [1972] 1 WLR 443: company directors (fiduciaries analogous to trustees, to whom the same rule applies) were not to take up for themselves business opportunities which it was their duty to try to secure for their firms.

[85] [1967] 2 AC 46.

rule,[86] discovered a business opportunity when working on the trust's behalf. He seized this opportunity to make a profit for himself (and also for the trust). Although there seems to have been no realistic prospect of the trust pursuing the opportunity in question, it was held that he should not have done so. His duties required him to give uncontaminated consideration to the questions whether the trust could take the opportunity, and if so how this might be achieved.

The argument for this approach is that, by giving an unmistakably stern message, it encourages trustees to err on the side of avoiding distraction, and that that maximizes the effectiveness of the rule in securing a good performance. But some judges regard such sternness as excessive. They think it right to require trustees to lay aside their own interests only where there is a 'real sensible possibility of conflict'. The words are those of Lord Upjohn, whose opinion in *Boardman v Phipps*[87] best exemplifies this viewpoint. He dissented from the decision just described because he thought, given the unlikelihood of the trust pursuing the opportunity whether it had uncontaminated advice from the solicitor or not, that the solicitor's pursuit of it could not have distracted him from his responsibilities to the trust.[88] An important factor behind this leaning is the fact that, in practice, the rule is normally used not merely prospectively, to enjoin trustees from entering a situation of potential conflict, but retrospectively, to hold them liable for breach of the duty to avoid such a situation.[89]

It can also be argued that the rule, even in its more lenient version, is counterproductive: that (like the rule against trustees' remuneration), far from safeguarding the quality of the trust's performance, it damages it. Notwithstanding the general duty to serve the trust's interests, there is usually no positive duty to exploit a particular opportunity. (Investment being the unscientific business that it is, such a rule—as opposed to the existing law's discretion—would be hard to justify.)[90] Given the rule

---

[86] The solicitor was a fiduciary *vis-à-vis* the trustees, who employed him. But since they had a duty undistractedly to promote their beneficiaries' interests, they could not allow the solicitor to do otherwise. There was a second defendant, one of the beneficiaries. He was in the same position as the solicitor since, though not paid to do so, he too acted on the trust's behalf.

[87] [1967] 2 AC 46, 124.

[88] Note also *Queensland Mines Ltd v Hudson* (1978) 18 ALR 1, Australia: the facts were extremely similar to those of *Industrial Development Consultants Ltd v Cooley* [1972] 1 WLR 443 (n 84 above), but the opposite outcome was reached.

[89] For the form of liability, see section 8.5.

[90] On trustees' duties regarding investment, see section 9.4.

against self-interested actions, the trustee therefore lacks any incentive to exploit it. The trust would apparently be better served if it could benefit from an exploitation motivated by self-interest. That suggests not an anti-distraction rule but a profit-sharing regime.[91] This was in fact the spirit in which the solicitor acted in *Boardman v Phipps*.[92] And while the law stripped him of his share on account of the rule as it stands, he was awarded remuneration for his efforts.[93] As an outcome, this to some extent reflected the argument here. But the jurisdiction to award remuneration operates after the event and opaquely, so cannot incentivize trustees in the way that an upfront provision would. Partly in reflection of this argument, but more especially so as to avoid impracticability, corporate trustees normally decline to act unless the rule is excluded, so that opportunities encountered in their dealings for one trust can be exploited for their other trusts and/or for themselves.

13.11 LEGAL ENFORCEMENT

A final factor conducing to satisfactory performance of trusts is the possibility of trustees who fail in their duties being legally liable.

This liability is normally civil. The civil remedies against trustees will be detailed in sections 15.2–15.5, but in essence they operate to put matters into the position that they should have been in if the trustees had performed their duty. For instance, if trustees pay someone (as though a beneficiary) whom they should not, they can be sued to make good the loss.

Sometimes, though comparatively rarely, trustees' misbehaviour will also result in criminal liability. The principal crimes relevant to trustees are theft,[94] false accounting,[95] and conspiracy to defraud.[96] These offences have in common a requirement of dishonesty on the part of the accused, meaning that his behaviour must have been what reasonable people would regard as dishonest, and that he should have realized this.[97] This is in

---

[91] W Bishop and D Prentice (1983) 46 MLR 289.

[92] [1967] 2 AC 46.

[93] Similarly *O'Sullivan v Management Agency and Music Ltd* [1985] QB 428; cf *Guinness v Saunders* [1990] 2 AC 663.

[94] Theft Act 1968 s 1. S 5(2), (3) removes difficulties which would otherwise affect the application of the offence to trustees.

[95] Theft Act 1968 s 17.

[96] *Scott v Metropolitan Police Commissioner* [1975] AC 819; *Wai Yu-tsang v R* [1992] 1 AC 269.

[97] *R v Ghosh* [1982] QB 1053.

contrast with trustees' civil liability, which can arise for failure to reach the prescribed standard (say, 'such care and skill as is reasonable in the circumstances')[98] through laziness or gullibility or even well-intentioned incompetence as much as through dishonesty. A trustee incurring criminal liability may be punished in the usual ways: fine, imprisonment, etc. The fact that the crime was committed by a trustee means that it attracts a more severe punishment than would otherwise have been given.[99]

Some trustees are also subject to a further kind of legal intervention. The Charity Commission can make orders against trustees of charities, eg removing them or freezing the trust assets.[100] The Occupational Pensions Regulatory Authority may intervene in various ways against trustees of occupational pension fund trusts,[101] and the Pensions Ombudsman[102] can investigate maladministration and make such orders as are open to a court.[103] The Financial Ombudsman Service, which has jurisdiction over most corporate and unit trust trustees, can order them to pay such compensation as seems fair.[104]

Legal liability helps secure the good performance of trusts in two ways. One is prophylactic, helping to ensure that trustees do not break their duties, like the factors considered earlier in this chapter. The other is corrective, putting matters right if there is a breach. The prophylactic effect depends upon the value of legal liability as a deterrent. All the forms of liability discussed above can have a deterrent effect. The effect arises from the shame of liability, together with the pain of the punishment or of having to pay compensation. The efficacy of deterrence is ethically and methodologically difficult to assess, and the limited extant evidence is hard to interpret.[105] But the prospect of legal liability probably contributes something to people's general inclination to keep the law, and more specifically the exposure of trustees to liability probably helps promote the satisfactory performance of trusts. The corrective effect of legal liability takes over where the prophylactic effect leaves off. It aims to secure the performance of trusts by putting matters right if the trustees fall down. This is the province of civil liability and the ombudsman jurisdictions (criminal liability concerns the fate of the delinquent

---

[98] Trustee Act 2000 s 1: see section 9.2.
[99] *R v Barrick* (1985) 7 Cr App R (S) 143; *R v Clark* [1998] 2 Cr App R (S) 137.
[100] Charities Act 1993 s 18.
[101] Pensions Act 1995 ss 1–15.
[102] Pension Schemes Act 1993 ss 146–51; Pensions Act 1995 s 157.
[103] *Hillsdown Holdings plc v Pensions Ombudsman* [1997] 1 All ER 862.
[104] Financial Services and Markets Act 2000 Part XVI and Sch 17.
[105] A Ashworth *Sentencing & Criminal Justice* 3rd edn (2000) 64–8.

trustees):[106] as we noted, the civil remedies are designed to restore matters to the position that they should have been in had the trustees performed properly. As such, they provide an ultimate safety net for securing the proper performance of trusts.

The availability of legal remedies does not, however, offer a panacea against unsatisfactory performance. Many factors (lack of information or resources, for example) can prevent the invocation of such remedies from being a practical possibility. The bulk of the work of eliciting a good performance from trustees therefore falls to the other factors considered in this chapter.

---

[106] Though criminal liability may be accompanied by a compensation order, which is roughly the same in effect as a civil judgment, so as to spare the victim the need to take additional civil proceedings.

14

Trustees' duties and beneficiaries' rights

The 'definition' of the trust concept sketched in section 1.1 asserted in part that 'a trust is a situation in which property is vested in someone (a trustee), who is under legally recognized obligations, at least some of which are of a proprietary kind, to handle it in a certain way'.

In Chapters 9–11 and 13, we discussed the main types of obligations resting on trustees: their duties to respect the fact that the property is not beneficially their own and to keep it safe, to manage and invest it, to pay out to the trust's objects (with or without a preceding discretionary choice), and to avoid distraction. We saw that the incidence and content of these duties varies to some extent from one trust, or class of trust, to another. This chapter begins by thinking generally about the nature of these duties.

Where a trust has beneficiaries, the trustees' duties are mirrored by rights on the part of those beneficiaries. This chapter also considers the significance of this, and in particular examines an argument that it is the interest of a beneficiary in the trust property, rather than the trustees' duties, that lies at the heart of the trust concept.

14.1 THE NATURE OF TRUSTEES' DUTIES

Legal duties are commonly divided into two classes, 'proprietary' (or '*in rem*') and 'personal' (or '*in personam*'). In early times, trust obligations were probably personal. But over time, the law has come to the view that some of these obligations are necessarily proprietary.[1] This means, essentially, that they do not simply rest on the trustees personally, but are in effect charged on to, or attached to, the trust property.[2] Personal duties,

---

[1] *Tinsley v Milligan* [1994] 1 AC 340, 371; *Westdeutsche Landesbank Girozentrale v Islington LBC* [1996] AC 669, 705; *Foskett v McKeown* [2001] 1 AC 102, 108, 127. The European Court of Justice, however, treats English trustees' duties as personal: *Webb v Webb* (Case C–294/92) [1994] QB 696; not followed (nominally distinguished) in *Re Hayward* [1997] Ch 45.

[2] To say that such obligations are proprietary does not necessarily mean that they confer ownership of the trust property on the beneficiary. In principle an obligation can be

by contrast, apply to particular individuals, and follow from their actions or their particular characteristics.

Although the proprietary characterization of at least some trust duties seems now beyond doubt, the issue was once much debated.[3] The debate has potential for continued vitality as part of the question whether equitable notions are to be seen as indeterminate supplements on the law: the view that they are is noted in section 1.12. Seeing obligations as configured on a case-by-case basis, that view must wish them to apply only personally. (Though the converse argument, that personal applicability necessarily predicates indeterminacy, would be incorrect.)

The attachment of trust obligations to the trust property manifests itself in various features of the law. Two are especially important.

The first concerns the impact of the trustee's bankruptcy. If I become bankrupt, my assets are taken and if necessary sold, to pay off my creditors. But assets in my hands are not mine to the extent that attached to them are obligations I owe to others. If I borrow money from you, it is purely mine. My obligation to repay you does not attach to the money itself: it is only a personal obligation. But if I am your trustee, duties I owe you are attached to the trust property. Therefore, the property cannot be taken to pay my creditors as though unaffected by those obligations, in the way that borrowed money can. The matter is sometimes expressed in the form that those to whom I owe trust obligations and other proprietary obligations have 'priority in bankruptcy', ie priority over my ordinary creditors, to whom I owe only personal obligations. The latter can demand only that my obligation to pay them be so far as possible met out of the proceeds of sale of the assets which have been taken from me. But the former can assert their claims in respect of the particular assets in my hands to which the obligation in question is attached: in the case of trust obligations, the trust property.

The second principal manifestation of the proprietary quality of trust obligations, ie attachment to the trust property, is that the obligations stay with that property when it is transferred from the trustees to other

---

attached to property, and thus proprietary, even though it confers less than ownership of that property: *Re Nisbet and Potts' Contract* [1905] 1 Ch 391, [1906] 1 Ch 386; *National Provincial Bank Ltd v Ainsworth* [1965] AC 1175, 1237–8. The extent to which beneficiaries do in fact enjoy ownership of trust property is considered in section 14.3.

[3] The victorious view was most famously stated by A Scott (1917) 17 Columbia LR 269; the defeated view by F Maitland *Equity* ed J Brunyate (1936) especially 106–16, and H Stone (1917) 17 Columbia LR 467.

people, and so can affect those other people.[4] Say the trustee gives trust property to his wife. She is not free to enjoy it for herself, any more than the trustee was: just as he held it on trust, so now does she. The duties, being charged on to it, have accompanied it into her hands. Not every recipient of trust property is so bound, however. Classically, a recipient is not bound if she is a 'bona fide purchaser of the property for value without notice'. Broadly, this formula exempts someone who buys the piece of property, rather than being given it ('purchaser . . . for value'); and who, when she bought, neither knew nor ought reasonably to have known that it was trust property ('bona fide . . . without notice').[5] In the modern law, this rule has been replaced in certain contexts by others having somewhat different profiles. In particular, where the trust property is land, a purchaser is generally speaking immune if the trust was not entered in the state register and the beneficiary was not himself in actual occupation of the land.[6]

It is sometimes argued that true proprietary obligations will affect *every* holder of the property to which they attach, and that the exceptions just mentioned therefore mean that trust obligations cannot be proprietary and must be personal.[7] The argument is false, however. These obligations affect those whom they do affect not because of some action or characteristic personal to the latter, but because they are attached to the property so that they affect all save the excepted categories. They cannot properly be termed personal, therefore. If one insists on not terming them proprietary, some third label is thus required. In fact, in English law traditionally no obligation is binding on absolutely all holders of the property to which it relates. A third label has not been sought: instead, the premise of the argument is rejected, and the term proprietary used after all.

It is however likely that some trust obligations are indeed personal rather than proprietary, precisely because they cannot sensibly affect subsequent holders of the trust property in this way. Some obligations

---

[4] See section 8.3. Note that even personal obligations can sometimes affect other people, but the way in which they do so is different and characteristically less comprehensive than that associated with proprietary obligations. It involves finding a wrong in someone's interference with the performance of the obligation between the two persons who are privy to that obligation. The prime example is the tort of interference with contractual relations (see T Weir *Tort Law* (2002) 180–1).

[5] For details, see eg J McGhee *Snell's Equity* 30th edn (2000) 48–61.

[6] Land Registration Act 2002 s 29.

[7] This was the main ground on which the European Court of Justice held trust obligations personal in *Webb v Webb* (Case C-294/92) [1994] QB 696.

require trustees to form a judgement: to decide how to manage the trust, for example, or whom to pay in a discretionary trust. The trustees' individual perceptions and ways of thinking will naturally be influential in that process. Trustees appointed as such (either initially by the settlor, or subsequently under the relevant mechanisms)[8] will thus generally be selected with an eye to their perceptions and ways of thinking. The courts have attached importance to this factor of selection as a reason for interfering little with the judgements that trustees make.[9] A transferee of the trust property would not be so selected, however. To impose on her the transferring trustee's duties to form judgements might thus be inappropriate. It makes sense therefore (though authority for the contention is scant) to treat duties of that kind as binding only on properly appointed trustees, ie as personal; and to regard proprietary quality as limited to the more basic duties of respecting the fact that the property is not beneficially the trustees' own, and of safeguarding it pending transfer, described in sections 9.1 and 9.2.

14.2 BENEFICIARIES' RIGHTS; THE INTEREST THESIS AND THE BENEFICIARY RULE

Where a trust has beneficiaries, the beneficiaries have rights mirroring its trustees' duties. Whatever the trustees are required to do is for the benefit of the beneficiaries, and the beneficiaries are entitled to have it done. The trustees must pay the beneficiaries as the settlor has stipulated: and the beneficiaries are entitled to have them do so. The beneficiaries' rights are said to be 'correlative' to the trustees' duties. Because beneficiaries' rights relate to trustees' duties in this way, information about the duties can be read across to the rights. So rights correlative to trustees' proprietary duties are themselves proprietary.

According to one thesis,[10] however, the last paragraph distorts the true picture. It is wrong, this thesis maintains, to see trustees' duties as central

---

[8] Section 13.1.

[9] *Edge v Pensions Ombudsman* [2000] Ch 602, 630.

[10] Described especially in *Re Astor's Settlement Trusts* [1952] Ch 534, 541–2; P Millett (1985) 101 LQR 269; P Matthews in A Oakley *Trends in Contemporary Trust Law* (1996) ch 1; J Penner *The Law of Trusts* 3rd edn (2002) 254. *Commissioner of Stamp Duties (Queensland) v Livingston* [1965] AC 694, 708 contrasts this view of trusts with the duty-centred account, which it applies to the relationship between the executor of a deceased person's estate and someone entitled to the as yet unestablished residue of that estate, who by the nature of things cannot yet have an interest in particular property. For discussion, see R Cotterrell in S Goldstein (ed) *Equity and Contemporary Legal Developments* (1992) 302; (1993) CLP 75.

to the trust concept, and the rights of any beneficiaries as merely the obverse of whatever those duties might be. On the contrary, the thesis continues, the very mission of the trust concept is to permit beneficiaries to have interests in the trust property: and trustees' duties ensue to effectuate these interests. Trusts must therefore have beneficiaries. This latter element in the thesis, insisted on in a number of decisions,[11] is known as the 'beneficiary rule'. It may even be better known than the full form of the thesis. The latter, however, places the rule in a justifying context. Beneficiaries are required as the repositories of the interests in the trust property which are the true heart of the trust concept. Call this thesis, therefore, the 'interest thesis'.

Accounts of the interest thesis[12] are often imprecise on the question of the exact nature of the 'interest in the trust property' which they demand. The requirement might simply be for rights attached to the trust property.[13] As we saw in the last section, all trustees have duties attached to the trust property (whether or not all their duties are so attached); so the beneficiaries' rights correlative to these duties are necessarily likewise attached. This conception of the required interest would therefore accommodate the thesis to all arrangements, otherwise recognizable as trusts, in which trustees owe proprietary duties to beneficiaries. That is, the substantive impact of the thesis would consist only in the beneficiary rule, ie a demand that trusts have beneficiaries. It is possible, however, to sense another, narrower, reading of the required 'interest in the trust property'.[14] This reading demands that the beneficiaries' rights amount to a claim to the property itself, rather than merely a claim (attached to the property) to the trustees' proper performance of their duties. On this narrower view, the interest thesis has a substantive message over and above the beneficiary rule: that the trust concept is confined to arrangements in which the beneficiaries have such a claim to the very trust property.

14.3 RIGHTS AND DUTIES IN THE CURRENT LAW

The matter has a history. There seems to be no evidence that the earliest ancestors of today's trusts did not always feature beneficiaries, but that

[11] *Bowman v Secular Society Ltd* [1917] AC 406, 441; *Re Wood* [1949] Ch 498, 501–2; *Re Shaw* [1957] 1 WLR 729, 744–6; *Leahy v AG for New South Wales* [1959] AC 457, 478–9, 484; *Re Endacott* [1960] Ch 232, 246, 250–1.

[12] N 10 above.

[13] This view seems to be taken by P Matthews (1998) 12 TLI 98, 99.

[14] See eg J Harris (1971) 87 LQR 31; J Davies [1970] ASCL 189.

could merely be because no one tried any variation; and even if that in turn was the result of the contemporary mind-set, it could hardly be eternally determinative. Originally the beneficiaries were regarded as having merely a right to the performance of the trustee's obligation, which they could neither enforce against a third party (ie the obligation and right were personal) nor assign themselves. The latter point was especially insisted upon by Sir Edward Coke at the end of the sixteenth century. Coke's view however was reversed in the seventeenth century, especially by Lord Nottingham who promoted the vision of beneficiaries' rights as analogous to legal estates, ie slices of the ownership of the assets.[15] The interest thesis, in its narrower and so quite distinctive version, thus certainly reflects Lord Nottingham's view. The question for us is whether matters rested there, or whether that view has in turn been replaced by a further new conception, in particular one focusing on the trustees' duties and holding beneficiaries and their rights inessential to the idea of a trust.

It seems that it has. Neither the demand for a claim to the trust property, nor that for beneficiaries with or without such a claim, is reconcilable with the trust phenomenon as it has been developed. The law has accepted various kinds of trusts where the trustees' duties do not mirror claims to the trust property, or in many cases rights of any kind, on the part of beneficiaries.[16]

Vast numbers of trusts do involve beneficiaries, of course; and such beneficiaries have rights to the performance of the trustees' duties, in at least some cases attached to the trust property. Furthermore, there certainly exist cases in which a beneficiary can be said to have a claim to the trust property. This is least controversially so where the trust is a 'bare' one, ie one in which the trustees hold the property for a sole adult beneficiary of full capacity, upon whose entitlement there are no conditions, and must transfer it to her on demand. Even if the trust arrangement contains features attenuating the beneficiary's entitlement to the trust

---

[15] D Yale *Lord Nottingham's Chancery Cases* vol II (1961) introduction 88–101. Lord Hardwicke LC therefore said in *Hopkins v Hopkins* (1739) West t Hard 606, 619:'It is the maxim of this court that trust estates, which are the creatures of equity, shall be governed by the same rules as legal estates, in order to preserve the uniform rule of property: and that the owner of the trust shall have the same power over the trust as he should have had if he had had the legal estate for the like interest or extent'.

[16] Though Lord Millett in *Twinsectra Ltd v Yardley* [2002] 2 WLR 802, 827 paras 90–1, equates the absence of a beneficial interest with a failure to make a complete trust, generating a resulting trust. The correctness of that equation is the issue under discussion; Lord Millett fails to deal with the evidence against it.

property in the meantime, such as the trustees' right to deduct expenses from periodic transfers of income to her, those features can be regarded as mandated by her, and so not antithetical to her having a claim to the property.

A beneficiary entitled to 'the trust income' for her life has also been judicially viewed as having a claim to the very income arising from the trust assets.[17] This is more controversial, however. Since such a beneficiary cannot alone demand transfer of the trust property,[18] we cannot on that account overlook qualifications upon her entitlement such as the fact that it extends not to the whole income but only to the balance left after deductions. Unsurprisingly, therefore, dissenting judges denied that the beneficiary had a claim to the very income, implicitly regarding her as having only a right to the proper performance of the trustees' duties. This dissenting view was found by a further decision[19] correctly to state New York law, which in principle had no reason to be different.

Some kinds of beneficiaries' rights, indeed, cannot possibly be regarded as claims to the trust property. Take trusts involving dispositive discretions: discretionary trusts, or trusts with powers to appoint, advance, maintain, or accumulate.[20] A beneficiary of such a trust certainly has a right that the trustees shall take their discretionary decisions in a proper way. But he has no claim to the assets (income or capital) which the trustees may, but need not, pay over to him. The point is most obvious in the case of a discretionary trust for a large number of potential payees, but analytically it is equally applicable to narrower situations, and it has been judicially accepted in the latter type of case.[21]

Moreover, some trusts have no beneficiaries. The most notable are trusts for charitable purposes.[22] Charitable trusts are usually aimed at an object such as providing education, and the provision must be for the benefit of the public rather than of particular individuals. Charities for the relief of poverty can stipulate for payments to individuals, but must be differentiated from trusts for individuals (beneficiaries) required to be

---

[17] *Baker v Archer-Shee* [1927] AC 844.

[18] Under *Saunders v Vautier* (1841) 4 Beav 115, Cr & Ph 240; see section 12.4.

[19] *Archer-Shee v Garland* [1931] AC 212.

[20] See section 11.2. Beneficiaries' rights in trusts of land (governed by the Trusts of Land and Appointment of Trustees Act 1996) are in some respects, especially that of occupation (s 12), also too dependent on discretion to amount to firm claims.

[21] *Gartside v IRC* [1968] AC 553; *Sainsbury v IRC* [1970] Ch 712. The beneficiaries of a discretionary trust may, if adult and of full capacity, unite to invoke *Saunders v Vautier* (1841) 4 Beav 115, Cr & Ph 240: *Re Smith* [1928] Ch 915. This seems not however to entail that the rights enjoyed by *each* beneficiary amount to a sufficient 'interest'.

[22] See ch 6. See *A-G v Cocke* [1988] Ch 414, 419–20.

poor;[23] the distinction is elusive, but the difference of principle is that the latter have the right to enforce the trust, while the former do not. Charitable trusts are enforced by the Charity Commission or Attorney-General,[24] who are not however beneficiaries, because they are not themselves benefited. Statements of the interest thesis and beneficiary rule note, but do not cavil at, the non-conformity of charities: they portray it as exceptional.

The courts have also held valid certain non-charitable purpose trusts. The cases fall into two classes. One class is usually indicated by reference to *Re Denley's Trust Deed*.[25] The trust there provided a sportsfield for a company's employees. Some view the trust as being for the employees as beneficiaries in the ordinary sense.[26] If this were correct, the employees could have claimed the money instead of the sportsfield.[27] The judge, however, took the trust as being for the purpose of providing the employees with a sportsfield,[28] and accepted it on the footing that a trust without beneficiaries in the ordinary sense is nonetheless valid if there are people directly and tangibly benefited by its performance.[29] Arguably, the logic of this decision also makes a trust valid if there is someone closely enough interested in its performance to be a reliable complainant against errant trustees, even if her interest is altruistic.[30] The other class

---

[23] *Re Scarisbrick* [1951] Ch 622; *Re Cohen* [1973] 1 WLR 415; *Re Segelman* [1996] Ch 171.

[24] Persons 'interested in the charity' can enforce, but only with the leave of the Charity Commission, which may not normally be given if the Commission could proceed itself: Charities Act 1993 s 33. Evidently, the section uses the word 'interested' in a different sense from the interest thesis.

[25] [1969] 1 Ch 373; for the relationship with the interest thesis see J Davies [1968] ASCL 438. For further instances, see *Re Trusts of the Abbott Fund* [1900] 2 Ch 326; *Re Aberconway's Settlement Trusts* [1953] Ch 647; *Re West Sussex Constabulary's Widows, Children and Benevolent (1930) Fund Trusts* [1971] Ch 1; *Carreras Rothmans Ltd v Freeman Mathews Treasure Ltd* [1985] Ch 207.

[26] See especially *Re Grant's Will Trusts* [1980] 1 WLR 360, 370–1; seemingly also *Re Lipinski's Will Trusts* [1976] Ch 235. These rely on *Re Bowes* [1896] 1 Ch 507, reading an apparent purpose trust as one for beneficiaries by treating the purpose as merely the motive with which an unrestricted entitlement is conferred (see section 3.5).

[27] *Saunders v Vautier* (1841) 4 Beav 115, Cr & Ph 240: see section 12.4.

[28] The lack of a beneficial interest in this class of case is also explicitly noted in *Carreras Rothmans Ltd v Freeman Mathews Treasure Ltd* [1985] Ch 207, 223. Explanation of another type of trust (that in *Barclay's Bank Ltd v Quistclose Investments Ltd* [1970] AC 567) in terms involving the lack of a beneficial interest was eschewed in *Twinsectra Ltd v Yardley* [2002] 2 WLR 802; but not expressly so as to rule out trusts of such a cast generally.

[29] Who may include the settlor, where she is directly and tangibly benefited by the trust's performance: *Carreras Rothmans Ltd v Freeman Mathews Treasure Ltd* [1985] Ch 207.

[30] The argument runs thus. Accepting de facto benefit as a substitute for status as a beneficiary depends on reading the fundamental authority's demand for 'somebody in whose favour the court can decree performance' (*Morice v Bishop of Durham* (1804) 9 Ves

comprises decisions declaring valid trusts for constructing and/or main-taining particular graves and monuments;[31] privately saying masses;[32] maintaining particular animals;[33] and 'miscellaneous' other purposes, a category apparently consisting solely of the promotion of fox-hunting.[34] Extension of the list, even by analogy, has been discountenanced,[35] for these trusts have been characterized as 'anomalous'. They fail to conform not only with the interest thesis and beneficiary rule, but also with the thinking in *Re Denley's Trust Deed*:[36] they do not feature people particu-larly benefited by, or indeed otherwise concerned about, the achievement of the purpose. To these classes of English decisions should be added the statutory regimes introduced in a number of other jurisdictions under which non-charitable purpose trusts are in principle valid, commonly so long as there is someone to enforce them:[37] perhaps the most famous being that of the Cayman Islands, known as STAR.[38]

So the interest thesis and beneficiary rule do not satisfactorily describe the shape which the existing law gives the trust concept. That is why the 'definition' given in section 1.1 does not reflect them but instead focuses on the trustees' obligations, a factor common to all the kinds of arrangement denominated trusts.[39]

399, 404) as a demand not for a beneficiary as required by the interest thesis but, more loosely, for somebody at whose suit the trust can be enforced against the trustees. Once the demand (based on the interest thesis) for a beneficiary is abandoned, there is no rule or reason why this 'somebody' should have to be benefited by the trust rather than otherwise keen to see it performed.

[31] eg *Trimmer v Danby* (1856) 25 LJ Ch 424; *Re Hooper* [1932] 1 Ch 38. Trusts to enhance or maintain churches or graveyards as such are charitable: *Re Vaughan* (1886) 33 Ch D 187.

[32] *Bourne v Keane* [1919] AC 815. Trusts for public masses are charitable: *Re Hetherington* [1990] Ch 1.

[33] eg *Pettingall v Pettingall* (1842) 11 LJ Ch 176; *Re Dean* (1889) 41 Ch D 552. The latter overlooks the requirement (see section 2.5) that such trusts have a maximum duration of 21 years. Trusts for animals generally may be charitable: see section 6.4.

[34] *Re Thompson* [1934] Ch 342. If fox-hunting is made illegal, of course, a trust to promote it would no longer be valid.

[35] *Re Endacott* [1960] Ch 232. It was thought that trusts for unincorporated associations had a place on the list, but they are nowadays handled by other analyses: see section 3.11.

[36] [1969] 1 Ch 373.

[37] See P Matthews in A Oakley (ed) *Trends in Contemporary Trust Law* 1996 ch 1. D Hayton (2001) 117 LQR 96 argues that English law should accept the presence of an enforcer, appointed by the settlor, as validating an otherwise invalid purpose trust. The first step may be the recognition of such trusts established in offshore jurisdictions.

[38] Introduced by the Cayman Special Trusts (Alternative Regime) Law 1997; see P Matthews (1997) 11 TLI 67; A Duckworth (1998) 12 TLI 16; P Matthews (1998) 12 TLI 98.

[39] The definitions given in the Hague Convention on the Law Applicable to Trusts and on their Recognition, and in D Hayton et al *Principles of European Trust Law* (1999), are to like effect.

14.4 RIGHTS AND DUTIES: ARGUMENTS OF PRINCIPLE

Is it better in principle to conceive trusts in terms of trustees' duties, regarding correlative beneficial rights as inessential; or do the interest thesis and beneficiary rule reflect persuasive considerations?

The basis of a conception in terms of trustees' duties is the logic of the facilitative project.[40] The law maintains express trusts so as to give settlors the means to do as they will with their property. Some wish to put their property to purposes other than payments to beneficiaries. The trust notion should accommodate that wish.

As explained in Chapter 2, facilitative logic should however yield, and does, where the settlor's goal is sufficiently inimical to some other policy consideration. A trust to promote genocide, whilst as valuable as any other in facilitative terms, should and would be rejected as heavily objectionable to rights concerns. An argument of this kind can be put for restricting the trust device in the way proposed by the interest thesis.

The concerns relevant to this argument are those regarding rights and economic utility.[41] The former asks that people be able to enjoy their property (as other aspects of their identity) in a full way; the latter that property be exposed to market influences, which means its being owned by someone with full liberty over its disposal. A facility for settlors to make trusts howsoever they please is likely to result in infringement of both these precepts, as they seek to confer heavily qualified entitlements on beneficiaries or to have money spent in particular ways rather than being paid to beneficiaries as cash. A beneficiary under a dispositive discretion, for example, while able freely to spend what the trustees decide to pay her, lacks untrammelled entitlement to particular property. A trust to promote a purpose advantageous to certain people, say by providing a sports field for a company's employees, prevents those advantaged from spending the money as they wish. Trusts for purposes not advantageous to particular people, say those to erect monuments, in a sense escape this criticism: but only because the settlors of such trusts commit what these precepts should deem the greater sin of directing the money altogether away from enjoyment by people. The money provided by every purpose trust, moreover, has to be spent on particular commodities needed to achieve the purpose: in the case of a sportsfield, land, turf, drainage

---

[40] See section 2.2.   [41] See sections 2.5–2.6.

pipes, etc. Except within the limits of those commodities, therefore, the use of the money is immune to market influences.

The kinds of trust arrangement acceptable to the interest thesis do not raise these concerns. A beneficiary with a full claim to the trust assets, especially one able to invoke *Saunders v Vautier*[42] so as to free them from the trust, can enjoy those assets as she herself wishes rather than as prescribed by the settlor; and in that enjoyment she will be open to market influences. A beneficiary having a claim on only the income from the trust assets, as Adam in the arrangement 'for Adam for life, thereafter to his children', is in a weaker but essentially similar position.[43] Whilst unable alone to take the capital assets using *Saunders v Vautier*,[44] he can likewise enjoy the income in his own way, and in that enjoyment will again be exposed to market influences. (Note that this holds good whether or not one considers[45] the beneficiary's claim to be to the gross income, rather than only to the sum properly payable, after deductions, by the trustees. There seems to be no advantage from the viewpoint of the present arguments in requiring interests to be of the former kind.)

The interest thesis can thus be understood as reflecting limits which rights and economic utility arguments would put on the facilitative project. But those arguments do not have a monopoly on this area of discourse. Some putative trusts inimical to them can nevertheless be supported by, especially, utilitarian and communitarian arguments,[46] where the trust in question is calculated to do good in a way intelligible to those arguments. At least some types of trusts accepted by the law but not reconcilable with the interest thesis can be accounted for as of this kind. This is especially so as regards charitable trusts, which must by definition benefit the public, albeit only in certain recognized ways. Large discretionary trusts, say for a company's workforce, and perhaps also those for the benefit of particular individuals, can be seen in a similar way. Likewise trusts for the kinds of purposes tolerated in the 'anomalous' cases: significantly, these (care of a testator's pets, provision of memorials)

---

[42] (1841) 4 Beav 115, Cr & Ph 240; see section 12.4.

[43] But note the likely reading of the arrangement 'for my widow, in the knowledge that she will look after our children' not as a trust for the widow for life, then for the children, but as conferring a capital entitlement on the widow, with only a moral duty on her to provide for the children: see section 3.4.

[44] (1841) 4 Beav 115, Cr & Ph 240. If and when Adam and his children are all adult and of full capacity, they can however agree together to use this facility.

[45] *Baker v Archer-Shee* [1927] AC 844, n 17 above.   [46] See sections 2.4–2.5.

are located in the culture of the family. This aspect of the law is untidy, but in broad terms far from indefensible.

It seems wrong, therefore, to think that as a matter of principle trustees' duties can only mirror beneficiaries' rights, and especially beneficiaries' interests in the sense of claims to the trust property. Trusts featuring duties not correlative to such rights or interests can be justified in the way, and to the extent, discussed.

14.5 THE ENFORCEMENT OF TRUSTEES' DUTIES

Where trustees' duties do correlate to beneficiaries' rights (claims to the trust property or otherwise), they can be enforced by the beneficiaries: and by the beneficiaries alone, so by no one else if the beneficiaries choose not to.[47]

Charities are enforceable by the Attorney-General and Charity Commission, and by no one else except interested individuals with the Commission's permission.[48] Trusts for purposes beneficial to particular individuals (or of interest to particular individuals, if the law goes this far) are enforceable by those individuals. In *Re Denley's Trust Deed*,[49] for example, the employees could have enforced if the trustees erred from their duty to provide the sports field. If the benefited individuals include the settlor, he can enforce. In *Carreras Rothmans Ltd v Freeman Mathews Treasure Ltd*,[50] the settlor, a tobacco company, placed money in trust so as to ensure that newspapers were paid for carrying its advertisements. It wanted this trust performed so that the newspapers would continue to accept its advertising. It was able to enforce. But again, if the benefited (or interested) individuals choose not to enforce, no one else can. So if a trust provided for a company's employees to have a sportsfield, but they did not want the sports field and the trustees proposed to sell it for building, neighbouring landowners opposed to the building could not enforce.

So far as 'anomalous' purpose trusts are concerned, the remaindermen, ie the people entitled to the sum remaining after the achievement of the purpose, have the right to enforce;[51] no suggestion of any alternative enforcer has been made. The remaindermen will want to sue if the trustees wrongfully reduce that sum, say by overspending on the monuments

---

[47] *Shaw v Lawless* (1838) 5 Cl & Fin 129; *Gandy v Gandy* (1885) LR 30 Ch D 57.
[48] Charities Act 1993 s 33.
[49] [1969] 1 Ch 373.
[50] [1985] Ch 207.
[51] *Pettingall v Pettingall* (1842) 11 LJ Ch 176; *Re Thompson* [1934] Ch 342.

or animals. But they have no incentive to sue, indeed have an incentive not to sue, where the trustees underspend on the purpose, so maximizing the amount remaining.

Two features of the picture regarding enforcement should be noticed. First, the regime is by and large not one calculated to secure the trustees' performance of their duties *as established by the settlor*. Where the person having the right of enforcement chooses not to enforce, that choice prevails, even if the settlor is or would have been chagrined thereby. It is easy to discern this in the case of trusts for beneficiaries: the beneficiaries' preferences might easily differ from the settlor's stipulations, and the law attaches positive importance to the precedence of the former, as announced in the consent principle[52] and *Saunders v Vautier*.[53] But, albeit without such an announcement, precedence is also given to the enforcer's wishes in other cases. This is true even as regards charities, where in reality the Attorney-General and Charity Commission can be expected not necessarily to enforce the settlor's stipulations without compromise. At least in jurisdictions which have introduced the appropriate regime,[54] however, a settlor can appoint an enforcer[55] or 'protector'[56] with the right to enforce against the trustees. Unless the appointment has been made with some other aim (a particular beneficiary could for example be appointed protector, with the aim of privileging her position *vis-à-vis* that of her fellow beneficiaries), the enforcer or protector can be expected generally to seek performance of the settlor's stipulations: though again, not in the last resort necessarily without compromise.

Secondly, there will not be enforcement in every case where the person entitled to enforce would in principle wish to do so. Theoretical rights to enforce are in practice diminished by lack of information, energy, strength, or resources, deficiencies in all these respects being routine features of life, even in the case of the Attorney-General and Charity Commission. Institutions such as legal aid, where available, help to remove some obstacles, but in the nature of things perfection cannot be achieved.

---

[52] See section 12.3.   [53] (1841) 4 Beav 115, Cr & Ph 240; see section 12.4.
[54] D Hayton (2001) 117 LQR 96 explores the importability to English law of purpose trusts with enforcers.
[55] Where the law permits it, enforcers can be used to validate otherwise invalid purpose trusts; but the device can also be extended to a trust with beneficiaries, to the exclusion of the beneficiaries' rights of enforcement (and non-enforcement) or otherwise. That is the position in, especially, the Cayman Islands. For a discussion of the latter, see P Matthews (1997) 11 TLI 67; A Duckworth (1998) 12 TLI 16; P Matthews (1998) TLI 98.
[56] D Waters in A Oakley (ed) *Trends in Contemporary Trust Law* (1996) ch 4.

14.6 MUST TRUSTEES' DUTIES BE ENFORCEABLE?

Prominent judicial statements can be found of an 'enforceability principle': ie that a trust cannot be validly created unless its trustees' duties will be enforceable against them. The most celebrated such statements are by Sir William Grant MR and Lord Eldon LC in *Morice v Bishop of Durham*.[57] That decision focused on the need[58] for certainty in the detailing of the trustees' duties, as explained in Chapters 10 and 11: for instance, the requirement, in the case of a trust requiring equal division of property between the beneficiaries, that the number of beneficiaries be known. Certainty was however required so that the trustees' duties could be defined, this in turn being necessary so that the court could enforce them.

These statements lead to assertions[59] that a trust must have a beneficiary or other enforcer, thus denying validity to trusts for purposes which are neither charitable nor, as *Re Denley's Trust Deed*[60] points out, to the advantage of, or perhaps otherwise of interest to, identifiable people. Although enforceable by their remaindermen, trusts for other purposes (whether or not 'anomalously' accepted as valid) are not enforceable as this principle requires,[61] for the remaindermen have no reason to intervene against underspending, as opposed to overspending, on the purpose.

Whether or not the judges stating the enforceability principle so intended, the principle can be presented as independent of the interest thesis, which places the need for an interest, and a beneficiary to possess it, at the heart of the trust concept.[62] The enforceability principle does not demand a beneficiary's presence for its own sake in this way; merely as a means (in fact, one among several, as noted: it is a strength of this analysis that it has no need to see charities, in particular, as exceptional) to the end of producing the supposedly necessary enforceability.

[57] (1804) 9 Ves 399, 404–5, (1805) 10 Ves 522, 539. See also *Re Astor's Settlement Trusts* [1952] Ch 534, 541–2; *Re Shaw* [1957] 1 WLR 729, 744–5; *Leahy v AG for New South Wales* [1959] AC 457, 479, 484.

[58] Except in charitable trusts: an insufficiently defined charitable purpose will be given shape by the Charity Commission (Charities Act 1993 s 16) or court.

[59] *Bowman v Secular Society Ltd* [1917] AC 406, 441; *Re Diplock* [1941] Ch 253, 259; *Re Wood* [1949] Ch 498, 501–2; *Re Endacott* [1960] Ch 232, 246.

[60] [1969] 1 Ch 373.

[61] *Re Shaw* [1957] 1 WLR 729, 745.

[62] This is the position of *Re Denley's Trust Deed* [1969] 1 Ch 373, which accepts (and fulfils) the need for enforceability, but rejects the need for a beneficiary, especially one with an interest in the trust property. See H Ford in P Finn (ed) *Essays in Equity* (1985) ch 9.

Is it correct to see the enforceability of the trustees' duties as essential to the trust concept?

It might be said that it is correct, on the basis of facilitative logic. The argument would be this. If the law offers the trust as a vehicle whereby a settlor can effectuate his intentions, but it cannot guarantee the trustees' performance of their duties embodying those intentions, the settlor is potentially led up the garden path: he may put assets into the trust only for his intentions to be subverted, say by the trustees keeping the money for themselves.[63] There are two difficulties about a justification for the enforceability principle in these terms, however.

The first is that a requirement of enforceability would not necessarily serve facilitative policy well. By holding the trustees to their duties, such a requirement facilitates projects which can be enforced. These cases are easy. But there is a dilemma for the policy regarding projects which cannot be enforced, notably purpose trusts (other than those caught by *Re Denley's Trust Deed*,[64] or charities). Demanding enforceability prevents frustration of settlors by the subversion of their intentions, but simultaneously itself frustrates them by denying such projects validity as trusts at all. Not demanding enforceability allows such trusts to exist, but at the cost of a risk of subversion. Either response promises only a partial vindication of settlors' wishes, therefore. It is not inevitable that the preference should be for enforceability and so invalidity. There is a parallel here with the treatment of certainty. Take, for example, the trustees' apparently simple duty to pay the settlor's designated objects and no one else. As we saw in section 10.6, a duty in this form might well be what settlors want; but it would require so much certainty that trusts would commonly fail for uncertainty. Reducing the duty to something more practicable would allow people to make valid trusts, but it would mean sacrificing strict fidelity to their wishes. The facilitative policy finds itself in a dilemma between these two positions. The latter approach has in fact prevailed: the duties are relaxed, and trusts upheld. Half a loaf is treated as better than none. Consistency argues that purpose trusts should be upheld too. Their being valid but unenforceable can be seen as the half a loaf that is better than the no bread of invalidity.

The second difficulty about ascribing the enforceability principle to facilitative thought is that, as we saw in the last section, the law's prevailing enforcement regime is not in fact generally calculated to secure the

---

[63] *Leahy v AG for New South Wales* [1959] AC 457, 484 explicitly puts the enforceability principle in terms of enforcement *of the settlor's wishes*.

[64] [1969] 1 Ch 373.

trustees' performance of their duties *as established by the settlor*. In an ordinary trust for beneficiaries, especially, the settlor's stipulations will be enforced only to the extent that this suits the beneficiaries; the settlor himself has no legal right to intervene. Facilitative logic is overlain with considerations about maximizing the rights of the recipients.

The loss of a foundation in facilitative logic is not necessarily fatal to the enforceability principle, however. It might be justified instead on another basis. The obvious candidate is an argument that the availability of legal enforcement is intrinsic to the concept of a legal duty (and, where applicable, a legal right). Owners without duties to the contrary can enjoy their property as they wish. Trustees are in principle owners of the trust property: the trust consists in the fact that their duties oblige them not to enjoy it themselves but to deploy it in the required way. Unless these duties can be enforced, it might be said, they amount to nothing, leaving the trustees with full ownership. Such thinking is perceptible in at least some statements of the enforceability principle.[65] It is certainly intelligible. But on examination, certainly as applied to express trusts, it fails to capture the whole truth.

The argument certainly cannot be that legal enforcement is all that prevents trustees from breaching their duties. In the vast majority of cases, trustees perform their duties regardless of the prospect of legal enforcement, for the kinds of reasons described in Chapter 13. (Express trust duties may differ in this respect from some others: perhaps legal enforcement is required to give practical substance to family provision law, for example.) Trusts containing wide exclusion clauses are illuminating. It is unlikely that trustees actually seek to perform at the undemanding levelpermitted; they breach their unexcludable duty to act honestly in the trust's interest if they do,[66] but this is surely not the only influence upon them. The situation is best regarded as one in which trustees try to perform what would otherwise be their duties, but cannot be sanctioned if they fail.

Rather, the argument needs to be that trusts cannot intelligibly exist *as legal institutions* unless trustees' duties are legally enforceable: that we cannot intelligibly speak of legal duties, such as would have to exist in an unenforceable trust, if these duties could not be legally enforced. That seems implausible, however. As we saw in the last section, even those duties which someone has the right and motivation to enforce are only

---

[65] *Morice v Bishop of Durham* (1804) 9 Ves 399, 404–5; *Re Astor's Settlement Trusts* [1952] Ch 534, 541–2; *Armitage v Nurse* [1998] Ch 241, 253.

[66] *Armitage v Nurse* [1998] Ch 241, 254.

adventitiously enforceable in practice (and the point is hardly confined to trusts); yet this does not prevent us thinking of them as legal duties. Their legal quality makes a difference in the eyes of the trustee who wishes to perform them despite the lack of legal sanction if she does not. For the same reason, one can intelligibly identify as involving distinctively legal duties a trust, such as a purpose trust, which no one has the right and motivation to enforce.

In the hands of compliant trustees of this kind, indeed, an unenforceable trust is not only an intelligible concept; but also one distinct from other concepts such as a power, a moral obligation, and absolute ownership. Telling such trustees that they had any of these would create different effects in their minds, and thus in their behaviour, from telling them that they had a trust. A power would signify that it was for them to choose whether to carry out the object in question or not.[67] A moral obligation would point definitely towards the promotion of the object; but its merely moral character means that even a trustee seeking to perform her legal duties would be right to weigh it against, and where appropriate postpone it to, contradictory moral obligations: for example, someone given money with a merely moral obligation to care for a horse could validly conclude that it should be spent on her starving children instead. And a person prepared to be a compliant trustee but in fact given absolute ownership would see herself, correctly, as under no relevant duties. Uncompliant trustees with unenforceable duties might treat these as of no moment; but compliant trustees regard their legal duties as such and try to perform them properly, irrespective of their enforceability. As most trustees seem to be compliant, this observation can properly persuade us to regard trusts without legally enforceable duties as nonetheless legal institutions.

Indeed, not only is it intelligible to see trusts as legal institutions notwithstanding that the duties in them may not be legally enforceable. Arguably, at least some express trusts *ought not to be* the subject of legal enforcement. The proposition here is that such trusts are to that extent best seen as self-contained, autonomous, institutions, zones of self-regulation into which judges positively should not intrude themselves. The origins of many express trusts in an act of generosity, and their place

---

[67] It is sometimes suggested that unenforceable purpose trusts should be salvaged from failure, if that would otherwise be their fate, by regarding them as purpose powers. (That is the effect of the Ontario Perpetuities Act 1966 s 16 and similar statutory provisions, but English decisions have ruled it out: *Re Shaw* [1957] 1 WLR 729, 746; *Re Endacott* [1960] Ch 232, 246.) The point in the text weighs against such an easy equation of unenforceable trust with power. It is also not clear that objections to purpose trusts are inapplicable to powers: see section 11.2.

in contexts such as the family, make this proposition plausible: they lend themselves to an argument that legalism, and so judicial enforcement, is inappropriate to them on communitarian grounds.[68] This observation has less relevance to other kinds of express trusts, such as pension fund trusts. But one could defensibly argue against judicial intervention more widely, for a further reason. The operation of most express trusts is not a purely mechanical exercise, but requires finesse and judgement. Trustees being chosen for their personal qualities in these respects,[69] their oversight by an outsider such as a judge might easily be inappropriate. This point seems to be taken in several features of the law itself, revealing a judicial reluctance to intervene in trusts. If trustees run into difficulty, the normal course is for the court to deal only with the specific problem, rather than to take on the whole administration of the trust. Trustees do not have to disclose the thinking behind their discretionary decisions.[70] If a discretionary decision is questioned in court, the judge considers merely whether the discretion has been exercised properly, not whether she herself agrees with the conclusion reached.[71] And if trustees are found to have gone wrong in the exercise of their discretion, the remedy is as conservative as possible: they may be told to try again,[72] or an order may be made to carry out a course of action favoured by some of them but blocked by others,[73] or else to give effect to the beneficiaries' own wishes; the judge may exercise the discretion herself,[74] but generally[75] only as a last resort.[76]

In the end, then, the notion that trustees' duties (and, where they arise, beneficiaries' rights) must necessarily be legally enforceable seems less supportable than the contrary view.

---

[68] See section 2.4. Compare the way that agreements between members of families are not normally enforceable as contracts, as 'lacking intention to create contractual relations'.

[69] See section 13.8.

[70] See section 13.9: *Re Beloved Wilkes' Charity* (1851) 3 Mac & G 440 (charity); *Re Londonderry's Settlement* [1965] Ch 918 (family trust); *Wilson v Law Debenture Trust Corp plc* [1995] 2 All ER 337 (pension fund). The Australian decision *Hartigan Nominees Pty Ltd v Rydge* (1992) 29 NSWLR 405 puts pressure on the rule, but does not ultimately reject it.

[71] *Gisborne v Gisborne* (1877) 2 App Cas 300; *Tabor v Brooks* (1878) 10 Ch D 273; *Tempest v Lord Camoys* (1882) 21 Ch D 571; *Edge v Pensions Ombudsman* [2000] Ch 602, 630 (expressly referring this attitude to the importance of the trustees' identity). Review of protectors' decisions may be especially attenuated: D Waters in A Oakley (ed) *Trends in Contemporary Trust Law* (1996) ch 4.

[72] *Re Locker's Settlement Trusts* [1977] 1 WLR 1323; *Turner v Turner* [1984] Ch 100.

[73] *Klug v Klug* [1918] 2 Ch 67.

[74] *McPhail v Doulton* [1971] AC 424, 457; *Mettoy Pension Trustees Ltd v Evans* [1990] 1 WLR 1587, 1617, 1632; *Thrells Ltd v Lomas* [1993] 1 WLR 456.

[75] Aberrantly, judicial exercise is the norm in the case of the discretions given to trustees of land: Trusts of Land and Appointment of Trustees Act 1996 s 14.

[76] Cf section 15.3.

15

Breach of trust and remedies

Chapter 13 concerned the factors helping to ensure that trustees perform their duties properly. Sometimes, however, trustees go wrong, and commit a breach of trust. In that event they can be sued, ie a legal remedy sought against them.[1] This chapter examines what counts as a breach of trust, the possible remedies, and their availability.

Under certain circumstances, people can incur liability for wronging a trust by breaking a duty which is not simply one of the duties incumbent on trustees as such. Later sections of this chapter also consider this phenomenon.

15.1 BREACH OF TRUST

A breach of trust is a failure by a trustee to perform a duty binding her: as modified, if relevant, either by an exclusion clause in the individual trust or by a general rule.[2] The essential principle is the same whether the trust is express, resulting, or constructive. The trustee's duties may however vary between the categories,[3] and certainly vary from one trust to another within them. Chapters 9–11 contained a survey of some of the main kinds of duty.

Many trust duties demand a reasonable performance rather than an impeccable one: for example, in management operations trustees are generally required to show 'such care and skill as is reasonable in the circumstances'.[4] Breach of such a duty consists in failing to display this level of care and skill, rather than in mismanagement in an absolute sense. Some duties, however, demand the performance of a particular task, positive or negative: eg avoidance of certain investments.[5] Here, non-performance

---

[1] Section 13.11 explains, however, that it will not always be practical to sue trustees in breach; and section 14.6 suggests that the possibility of doing so should not be seen as essential to the trust concept.

[2] See ch 12.

[3] See section 9.1.

[4] Trustee Act 2000 s 1, Sch 1 para 1.

[5] The Trustee Act 2000 s 6 allows settlors to restrict the range of investments open to the trustees: eg so as to confine them to ethical investments.

will be a breach even if reasonable, as where trustees pardonably mis-understand their investment instructions (though such a breach may well be excused, ie the trustees exonerated from liability).[6]

In regard to discretions, the trustees' duty is to consider the question properly: that is, give it active thought, taking relevant matters into account and leaving irrelevant ones aside.[7] Breach consists in a failure to do so, so long as the trustees would have come to a different determin-ation if they had thought properly.[8] The question is not whether the judge would have come to a different determination in the trustees' place.[9] There will however be a breach, even if it is impossible to identify a failure in their thinking, if trustees reach a conclusion that is unreason-able, in the sense[10] that no reasonable trustees thinking about the question properly could have arrived at it.[11] The latter rule has been little relied on, but is potentially useful against trustees who decline to disclose their thinking, as they are permitted to do.[12]

[6] Trustee Act 1925 s 61: see section 12.2.

[7] See sections 9.3–9.4 and 11.5–11.6.

[8] *Re Hastings-Bass* [1975] Ch 25, 36, 41; *Mettoy Pension Trustees Ltd v Evans* [1990] 1 WLR 1587, 1621, 1624–6. The requirement that the trustees would have reached a different determination had they thought properly reduces the likelihood of a breach, but the courts have continued to worry over the ease with which trustees can find themselves breaching in this way: *Scott v National Trust for Places of Historic Interest or Natural Beauty* [1998] 2 All ER 705, 718; *Breadner v Granville-Grossman* [2001] Ch 523, 542–3 paras 58–61.

[9] *Gisborne v Gisborne* (1877) 2 App Cas 300; *Tabor v Brooks* (1878) 10 Ch D 273; *Tempest v Lord Camoys* (1882) 21 Ch D 571; *Edge v Pensions Ombudsman* [2000] Ch 602. A contrary position was taken in earlier decisions, of which the final examples are *Re Hodges* (1878) 7 Ch D 754; *Re Roper's Trusts* (1879) 11 Ch D 272; it is probably significant that the bene-ficiaries in these cases were wards of court, in the protection of whose interests judges are abnormally interventionist. This more interventionist approach is however revived where the trust is of land: Trusts of Land and Appointment of Trustees Act 1996 s 14 (though perhaps a breach by the trustees is not a prerequisite for the court to exercise its own discretion under this section).

[10] Sometimes called '*Wednesbury* unreasonableness', after the reference to it in the public law decision *Associated Provincial Picture Houses Ltd v Wednesbury Corp* [1948] 1 KB 223, 230.

[11] *Edge v Pensions Ombudsman* [2000] Ch 602, 627–30, 636.

[12] *Re Londonderry's Settlement* [1965] Ch 918; *Wilson v Law Debenture Trust Corp plc* [1995] 2 All ER 337; see section 13.9. In *Re Beloved Wilkes' Charity* (1851) 3 Mac & G 440, 448 it is said that trustees who disclose their reasoning will be in breach if it does not support their conclusion, but that was rejected (disclosure of reasoning makes it easier to apply the usual rule, but nothing more) in *Dundee General Hospitals Board of Management v Walker* [1952] 1 All ER 896, 900; *Scott v National Trust for Places of Historic Interest or Natural Beauty* [1998] 2 All ER 705, 718–19.

15.2 REMEDIES

The legal remedies for breach of trust aim to correct the breach: ie to bring matters as close as possible to the state they would have been in if there had been no breach. There are two types of remedy, approaching this aim in different ways. The first seeks to have the duty in question performed after all. The second recognizes that harm has been done by the breach, and seeks to redress that harm.[13]

Say trustees have invested trust money in a prohibited way. A remedy of the first type will consist in their being ordered to sell that investment and to reinvest the proceeds properly. A remedy of the second type will treat that money as lost to the trust, and will consist in an order that the trustees shall make good the loss from their own pockets. Or say that a fiduciary has taken a bribe, and now holds it on a constructive trust. A remedy of the first type will demand that she performs her duties under that trust by paying the property it now contains over to her principal. A remedy of the second type will instead observe that the fiduciary broke her duty by accepting the bribe, and require her to reimburse her principal the amount in question.

The two types of remedy will be considered in turn.

15.3 ORDERING PERFORMANCE OF A DUTY

We look first at ordering trustees to perform their duty. Fundamentally, someone holding assets on trust but failing to behave accordingly can be ordered to do so. For example, trustees who fail to pay some money to the beneficiary entitled to it, and who still have it available, can be told to repair the omission. Trustees who fail to think properly about a discretion can be told to do so.[14]

This type of remedy is possible only where the person against whom it is sought holds trust property to which the duty is attached. A trustee who, having embezzled the trust property, has simply squandered it, can

---

[13] Broadly, these correspond respectively to specific performance and the award of damages in the law of contract.

[14] *Re Locker's Settlement Trusts* [1977] 1 WLR 1323; *Turner v Turner* [1984] Ch 100. It is said that where a power of appointment must be exercised, if at all, by a date which has now passed, the trustees cannot be ordered to consider exercising it: *Re Allen-Meyrick's Will Trusts* [1966] 1 WLR 499, 505; *Breadner v Granville-Grossman* [2001] Ch 523, 540 para 52. But this rule ignores the *duty* that the trustees have to consider exercise; performance of a duty was ordered out of time in *Re Locker's Settlement Trusts*.

no longer be ordered to perform her duties as trustee regarding it. And someone who should have acquired certain property so as to hold it on trust, but did not, cannot be ordered nonetheless to perform a trustee's duties in respect of it.

This type of remedy has two main advantages over one accepting the default and requiring the trustee to make it good out of his own pocket. First, it has priority in the trustee's bankruptcy. An obligation to pay from one's own pocket is a debt like any other,[15] and in the event of bankruptcy will be payable to the same reduced extent as all the trustee's other debts from his necessarily insufficient property. An order requiring the trustee to treat an asset in his hands as the trust's, however, means that asset's removal from the pool of the trustee's property and devotion to the trust's requirements. This can be a valuable advantage, and often underlies the choice of this type of remedy where otherwise it holds no advantage (and indeed has the disadvantage of requiring proof that the trustee still holds trust property). Secondly, a remedy ordering the trustee to treat an asset as the trust's gives the trust the benefit of any increase in the asset's value,[16] whilst one accepting the asset as lost to the trust and ordering the trustee to make good the loss requires him only to restore its original value. Conversely, of course, the latter is preferable where the asset has lost value.

Sometimes it is not satisfactory simply to order the trustees now to perform their duty. If for some reason the trustees can no longer act, or if there are misgivings about their continued handling of the trust, the court may replace them[17] and leave the new trustees to perform.[18] It has also been said that the judge may if necessary act in the trustees' place. This response is unproblematic if the duty in question requires a specific action, such as the transfer of some property. There is greater difficulty in the case of a duty properly to reach a decision, such as a duty to choose an investment or a beneficiary for payment in a discretionary trust.[19] The rule that trustees will not be in breach merely because the judge might

---

[15] A claimant for compensation may sometimes however be able to point to a charge over the trustee's assets and so to obtain priority in the trustee's bankruptcy: see section 8.6.

[16] *Foskett v McKeown* [2001] AC 102.

[17] See sections 13.1 and 13.8.

[18] This used to be thought the only response when trustees with a power of appointment neglect their duties of consideration (*Re Gestetner Settlement* [1953] Ch 672, 688; *Re Manisty's Settlement* [1974] Ch 17, 25–6); but that restrictive view no longer obtains: *Mettoy Pension Trustees Ltd v Evans* [1990] 1 WLR 1587, 1617–18.

[19] The possibility of judicial performance of such a duty was accepted in *McPhail v Doulton* [1971] AC 424, 457; *Mettoy Pension Trustees Ltd v Evans* [1990] 1 WLR 1587, 1617, 1632; *Thrells Ltd v Lomas* [1993] 1 WLR 456.

have chosen differently[20] commits the law to the view that there is no single right way of performing such a duty. In making what the law thus constructs as a free choice, a judge will do something which many believe antithetical to the judicial function.[21]

15.4 RECOVERY OF LOSSES AND PROFITS

The second type of remedy accepts that the trust will not be performed, and instead requires the trustee to pay over the amount of money at issue, from her own resources.

So where the breach has resulted in a loss to the trust, such as where the trustee made an improper investment which then lost value, or paid out to someone who was not entitled, the trustee can be ordered to pay compensation for the amount of the loss. And where the breach has produced a profit to the trustee, say by buying in her own name a piece of land which she was supposed to be seeking for the trust and then reselling it at a profit, she can be ordered to pay the amount of the profit. A trustee's liability to make a payment in one of these ways is often referred to as a liability to 'account' for the loss or profit.

Where the trust has a number of beneficiaries, especially with successive interests (eg 'for Adam for his life, then for Briony'), the order will require the breaching trustee to pay the money in question not direct to particular objects, but to the trust itself (usually to newly appointed trustees). This is because the individual objects will not be immediately entitled to the trust's capital assets: the order sets out to reinstate the capital assets. A payment direct to the objects is however appropriate if they simultaneously wind the trust up;[22] and where there is a single, immediately entitled, object the law short-circuits the process of payment to the trust's capital assets followed by delivery of those assets to the object, and instead orders payment direct to the object.[23]

Some decisions have given the compensation remedy two striking features.[24] First, the trustee has been ordered to pay the amount taken from the trust in her breach, even though some or all of this amount would still

---

[20] N 9 above.
[21] For an account of this view, see eg R Dworkin *Taking Rights Seriously* (1977) 68–71. Judges have however been asked routinely to exercise trustees' discretions as regards trusts of land: Trusts of Land and Appointment of Trustees Act 1996 s 14.
[22] Under the rule in *Saunders v Vautier* (1841) 4 Beav 115, Cr & Ph 240: see section 12.4.
[23] *Target Holdings Ltd v Redferns* [1996] AC 421, 434–5.
[24] Cf S Elliott (2002) 65 MLR 588.

have been lost to the trust 'but for' the breach, for other reasons. Say I hold money on trust for Adam, which Adam was committed to lend to you; that I pay it to you before receiving Adam's order to do so; and that you then disappear, so that the loan cannot be recovered from you. Some decisions suggest that I will be liable for the sum paid to you even though Adam would have suffered the same loss if I had waited for his order before making the payment.[25] Secondly, the trustee has been ordered to pay for a loss which would not have occurred 'but for' the trustee's breach, but which was mainly attributable to the activities—even the negligence or dishonesty—of a third party. Say I am permitted to invest trust assets only in ethical funds, and breach my duty by choosing a non-ethical fund. Even though non-ethical, the fund I choose should have been financially satisfactory: but it was sold to me by someone trading fraudulently, having insider knowledge that its value was about to fall, as it then did. Some decisions suggest that I will be liable for the loss even though my breach did no more than set the scene in which the loss then occurred for other reasons.[26]

Both these positions have now been disapproved, however, in favour of rules requiring the trustee to pay only such amount as is required to put the trust in the same position as hindsight shows it would have been in if no breach had occurred, ie not requiring her to pay for losses which would still have occurred 'but for' the breach; and only for losses which 'common sense'[27] tells us to attribute to the breach.[28] So I am apparently not liable for the loss in either example.[29] The rejected stricter approach seems to have been another measure calculated to redress the vulnerability inherent in trusts in the shape of the practical free hand

---

[25] eg *Bartlett v Barclays Bank Trust Co Ltd (No 2)* [1980] Ch 515, 543–5; *Re Bell's Indenture* [1980] 1 WLR 1217. There, trustees causing loss were liable for its full value, taking no account of the tax liability which the trust would have incurred if the breach had not occurred. In tort, by comparison, the claimant's tax exposure had there been no breach is deducted from the loss which the defendant is required to make good: *British Transport Commission v Gourley* [1956] AC 185.

[26] eg *Bartlett v Barclays Bank Trust Co Ltd (No 2)* [1980] Ch 515, 545–6.

[27] Further litigation can of course be expected as to the significance of this expression.

[28] *Target Holdings Ltd v Redferns* [1996] AC 421, 432, 435, 438–9. The case was one in which any compensation payment would have been direct to the object, rather than to the trust; but there is no reason why that should affect the issues under discussion.

[29] Cf however the case where I fail to take care of jewellery which I hold on trust, and it is stolen by a thief. Since theft is one of the very things against which my duty is calculated to guard, my breach does more than 'set the scene' for the loss, so I should be liable (together with the thief): cf *Stansbie v Troman* [1948] 2 KB 48; *Reeves v Commissioner of Police of the Metropolis* [2000] AC 360.

trustees necessarily have with the objects' interests and property.[30] The redress took the form of charging trustees with all losses which might have arisen from their breaches, sparing objects the trouble of navigating their way through arguments about alternative causes. But since that approach required trustees to bear losses which reflection showed were not attributable to their breaches, it is unsurprising that it came to be perceived as too severe.[31]

The advantages and disadvantages of this second type of remedy are broadly the converse of the advantages and disadvantages of the first type of remedy. The latter is limited by its necessity for the trustee currently to have the trust property: the second type of remedy has no such limitation, being specifically designed to provide relief where the trust is no longer performable. On the other hand, where the first type of remedy involves enforcing duties attached to the trust property and so can survive the trustee's bankruptcy or the transfer of that property to a third party, the second type, ordering an individual trustee to pay a sum of money from her own resources, lacks those advantages. If she goes bankrupt, therefore, the claimant is left as one amongst her creditors.

There is a qualification to the latter proposition, however. If the loss for which a claimant seeks compensation consists in the trustee's wrongful mixture of trust property with her own, such that the trust property can be traced into what remains of the mixture or its proceeds, the right to compensation is secured by a charge over the latter assets.[32] So if I, trustee for you, mix £500 trust money with £1,000 of my own, and spend £800 of the resulting mixture on a holiday, you can sue me for the £500 and point to the £700 remaining in the mixture as carrying a charge for £500 in the trust's favour. I shall still be ordered to pay the required compensation, £500, from my own resources. But the charge means that, if my resources are insufficient to meet all my liabilities, you can demand that your claim is met from the £700 before any other use is made of the £700. That is, the charge gives the claim priority in my bankruptcy.

---

[30] Cf sections 8.4–8.6.

[31] The approach of charging losses to trustees in neglect of causal arguments to the contrary might also have been assailable under Protocol 1, Art 1 of the ECHR as of a severity disproportionate to the public interest (correction of the agency problem) at which it was aimed. Cf *Wilson v First County Trust Ltd (No 2)* [2002] QB 74.

[32] See section 8.6.

15.5 A CHOICE OF REMEDIES

Sometimes a claimant will find that only one type of remedy is available. In particular, as explained, if a remedy is sought against someone who no longer has the trust property to which the relevant duty is attached, it will be impossible to seek a remedy of the first type. Sometimes, both types of remedy are in principle available, but only one is realistically useful. Where the defendant is bankrupt, a remedy of the second type will remain available, but will (unless secured by a charge) yield little: whereas one of the first type will in principle yield as much in this case as in the case where the defendant is not bankrupt.

At other times, however, the claimant's choice is less constrained. One type of remedy or the other will be chosen with an eye to the overall balance of advantage. The advantage looked to might be one of quantum. Thus, the first type of remedy can be used to recover a rise in value of the maltreated asset, whereas the second type yields the original value of the asset and so protects the claimant against a subsequent fall. Or the advantage might be thought of in forensic terms. The tracing exercise which might be needed to found a claim of the first kind (demanding the transfer of property held on a constructive trust) could be both factually and legally complex, a drawback avoidable by claiming a remedy of the second kind, assuming it is not sought to invoke a charge in its support.

Another factor influencing claimants in the way they present their claim might be a difference in the limitation rules applicable to their options. The limitation rules are those preventing a claim being mounted once a certain period has elapsed from the moment it first arose. Most claims in respect of trusts are governed by the Limitation Act 1980. There is no period of limitation (ie claims can in principle be brought indefinitely) in respect of claims of the first type.[33] Claims of the second type have a limitation period of six years[34] unless they involve a factor making it right to be abnormally ungenerous to the defendant, namely that the breach was fraudulent,[35] or the loss consisted in the trustee's taking the assets for herself.[36]

Where a claimant can make what is essentially the same claim in more

---

[33] S 21(1)(b), 'to recover from the trustee trust property or the proceeds of trust property in the possession of the trustee'.

[34] S 21(3).

[35] S 21(1)(a).

[36] S 21(1)(b), 'to recover from the trustee trust property or the proceeds of trust property . . . previously received by the trustee and converted to his use'.

than one way, he is of course made to choose one way, rather than recover multiple remedies. If I invest trust assets improperly, say, you cannot demand *both* that I liquidate the improper investment and reinvest the proceeds properly *and*, treating those assets as lost altogether, that I reimburse the amount so taken. You can, however, demand that I both liquidate the improper investment and reinvest the proceeds properly, and pay compensation for any loss, caused by the improper investment, which that leaves outstanding.

15.6 LIABILITY OTHER THAN FOR BREACH OF A TRUSTEE'S DUTIES

So far, we have focused on the liability of a trustee arising from a breach by him of one of the duties he owes as such, a number of which were discussed earlier in the book. We turn now to liability of a different kind. People can sometimes be sued by trust objects for breaching duties distinct from those which rest on trustees as such. There seem to be three classes of this form of liability, known as 'dishonest assistance', 'trusteeship *de son tort*', 'knowing receipt' (though we shall see that the latter may itself comprise more than one class); and no others.[37] We shall consider them in turn.

15.7 DISHONEST ASSISTANCE

A person who dishonestly helps trustees to commit a breach of trust is liable to reimburse the trust the sum involved, alongside the breaching trustees. This form of liability is termed 'dishonest assistance'.[38] The remedy, evidently, is one of the second type.

Losses caused by breach of trust are ones that the law regards as meriting compensation, and this rule treats this compensation as exigible from not only the breaching trustees themselves but also others sufficiently culpably involved in the occurrence of the breach and loss: it imposes on them a duty not to so involve themselves. (Arguably, the rule should apply also to the reimbursement of gains made by a breaching trustee, but there is little evidence of its being used in this way.) Given the trust institution's proprietary quality, it is unsurprising that the law

---

[37] *Metall und Rohstoff AG v Donaldson Lufkin & Jenrette Inc* [1990] 1 QB 391, 481, denying especially that there is a further ground of liability in the shape of a tort of 'procuring a breach of trust' analogous to the tort of interference with contractual relations.
[38] C Mitchell in P Birks and A Pretto (eds) *Breach of Trust* (2002) ch 6.

requires others to respect it in this way (as well as imposing duties on those who acquire trust property). Similar duties not to contribute to legally recognized wrongs are found more widely, however. They exist in respect of crimes,[39] torts, and breaches of contract.[40] At any rate contractual obligations are not proprietary, as trust obligations are. This suggests that acting as accessory to a legally recognized wrong is objectionable in its own right. That is intelligible: by definition, accessories increase the chances of the wrong occurring or of harm resulting, and those are the evils against which the law aims the wrong in the first place.

So say I am trustee of a pension fund, and that you are not a trustee but the fund's auditor. I embezzle £1 million from the fund. You know what I am doing, but cover it up, hoping that this will make me want to continue employing you. Assuming that a judge would regard you as dishonest in this, as seems likely, you are liable (in dishonest assistance) alongside me (in breach of trust) to reimburse the £1 million. The portrayal of the helper in this example as an auditor reflects the fact that a trust's professional agents—auditors, solicitors, bankers—will routinely, given the nature of their work, be caught up in a breaching trustee's activities. Whether, as a result, they find themselves liable for the trustees' breaches depends on the exact profile of the liability.

At one time, there could be no liability of this kind unless the trustee's breach was itself dishonest,[41] but that limitation has now been removed in English law,[42] so someone who dishonestly helps in even a careless or unwitting breach will be liable. (Then, the dishonest 'helper' may well be the prime mover of the breach, the trustee committing his breach as the helper's tool.) The help must be of some substance: cooking a good breakfast for a trustee about to embezzle from his trust does not entail liability for the cook.[43]

---

[39] 'Complicity'.

[40] 'Interference with contractual relations'.

[41] *Barnes v Addy* (1874) 9 Ch App 244. At the time of this decision, trustees would breach certain important stewardship duties by doing anything which hindsight revealed to have been a mistake, however sound it seemed at the time. This rule was thought too harsh, and *Speight v Gaunt* (1883) 9 App Cas 1 changed it so that trustees were liable only if careless. *Barnes v Addy* can be seen as anticipating that move, so that meanwhile at any rate trustees' helpers should not incur liability too easily.

[42] *Royal Brunei Airlines Sdn Bhd v Tan* [1995] 2 AC 378; *Twinsectra Ltd v Yardley* [2002] 2 WLR 802. The limitation remains in Canada: *Air Canada v M & L Travel Ltd* [1993] 3 SCR 787; *Gold v Rosenberg* [1997] 3 SCR 767; *Citadel General Assurance Co v Lloyds Bank Canada* [1997] 3 SCR 805.

[43] *Brinks Ltd v Abu-Saleh (No 3)* [1996] CLC 133.

In English law, the helper incurs liability only if she acts dishonestly.[44] In this context, she acts 'dishonestly' if her deeds,[45] seen in the context of the circumstances and her motives and attitudes,[46] are dishonest by the ordinary standards of reasonable and honest people, and if she herself is aware that that is so.[47] Both elements refer the law to a value judgement. The first requires a value judgement by the judge. Ordinary standards of honesty are not free of doubt or unchanging. A proxy for this element of dishonesty, formulated appropriately to a commercial context but applicable *mutatis mutandis* more generally, is the question whether the assister is 'guilty of commercially unacceptable conduct in the particular context involved':[48] a formulation which leaves unmistakable the standard's variability. Take someone who knows about a breach of trust, could stop it by reporting it, but fails to do so because she regards it as 'none of her business'. Deciding whether she is dishonest by the ordinary standards of reasonable and honest people requires the judge in effect to legislate whether, in the context concerned, there is a duty not to turn a blind eye to wrongdoing in this way. At first sight, the second element of the dishonesty test seems to pose a mere question of fact as to the state of the helper's awareness. But it requires the exculpation of a helper 'guilty of . . . unacceptable conduct in the particular context involved' if the helper has lower standards, by which her conduct is acceptable, and she believes in their prevalence, sincerely if myopically.[49] There is liability for dishonest assistance only if both value judgements are unfavourable to what the helper did. Arguably, the reference to the helper's own value judgement is

---

[44] *Royal Brunei Airlines Sdn Bhd v Tan* [1995] 2 AC 378; *Twinsectra Ltd v Yardley* [2002] 2 WLR 802.

[45] The question 'are her deeds dishonest?' must probably be applied to the deeds she actually commits, not to the deeds she may have wrongly believed herself committing. Say someone helps in a breach of trust but thinks she is helping in tax evasion. Say further that she would be dishonest if she were right. It does not follow that the help she gives in what is actually a breach of trust is necessarily dishonest: *Brinks Ltd v Abu-Saleh (No 3)* [1996] CLC 133. (The contrary view was taken in *Agip (Africa) Ltd v Jackson* [1990] Ch 265, 295, affirmed [1991] Ch 547, but this pre-dated the ruling requiring dishonesty.)

[46] *Royal Brunei Airlines Sdn Bhd v Tan* [1995] 2 AC 378, 390–1.

[47] *Twinsectra Ltd v Yardley* [2002] 2 WLR 802. The formulation of dishonesty in these terms is taken from the criminal law case *R v Ghosh* [1982] QB 1053.

[48] *Cowan de Groot Properties Ltd v Eagle Trust plc* [1992] 4 All ER 700, 761; adopted in *Royal Brunei Airlines Sdn Bhd v Tan* [1995] 2 AC 378, 390.

[49] This was the result in *Twinsectra Ltd v Yardley* [2002] 2 WLR 802 itself. The helper, a solicitor, believed that his responsibility was purely to assist his client, and that he had no duty to attend to the terms on which money came to his client and which the client broke. It was held that his conduct was contrary to ordinary standards of honesty, but that his belief prevented liability.

too generous. It prevents the law from imposing its own standards, which is its very function.

What should be the courts' vision of 'unacceptable conduct' in respect of the kind of situation at issue here? There are many variables, so a comprehensive discussion is impossible. But one central question is whether a person, especially a professional agent, should guard against the possibility that those with whom she deals are trustees in breach of their trust, or may content herself with the appearance that they are not. The answer is not self-evident, and before the establishment of the dishonesty rule, different judges came out for[50] and against[51] a rule requiring people so to guard. The principal considerations can however be explained.[52]

A vision of dishonesty demanding knowledge of the breach generates liability less frequently, and generates incentives to less work, than one requiring alertness as to the possibility. The former vision thus tracks a public interest in minimizing the financial exposure and the amount of 'red tape' to which commercial undertakings, such as trustees' professional agents, are subject: their competitiveness is thus enhanced, and more wealth is created. It also tracks a further interest in not undermining such agents' willingness to work for trusts, in that their work conduces importantly to the satisfactory performance of trusts; though there was more anxiety over this in the past than there is today. Conversely, a vision requiring alertness as to the possibility of breach generates liability more frequently, and creates incentives to more work. As professional agents will carry insurance against this liability, the cost of the premiums being reflected in their charges to the trust and so deducted from the payments out to the objects, such a vision thus comes closer to requiring objects to insure themselves against the possibility of depredation by their trustees: which may be felt desirable, especially in contexts such as family and especially pension trusts, where the objects' prosperity is substantially at stake but they might well not take insurance on their own initiative. And incentivizing such agents to police their trustee clients' activities may also be thought desirable: experience suggests the job to be

---

[50] Thus eg *Selangor United Rubber Estates Ltd v Cradock (No 3)* [1968] 1 WLR 1555, 1590.

[51] Thus eg *Agip (Africa) Ltd v Jackson* [1990] Ch 265, 292–3. (The decision was affirmed, but more equivocal statements made as to the present issue, [1991] Ch 547, 567, 569–70.) This view represents Canadian law: *Air Canada v M & L Travel Ltd* [1993] 3 SCR 787; *Gold v Rosenberg* [1997] 3 SCR 767; *Citadel General Assurance Co v Lloyds Bank Canada* [1997] 3 SCR 805.

[52] For expansion of what follows, see S Gardner (1996) 112 LQR 56, 71–85.

worthwhile, these agents are particularly well placed to perform it, and it chimes with what is already required of them by their own professional standards and by anti-money laundering legislation.[53] In recent times the dominant judicial proclivity has been to minimize professional agents' liabilities. In 2002, however, striking evidence emerged of complacency on auditors' part to the possibility of fraud, to which there was a strong reaction demanding higher standards. It would be unsurprising if there ensued a tendency to treat slackness on professional agents' part as 'unacceptable conduct', falling short of ordinary standards of honesty.

One factor distorts the natural calculus, pushing the law to narrow the liability. Someone liable in dishonest assistance is liable, alongside the breaching trustees, to reimburse the trust for the whole loss following from the breach of trust. Say I, a trustee, embezzle £1 million, and you dishonestly help me. We shall both be liable for £1 million. That is, the claimant can sue either or both of us for all or any part of that sum, so long as she does not recover more than £1 million overall. Liability of multiple defendants organized in this way is called 'joint and several', and is a characteristic, but controversial,[54] feature of English law. A defendant made to pay for all of a loss under this doctrine can recoup himself against others who might have been sued using a process known as 'contribution', whereby the loss is apportioned amongst those responsible for it;[55] but any difficulty in doing so, eg the disappearance or bankruptcy of another defendant, is his problem rather than the claimant's. This rule has an especially significant impact in the context of dishonest assistance. A claimant will commonly have little chance of recovering the loss from the breaching trustee, but a much better chance of recovering it from the trustee's professional agent helpers, if they are liable at all. The agents' correct share will normally be less than half, as the main instigator will have been the breaching trustee. But the agents will have equally little chance of obtaining contribution from the trustee. So they will in practice be left bearing the entire loss, rather than their correct share. This is an unsatisfactory outcome. A narrow construction of the first element of dishonesty (and indeed the addition of the second element can be seen in the same light) helps to avoid it, by making it likely that the helper will

---

[53] In especially the Proceeds of Crime Act 2002 Part 7 (superseding similar provisions in the Criminal Justice Act 1993); Money Laundering Regulations 1993 SI No 1933.

[54] In 1995 the Law Commission concluded that it would nevertheless not be justified in exploring reform. This surprised many and caused the government to consult more widely: Department of Trade and Industry *Feasibility Investigation of Joint and Several Liability* (1996). No reform has ensued, however.

[55] Civil Liability (Contribution) Act 1978 s 1.

not be liable at all. Having the helper emerge not liable at all is also an unsatisfactory outcome, but no liability is closer to the correct outcome, a less-than-half share, than is full liability.

15.8 TRUSTEESHIP *DE SON TORT*

A person who is not a trustee, but who acts as though he were, is known as a 'trustee *de son tort*'. As such, he becomes subject to all the duties incumbent on the genuine trustees of the trust in question (these of course vary from one trust to another). He is accordingly liable to the same remedies as are available against trustees if he breaches any of those duties, though it would be curious to seek a remedy of the first kind (ie a demand for the performance of the trust obligations) against someone who is not in fact a trustee. The special feature of this liability thus lies not in the duties and remedies it involves, but in its application of the duties normally incumbent on trustees to non-trustees. Making a non-trustee liable for his malperformance of trust duties is justifiable where he makes himself responsible for their proper performance: and that is, by definition, what someone acting as though he were a trustee does.

Say I am personal assistant to the single trustee of a trust, and when she dies I carry the trust on. Or say I am clerk to a group of elderly trustees and take all their decisions for them. If for example I invest the trust's assets in an unauthorized way and at a loss, I have come under and broken the duty not to invest improperly, and can therefore be required to make good the loss.[56]

There is no requirement of culpability before someone is held a trustee *de son tort* (though presumably some kind of awareness that one is encroaching on the role of trustee is required). The only culpability required for this kind of liability is that, if any, required for breach of the duty in question by a proper trustee. So someone who helps trustees as they put themselves in breach of trust, and who is honest and so not liable in dishonest assistance, is nonetheless liable for the breach if he is a trustee *de son tort*. The concept of 'acting as though one were a trustee', limiting the scope of the latter possibility, thus decides where the requirements for dishonest assistance can in effect be undermined. The courts have been mindful of this point,[57] and once again concerned to

---

[56] *Blyth v Fladgate* [1891] 1 Ch 337.
[57] *Barnes v Addy* (1874) LR 9 Ch App 244, 251; *Williams-Ashman v Price & Williams* [1942] Ch 219, 228.

protect, in particular, professional agents from liability,[58] a position intelligible (though not inevitable) for the kinds of reasons considered in the last section. They have accordingly circumscribed the concept of 'acting as though one were a trustee' by contrasting it emphatically with the phenomenon of associating oneself with the carrying on of the trust while acknowledging one's non-trusteeship.[59]

Some judicial treatments assert that a person becomes a trustee *de son tort* only where he takes control of the trust assets.[60] Others, while not expressly denying such a requirement, do not assert it.[61] The demand is presumably not for the acquisition of title to the trust assets alongside or in place of the proper trustees: someone who acquires title to the trust assets incurs a constructive trust,[62] and is thus liable *as* a trustee, rather than *as though he were* a trustee. The demand should therefore be understood as one for de facto control. It is calculated to narrow further the ambit of this liability. It seems essentially unprincipled, however. As noted above, trusteeship *de son tort* is justifiable as imposing liability for malperformance of trust duties on someone who makes himself responsible for the proper performance of those duties. And it seems possible for a person to fit the latter description even if he does not take control of the trust assets: as where the trustees defer to him, and he colludes in their doing so, specifically in the operation of a trust's dispositive discretions.

15.9 KNOWING RECEIPT

If someone acquires trust property transferred by a trustee acting in breach of trust,[63] then, unless she acquires as a bona fide purchaser of the property for value without notice of its provenance, she holds it on a constructive trust, as explained in section 8.3. So long as she still has this property or further property identified by the tracing rules,[64] a remedy of the first kind is thus available against her, requiring her to transfer the property to new trustees, or if appropriate to the trust objects.

Additionally, however, a remedy of the second kind is available not only

---

[58] *Barnes v Addy* (1874) LR 9 Ch App 244, 251–2, 255.
[59] *Mara v Browne* [1896] 1 Ch 199; *Williams-Ashman v Price & Williams* [1942] Ch 219.
[60] *Morgan v Stephens* (1861) 3 Giff 226, 236; *Re Barney* [1892] 2 Ch 265; *Williams-Ashman v Price & Williams* [1942] Ch 219, 228.
[61] *Mara v Browne* [1896] 1 Ch 199.
[62] See section 8.3.
[63] If the trustee transfers the property legitimately, the obligations attached to it will be overreached, so that it ceases to be trust property: see section 8.3.
[64] See section 8.6.

against the trustee responsible for the wrongful transfer, but also against such a transferee. If, when the latter knows or ought to know that her acquisition is trust property, she misappropriates or loses it, she is liable in 'knowing receipt'. (This term undeniably obscures some of these details of the liability's make-up. 'Knowing' is not quite exact, and the time at which the transferee has to 'know' of the property's provenance is not the time when she receives it, but any time before she does the act causing the loss for which compensation is sought.) As with dishonest assistance and trusteeship *de son tort*, therefore, trust objects are thus valuably enabled to increase the number of those against whom they have an action in respect of a given loss.

Say I give you some money as a present. The money is in fact money that I hold on trust for Adam, and I break my trust in giving it to you. You spend it so that there are no traceable proceeds, eg on a holiday. If you know or ought to know that it came to you in breach of trust before you spend it, you are liable to reimburse Adam's trust.

According to this outline, the transferee is liable in knowing receipt if, before causing the loss, she 'knows or ought to know' that her acquisition is trust property. The formulation used by the principal English authority at the time of writing is that 'the recipient's state of knowledge must be such as to make it unconscionable' for her, having had the trust's property, not now to repay the trust.[65] Once the latter is deciphered, the two accounts seem to come to the same thing.

A formulation in terms of 'unconscionability' is opaque, and was rejected on this ground in the context of dishonest assistance.[66] But the court seems to have chosen it as offering the flexibility to have the best of both worlds between two other positions, acknowledging each as to an extent attractive. According to one, there should be liability only if the recipient actually knows of the property's provenance. This view is especially calculated to eliminate the delays and costs, and so damage to commerce, which would ensue if recipients of property could not accept it at face value but had to check its provenance;[67] and to recognize that those presented with property as a gift will find it hard not simply to accept it at face value.[68] According to the other position, there should be liability also if, with a certain amount of diligence, the recipient could

---

[65] *Bank of Credit and Commerce International Ltd v Akindele* [2001] Ch 437, 455.
[66] *Royal Brunei Airlines Sdn Bhd v Tan* [1995] 2 AC 378, 392.
[67] *Manchester Trust v Furness* [1895] 2 QB 539, 545.
[68] *Re Montagu's Settlement Trusts* [1987] Ch 264.

have discovered the property's provenance, whether she did or not:[69] a view conducing more to commercial responsibility.[70] The reference to unconscionability instructs the judge to decide how far it is right to go in the direction of the second of these positions, not as a general proposition but for the purposes of the individual case. A transferee's failure to discover the property's provenance will be unconscionable if, but only if, she not only *could* have discovered it but also *should* have exercised the diligence necessary to discover it. And that judgement depends on the context (traditionally, for example, great diligence has been expected where the property is land), and will also vary over time. One could thus paraphrase the inquiry as one whether the transferee, in failing to discover the property's provenance, is guilty of unacceptable conduct in the particular context involved. In effect, then, 'unconscionability' seems to be identical to the first element of 'dishonesty' as used in dishonest assistance, discussed in section 15.7.[71] Judges applying it will be influenced by the same kinds of considerations as were explored in that discussion.

Section 15.6 presented knowing receipt as a liability distinct from those arising from a breach of their duties by trustees as such. This is a widely held view, but it may not be correct. Knowing receipt can be seen as the application to the particular context under discussion of the principles governing the ordinary liability of trustees, explained in early sections of this chapter. Remember that the transferee is in fact trustee of the acquired assets, as explained at the start of this section. As such, once she realizes or should realize the assets to be trust property, she owes a duty to take care of them.[72] If she then misappropriates or loses them, say

---

[69] A state of affairs commonly described as 'notice', but that term has been used with a number of meanings, including sometimes merely knowledge: eg *Eagle Trust plc v SBC Securities Ltd* [1993] 1 WLR 484, 494–5, 504–6.

[70] *Agip (Africa) Ltd v Jackson* [1990] Ch 265, 291; *Houghton v Fayers* [2000] 1 BCLC 511, 516; *Westpac Banking Corp v Savin* [1985] 2 NZLR 41, 53, New Zealand; *Gold v Rosenberg* [1997] 3 SCR 767, Canada; *Citadel General Assurance Co v Lloyds Bank Canada* [1997] 3 SCR 805, Canada.

[71] The court in *Bank of Credit and Commerce International Ltd v Akindele* [2001] Ch 437, 448–50 rejected a 'dishonesty' test. As in the dishonest assistance decision *Twinsectra Ltd v Yardley* [2002] 2 WLR 802, 'dishonesty' is viewed as meaning not only that the defendant's conduct was unacceptable by ordinary standards, but also that the defendant should have been aware of this. The rejection is on account of the latter element. In section 15.7 it was argued that that element is inappropriate in dishonest assistance too. On that view, the test would be the same (the defendant has the required degree of fault if either he knew of the breach, or he failed to do so as a result of unacceptable conduct) in both dishonest assistance and knowing receipt.

[72] See section 9.2. Lord Browne-Wilkinson in *Westdeutsche Landesbank Girozentrale v Islington LBC* [1996] AC 669, 705 proposes that the transferee does not hold the property

by spending them on a holiday, she breaks this duty and can be sued for compensation accordingly. This form of liability seems exactly to correspond with knowing receipt.[73]

Many nonetheless regard knowing receipt as not simply a liability arising from a breach of her duties by a trustee as such. They hold two views as to what the basis of the liability then is. Some see knowing receipt as essentially a standard restitutionary liability, aimed at reversing the unjust enrichment at the trust's expense that the acquisition of trust property brings the recipient.[74] Applying the classic account of restitution to this view, the law should not ask whether the recipient knew or should have known of the property's provenance before imposing liability, but should make the recipient repay on a strict liability basis, ie on the basis of having had the enrichment pure and simple.[75] A liability seemingly of this kind does exist not far from, though not quite in, the context of misapplied trust property: if someone receives property to which he is not entitled in the distribution of a deceased person's estate (rather than from a trustee, but there are similarities), he is liable to repay the estate even if he had no reason to doubt his entitlement.[76] But the courts have been slow to mould knowing receipt on similar lines: even when attracted by the restitutionary view of knowing receipt, they have rejected a strict liability treatment of it.[77] The restitutionary vision of knowing receipt also has a more fundamental difficulty. As noted earlier, a recipient of

on trust until she knows or should know it to be trust property (section 1.13 disputes this); but continues (707) that on acquiring the necessary knowledge, she may 'become a constructive trustee . . . on the basis of knowing receipt', thus also arriving at the suggestion in the text.

[73] Knowing receipt seems to be depicted thus in *Re Montagu's Settlement Trusts* [1987] Ch 264, 272–3; *Westdeutsche Landesbank Girozentrale v Islington LBC* [1996] AC 669, 707.

[74] P Millett (1991) 107 LQR 71; P Birks in P Birks (ed) *The Frontiers of Liability Volume 1* (1994) ch 3; Lord Nicholls in W Cornish et al (eds) *Restitution: Past Present and Future* (1998) ch 15; P Birks in P Birks and A Pretto (eds) *Breach of Trust* (2002) ch 7; *El Ajou v Dollar Land Holdings Plc* [1993] 3 All ER 717, 736–9; *Royal Brunei Airlines Sdn Bhd v Tan* [1995] 2 AC 378, 386; *Twinsectra Ltd v Yardley* [2002] 2 WLR 802, 831–2 para 105.

[75] In the law of restitution, however, an ignorant recipient is not liable to the extent that he incurs additional expenditure on the footing that the enrichment is his to keep, under the defence of 'change of position': *Lipkin Gorman v Karpnale Ltd* [1991] 2 AC 548.

[76] *Ministry of Health v Simpson* [1951] AC 251.

[77] *Bank of Credit and Commerce International Ltd v Akindele* [2001] Ch 437, 455–6; *Citadel General Assurance Co v Lloyds Bank Canada* [1997] 3 SCR 805 para 51, Canada. Perhaps these contributions can be viewed as questioning the strict liability orthodoxy regarding restitution generally (cf N McBride and P McGrath (1995) 15 OJLS 33, 38–9). That orthodoxy is harsh on defendants: one having to prove that he incurred additional expenditure on the footing of a belief that the enrichment was his to keep is in a weaker position than one against whom a claimant has to show knowledge or the ability to know.

improperly transferred trust property takes the property not as her own, but on constructive trust.[78] So she is not enriched at the trust's expense in the way that, outside the trust context, a recipient of a simple mistaken payment is enriched (because he becomes owner of the money paid) at the payer's expense.[79]

Others agree in seeing knowing receipt as based not simply on breach of her duties by a trustee as such, but suggest a different basis. They regard it as a wrong similar to the tort of conversion:[80] as a breach of a duty, aimed at all the world, not to misappropriate or lose property coming into one's hands but which belongs to another. In knowing receipt, one acquires the legal title, but the property belongs to another in the sense that it remains the subject matter of a trust. This account is easier to reconcile with the law as it stands, and might be thought particularly to explain the requirement that the recipient knows or should know of the property's provenance, though conversion itself is of strict liability. There is still this difficulty, however. The alleged duty seems to be aimed not at all the world, but at all the world except trustees of the property in question: the latter are under a duty not to misappropriate or lose the property simply because they are its trustees. And, as we have already seen, anyone incurring liability in knowing receipt is at that moment necessarily a trustee of the property in question, and her liability can be explained on that basis.

There is an important exception from knowing receipt. It does not catch someone who, in receiving and then misappropriating or otherwise depriving the trust of the property, acts as agent for someone else. Imagine a situation in which I would be liable. Now imagine a situation which is otherwise the same but in which I acquired the improperly transferred trust property not in my own right but as agent for you, and I was adhering to your instructions when I deprived the trust of it. In the latter case, I am not liable. You are probably liable instead, however: even if, at the time when I deprive the trust of the property, you yourself neither knew nor ought to have known of the property's provenance, I did, and since I am your agent that is imputed to you.

---

[78] Or, on Lord Browne-Wilkinson's view in *Westdeutsche Landesbank Girozentrale v Islington LBC* [1996] AC 669, 705, subject to a 'proprietary interest': this makes no difference to the argument in the text.

[79] *Lipkin Gorman v Karpnale Ltd* [1991] 2 AC 548 seems to show that a defendant can be liable as though for unjust enrichment even though he never acquires the asset, which remains the claimant's throughout: but the thinking behind this is difficult, and its message for knowing receipt conjectural: L Smith (2000) 116 LQR 412.

[80] On conversion generally, see T Weir *Tort Law* (2002) ch 11.

The exemption is available not only to agents properly so called, but also to banks: in the example above, I am not liable if I am your bank and receive the improperly transferred trust assets as a payment into your account with me.[81] Technically, that is surprising. When money is 'paid into' a customer's account, the bank acquires it not as the account-holder's agent but in its own right: the credit to the customer's account is a debt which the bank undertakes to the customer in return. That the law nonetheless treats the bank as the customer's agent, so immunizing it against liability in knowing receipt, suggests that, like certain aspects of the law on dishonest assistance and trusteeship *de son tort*, the immunity reflects a project of protecting 'professional agents'. Within such a project, banks are indeed bracketed with agents proper.

One would wish the immunity to be explicable in a principled way, however. The best approach might be the following. Remember the thesis, explicating the test of unconscionability, that the liability should be imposed only where the recipient knows of the property's provenance, or, in not knowing, is guilty of unacceptable conduct. Arguably, it should be seen as acceptable for agents and banks not to probe their customers' dealings, so that they should incur no liability if they take matters at face value (though it ought to follow that they should be liable if they actually know of the impropriety). But one could controvert that argument, and, regarding it (as the money laundering legislation does) as both feasible and desirable for professional agents to undertake such probing, aver that they should incur liability for knowing receipt accordingly. The question is once again distorted, however, by the consideration of joint and several liability, described in section 15.7. If an agent could be liable in knowing receipt, it would theoretically be alongside its customer and the trustees responsible for the wrongful transfer. But in practice, the agent would commonly bear the whole burden, as the jointly and severally liable defendant with much the deepest pocket. Once again, the courts may be prepared to skew the law so as to prevent that.

Take finally a different kind of case: that where trustees lawfully trans-fer trust property to their own agent. The agent is of course liable to the trustees for any breaches of his duties to them. But if he is or should be aware[82] of the property's status as trust property and of the trust's terms,

---

[81] *Agip (Africa) Ltd v Jackson* [1990] Ch 265, 292.

[82] This formulation, analogous to the rule for knowing receipt and with the preferable position regarding dishonest assistance, is broadly suggested by *Williams v Williams* (1881) 17 Ch D 437. The defendant there was a solicitor, and there is a flavour of the accustomed leniency towards professional agents in the decision that it was permissible for him not to have been aware of the trust in question.

and he treats it inconsistently with those terms, he is also liable to the trust objects for the loss.[83] Some accounts conflate this liability with knowing receipt proper; others insist on its distinctness.[84] It certainly cannot be explained as a breach by the agent of a duty which he owes simply as the property's trustee, for he does not hold the property on trust for the objects.[85] Perhaps in this limited context, therefore, we do indeed encounter a liability aimed at protecting trusts but which must be distinct from that applicable to trustees as such. An explanation in unjust enrichment seems untenable, for at no point is the agent enriched (he at first holds the property as lawful agent, then wrongfully causes its loss). An analogy with conversion is plausible, however.

[83] *Lee v Sankey* (1873) LR 15 Eq 204.
[84] *Agip (Africa) Ltd v Jackson* [1990] Ch 265, 291.
[85] He may however hold it on trust for the trustees, as being an authorized acquisition by a fiduciary (see section 8.4).

Index

Index